Figures in a Renaissance Context

Figures in a Renaissance Context

C. A. PATRIDES

Edited by
Claude J. Summers and Ted-Larry Pebworth

Ann Arbor
THE UNIVERSITY OF MICHIGAN PRESS

Copyright © by The University of Michigan 1989
All rights reserved
Published in the United States of America by
The University of Michigan Press
Manufactured in the United States of America

1992   1991   1990   1989   4   3   2   1

Library of Congress Cataloging-in-Publication Data

Patrides, C. A.
 Figures in a Renaissance context / C. A. Patrides; edited by Claude J. Summers and Ted-Larry Pebworth.
   p.   cm.
 Bibliography: p.
 Includes index.
 ISBN 0-472-10119-6 (alk. paper)
  1. English literature—Early modern, 1500–1700—History and criticism.   2. Renaissance—England.   I. Summers, Claude J.
II. Pebworth, Ted-Larry.   III. Title.
PR411.P38   1989
820.9'003—dc20   89-34015
                                                                  CIP

For Helen Valioulis, Dean's Mother

Σ' ἀγαπῶ' δεν μπορῶ
τίποτ' ἄλλο νὰ πῶ
πιὸ βαθύ, πιὸ ἁπλὸ,
πιὸ μεγάλο!

Contents

Introduction	1
1. Erasmus and More: Dialogues with Reality	7
2. Edmund Spenser: The Definition of Poetry	29
3. Shakespeare: The Comedy beyond Comedy	47
4. Ben Jonson: A Poet Nearly Anonymous	73
5. John Donne: The Aesthetics of Morality	89
6. George Herbert: The Transfiguration of Plainness	117
7. Richard Crashaw: The Merging of Contrarieties	141
8. Sir Thomas Browne: The Strategy of Indirection	161
9. Milton: Apocalyptic Configurations	181
10. *Paradise Lost:* The Language of Theology	215
11. *Samson Agonistes:* The Comic Dimension	231
12. Milton's Prose: The Adjustment of Idealism	249
13. Andrew Marvell: Engagements with Reality	273
14. The Experience of Otherness: Theology as a Means of Life	295
Bibliography of C. A. Patrides	325
Index	331

Introduction

On Tuesday morning, September 23, 1986, C. A. Patrides died in Ann Arbor, Michigan, at the age of fifty-six. With his death, the scholarly community sustained a severe loss. For those of us who knew him personally, who were touched by his colorful personality and his passion for friendship, the loss is still more grievous.

He was born in New York City and educated in Athens and at Kenyon College, where he studied with John Crowe Ransom and Charles M. Coffin, and at Oxford University, where he studied with Ethel Seaton. After a distinguished record of research and teaching at the University of California, Berkeley, and at the University of York in England, and after visiting professorships at the University of Pennsylvania and at New York University, he came to the University of Michigan in 1978, where he was named the G. B. Harrison Distinguished Professor of English in 1981. Designated an Honored Scholar by the Milton Society of America and twice the recipient of Guggenheim fellowships, he received numerous awards for his outstanding teaching and research, including the University of Michigan Distinguished Faculty Achievement Award.

He was, as John Knott described him, one of the preeminent scholars of his generation. Enormously erudite, he brought to the study of literature an extraordinarily broad and equally deep understanding of Renaissance theology and philosophy. Yet he was neither a pedant nor simply a hoarder of an impressive body of arcane knowledge. Rather, he was a remarkably creative scholar, who interpreted the past with amazing sensitivity and tact and with an unfailing fidelity to truth. Gifted with an extraordinarily subtle intelligence, he was as well a critic of uncommon brilliance. As a historian of ideas, a penetrating critic, and a distinctive stylist, he made a major contribution to our understanding of sixteenth- and seventeenth-century literature and thought. In addition, he also wrote memorable essays and lectures on ancient Greek poetry and art, on Patristic and medieval literature, and on twentieth-century figures such as Eliot and Yeats. As a lecturer, he embodied in his presentations a kind of sophistication and elegance exceedingly rare in our profession.

As the bibliography appended to this volume attests, his publications total more than one hundred twenty-five in number, including twenty-three books. *Milton and the Christian Tradition, "The Grand Design of God": The Literary Form of the Christian View of History, Bright Essence: Studies in Milton's Theology, George Herbert: The Critical Heritage,* and *Premises and Motifs in Renaissance Thought and Literature;* his collections of essays on *Lycidas,* on Milton's epic poetry, on *Paradise Lost,* on aspects of time, on Marvell, on Sir Thomas Browne, on the Apocalypse, and on the Age of Milton; and his editions of the Cambridge Platonists, of Sir Walter Ralegh's *The History of the World,* of Milton's selected prose, of Browne, of Herbert, and of Donne: these constitute an extraordinary achievement, one that will continue to influence the study of literature for generations to come.

In a tribute delivered on December 29, 1986, at the annual dinner of the Milton Society of America, Roland Mushat Frye observed that

> In our time, certainly, no one has excelled [Patrides'] breadth and depth of learning, shaped throughout by superb critical judgment. For him, a poem or other literary piece was never an excuse for displaying the kinds of critical bravura and virtuosity that can smother a text in order to glorify the critic. On the contrary, Dean Patrides approached great poetry with awe and reverence, mixed with joy. His vast historical and critical erudition illumined classic texts afresh and enabled us to see familiar passages as if for the first time. The "newness" he revealed was not, however, merely an ingenious construct, but so far as possible was a recovery of the freshness of the original work itself, its time and place, its author, audience and tradition, its ambience and its essence—all done to advance critical understanding and appreciation in our own time."[1]

Patrides excelled above all at the practice of contextualization. In his hands, this process alternatively (and sometimes simultaneously) recovered works from the misty obscurities of an earlier age and antiquated pattern of thought, on the one hand, and, on the other, estranged classic texts that had grown stale through over-familiarity, in order to render them as fresh and new works.

These qualities are apparent in the fourteen essays collected in this volume, which illustrate their author's characteristic intellectual concerns and the remarkable range of his learning. Patrides' last major project, the collection was designed to betoken his sense of the Renaissance experience in literature. It may best be seen as a companion volume to *Premises and Motifs in Renaissance Thought and Literature* (1982). Like the essays collected there, the articles presented here are broad in conception and daunting in their scholarship. But whereas the earlier volume emphasized intellectual history and a Renaissance worldview, the present one focuses on individual talents, engaging the period's central literary texts as the joint products of particular sensibilities and pervasive Renaissance suppositions. Although always firmly grounded in literary and philosophical history and consistently enlivened by critical vitality, the essays were originally composed for a variety of occasions, and they are notably diverse in approach. For all their variety, however, as now revised and arranged, they cohere to form a broad survey of the major figures of the period, considering in depth almost every significant English Renaissance poet except Sidney, Herrick, and Vaughan. The book's intent, like the intent of Renaissance literature itself, is to apprehend variety diversely.

The final essay, "The Experience of Otherness: Theology as a Means of Life," may appear to diverge from the general pattern inasmuch as it is not concerned with a single figure or work. But its inclusion is deliberate and, indeed, necessary: the argument is intentionally expansive, even encyclopedic, in order to underline theology's pivotal significance for the literature of the Renaissance. Although it may have served an introductory function equally well, the essay as now placed collects in a broad summary many of the ideas and generalizations proposed earlier and applied locally. In identifying the experience of otherness as a central aspect of the period's theology, it simultaneously locates theology as a crucial background for comprehending the Renaissance literature at the book's foreground.

The collection is also unified by recurrent thematic and aesthetic concerns. The opening essay on Erasmus and More, for example, charts two different, yet parallel, endorsements of "reality" in the confluence of the serious and the playful, and by extension the tragic and the comic. This pattern is then amplified in five subsequent essays: those devoted to Shakespeare, Crashaw, Sir Thomas Browne, *Samson Agonistes,* and Marvell. In addition, another motif, one more centrally concerned with the criticism of poetry *qua* poetry, is initially explored in the essay on Spenser and then delineated in the studies of Jonson, Donne, Herbert, and *Paradise Lost*. But despite the varying emphases of the individual essays, they all engage thematic and aesthetic concerns simultaneously. For example, even where the first essay argues essentially thematic dimensions in the experiential lives and works of Erasmus and More, the interest never strays far from the strategies used by the two writers to advance their respective theses. Similarly, the second essay, which emphasizes Spenser's poetic virtuosity, also probes that expertise in light of the poet's thematic preoccupations. The crucial third essay on Shakespeare gathers the premises articulated in the first two studies and then projects them in the direction of the figures examined thereafter. The collection, then, incorporates as its own principle of unity that method of "indirection" observed at the outset in Erasmus and More, and later scanned expansively in the essay on Browne.

In addition, the essays are also indissolubly linked by their style. This is not to say that the style is the same throughout, undifferentiated as essay follows essay. On the contrary, Patrides, in his own version of mimetic criticism, varies his manner of expression to suit the matter expressed. For example, the diametrically different approaches of the essays on Jonson and Browne necessitate radically different diction and phrasing, as Patrides imitates the restraint of Jonson in one essay and the luxuriousness of Browne in the other. But notwithstanding this range and variety, Patrides' Olympian style remains distinctive, characterized not only by its mannered elegance of phrasing, but preeminently by a kind of sophisticated wit that incorporates playfulness and amusement even in the most serious of observations and that prevents even the most magisterial pronouncements from ever sounding pompous or self-important. The playfulness of Patrides' scholarly voice is a function not merely of his style, but also of his approach, communicating the joy he found in literature, sometimes in the most unexpected places.

Unity is further imposed on the collection by the numerous cross-references between the essays, which serve to correlate and integrate the individual pieces, and by the epigraphs to the various chapters, all quotations from Shakespeare. The Shakespearean headnotes are not gratuitous. They symbolize the pertinence and centrality of Shakespeare's practice to the literature of the Renaissance generally.

The essays collected here all originated as lectures, and they were quite literally delivered all over the world, from Berkeley to Wurzburg, and from Notre Dame to Tel Aviv. All but the essay on Crashaw have been previously published. As they now appear, however, they have all been yet again revised, frequently lengthened and more fully documented. Most significantly, they are now placed within a broad and meaningful context that serves to amplify the individual studies and to focus them as contributions to a larger cultural project than they originally served. That is to say, the collection is finally more than the sum of its parts. The book's approach is contextual not only in the sense that it places the individual authors in various Renaissance contexts, but also—and perhaps more importantly—in that it creates a Renaissance context in which to examine the diverse figures that it considers.

Although he died before it was entirely completed, Patrides conceived and designed the shape of this book. He selected the essays to be included and began the process of revising and interlinking the essays and updating the references. By the time of his death, he had substantially completed the task. In the case of several essays (including the previously unpublished study of Crashaw), he had not yet finished the revisions; but in these instances he left clear and specific instructions as to the nature of the revisions he intended. In editing the collection, we have attempted to honor these instructions, using his own words whenever possible. Except for corrections of a few factual errors and misquotations, we have neither departed from his original text nor introduced new ideas without explicit authorization from his notes.

The present volume deviates from Patrides' original conception principally in that it omits two essays that he planned to include: the essays that served as the introductions to his editions of Ralegh's *The History of the World* and of *The Cambridge Platonists*. Dictated by the need to shorten a lengthy manuscript, the decision to exclude these essays was a painful one, particularly since they offer the kind of intellectual history at which Patrides excelled and focus on historical and philosophical issues that he illuminated more than any other scholar of his time. But because they are fairly readily available in standard editions and because the extent of his revisions of these two essays was slighter than that of the other essays, they were logical choices to cut.

Finally, the dedication was dictated by Patrides, who was nursed through his final illness by his heroic mother and devoted sister.

We are grateful to the following editors and publishers for permission to use the material indicated: for the essay on Erasmus and More, the editors of the *Kenyon Review*; for the essay on Spenser, the editor of the *Yale Review*; for the essay on Shakespeare, the editors of the *Kenyon Review*; for the essay on Jonson, the director of the University of Pittsburgh Press and the editors of *Classic and Cavalier: Essays on Jonson and the Sons of Ben,* edited by Claude J. Summers and Ted-Larry Pebworth; for the essays on Donne and Herbert, the director of J. M. Dent and Sons Ltd.; for the essay on Browne, the director of the University of Missouri Press; for the essay on Milton's apocalyptic configurations, the editors of *English Language Notes* and the directors of the University of Manchester Press and the Cornell University Press; for the essay on the language of theology in *Paradise Lost,* the director of Frederick Ungar Publishing Company and the editors of *Language and Style in Milton,* edited by Ronald D. Emma and John T. Shawcross, as well as the director of the University of Utah Press; for the essay on the comic dimension of *Samson Agonistes,* the director of the University of Pittsburgh Press and the editor of *Milton Studies,* James D. Simmonds; for the essay on Milton's prose, the directors of Penguin Books Ltd. and the University of Missouri Press; for the essay on Marvell, the director of Routledge and Kegan Paul Ltd.; and for "The Experience of Otherness," the directors of the University of Manchester Press and Barnes and Noble.

Claude J. Summers
Ted-Larry Pebworth
Dearborn, Spring, 1988

NOTE

1. Frye's generous assessment of Patrides' work appears in *Milton Quarterly* 21 (1987): 36–37. But the man was yet more remarkable than his work, and more personal tributes by Claude Summers and Gordon Campbell also appear in *Milton Quarterly* 21 (1987): 37–39, and 39–40, respectively.

Erasmus and More: Dialogues with Reality

> to perform an act
> Whereof what's past is prologue
> —*The Tempest*

I. "The jester of the gods"

"Sancte Socrates, ora pro nobis!" ["Saint Socrates, pray for us!"] So exclaims a character in one of Erasmus' colloquies;[1] and, ever since, readers have been either dazzled by the boldness of the great humanist or distressed by the limitations of his spiritual horizons. But perhaps we are not often enough inclined to be amused, unprepared as we are to grant readily that the intent of Erasmus, here as elsewhere, was to delineate a vision essentially dependent on a lusory apprehension of reality.

The notorious exclamation I have just quoted occurs in a particular colloquy, the *Convivium religiosum* (*The Godly Feast*), which Erasmus deliberately made to resound with echoes of Plato's *Symposium*. In deploying a dramatic form reminiscent of the greatest Platonic dialogue, Erasmus had clearly hoped to elicit responses within the framework provided. In the event, however, he was disappointed repeatedly, for readers responded in the light of personal visions not always cognizant either of Platonism or of its preferred means of exposition, the dialogue. Where satire was also present, the reaction tended to be even more adverse. In the *Julius exclusus* (1517?) and the *Ciceronianus* (1528), two works yet again cast in dramatic form molded by a satiric spirit not devoid of invective, Erasmus censured abuses of ecclesiastical power in the former and abuses of style in the latter. Most of the *Ciceronianus* was not intended to enthrall scholars given to extravagant Ciceronian flourishes, any more than the following exchange in the *Julius exclusus* between St. Peter and Pope Julius II before the gates of heaven could be expected to delight the members of the Catholic hierarchy:

> *Julius:* ... I always wanted the Church to be adorned with all good things. They say that Aristotle established three categories of goods, of which some come from fortune, some from the body, and some from the mind. So I did not want to reverse the order of goods; I began with the goods of fortune. Perhaps I would gradually have reached the goods of the mind if a premature death had not snatched me from the earth.

Peter: Premature indeed—and you a septuagenarian! Still, why did you need to mix water with fire?

Julius: Well, if those benefits are lacking, the people won't give a hoot for us; even as it is they fear and hate us. So the whole Christian state would collapse if it could not protect itself against the power of its enemies.

Peter: On the contrary, if the Christian peoples saw in you the true gifts of Christ—namely, holiness of life, sacred learning, burning love, prophecy, virtues—the more they thought you cleansed of worldly goods, the more they would admire you; and the Christian state would flourish more widely if it were a wonder to the world through its contempts for pleasures, for wealth, for power, and for death. As it is now, not only has it been very narrowly constricted, but, if you examine the matter closely you will even find that many Christians are that in name only. . . .[2]

One reader who was bound to have concurred was Luther, not simply because he approved of the argument but because as a stylist himself—on occasion indeed, a brilliantly sensitive stylist—he was in a position to appreciate the stylistic greatness of Erasmus. But the possibility of endorsements was becoming daily less likely, in that Luther and Erasmus were advancing steadily toward their historic debate over free will (1524–25) that defined, as it unfolded, the mutually exclusive visions of the two men.

Their different paths once carved, Erasmus and Luther moved ever further apart. The publication of Erasmus' *Moriae encomium* in 1511, and its astonishing popularity as edition followed edition to a total of thirty-six within his lifetime, drove an irate Luther to propose that "When Erasmus wrote his *Folly,* he begot a daughter like himself. He turns, twists, and bites like an owl, but he, as a fool, has written true folly."[3] How incensing for Luther, however, that Erasmus was likely to have misconstrued the charge as a compliment! After all, Erasmus' self-eulogizing protagonist had already enrolled "my friend Erasmus" among her loyal subjects—a deflation much like to that in the *Ciceronianus,* where one of the speakers explodes on hearing Erasmus termed a scholar: "You said you were going to talk of *writers*! Far from numbering him among the Ciceronians, I don't even count him a writer at all."[4] Characteristically Erasmian, the stand was not intended to captivate readers such as Luther. It was designed for minds which, like Sir Thomas More's, were temperamentally attuned to the model provided especially by Lucian.

Erasmus and More were intimately familiar with Lucian, most obviously once they merged their efforts to translate several of his dialogues from Greek into Latin (1506). Erasmus was responsible for the translation of eighteen short dialogues and ten longer ones; More, for an additional four. The two humanists also composed elaborate "declamations" against the *Tyrannicida,* which at the time was thought to be Lucian's.[5] Such efforts were by no means unique since other humanists—among them Ulrich von Hutten, Reuchlin, and Melanchthon—were also concerned to make Lucian available in Latin. Even so, the translations by Erasmus and More were determinative because they were the most popular—so much so, indeed, that More's versions outstripped the popularity even of his *Utopia.* To have made Lucian more generally accessible was reward enough, of course, for any humanist. But Erasmus and More were also motivated in their translations by the boundless respect they both had for Lucian's rhetoric, especially its wit and its detachment which appeared so obviously to correspond to their own. "These dialogues," Erasmus said of the ones he translated, "are better than any comedy or any satire, whether you are looking for pleasure or profit."[6] The pleasure is only too clearly evident, derived as it is from Lucian's explicit playfulness. But the "profit" claimed to inhere in Lucian may well surprise, conditioned as we are to think of him as a cynic negative in his proclivities rather than positive. Certainly Erasmus was fully persuaded that "nothing commonplace could come out of Lucian."[7] If in later assessments Lucian was to be viewed as an "atheist," during the Renaissance most humanists would have agreed with More's refusal to be perturbed just because Lucian "appears to have been disposed to doubt immortality and that he was in the same error as Democritus, Lucretius, Pliny, and many others likewise were. For why should it concern me," he went on to ask disingenuously, "what a pagan thinks about those matters that are contained in the peculiar mysteries of the Christian faith?"[8]

Lucian's diffusive impact on Erasmus can best be demonstrated paradoxically, through an idea as utterly absent from Lucian as it is obsessively present in Erasmus. The idea occurred first in Plato's *Symposium,* where it concerns Alcibiades' celebrated comparison of Socrates to a statuette of Silenus which, once opened, reveals treasures not apparent before. Erasmus' increasing fascination with the comparison was never focused exclusively on any one individual, however. The expansive context he favored is evident in his first relevant statement, in the *Enchiridion militis christiani* ("The Handbook [lit., Poniard] of the Christian Soldier," 1503), where he concluded that "especially do the Holy Scriptures, like the Silenus of Alcibiades, conceal their real divinity beneath a surface that is crude and almost laughable."[9] The implied contrast between appearance and reality assumed in time a cosmic significance distinctly Erasmian. According to the detailed explication in the splendid adage *Sileni Alcibiadis* (1515), the statuettes of "the jester of the gods" are said to have been used often by the learned Greeks "either with reference to a thing which in appearance (at first blush, as they say) seems ridiculous and contemptible, but closer and deeper examination proves to be admirable, or else with reference to a person whose looks and dress do not correspond at all to what he conceals in his soul."[10] The prototype of these Sileni was Socrates, who in his physical demeanor and manner of argument may have suggested a fool ("his eternal jesting gave him the air of a clown") but who was very different in fact:

> Once you have opened out this Silenus, absurd as it is, you find a god rather than a man, a great, lofty and truly philosophical soul, despising all those things for which other mortals jostle and steer, sweat and dispute and struggle—one who rose above all insults, over whom fortune had no power, and who feared nothing, so that he treated lightly even death, which all men fear; drinking the hemlock with as cheerful a face as he wore when drinking wine, and joking with his friend Phaedo even as he lay dying.

The prototypical Socrates was followed by many another Silenus, for example Epictetus ("a slave, and poor, and crippled, as his epitaph tells; but, greatest fortune of all, he was dear to the gods, something which can only be attained by purity of life combined with wisdom"). Under the Christian dispensation the Sileni assumed their greatest import yet, beginning with John the Baptist, encompassing the Apostles, and culminating in the God-man:

> Is not Christ the most extraordinary Silenus of all? . . . If you look on the face only of the Silenus-image, what would be lower or more contemptible, measured by popular standards? Obscure and poverty-stricken parents, a humble home; poor himself, he had a few poor men for disciples. . . . But if one may attain to a closer look at this Silenus-image, that is if he deigns to show himself to the purified eyes of the soul, what unspeakable riches you will find there: in such service to mankind, there is a pearl of great price, in such humility, what grandeur! in such poverty, what riches! in such weakness, what immeasurable strength! . . .

But Sileni should not be sought only in individuals led by the Christ. They will also be discovered—as the *Enchiridion* had already proposed—in the Scriptures, especially in the parables, and eventually in the sacraments too. In short, the statuettes in Alcibiades' discourse were transformed by Erasmus into an "allegory" of the ultimate spiritual reality.[11]

Erasmus' adage on the Sileni concludes with a passionate plea for purity of life. Lucian, one suspects, would not have approved of the thesis;

but he would certainly have assented to the manner of its presentation, particularly the wit that informs the "allegory." The assent would have been extended even more enthusiastically to the similar attitude in the *Moriae encomium:*

> It is clear that all human affairs, like the Sileni of Alcibiades, have two aspects quite different from each other. Hence, what appears "at first blush" (as they say) to be death, will, if you examine it more closely, turn out to be life; conversely, life will turn out to be death; beauty will become ugliness; riches will turn to poverty; notoriety will become fame; learning will be ignorance; strength, weakness; noble birth will be ignoble; joy will become sadness; success, failure; friendship, enmity; what is helpful will seem hurtful; in brief, you will find everything suddenly reversed if you open the Silenus. (Pp. 42–43)

The attitude inclusive of the phrasing is almost identical to Erasmus' argument in the *Sileni Alcibiadis*. One difference makes all the difference, however, for presently the speaker is not Erasmus "in propria persona" but Folly herself, Moria. Within the dramatic context, Moria speaks on behalf of Erasmus only coincidentally, and scarcely ever without irony.

II. "The plain, unvarnished truth"

Silenus-like, Erasmus' title warns against expeditious conclusions. *Moriae encomium* (written 1509 [?], published 1511) is the Latinized Greek of Μωρίας ἐνκώμιον, itself translated into Latin as *Stultitia laus*; but while Stultitia carries a restrictive single meaning, Moria stands as much for Folly as for the book's recipient, Sir Thomas More. Erasmus did not fail to mention the "coincidence" in his dedicatory epistle to More; and written as the work was in More's house, it prompted Erasmus to remark playfully on another occasion, "Moriam lusimus apud Thomam Morum" ("I played the fool at the house of Thomas More").[12] More enjoyed toying with his name equally, much as his distant kin John Donne was to play both with "More" and with "Donne" in one of his greater poems, "A Hymne to God the Father."

The double reference of the *Moriae encomium*—"The Praise of Folly" as well as "The Praise of More"—insists that Moria is less like folly than she is like More. Girardus Listrius, in the important commentary he annexed to the work (1515ff.), was particularly laudatory of the wit involved, formulating a principle appropriate to the implicit Erasmian strategies: "Nothing requires more talent than to joke learnedly."[13] But it was in fact

Erasmus who best placed his work within an ongoing literary tradition. As he noted in the dedicatory epistle to More:

> As for those who are offended by the levity and playfulness of the subject matter, they should consider that I am not setting any precedent but following one set long ago by great writers: ages ago Homer amused himself with *The Battle of the Frogs and Mice,* as Virgil did with the Gnat and the Rustic Salad, and Ovid with the Walnut-Tree. So too Polycrates and his corrector Isocrates both wrote encomia of Busiris; Glauco praised injustice; Favorinus, Thersites and the quartan fever; Synesius, baldness; Lucian, the fly and the art of the parasite.... (Pp. 2–3)

The literary tradition outlined by Erasmus is essentially twofold: one aspect rests on parody, as with the works which in his time were still attributed to Homer, Virgil, and Ovid, while another aspect depends on the paradoxical encomium, as with Synesius' famous praise of baldness and the numerous works that were to be written well into the eighteenth century.[14] Erasmus' own contribution to the tradition was both immediate and lasting, witness his influence on Rabelais and Ariosto and Shakespeare and Cervantes, but also the inclusion of the *Moriae encomium* in Milton's list of "laughable topics" by "distinguished orators." "There is now in the hands of everyone," Milton reported in the late 1620s, "that most clever *Praise of Folly,* a work not by a writer of the lowest rank."[15]

The *Moriae encomium* embraces many other traditions too, however. In terms of its rhetorical structure, it is a "declamation"— a *declamatio* or μελέτη—in that, as Listrius reminds us, "it was written as a witty exercise, for fun and enjoyment" (p. 9). Popular culture also left its imprint.[16] But the extensive fool literature of the later Middle Ages was even more influential, largely through the pressures exerted by the variegated personalities of Mère-Folle in the sotties and by the aspirations however unrealized in works like Sebastian Brant's *Narrenschiff* ("The Ship of Fools"). It may be noted that Brant commended the *Moriae encomium* in a few doggerel verses prefixed to the Schürer edition of 1511, quite unaware that his own work was destined never thereafter to affect the creative mind. Incapable of a lusory apprehension of reality, Brant could not have applied the indirection that Erasmus upheld, with suitable indirection, in his prefatory address to More: "Just as nothing is more trivial than to treat serious matters in a trivial way, so too nothing is more delightful than to treat trifles in such a way that you do not seem to be trifling at all" (p. 4). The *Narrenschiff* looks to the past; but the *Moriae encomium* is perpetually of the present.[17]

On the face of it, Moria's links with her predecessors in medieval literature seem substantial. Her discourse—or is it yet another of the "sermons joyeux"?—appears to have taken as its text the motto of the *compagnies de fous,* "Numerus stultorum est infinitus." Besides, the cap with the bells of the jester she wears suggests the fool's traditional license to speak freely: "Don't forget," as she tells us, "another talent, by no means contemptible, that is peculiar to fools: they alone speak the plain, unvarnished truth" (p. 55). Yet Moria's medieval predecessors would have taken exception to the skepticism induced by the tendency of the dramatic context to qualify repeatedly the claims she advances. When she observes ever so casually that "I never wear disguises, nor do I say one thing and think another" (p. 13), it is indicative that the comment is ventured while she is in disguise, so that in effect she says one thing and thinks quite another. Are we simply to invert her claims in order to reap "the plain, unvarnished truth"? But that were to compound our problems since we would in consequence repudiate every noble Erasmian principle upheld by Moria, inclusive of her eloquent denunciation of war:

> War is so inhuman that it befits beasts, not men, so insane that even the poets imagine that it is unleashed by the Furies, so noxious that it spreads moral corruption far and wide, so unjust that it is normally carried on best by robbers, so impious that it is utterly foreign to Christ.... (P. 114)

The statement is characteristic of those moments in the *Moriae encomium* where one's talents at discrimination fail to serve. Erasmus' mercurial protagonist is wont to disavow a number of specifically Erasmian tenets, admit as many others, and—more often than not—disavow and admit them at once.[18] Moria's own confusion (e.g., "none of you is so wise, or rather foolish—no, I mean wise—as to be . . ." and so forth [p. 19]) is so far from being an indication of Erasmus' inability to control his work that it is part of the overall dramatic pose. But here, to allay our mounting despair over the validity of *any* approach, Erasmus intervenes with the metaphor of the world as a stage.

The metaphor, Silenic in nature, has antecedents throughout European literature before and after it was iterated by Lucian too.[19] Erasmus' authoritative formulation was disseminated so much further, however, that its impact cannot be measured with any precision:

> The whole life of mortal men, what is it but a sort of play, in which various persons make their entrances in various costumes, and each one plays his own part until the director gives him his cue to leave the stage? Often he also orders one and the same actor to come on in different costumes, so that the actor who just now played the king

in royal scarlet now comes on in rags to play a miserable servant. (Pp. 43-44)

As with art, so with life; but—equally—as with life, so with art. If in life we act roles given, Erasmus in the *Moriae encomium* is at once director in that he gives everyone their cues, and actor in that he performs an assigned role. "I assumed," he informed a correspondent, "I assumed a mask to play this part"—"the mask of folly."[20] As the dramatic form of life and the dramatic form of Erasmus' artifact coincide, however, we observe that the actors in both are other than they appear to be. In brief, the mask is a disguise—more explicitly, a premeditated attempt at deception—which is meant profoundly to disturb us. But as Erasmus' purpose was not to provoke only disquiet, he also invites us to regard the mask as testimony to the boundless gaiety of life. Thus the *Moriae encomium* is "like" life in that within the one as within the other converge the tragic and the comic, the serious and the playful, the rational and the irrational, the positive and the negative—and, after all is said, the wisdom that is folly and the folly that is wisdom. If Erasmus praises folly when he meant to celebrate wisdom, and next praises wisdom when he ought to have commended folly, it is because he recognized that life's complexities are intolerant of all either/or dichotomies. Indeed, as the Silenic metaphor we have just considered attests, there is no line of demarcation even between appearance and reality. In the convergence of the twain here as elsewhere, Moria has merged with Athena; yet insofar as her name μωρία is not only classical but Pauline, she has also fused with the supernal folly upheld in St. Paul's first letter to the Corinthians (1.21-30).

The *Moriae encomium* is the boldest annotation of the Pauline position ever. It was anticipated in the *Enchiridion,* less through any ringing generalization ("He is happily a fool who is wise in Christ, miserably a fool who does not know him") than through the exhortation that worldly wisdom should be "unlearned by one who wishes to be truly wise" so as to empower him to comprehend the language of "holy Wisdom" which, by definition partial to the innocent, "stammers childishly" (pp. 53-54, 60, 160). Erasmus' emphasis partakes of that "philosophy of Christ" which in his vision was constituted of the childlike, unadorned "inner piety" he explicated on one occasion thus:

> In this kind of philosophy, located as it is more truly in the disposition of the mind than in syllogisms, life means more than debate, inspiration is preferable to erudition, transformation is a more important matter than intellectual comprehension. Only a very few can be learned, but all can be Christian, all can be devout, and—I shall boldly add—all can be theologians.[21]

Erasmus once professed that the difference between the *Enchiridion* and the *Moriae encomium* is one of ends, not of means. The ends are much "the same" in the two works, he wrote, while their means diverge insofar as the *Moriae encomium* was composed "under the appearance of a joke."[22] Yet the two works also differ in their tone, especially the tone of assurance with which Erasmus approached the paradox of that higher folly which alone defines wisdom. The boldness is unmistakable, and massively impressive. Having collected a number of Biblical references to "fools," he inquired rhetorically:

> Do not all these witnesses cry out with one voice that all mortals are fools, even the pious? And that even Christ, though he was the wisdom of the Father, became somehow foolish in order to relieve the folly of mortals when he took on human nature and appeared in the form of a man? Just as he became sin in order to heal sins. Nor did he choose any other way to heal them but through the folly of the cross, through ignorant and doltish apostles. For them, too, he carefully prescribed folly, warning them against wisdom, when he set before them the example of children, lilies, mustard seed, and sparrows—stupid creatures lacking all intelligence, leading their lives according to the dictates of nature, artless and carefree.... (P. 130)

Only here, in the later part of Moria's dramatic monologue, are we in a position to appreciate fully the understatement in Erasmus' remark to More that "my praise of Folly is not altogether foolish" (p. 4). Obedient to the Divine Purpose as all creatures must finally be, Moria has been obliged to curtail her irony and to still her fluctuating moods before being permitted to speak on behalf of the Christ—or, in terms of Erasmus' favorite "allegory," to open the statuette of "the most extraordinary Silenus of all." But uncharacteristic as it would have been for her to dwell in transcendent regions longer than absolutely necessary, near the end of her discourse she reverts to the stage of the world on which the play of our lives must be enacted. The final salutation is typically buoyant: "valete, plaudite, vivite, bibite"—"farewell, clap your hands, live well, drink your fill" (p. 138).

Is it any wonder that Rabelais approved mightily?

III. "Setting a camel to dance"

As approval of the *Moriae encomium* depends on one's affinitive response to its lusory apprehension of reality, readers who cannot be amused are automatically distanced from its argument. Erasmus evidently expected his kaleidoscopic vision to be regarded askance in many quarters, for in his epistle dedicatory to More he expressed his concern that he might be accused "of ripping everything to shreds" (p. 2). His fears were, in fact, fully justified. In particular, the lack of understanding on the part of Martin Dorp, professor of philosophy at Louvain and overseer of Erasmus' *Opuscula* through the press, must have confirmed him in his judgment that professors are not exempt from folly—alas! quite the contrary.

"It is not for me to advise," Dorp advised Erasmus in 1514, "but I humbly trust that you will do all that is required, if you compose and publish in reply to Folly, a Defence of Wisdom."[23] Erasmus' immediate reaction must have been not unlike Milton's on being counseled by Thomas Ellwood that the poem on the lost Paradise—so manifestly incomplete!—demanded another one on Paradise recovered.[24] Publicly, at any rate, Erasmus elected to deploy his irony in order to address readers beyond Dorp, both present and to come. "I am most eager that you should approve whatever I do," he wrote in formal reply, "for I have such a high opinion of your almost divine intelligence, your preeminent learning, your superlatively acute judgment that I would rather have Dorp alone on my side than a thousand others."[25] The rest of the letter demonstrates conclusively that Dorp's intelligence was not necessarily divine, his learning not quite so preeminent, and his judgment less than superlatively acute. In the process, the letter refuses to confine itself solely to an exposition of Erasmus' method of approach in the *Moriae encomium*. Affirming the ideal reader to be widely read and sensitively perceptive, it forms part of the expressly humanistic commitment to education.

Dorp's engagement with literature was, we must presume, negligible. In educating him into the proper reading of the *Moriae encomium,* Erasmus ranges from explicit suggestions as to how "wise folly" ought to be understood ("the language is figurative, not literal") to pleas for the recognition of the delight generated by literature as an experience common to "all alike"—"except for those," he adds almost coincidentally, "who are so insensitive that they are completely impervious to the pleasures of literature" (pp. 160, 148). The irenic temper is unmistakably Erasmian, its broad dissemination through the *Moriae encomium* displayed variously as gentleness, lightheartedness, gaiety, playfulness. Like her creator, however, Moria is capable of sudden explosions of baleful satire that often veers toward invective similar to that of the *Ciceronianus* and the *Julius exclusus*. Such shifts in Moria's moods parallel her assumption of an increasingly serious mood as she maps the Christian contours of folly; and the strategy signals in each case, not Erasmus' faltering control over his work, but the nature of Moria's inner character: the fluctuating moods, that is to say, validate the multiformity of folly. It may be that the strategy is not inapposite to a work which propounds a wise folly but also, as Erasmus informed a baffled Martin Dorp, "a sane insanity and a sagacious madness" (p. 157).

The *Moriae encomium* is a playful demonstration that playfulness need not be merely playful. Erasmus knew that the task he had set for himself was formidable, yet he chose lightheartedly to describe it as "much the same thing as setting a camel to dance."[26] In the event, Sir Thomas More would most likely have pronounced that the camel had danced all too creditably.

IV. "Every inch pure jest"

The friendship between Erasmus and More was like to that between George Herbert and Nicholas Ferrar: "Their very souls cleaved together most intimately."[27] An apocryphal story holds that Erasmus and More seem to have known one another before they were introduced. It is said that Erasmus on first meeting More remarked, "Aut tu es Morus aut nullus" ("You are More or no one"); and that More replied, "Et tu es aut Deus aut demon aut meus Erasmus" ("You are either God or the devil or my own Erasmus"). Years later, while evincing the diverse ways an idea can be expressed, Erasmus repeated two hundred different ways a sentence pertained to More: "semper dum vitam tui meminero" ("always, as long as I live, I shall be mindful of you"). The generalization of an early biographer must clearly be accepted as given: "Erasmus of all men in the world delighted in the companye of Sir Thomas More."[28]

Erasmus' delight is best testified in the celebrated "portrait of More" he sketched for another great humanist, Ulrich von Hutten, in 1517. "From boyhood he was always so pleased with a joke," Erasmus wrote of More, "that it might seem that jesting was the main object of his life; but with all that, he did not go so far as buffoonery, nor had ever any inclination to bitterness. . . ." In maturity, added Erasmus, More did not forego his fondness for play:

> There is nothing that occurs in human life, from which he does not seek to extract some pleasure, although the matter may be serious in itself. If he has to do with the learned and intelligent, he is delighted with their cleverness, if with unlearned or stupid people, he finds amusement in their folly. He is not offended even by professed clowns, as he adapts himself with marvellous dexterity to the tastes of all. . . . You would say it was a second Democritus, or rather that Pythagorean philosopher, who strolls in leisurely mood through the market-place, contemplating the turmoil of those who buy and sell. . . .[29]

All of the extant Renaissance documents on More dwell on his "merry" disposition. "His sense of fun," wrote Richard Pace in 1517, "is joined with public refinement—you may call humor his father and wit his mother."

Another early biographer, Beatus Rhenanus, described More as "every inch pure jest," while still another, his son-in-law William Roper, quoted him as attributing his irrepressible playfulness to a metaphysical source: "me thinckethe god maketh me a wanton and settethe me on his lappe and dandlethe me."[30] More's premises inevitably affected his writings. Some of his more noteworthy dialogues use a number of "fonde chyldyshe tales," not indeed for any mistaken need of "comic relief" but because, as he wrote in A *Dialogue of Comfort,* "no tale [is] so foolishe, but that yet in one matter or other to some purpose it may hap to serve."[31] However, none of More's "merry tales" even remotely compares with the one he stretched the entire length of his *Utopia* (1515–16).

It was a tale which additionally involved many other humanists in a lively—and certainly unprecedented—conspiracy of amusement. Expert students of Greek that they all were, they never misconstrued "utopia" to mean an ideal state. They knew that it meant, quite simply, No-place, so that in effect it is fully as "realistic" as Aristophanes' Cloudcuckooland. At the same time, determined as they were to display their ingenuity— the "invention" so often commended during the Renaissance—they set to endow their nonexistent place with a sense of place replete with people, customs, ideals (but not, we are meant to mark, any history). One of the wittier conspirators, the City of Antwerp's chief secretary Peter Giles, went so far as to furnish both the Utopian alphabet and "a little scrap of verse" which he not only translated but, much more cleverly, transliterated ("Utopos ha Boccas peula chama . . ."—and such sensible-sounding nonsense).[32] One can imagine the common amusement as details accumulated about More's original design, thereby creating an aura of reality about a place devoid of reality in that it was, by definition, no place! A potentially vexing problem, Utopia's actual location, was also bypassed with alacrity. More, in his first letter to Peter Giles, pretended to remind him that when they both met their informant, they regrettably forgot to raise the question ("it didn't occur to us to ask, nor him to say, in what area of the New World Utopia is to be found"). Giles proved even more inventive, however, for in addressing another correspondent he claimed that the informant had in fact revealed the place of No-place but—a wretched coincidence!—at that very moment someone coughed so loudly that he did not quite catch what was said. The intorted joke was said by More to have affected at least one individual, a devout man who wanted to proselytize the Utopians at least as fervently as he wanted to be named their first bishop. But More and his fellow-conspirators would have been equally amused had they been told that, several centuries later, some readers would continue to behave as if No-place is, or could ever be, somewhere.

So far we have glanced at the side of More's personality which is most like to that of Erasmus, humane in outlook and playful in tone. But there is another side, darker and altogether more mysterious. He practiced, for one, self-flagellation. As his son-in-law William Roper testified, More tended frequently to "punishe his body with whippes, the cords knotted"; additionally, he wore a hair shirt "secreatly next his body."[33] Such details are not relevant only to the inner life of the saint; they are also relevant to the public life of the humanist who was often a fanatic polemicist, and of the fanatic who as Lord Chancellor condemned equally pious spirits to be burned at the stake. One must read the grim works More penned between the first and the last of his dialogues—the *Dialogue concerning Heresies* (1528) and the *Dialogue of Comfort* (1534)—in order to appreciate the extent to which "our Christian Socrates" could suspend the spirit of both Christian charity and Socratic humanity. Sir Thomas More the militant partisan is not inevitably a man for all seasons.

The highly praised *Dialogue of Comfort,* rightly called "one of the greatest dialogues in the English language,"[34] signals the recovery of More's playfulness. The *Dialogue,* like the *Utopia,* cannot be understood apart from that mood; nor can either work be understood solely by that mood. The clouds hovering over More's years of polemical engagement envelop the *Utopia* too, qualifying its argument very much this side of mere amusement. The outlook of More in general, like the outlook of the *Utopia* in particular, is far more consistent than we have been inclined to admit.

V. "The ills of the body politic"

The initial conspiracy of amusement over the meaning of "utopia" should have included the one important individual that it happens to exclude, More's informant about the Commonwealth of Utopia, Raphael Hythloday. We are after all told that he is a linguist, "better versed in Greek than in Latin" (p. 110); and we naturally expect him to have perceived at once that "No-place" is just that: no place. But our expectations are met with silence; and because they are, we are at liberty to conclude either that Hythloday's Greek is very small indeed and his Latin even less, or that he is not fairly perceptive—or, quite possibly, both. Yet presently our confidence in him is shaken further still, for he appears to be unaware of the import even of his own name!

"Raphael Hythloday" is among the most elaborate scholarly jokes of the Renaissance. The Hebraic "Raphael" represents the messenger of God and literally means "God heals," while "Hythloday" transliterates the Greek ὑθλοδαῖος or "speaker of nonsense."[35] In effect, then, the full name could be said to suggest one who is meant to heal but, incapable of doing so, dispenses nonsense instead. But an even more remarkable pun, this time trilingual, would reverse the judgment in Hythloday's favor: "God heals

[Hebr., *Raphael*] through the nonsense [Gr., *huthlos*] of God [Lat., *dei*]."[36] Whether actual or presumed, etymological expertise of this order underlines that we are asked to credit the existence of No-place as related by a man essentially called No-sense. But it underlines More's achievement too, in that we are soon embroiled in the nonexistent political and social structure of No-place, and allow more sense to No-sense than even common sense allows we should.

The *Utopia* is akin to the *Moriae encomium* in more ways than one. The relationship is in the first instance asserted by the original title pages, for where More's work was described as "a truly golden book, no less beneficial than entertaining," Erasmus' was described in 1519 as "a truly golden book, no less learned and beneficial than entertaining."[37] Within, the two works—the two Aristophanic works, I should perhaps insist—are alike distinguished by their dramatic framework, and alike obstruct our immediate apprehension of "the plain, unvarnished truth." More had of course studied the dialogue form in depth through the Lucianic dialogues and the *Moriae encomium*; and he would use it again in the more splendid of his later dialogues. Significantly, of the composition of the *Utopia* we know from a comment by Erasmus[38] that More first wrote Book II—the monologue by Raphael Hythloday—which he later qualified by placing it within the broader context of the dialogue in Book I. The new context alone permitted a character named More to observe at the end of Hythloday's exposition, "I cannot agree with everything he said."

I speak of "a character named More" deliberately, in opposition to our frequent assumption that More who figures within the *Utopia* articulates the viewpoint of his creator. Such an assumption is correct only insofar as we are prepared to accept that the narrating voice of *The Faerie Queene* or of *Paradise Lost* necessarily represents Spenser or Milton. To distinguish More the character from More the creator is to appreciate More as the master of an indirection—and certainly of an architectonic irony—worthy of Lucian or Erasmus. In this respect Hythloday is of course even further removed from More the creator, witness his total lack of the qualities Erasmus praised in his "portrait of More": the humanity, the objectivity, the gravity enjoined to a perpetual amusement. Hythloday among the Utopians is like his descendant Gulliver among the Houyhnhnms, his reason suspended about a land of reason, and his passion aroused over a land devoid of passion. No wonder that More carried on with his stroll "in leisurely mood through the market-place, contemplating the turmoil of those who buy and sell . . ." He was not, I think, a Utopian.

Might the *Utopia* be only entertainment—"a holiday work, a spontaneous overflow of intellectual high spirits, a revel of debate, paradox, comedy and (above all) of invention?"[39] The possibility attracts, indisputably true as it is that a side of More was "every inch pure jest." But

Erasmus' commendation appears more sensitively balanced. "If you have not read More's *Utopia*," he told a correspondent, "do look out for it, whenever you wish to be amused, or rather I should say, if you ever want to see the sources from which almost all the ills of the body politic arise."[40] More's serious aims were recognized during the Renaissance by many others besides Erasmus, witness George Puttenham's grouping of the *Utopia* with Plato's *Republic* as prime examples of the tendency of "the learned and wittie men of those times to devise many historicall matters of no veritie at all, but with purpose to do good and no hurt, as using them for a maner of discipline and president of [i.e., precedent for] commendable life."[41] Yet for Erasmus, it is clear, the *Utopia* was amusing and serious not successively but simultaneously: the humor reinforces the argument, much as it does in the *Moriae encomium*. But Erasmus perceived More's central argument too. He thought it focused on "the ills of the body politic," with the "sources" of those ills left unspecified in the expectation that they would be descried readily by the individual reader.

Erasmus' expectation was mistaken, however. More's self-effacement was so immaculate that readers have wandered ever since in a variety of directions. By way of example, one authority alleges that the *Utopia* endorses "the ideal of religion without dogma as the purest and best worship of the divine being,"[42] even though More would eventually be executed for his unswerving loyalty to a religion not usually noted for its lack of dogma. Another authority urges that More "truly believed" in the need for the abolition of a money economy,[43] even though More somehow failed so much as to hint his radical views in contexts other than the strictly dramatic one of the *Utopia*. By the same token, Marxists who have enlisted More under their banner should consider that in another work he denounced communism as one of the "horrible heresies" of the Anabaptists.[44] Yet I will not suppose that the point is likely to be granted, since those who know their Marxism usually know nothing but their Marxism.

More shared a number of the Utopians' more estimable views, such as their disapprobation of astrology, and rejected as many others, such as their tolerance of religious opponents. In all likelihood, he agreed too with the Utopian prohibition of premarital intercourse. But did he also approve of the extraordinary penalty exacted for its violation, that the offending parties should not be allowed to marry during their entire lives? Did he approve of the premarital inspection of bride and groom naked, which even the usually uncritical Hythloday thinks "foolish and absurd in the extreme" (p. 66)? Did he approve of hedonism, which the Utopians considered "the goal of our actions," and in itself "virtue" (pp. 55–56)? Did he approve of the rule of reason at the expense of clemency and mercy?[45] Did he approve of slavery or of euthanasia? Did he approve of capital punishment for *any* political discussion outside the senate or the popular assembly? Did he approve of cunning and deceit as a matter of national policy? Did he approve of the identical clothes that everyone in Utopia is obliged to wear? Did he approve of the strict prohibition against travel without permission? Did he approve of the exchange of houses by lot every ten years or, even more astonishingly, of the transfer of individuals "from one household with too many into a household with not enough" (p. 44)? More's Utopia may represent the glorification of reason; but it is chilling in the extreme, even for a place that does not exist.

Our proliferating questions over the *Utopia* cannot always be answered so as to redound to the credit of More the enlightened and urbane humanist. The dark shadows that surround both the man and his work will continue to linger; and given More's pervasive irony, it is predetermined that we are not likely ever to conclude which aspects of No-place he favored, and which ones he—like his character More—could not agree with. Fortunately, the greatness of the *Utopia* does not reside in any display of our abilities to argue about it persuasively. It resides in its own ability to confront reality, not indeed by settling questions, but by raising them. True, we find it disconcerting that More punished his wayward body and tormented it further still with a hair-shirt; yet we ought to reflect on occasion whether such behavior should not under certain circumstances be preferred to that of Erasmus, whose experiential horizons never touched on any sense of sin profoundly felt.

The difference between Erasmus and More is the difference between the lusory apprehension of reality that colors the *Moriae encomium* and the more somber hues that enamel the *Utopia*. The Commonwealth of No-place is of course thoroughly amusing as the place that it is not. But what price amusement, when No-place is transformed—and transformed in accordance with More's premeditated design, I am arguing here—into an alarmingly realistic State at once politically totalitarian and socially claustrophobic? Hythloday persists, of course, with his paean; but the paean is scarcely relevant to our final estimate of Utopia, save where we do not mind accepting "the plain, unvarnished truth" from a scholar who does not know his name and, by extension, himself. All the same, at the end of his monomaniacal discourse, he serves More's purposes by denouncing pride as "one single monster, the prime plague and begetter of all others"—"a serpent from hell," he adds with increasing emotion, "which twines itself around the hearts of men" (p. 90). For Hythloday such pride is characteristic of Europeans, not of the Utopians he favors so indiscriminately; yet spacious as his generalization is, it subsumes the citizens of No-place too. Sir Thomas More was after all not likely to have exempted the Utopians from experiential cognizance of the serpent from hell. Its terrible reality was known to him at close quarters, all too intimately; and having once placed it within the *Utopia,* he made that work preferable to the *Moriae encomium* as a document impressively responsive to the richness and the complexity of the human condition. Erasmus' celebration of wise folly is one of the many works of the imagination we have termed, quite justly, "a Divine Comedy";[46] yet More's exhibition of No-place would seem to merit the designation no less justly, and quite possibly more.

NOTES

An earlier version of this chapter appeared in the *Kenyon Review* 8 (1986): 34–48. Copyright 1986 by Kenyon College. Reprinted by permission. Erasmus is here quoted from the translations by Clarence H. Miller of the *Moriae encomium* and the *Letter to Martin Dorp* (New Haven, 1979), by Raymond Himelick of the *Enchiridion* (Bloomington, 1963), by Paul Pascal of the *Julius exclusus* (Bloomington, 1968), and by Margaret Mann Phillips of *The "Adages"* (Cambridge, 1964). Sir Thomas More is quoted from the translation of the *Utopia* by Robert M. Adams (New York, 1975).

1. *Ten Colloquies,* trans. Craig R. Thompson (New York, 1957), p. 158.
2. *Julius exclusus,* pp. 88–89. The work has not always been attributed to Erasmus with certainty; but the evidence in favor of his authorship appears to be conclusive, as shown by J. B. Pineau, "Érasme est-il l'auteur du Julius?" *Revue de littérature comparée* 5 (1925): 385–415, and by J. Kelley Edwards in his introduction to Paul Pascal's translation. For a reading of the "stark comedy" of the other dialogue, see Emile V. Telle, "Erasmus's *Ciceronianus:* A Comical Colloquy," in *Essays on the Works of Erasmus,* ed. Richard L. DeMolen (New Haven, 1978), chap. 11.
3. Quoted by Preserved Smith in *Erasmus* (1923), reprinted in *Twentieth-Century Interpretations of "The Praise of Folly,"* ed. Kathleen Williams (Englewood Cliffs, N.J., 1969), p. 19.
4. Margaret Mann Phillips, "Erasmus and the Classics," in *Erasmus,* ed. T. A. Dorey (London, 1970), p. 24. The quotation on "my friend Erasmus" is from p. 116 of Clarence H. Miller's translation.
5. For details, consult Craig R. Thompson, *The Translations of Lucian by Erasmus and St. Thomas More* (Ithaca, N.Y., 1940). It may be noted that Erasmus—but not More—later translated still other pieces by Lucian.
6. Phillips, in *Erasmus,* ed. Dorey, p. 9. On More's efforts, see T. S. Dorsch, "Sir Thomas More and Lucian: An Interpretation of *Utopia,*" *Archiv für das Studium der neueren Sprachen und Literaturen* 203 (1966–67): 345–63, and Warren W. Wooden, "Thomas More and Lucian: A Study in Satiric Influence and Technique," *Mississippi Studies in English* 13 (1972): 43–58.
7. Phillips, in *Erasmus,* ed. Dorey, p. 9.
8. Quoted in Thompson, *Translations of Lucian,* p. 26.
9. *Enchiridion,* p. 105.

10. The "*Adages*," p. 269; the *Sileni Alcibiadis* occupies pp. 269–96. One of the most persuasive of relevant studies is by Lynda G. Christian, "The Figure of Socrates in Erasmus' Works," *Sixteenth Century Journal* 3.2 (1972): 1–10.
11. The term is his own (*Letter to Martin Dorp*, p. 159).
12. *Opus Epistolarum Des. Erasmi*, ed. P. S. Allen et al. (Oxford, 1906–58), 1:19; quoted by Richard Sylvester in *English Literary Renaissance* 6 (1976): 126.
13. Quoted in W. David Kay, "Erasmus's Learned Joking: The Ironic Use of Classical Wisdom in *The Praise of Folly*," *Texas Studies in Literature and Language* 19 (1977): 248 and 264. Listrius' commentary was furnished by invitation; but as he appears to have fallen ill before the completion of his assignment, Erasmus rounded off the gathered materials and added the remaining notes. For details consult J. Austin Gavin and Thomas M. Walsh, "*The Praise of Folly* in Context: The Commentary of Girardus Listrius," *Renaissance Quarterly* 24 (1971), 193–209; and on the other supplementary materials published with the work: Genevieve Stenger, "*The Praise of Folly* and its Parerga," *Medievalia et Humanistica*, n.s. 2 (1971): 97–117.
14. See the detailed study by Henry K. Miller, "The Paradoxical Encomium with Special Reference to Its Vogue in England, 1600–1800," *Modern Philology* 53 (1956): 145–78.
15. *Works*, gen. ed. Frank A. Patterson (New York, 1931–40), 12:221.
16. See Donald G. Watson, "Erasmus' *Praise of Folly* and the Spirit of Carnival," *Renaissance Quarterly* 32 (1979): 333–53, with further references to other studies of the work's carnivalesque features.
17. In a classic paragraph, Erwin Panofsky differentiated between the Middle Ages and the Renaissance in terms of Brant and Erasmus (see "Renaissance and Renascences," *Kenyon Review* 6 [1944]: 234–35). But the line of demarcation is not quite so clearly evident, since the transition to Renaissance humanism was a process both slow in unfolding and difficult to assess. Consult the older essay by Hermann Schönfeld, "Die kirchliche Satire und religiöse Weltanschauung in Brants *Narrenschiff* und Erasmus *Narrenlob*, resp. in den Colloquia," *Modern Language Notes* 7 (1892): 78–92, 138–50, 346–48; and the subsequent studies by Robert Klein, "Un Aspect de l'hermeneutique à l'age de l'humanisme classique: le theme du fou et l'ironie humaniste," *Archivio di filosofia, umanesimo e ermeneutica* 3 (Padua, 1963), pp. 11–25; Barbara Könneker, *Wesen und Wandlung der Narrenidee im Zeitalter der Humanismus* (Wiesbaden, 1966); and E. Castelli et al., *L'umanesimo e "la Follia"* (Rome, 1971), notably the essays by Maurizio Bonicatti, "La tematica della follia in chiave moralistica: Sebastian Brant e Hieronymus Bosch" (pp. 20ff.), and Pierre Mesnard, "Erasme et la conception dialectique de la folie" (pp. 45ff.). Erasmus' immediate impact on a contemporary artist, Quentin Metsys, is examined by Caterina Limentari Virdis, "Moralismo e satira nella tarda produzione di Quentin Metsys," *Storia dell' Arte* 20 (1974): 19–24. But the best visual counterpart to the Erasmian vision of universal folly is the engraving by Pieter Bruegel the Elder, "The Feast of Fools" (reproduced in Max Seidel and R. H. Marijnissen, *Bruegel* [New York, 1971], p. 67). On the celebrated Holbein illustrations, see the essay by F. Saxl in the *Burlington Magazine* 83 (1943): 275–79.
18. For one of the more sensitive studies of the *Moriae encomium* along these

lines, consult Walter Kaiser, *Praisers of Folly* (Cambridge, Mass., 1963), Part I. Moria's fluctuating moods are also annotated by Geraldine Thompson, *Under Pretext of Praise: Satiric Mode in Erasmus' Fiction* (Toronto, 1973), chap 2.
19. In his dialogue *Menippus or Necromantia*, quoted by Leonard Dean in *Twentieth-Century Interpretations*, ed. Williams, pp. 51–52.
20. *Letter to Martin Dorp*, p. 145.
21. Quoted in Craig R. Thompson, "The Humanism of More Reappraised," *Thought* 52 (1977): 238.
22. *Letter to Martin Dorp*, p. 143. On the points of contact between the *Enchiridion* and the *Moriae encomium*, see Lynda G. Christian, "The Metamorphoses of Erasmus' Folly," *Journal of the History of Ideas* 32 (1971): 289–94.
23. *Epistles*, trans. F. M. Nichols (London, 1901–18), 2:170 [ep. 304].
24. Much to one's surprise, Milton's responsible biographer William R. Parker concluded that Ellwood "almost certainly inspired" the title of *Paradise Regained!* (*Milton* [Oxford, 1968], 1:616).
25. *Letter to Martin Dorp*, p. 140. The letter was first added to the *Moriae encomium* in 1516. More's own letter to Dorp is usually praised as much as—and sometimes more than—Erasmus'. For a detailed study of it as "a masterpiece of rhetorical balance, thematic consistency, and stylistic tact," see Daniel Kinney, "More's Letter to Dorp: Remapping the Trivium," *Renaissance Quarterly* 34 (1981): 179–210.
26. In his letter to Ulrich von Hutten (1517); in *Epistles*, trans. Nichols, 3:392 [ep. 585B].
27. As Barnabas Oley said in 1652; see *George Herbert: The Critical Heritage*, ed. C. A. Patrides (London, 1983), p. 79.
28. The apocryphal story is reported by G. R. Hibbard, "Erasmus and More in the Age of Shakespeare," *Erasmus in English* 12 (1983): 6. The reiterated sentence occurs in Erasmus' *De duplici copia verborum ac rerum* (1512ff.), chap. 33, and is noted by Thompson, "The Humanism of More Reappraised," p. 231. The early biographer is Nicholas Harpsfield, *The Life and Death of Sir Thomas More*, ed. E. V. Hitchcock (London, 1932), p. 136.
29. *Epistles*, trans. Nichols, 3:392 [ep. 585B]; also in Robert M. Adams's translation of the *Utopia*, p. 130.
30. Pace's remark is quoted by Warren W. Wooden, "The Wit of Thomas More's *Utopia*," *Studies in the Humanities* 7.3 (1979): 44, from T. E. Bridgett, *Life and Writings of Sir Thomas More* (London, 1891), pp. 12–13; Rhenanus' phrase is cited by Robert C. Elliott in the comments reprinted in Robert M. Adams's translation of the *Utopia*, p. 184; while Roper's report occurs in his *The Lyfe of Sir Thomas More*, ed. Elsie V. Hitchcock (London, 1935), p. 76. Roper also reports More's remarkable humor as he ascended the scaffold, requesting of the attending officer, "I pray you, good M. Lieutenant, see me safe up, & for my comming downe let me shift for my selfe."
31. Quoted in Willard Farnham, "The Medieval Comic Spirit in the English Renaissance," in *Joseph Quincy Adams Memorial Studies*, ed. James G. McManaway et al. (Washington, D.C., 1948), p. 431. The "merry tales" within another dialogue, the *Dialogue concerning Heresies*, have—not at all surprisingly!—been discovered to cohere with More's overall purpose; see Walter M. Gordon, "The Argument of Comedy in Thomas More's *Dialogue concerning Her-

esies," Renaissance and Reformation 16 (1980): 13–32, and his shorter if distinctly more polemical "In Defense of More's Merry Tales," *Moreana* 38 (1973): 5–12. It is certainly to be regretted that scholars persist both in interpreting More's humor as "comic relief" (e.g., Warren W. Wooden, "The Wit of Thomas More's *Utopia,*" p. 50) and in misinterpreting that humor as mere ridicule and sarcasm (e.g., Rainer Pineas, "Thomas More's Use of Humor as a Weapon of Religious Controversy," *Studies in Philology* 58 [1961]: 97–114).

32. The conspirators' letters are given—together with another letter by Erasmus to Ulrich von Hutten—in Robert M. Adams's translation, pp. 110–35 (the "little scrap of verse" is on p. 116). On the humanist aspect of these letters, see the informative and discriminating study by Peter A. Allen, "*Utopia* and European Humanism: The Function of the Prefatory Letters and Verses," *Studies in the Renaissance* 10 (1963): 91–107.

33. Roper, *Lyfe of Sir Thomas More,* pp. 48 and 49.

34. By R. J. Schoeck, in *Thought* 52 (1977): 325. The work is ably discussed by Leland Miles, "The Literary Artistry of Thomas More: *The Dialogue of Comfort,*" *SEL* 6 (1966): 7–33, and Louis L. Martz, "The Design of More's *Dialogue of Comfort,*" *Moreana* 15–16 (1967): 331–46.

35. On the rich lore that had gathered about Raphael, see Elizabeth McCutcheon, "Thomas More, Raphael Hythlodaeus, and the Angel Raphael," *SEL* 9 (1969): 21–38. Perhaps the most sophisticated reading of More's protagonist is by R. S. Sylvester, " 'Si Hythlodaeo credimus': Vision and Revision in Thomas More's *Utopia,*" in *Essential Articles for the Study of Thomas More,* ed. R. S. Sylvester and G. P. Marc'hadour (Hamden, Conn., 1977), pp. 290–301.

36. Proposed by Robert M. Adams in a note to his translation (p. 6).

37. As observed by Warren Wooden, "The Wit of Thomas More's *Utopia,*" p. 43.

38. In his letter to Ulrich von Hutten, in the Adams translation, p. 134. We may not overlook that, whatever More wrote, he invariably dramatized. This is true even of historical works, witness the argument by Arthur N. Kincaid, "The Dramatic Structure of Sir Thomas More's *History of King Richard III,*" *SEL* 12 (1972): 223–42.

39. C. S. Lewis, *English Literature in the Sixteenth Century* (Oxford, 1954), p. 169. Lewis's account of More (pp. 165–80) may be one-sided but it is also extremely useful because of his enthusiastic argument that "nearly all that is best in More is comic or close to comedy."

40. *Epistles,* trans. Nichols, 2:503 [ep. 519].

41. *The Arte of English Poesie* (1589), ed. Gladys D. Willcock and Alice Walker (Cambridge, 1936), pp. 40–41.

42. Ernst Cassirer, *The Platonic Renaissance in England,* trans. James P. Pettegrove (Austin, 1953), p. 108.

43. J. H. Hexter, *More's "Utopia": The Biography of an Idea* (1952; New York, 1965), p. 57. Hexter's argument is otherwise commendable.

44. In his *Confutation,* as cited by C. S. Lewis, *English Literature in the Sixteenth Century,* p. 169. The prototypical Marxist interpretation of More is by Karl Kautsky, *Thomas More und seine Utopie* (Stuttgart, 1888), trans. H. J. Stenning (New York and London, 1927).

45. On this, consult in particular H. W. Donner, *Introduction to "Utopia"* (London, 1945), pp.75ff. On the limitations of Utopia's institutions and customs, see also T. S. Dorsch, "Sir Thomas More and Lucian."
46. Edward K. Rand, "Horace and the Spirit of Comedy," *Rice Institute Pamphlets* 24 (1937): 115.

Edmund Spenser: The Definition of Poetry

> as imagination bodies forth
> The forms of things unknown, the poet's pen
> Turns them to shapes
> —*A Midsummer-Night's Dream*

I. "A better teacher than Scotus or Aquinas"

Spenser in our time is attended by several ample claims, each proposed ostensibly on his behalf but actually on ours. One of his most discriminating readers thus stipulates our commonest persuasion:

> We stress in him not the painter of ravishing pictures or the spellbinder who can draw us with him deep into wandering woods of fancy, but the maker, the creator of his own coherent universe, the serious, mature, and dedicated poet whose work is a personal vision of truth.[1]

Shared widely by other critics, this attitude appears also to inform the estimates by creators of the order of Virginia Woolf. Her judgment on Spenser was summarily stated on one occasion categorically enough. "He is alive," she said, "in all his parts."[2] Her diary bears witness that her main concern was with the general in Spenser, his "conception," his "idea." On January 23, 1935, she wrote:

> I am reading *The Faerie Queene*—with delight. . . . I can't think out what I mean about *conception*: the idea behind *F.Q.* How to express a kind of transition from state to state. And the air of natural beauty. It is better to read the originals.

A month later, on February 27, she added:

> I now feel a strong desire to stop reading *F.Q.*: to read Cicero's letters, and the Chateaubriand Memoirs. As far as I can see, this is the natural swing of the pendulum. To particularise after the generalisation of romantic poetry.[3]

Among creators, however, Virginia Woolf is an exception. The "idea" of *The Faerie Queene,* its "conception," appears not to have distressed anyone else; and because it has not, I propose here *inter alia* to speculate about the frequent and often obsessive way that the creators of literature in English tend to revert to Spenser. Certainly no poet save Shakespeare has fascinated other poets—and some of our finest prose writers too—quite as much; and this remarkable phenomenon, often enough marked but very rarely annotated, merits attention in that to regard Spenser from diverse vantage points is to appreciate the polymorphic nature of his appeal as well as to understand the motivation behind any given creator's response.

The direction of my inquiry is, I hope, clear. My interest is not primarily with Spenser as an influence, much less with Spenser as a "source." The detection of sources is entirely valid as a critical enterprise, and distinctly salutary in its consequences, witness the studies which in the case of Hawthorne, for example, have broadened our horizons by alerting us to the correspondence between the Bower of Bliss and Rappaccini's garden, or between the House of Pride and *The House of the Seven Gables*.[4] Yet we must explore further, not simply where the implicit evidence is conclusive, but especially where it is not. In the light of Virginia Woolf's favorable judgment on Spenser, what might we propose as the common ground, the connecting link, between *The Faerie Queene* on the one hand and *To the Lighthouse* or *Mrs. Dalloway* on the other? By the same token, knowing as we do that Sir Thomas Browne possessed a copy of *The Faerie Queene*—and he appears not to have owned works of the imagination as a mere collector—what might we claim about his own performance in *Hydriotaphia* or *The Garden of Cyrus*? I am reaching in each case after the nature of one artist's response to another; nor would I exclude instances where the evidence one way or the other is entirely lacking. On the negative side one thinks—as one is bound to think—notably of Bunyan. Are we lightly to dismiss Dr. Johnson's vigilant observation about Bunyan, that "There is reason to think that he had read Spenser"?[5] Johnson's well-attested prejudices notwithstanding, it were positively reckless to apostasize from his sagacity without reflection due.

As with our prose writers, so in particular with our poets. We are often reminded that Milton commended the "sage and serious" Spenser as "a better teacher than Scotus or Aquinas"; that Cowley attributed his poetic prowess to "the tinckling of the Rhyme and Dance of the Numbers" in *The Faerie Queene*; that Dryden expressly acknowledged "that Virgil in Latin, and Spenser in English, have been my masters"; that Pope regarded Spenser as "ever a favourite poet," indeed "like a mistress, whose faults we see, but love her with them all"; and that the genius of Keats was "awakened" once he had gone through *The Faerie Queene* "as a young horse would through a spring meadow—ramping!"[6] In themselves, however, each of these ringing declarations rather obscures than clarifies, in that each multiplies the questions we must necessarily raise. As with the apparent disparity already noted between Virginia Woolf's approbation of Spenser and her own artistic predilections, it should astonish that we have the comments from Milton to Keats in the form that we do have them. Especially where Cowley, Dryden, and Pope are concerned, their eulogies of Spenser are tantamount to oddities begotten by misconception upon implausibility; and it startles even more to learn that Pope had initially contemplated using a stanza from *The Faerie Queene* (I.i.23) as the motto for *The Dunciad* but, in due course, relented.[7] True, Milton's praise of Spenser, and the reportedly spontaneous response of Keats, may impress us as distinctly more apprehensible. Yet they are not devoid of their oddities too, in that Milton's comment is confined to Spenser the "teacher" when we are cognizant of his boundless respect for Spenser the artist, while Keats's reported enthusiasm is confined to Spenser as an initial catalyst when we are aware of his response to Spenser on the variety of fronts suggested by one of our greatest scholars:

> Keats is commonly linked with the Elizabethans by virtue of his sensuous richness, but there are less obvious and not less important links than that. For one thing, in Keats as in a number of Elizabethans, it is almost impossible to draw a line between sensuous and spiritual experience. For another, Keats was the only one among the romantic poets who could quite naturally accept and carry on the allegorical interpretation of myth as he found it in Spenser, Chapman, Sandys, and others. . . . Like Spenser, too, he loves beauty in its concrete and human forms, and sees in myth a treasury of the "material sublime."[8]

The expansive frame of reference here compares adversely with the one provided by Charles Cowden Clarke, who in citing Keats's response to *The Faerie Queene,* emphatically averred that the poet "especially singled out epithets, for that felicity and power in which Spenser is so eminent."[9] Yet Keats himself, in his verse epistle to Clarke, transferred the emphasis to Spenser's sound patterns, notably those

> Spenserian vowels that elope with ease,
> And float along like birds o'er summer seas,
> ("To Charles Cowden Clarke," ll. 56–57)

Such diversity of emphases should deflect us from an uncritical acceptance of comments by poets as by prose writers, whether penned by them or reported second-hand. In each case we rather need a context which, comprehensively based on the given creator's personal assumptions, involves in the first instance our sympathetic admission even of attitudes we may regard as intolerable. The example of Yeats is, I think, particularly instructive.

II. "Not to like Spenser is not to like poetry"

Yeats is instructive because in his 1906 edition of selections from Spenser, and in the introduction he wrote for the occasion, he seems determined to alienate those who share the common persuasion I cited at the outset, that Spenser is less the spellbinder than the "serious, mature, and dedicated poet." Yeats's extracts from *The Faerie Queene* are themselves revealing in that their common denominator is the evocative, the enchanted, the musical, the "poetic," witness the way that his selections begin with the celebrated stanzas on "Enchanted Trees" (I.ii.28–45), terminate with "Una among the Fauns and Satyrs" (I.vi.7–31), and in between include the descriptions of the Houses of Despair and of Richesse (I.ix.21–54; II.vii.3–66), the isles of Phaedria and Acrasia (II.v.28–34; vi.2–26; xii.1–87), the Garden of Adonis (III.vi.30–48), and the like. Yeats's introductory essay, moreover, translates the allegorical into the "mythological and symbolical" ("I am for the most part bored by allegory"), celebrates Spenser's "power of describing bodily happiness and bodily beauty," and concludes that Spenser is at his best

> when he is not quite serious, when he sets before us some procession like a Court pageant made to celebrate a wedding or a crowning. One cannot think that he should have occupied himself with moral and religious questions at all.... One is persuaded that his morality is official and impersonal—a system of life which it was his duty to support.... He is a poet of the delighted senses.[10]

We protest, of course; and leaping to Spenser's defense, we are likely to remark with polemical zeal on Yeats's extreme partiality. We should consider, however, that our defense of Spenser may well mask but a defense of our own interests; that poets like Spenser are in any case sufficiently spatial to accommodate attitudes which in appearance, and possibly in fact, are mutually exclusive; and that when all is said the statements by the creators in our midst are provident in their discretion, hortative in their perspicacity, and infinite in their suggestiveness. I know we behave at times as if "truth" in literature is like "truth" in the sciences, either cumulative or—when a novel concept inspires us—abruptly replaceable by that concept. But "truth" in literature is in its quintessence recurrent yet linearly continuous, apparently dated yet perpetually contemporary.

Yeats is in this respect an exemplar of those principles which, well-considered, involve in particular responses primarily if not exclusively aesthetic. In brief, Yeats the poet commenting on Spenser the poet is a forceful reminder of our own priorities.

Am I proposing that we should revert to Yeats's view of Spenser as the "poet of the delighted senses," discarding our current persuasion that Spenser is a "serious, mature, and dedicated poet"? To a certain extent, yes; for Spenser's sensuousness remains when all is said his most immediately irresistible quality, delighting even readers who were not initially prepared to be delighted, and ever compelling poets to imitate his verses (as did Pope and Blake among numerous others),[11] or to invoke his rhythms at crucial points (as did Marvell in "Clorinda and Damon," Milton in several poems inclusive of *Pardise Regained,* Tennyson in "The Lotos-Eaters," and so on endlessly),[12] or to liberate their energies so as to beget incantatory visions whether of sacred rivers running through caverns measureless to man, storms as if uplifted from the head of some fierce Maenad, or shadowy figures in elfin grots conceived "when reason fades" and magic sleep broods "o'er the troubled sea of mind / Till it is hush'd and smooth." The appropriate generalization was provided by a critic who is now mentioned only to be dismissed. Yet it was all too perceptively that Leigh Hunt wrote in 1833 that

> an admiration of Spenser is a test of poetical taste. Other poets may be preferred, and some few (such as Dante and Shakespeare) were greater men and profounder originals; but not to like Spenser is not to like poetry for its own sake—not to relish the beautiful and the luxurious, without the aid of other stimulants. All the poets have liked him. There has not been a more genuine favourite among them, a writer beloved more as a matter of course, or more imitated; and what is remarkable, he has been beloved by poets of all sorts, natural and artificial. To be poetical at all is to have a sympathy with him.[13]

However flawed by hyperbole, Hunt's statement coincides not with another Romantic manifesto—which in any case it is not—but with the observation predicated by Spenser's great editor, John Hughes, more than a century earlier, in 1715, that Spenser "has been the father of more poets among us than any other of our writers."[14] Incontestably just as I regard such statements to be, they invite a major study of Spenser's influence—yet a study, I believe, which can never be written in that it would have to be, by definition, the history of English literature since the 1590s. There is but one other poet who shares with Spenser the honor of having exerted an influence as ubiquitous, extensively diffused, and penetrating in its diverse manifestations. I refer, of course, to Ben Jonson; and if admissible that Jonson and Spenser between them determined the temper of English poetry thereafter (cf. p. 84), it may be that Jonson's notorious remark on the other's language ("*Spencer*, in affecting the Ancients, writ no Language: Yet I would have him read for his matter; but as *Virgil* read *Ennius*")[15] is rather a telling compliment than a censure. Ben Jonson's ire was usually directed against those of a prowess equal to his own.

In the light of Spenser's impact, emphases on the "serious, mature and dedicated poet" at the expense of other aspects of his achievement are fundamentally a disservice to his greatness. Alas, but Spenserian critics and scholars tend to respond with untoward nervousness. Suspicious of the slightest adverse criticism, they gallop to the opposite extreme with indefensible claims such as the ones in a popular account of Spenser, that *The Faerie Queene* is "the most imaginative" work written in English, that it is "the most human of epics," that its moral purpose is carried by the narrative "effortlessly"—and the like.[16] More formidable studies sin even more formidably, in that they accept similar platitudes as manifestly self-evident. But the testimony of the past—the testimony of adverse as of favorable judgments which I am resuscitating here—may not be eschewed. So far as Spenser's moral purpose is concerned, for instance, experience repeatedly confirms that he had (as Keats said on another occasion) "a palpable design upon us."[17] The report by Henry Reynolds in 1632 is still apposite, all the more because it is so cautiously phrased. Spenser in *The Faerie Queene,* he wrote, fashioned "an exact body of ethic doctrine; though some good judgments have wished, and perhaps not without cause, that he had therein been a little freer of his fiction, and not so close riveted to his moral."[18] But even Addison was not entirely mistaken when he remarked, however militantly, that "the dull moral lies too plain."[19] The reference here, we may assume, is not to an episode like Sir Guyon's destruction of the Bower of Bliss "with rigour pitilesse," since the Bower's artificial wantonness and metallic sterility—especially when opposed to the natural order and expansive fecundity of the Garden of Adonis—is Spenser's ultimate display of subtlety in the education of his reader. We may nevertheless accept that even the conception of the Bower of Bliss is marred by an occasional explicitness, as in the presence within it of "loose Ladies and lascivious boyes" (II.v.28), who reappear within a few cantos as "faire ladies, and lascivious boyes" (II.xii.72). Spenser's often insouciant adjectives stalk us indeed throughout *The Faerie Queene,* their impact frequently neutralized whether the poet indiscriminantly speaks of "fair Britomart," "fair Amoret," "fair Canace," and the like, or redundantly terms Braggadocchio "proud," Triamond "stout," Argante "vile and vicious," and Duessa "false" or "foul" or—usually—both. Yet the "palpable design" is even more widely disseminated than I have suggested, irritating us when a delightful episode such as Una's encounter with a "ramping lion" terminates in the explicit moral ("O how can beautie master the most strong, / And simple truth subdue avenging wrong?" [I.iii.6]). Worse in many ways is the unintended laughter generated when a promising allegorical figure such as Ate, "mother of debate," is not only vaguely said to be "fowle and filthy"—as Spenser pronounces, using two of his most persistent adjectives—but is specifically endowed with a "loathly mouth," "squinted eyes," "matchlesse eares," and even unequal hands! (IV.i.27–29). One is inadvertently reminded of Herrick at his most diverting:

> First, *Jollies* wife is lame; then next, loose-hipt:
> Squint-ey'd, hook-nos'd; and lastly, kidney-lipt.

Might it be that Spenser did not always discern that morality in poetry is vested not in the morality but in the poetry?

III. "Labouring under such a difficulty"

I will be reproached, I know, for failure to understand the nature of allegory—and perhaps for a lack of sympathy to the point of Yeats's boredom with the allegory *qua* allegory, or even of Macaulay's impatience with the absence of humanity from *The Faerie Queene*. "One unpardonable fault," Macaulay said of Spenser during an almost liturgical essay on Bunyan,

> One unpardonable fault, the fault of tediousness, pervades the whole of the Fairy Queen. We become sick of cardinal virtues and deadly sins, and long for the society of plain men and women. Of the persons who read the first canto, not one in ten reaches the end of the first book, and not one in a hundred perseveres to the end of the poem. Very few and very weary are those who are in at the death of the Blatant Beast.[20]

"At the death of the Blatant Beast": Macaulay himself, it is clear, did not persevere to the end. Yet for all its conspicuous bias, Macaulay's judgment is useful in that it focuses attention on an unvarying problem in Spenserian studies, the way our nervous defenders of Spenser present him as an allegorist who is yet committed to character delineation in recognizably dramatic and even psychological terms. The significant exceptions to this rule serve but to sustain the rule. The characters in *The Faerie Queene,* one reader admits, "are all flat and typical, and it is often hard to keep them straight. This is made worse by a similarity of names and situations: the same *kinds* of situation recur again and again, and the poet merely substitutes one set of figures for another." Spenser's genius, another reader states, "is to make us participate in attitudes and states of feeling, but this participation does not involve the pressure of feeling them as dramatic potentialities at the moment of reading. . . . The poetry is a mode of understanding, not of experience."[21] But on the other hand we are assured that Britomart is "a more dramatic characterization than any other in the poem," that "in human terms" Marinell and Florimell "are very recognizable," that often *The Faerie Queene* is "seen to analyse psychological experience in unusual depth," and—far more spectacularly—that "Spenser is very much the poet of humanity and of human relationships."[22]

With respect, I am less than certain of the advisability of defending Spenser along these lines. True, he often suggests implicitly—and sometimes proclaims explicitly—that his "perfect" knights inclusive of Prince Arthur are not necessarily perfect, subject as they are to an omnipresent pride.[23] But such a tendency is consciously perfunctory, the given protagonist remaining by and large static in every respect but the physical. In consequence, *The Faerie Queene* is only nominally an analysis of "psychological experience in unusual depth," its several characters being "too often mere names, with no bodies to back them,"[24] and actualized not as individuals but primarily as ideas, not as "felt" entities but largely as stated principles. Other literature may adhere in the first instance to individuals, to "felt" entities, and in the second to ideas, to principles; but allegory, we ought to acknowledge, reverses those priorities with sustained consistency. My intention, it should be noted, is not to speculate on whether Spenser's poetry betrays his failure to journey extensively through the broad landscape of human experience, alien of the arctic regions of solitude, the dark caves of remorse, the parching deserts of unfulfilled love. My emphasis is placed exclusively on the need to honor Spenser's choice of allegory, much as we honor the choices made by Milton or Blake or Yeats. The best commentary on *The Faerie Queene* is in this respect singular: it is *The Faerie Queene* itself.

The judgment is anaemic, and in appearance rather facetious. But I am arguing for a recognition of the poem's aesthetic symmetries within its own circumference. Within that circumference I would locate Spenser's "palpable design upon us," as already indicated. I would also locate there two more limitations, alike appertaining to that repetitiveness which was meant to strengthen the "design" but in the event results either in a distressing lack of economy or—if one wishes to be complimentary—in a splendid superfluousness.[25] Spenser's choice of stanza—"the ill choice of his stanza," as Dryden would have it[26]—might be said to have contributed to Spenser's lax utterance by obliging him to multiply his verses to the requisite nine; yet on the other hand, as Dryden was the first readily to grant, Spenser is arguably "the more to be admired, that, labouring under such a difficulty, his verses are so numerous, so various, and so harmonious." A much more serious limitation is Spenser's obsession with alliteration and assonance—"the dreariest commonplaces of Spenserian criticism," as one critic urges in an evident effort to prevent discussion.[27] But the obsession lingers, stubbornly; and writ large as it is in *The Faerie Queene,* it invites comment on the proliferation of similar sound patterns which, however musical in themselves, compromise the poem by their excess. After all, abused assonance and abused alliteration alike abstract us as we attend to the artifice apart from the argument, arrested by the Aeolian accents, moved by the mellifluous measures, seduced by the swarming sounds, dazzled by the diverting designs. Spenser, one hazards, cannot always be accused of tenacity.

IV. "A powerful and subtle language"

The limitations of Spenser have often been extended to encompass his language. By the mid-seventeenth century, indeed, Spenser's "obsolete language"—as Davenant reported in 1650—had already "grown the most vulgar accusation that is laid to his charge";[28] and I expect that the process began not with Jonson as before noted ("*Spencer,* in affecting the Ancients, writ no Language") but with Sidney, who earlier had imperiously "dare[d] not alowe" the deployment in *The Shepheardes Calender* of "an old rustick language."[29] Like Jonson, however, Sidney was not entirely impartial; and in any case his judgments coincided with the interests of his immediate contemporaries only spasmodically, witness his rejection of the confluence of tragedy and comedy—"mungrell Tragy-comedie," as he called it— on the very morning of its brightest advent on the horizons of invention (see p. 23). In all, Spenser's language may be censured solely where we deny poets the prerogative to create their own mode of articulation, else where we expect them to write in the language "really used by men"—a precept rather violated than ever implemented, not least by Wordsworth himself. Considered in itself, the language of *The Faerie Queene* as of *The Shepheardes Calender* is in fact neither "old" nor "rustic," nor indeed even coincidentally Chaucerian, in spite of Spenser's benediction on that "wel of English undefyled" (IV.ii.32). It is primarily and expressly Spenserian— a "powerful and subtle language," as Yeats correctly judged, "more full of youthful energy than even the language of the great playwrights."[30] In this sense, too, the best commentary on *The Faerie Queene* is *The Faerie Queene.*

Spenser's language is essentially distinguished by a polyvalency promoted by a rhythm at once ceremonious and ritualistic. Tension should not be sought because it will not be found, all frequent claims to the contrary notwithstanding. But the absence of tension is fully premeditated, the capital aim being a modulation in the sound patterns so as to suggest with extraordinary subtlety a diversity of emphases. Milton, I am persuaded, drew on Spenser for a parallel dimension in his poetry when he differentiated between Heaven and Hell largely in terms of fertile concourse in the one, and stagnant perversity in the other—a strategy obviously central to Spenser's conception of the Garden of Adonis on the one hand, and the Bower of Bliss on the other. But Milton also drew on Spenser for that excess of poetic texture which in the first two books of *Paradise Lost* constitutes a warning not to be swayed by the poetry alone, much as Spenser had warned that extravagantly rich evocations like that of the House of Pride are exempla of evil to be heeded especially when we are thereafter confronted by temptations far more subtle and therefore far more sinister. Spenser did not underestimate the infinite attraction of evil; and because he did not, the nominal opposites he intimates habitually—whether good and evil, order and chaos, concord and discord, grace and nature, *agape* and *eros*, eternity and time—are consciously rendered indistinct. Theoretically, the City of God is diametrically opposed to the City of Man, just as art may be held to be antithetic to nature. But our great poets accept such dichotomies only to abrogate them in their concerted efforts to intimate the multiformity of reality and, beyond, the existence of a transcendent order aesthetically apprehended. Spenser's "palpable design upon us" is at times much too explicit, as I have argued earlier; yet his interrogation of reality remains an impressive achievement all the same, in that his ceremonious and ritualistic rhythms unite what is apparently severed, and conflate what is nominally dispersed.

Spenser's "poetry of reconciliation"—to advocate the phrase fundamental to one of the more substantial studies of *The Faerie Queene* to date[31]—is best described in terms of unity, conflation, harmony, concourse. The same principle is of course applicable to any other major artistic vision too; but Spenser's espousal of it issues in the characteristic way that *The Faerie Queene* sanctions patterns of recurrence even as it is committed to a linear progress that advances from enclosed areas—the garden, the wood, the castle—to that broader prospect wherein (as Marvell was to maintain later) the industrious bee computes its time as well as we. In the end, Spenser's poem stands poised before an ongoing beginning. History will repeat itself with but a few variations, precisely as in the poetry "the same *kinds* of situation recur again and again" (see p. 35). Yet history is not finally either the nightmare from which Stephen Daedalus would endeavor to awaken, nor the horror which the narrator of *The Dry Salvages* would attest by crediting that "the past is all deception, / The future futureless." Spenser's knights—and Spenser's readers—emerge from his Fairyland vigilant of the present because cognizant of the past, and confident in the future because admonished by both. True, the Blatant Beast continues to slouch its way across the world; equally true, we are permitted a vision of the new Jerusalem only from afar. But to the extent that we are persuaded by the form of Spenser's poetry, we defer also to his optimistic creed about the form of history.

V. "Like bars of gold thrown ringing one upon another"

The form of poetry that issues in the form of history is one way of approaching the problem that exercised Virginia Woolf about Spenser's "conception," the "idea" behind *The Faerie Queene*. She had added, we recall, that her concern was with the nature of Spenser's transition "from state to state," which suggests an instinctive response to Spenser's conflation of the recurrent and the linear, and more precisely to his assertion of time at the very moment he was wont to abrogate it. Given Virginia Woolf's own artistic predilections, it does not surprise that this quality in Spenser should oddly parallel montage—"the filmic fourth dimension," as Sergei Eisenstein called it—where image is superimposed on image in a continuum that intimates rather states of mind than the literal dimensions of space and time.[32] Yet Coleridge, whom I dare be known to think a better critic than any before or since, had already marked the same quality in his perception of "the marvellous independence and true imaginative absence of all particular space or time in the 'Faery Queene.' "[33]

The unity of Spenser's major poem has of course been specified in other ways too. Some have sought it in the imagery, and others have found it in the "harmony of atmosphere";[34] while a determined cluster of readers have even emphasized the numerological connection, which I presume convinces only if we care to accept that a major prerequisite in poetry is the ability to count.[35] I myself prefer the less adventurous view that sees in *The Faerie Queene* "unity arising from multeity."[36] I would at most add that my particular emphasis involves, as before noted, Form—namely, that aesthetic consistency which conflates the many into the one by a felicitous coincidence of the intention ("the form of poetry") and the argument ("the form of history"). Least relevant here, it will be observed, is the much debated letter to Ralegh, post-fixed to the 1590 edition of the first three books of *The Faerie Queene*; for that letter is simply *a* reading of the poem before or after the event and in a dramatically different medium, comparable but to Dante's largely irrelevant claims in that wayward letter to Can Grande, Tasso's in the serpentine afterthoughts on the *Gerusalemme liberata,* Milton's in the myopic preface to *Samson Agonistes,* or Yeats's in the impossible convolutions of *A Vision*.[37] Spenser's letter to Ralegh restricts *The Faerie Queene* much in the way mere program notes limit, say, *The Magic Flute*. Spenser's poem and Mozart's opera if judged in themselves resound the inadequacy of their plots no less than the infirmity of their characterization; but they resound, too, the charm of their improbable tales, the potency of their magic, the passion of their lyricism, the liveliness of their comedy annexed to the gravity of their seriousness.[38] As allegory is essential to the one, so is symbolism to the other; and once accepted *qua* allegory and symbolism, we are liberated into a perception of those ideas and principles which inform the visionary aim of both Spenser and Mozart through the mythopoeic tactics of each. In effect, Yeats's translation of the allegorical into the "mythological and symbolical" was not totally misplaced, so far at least as we may say of allegory much as it was once said of a particular myth, that it "never happened but it always is" (ταῦτα δὲ ἐγένετο μὲν οὐδέποτε, ἔστι δὲ ἀεί).[39]

Yet to regard the judgments of our poets and prose writers in general terms is to be impressed by the incremental interest they have displayed not so much in Spenser's mythopoeic tactics as in the poetry of his poetry. The motivation was best stated by Yeats when he averred on behalf of his fellow-poets as of himself, that creators study their predecessors in order to understand "that impulse and method of creation that can only be learned with surety from the technical criticism of poets, and from the excitement of some movement in the artistic life."[40] In the case of Spenser, responses have abounded not simply because of the decorative nature of his poetry but capitally because of his creative language and phraseology, his critical adaptation and extension of traditional modes of poetic expression, his controlled diversity of meters, his sustained deployment of imagery, his variegated stanzas in spite of their predetermined compass, and of course his visual and aural imagination. "He seemed always," said Yeats, "to feel through the eyes, imagining everything in pictures."[41] Yet he felt even more acutely through the ears; and therefore his lines, as Yeats noted in a striking phrase, are "like bars of gold thrown ringing one upon another."[42]

We have reached, I think, the cardinal reason for Spenser's approbation by our creators. It is his sound patterns, so orchestrated as to define poetry at its most elemental. But "poetry at its most elemental" should not be misconstrued, *pace* Leigh Hunt, as "the beautiful, and the luxurious, without the aid of other stimulants"—in short, "poetry for its own sake." Our persuasion that Spenser is a "serious, mature, and dedicated poet" may at times be hyperbolic in the latitude of its claims; yet it were extravagant to deplore it utterly, all the more since a greater poet also acknowledged him to be at once "sage and serious." Nevertheless, the achievement of Spenser centers finally not on his unexceptionable "body of ethic doctrine," much less on his alleged analysis of "psychological experience in unusual depth." It centers on a measured poetic flair so far superior to his ideas that to neglect the flair for the sake of the ideas would be the ultimate aberration. We are admonished as much by Spenser himself, whenever he veers away from his "palpable design" to serve notice that the proper advance of his "poetry of reconciliation" is from the congregated strains to the single pattern, not the other way around. Hence, indeed, even the meaningfully assonant clusters of names like Phantastes, Eumnestes, and Anamnestes, or Triamond, Diamond, and Priamond—but also, habitually expansive as Spenser tended to be, the alarming enumeration within a single stanza of Gardante, Parlante, Iocante, Basciante, Bacchante, and Noctante (III.i.45). Spenser is no doubt maculate; yet the concord of his well-tuned sounds is often so highly wrought that, like Pope, we love him with all his faults. No other response is possible when we are confronted by his vibrant description of the nuptials of the Thames and the Medway, easily the most resonant of the Spenserian strains, and indeed a definition of "poetry at its most elemental." Lengthy though the procession of the wedding guests is, one would have wished it far longer so that we may joy in the symphonic presence of

> The rich *Cteatus,* and *Eurytus* long;
> *Neleus* and *Pelias* lovely brethren both;
> Mightie *Chrysaor,* and *Caïcus* strong;
> *Eurypulus,* that calmes the waters wroth . . .
>
> (IV.xi.14)

Or the founders of "puissant Nations":

> Ancient *Ogyges,* even th' auncientest,
> And *Inachus* renowmd above the rest;
> *Phœnix,* and *Aon,* and *Pelasgus* old,
> Great *Belus, Phœax,* and *Agenor* best;
> And mightie *Albion,* father of the bold
> And warlike people, which the *Britaine* Islands hold.
>
> (IV.xi.15)

Or the mighty rivers:

> Great Ganges, and immortall Euphrates,
>   Deepe Indus, and Maeander intricate,
>   Slow Peneus, and tempestuous Phasides,
>   Sweet Rhene, and Alpheus still immaculate:
> Ooraxes, feared for great *Cyrus* fate;
> Tybris, renowmed for the Romaines fame,
> Rich Oranochy, though but knowen late . . .
>
> (IV.xi.21)

—and, at the end of the same canto, the ultimate prosperity of resonance in the invocation of the sea nymphs:

> Fresh *Alimeda,* deckt with girlond greene;
>   *Hyponeo,* with salt bedewed wrests:
> *Laomedia,* like the christall sheene;
> *Liagore,* much praisd for wise behests;
> And *Psamathe,* for her brode snowy brests;
> *Cymo, Eupompe,* and *Themiste* just;
> And she that vertue loves and vice detests
> *Euarna,* and *Menippe* true in trust,
> And *Nemertea* learned well to rule her lust.
>
> (IV.xi.51)

Yet touchstone passages of the same level occur elsewhere in *The Faerie Queene* too; and in an effort to describe their impact, one borrows frantically from other poets to assert the "Aeolian visitations," the "planetary music heard in trance," the "soul-animating strains." Those other poets, certainly, were obliged to listen with great care whenever Spenser tuned his poetic universe through those wondrous musical descriptions of music:

> And all the way their merry pipes they sound,
>   That all the woods with doubled Eccho ring,
>   And with their horned feet do weare the ground,
>   Leaping like wanton kids in pleasant Spring.
>
> (I.vi.14)

Or again, in the celebrated Masque of Cupid:

> The whiles a most delitious harmony,
>   In full straunge notes was sweetly heard to sound,
> That the rare sweetnesse of the melody
>   The feeble senses wholly did confound,
>   And the fraile soule in deepe delight nigh dround:
> And when it ceast, shrill trumpets loud did bray,
>   That their report did farre away rebound,
> And when they ceast, it gan againe to play,
> The whiles the maskers marched forth in trim aray.
>
> (III.xii.6)

And finally, in that moment of auditory magic when Cymoent journeys with the other nymphs across the waters to Marinell, and Neptune with "all the griesly Monsters of the Sea / Stood gaping at their gate, and wondred them to see":

> A teme of Dolphins raunged in aray,
>   Drew the smooth charet of sad *Cymoent*;
>   They were all taught by *Triton,* to obay
>   To the long raynes, at her commaundement:
>   As swift as swallowes, on the waves they went,
>   That their broad flaggie finnes no fome did reare,
>   Ne bubbling roundell they behind them sent;
>   The rest of other fishes drawen weare,
> Which with their finny oars the swelling sea did sheare.
>
> (III.iv.33)

In part, certainly, Leigh Hunt was quite right: "not to like Spenser is not to like poetry."

NOTES

An earlier version of this essay appeared as "The Achievement of Edmund Spenser," *Yale Review* 69 (1980): 427–43. The *Yale Review* copyright 1980 Yale University. Reprinted by permission. *The Faerie Queene* is here quoted from the edition by J. C. Smith (Oxford, 1909, reprint 1964), 2 vols.

1. Kathleen Williams, *Spenser's "Faerie Queene": The World of Glass* (London, 1966), p. xi.
2. From a posthumously published essay, partially reprinted in *The Prince of Poets,* ed. John R. Elliott, Jr. (New York, 1968), p. 19.
3. *A Writer's Diary,* ed. Leonard Woolf (London, 1953), pp. 238, 239.
4. See Randall Stewart, "Hawthorne and *The Faerie Queene,*" *Philological Quarterly* 12 (1933): 196–206; Hazel T. Emry, "Two Houses of Pride: Spenser's and Hawthorne's," *PQ* 33 (1954): 91–94; John W. Shroeder, "Hawthorne's 'The Man of Adamant': A Spenserian Source-Study," *PQ* 41 (1962): 744–56; Herbert A. Leibowitz, "Hawthorne and Spenser: Two Sources," *American Literature* 30 (1959), 459–66; etc.
5. James Boswell, *Life of Johnson,* ed. G. B. Hill, revised by L. F. Powell (Oxford, 1934), 2:238. The thesis of Harold Golder that Spenser's influence is "unlikely" ("Bunyan and Spenser," *PMLA* 45 [1930]: 216–37) requires, I think, drastic reappraisal.
6. Milton, *Areopagitica* (1644), in *Prince of Poets,* ed. Elliott, p. 10; Cowley, "Of Myself" (1656), in Elliott, p. 11; Dryden, Dedication of his translation of *The Aeneid* (1697), in *Edmund Spenser: A Critical Anthology,* ed. Paul J. Alpers (Harmondsworth, England, 1969), p. 75; Pope, letter to John Hughes (1715),

in Elliott, p. 13; and Keats, as reported by Charles Armitage Brown, and by Charles and Mary Cowden Clarke, alike quoted by Walter Jackson Bate, *John Keats* (London, 1963), p. 33.
7. Joseph Spence, *Observations, Anecdotes, and Characters of Books and Men,* ed. James M. Osborn (Oxford, 1966), 1:182.
8. Douglas Bush, *Mythology and the Romantic Tradition in English Poetry* (Cambridge, Mass., 1937), p. 85.
9. Quoted in Bate, *John Keats,* p. 33.
10. From the prefatory essay to *Poems of Spenser: Selected and with an Introduction by W. B. Yeats* (Edinburgh, [1906], here quoted from Yeats's *Essays and Introductions* [London, 1961]). For a generalized account, see A. G. Stock, "Yeats on Spenser," in *In Excited Reverie,* ed. A. Norman Jeffares and K. G. W. Cross (London, 1965), pp. 93–101. Consult also the broader context provided by Cleanth Brooks in "William Butler Yeats as a Literary Critic," in *The Disciplines of Criticism,* ed. Peter Demetz et al. (New Haven, 1968), pp. 17–41, and Enoch Brater in "W. B. Yeats: The Poet as Critic," *Journal of Modern Literature* 3 (1975): 651–76.
11. See Pope's *Minor Poems,* ed. Norman Ault and John Butt (London, 1964), pp. 43–45, and Blake's *Poems,* ed. W. H. Stevenson (London, 1971), pp. 17–19.
12. Marvell's poem has been described as "predominantly Spenserian" by J. B. Leishman, *The Art of Marvell's Poetry* (London, 1966), p. 119. An excellent essay on Milton in relation to Spenser is by John M. Major, "*Paradise Regained* and Spenser's Legend of Holiness," *Renaissance Quarterly* 20 (1967): 465–70. On Tennyson, consult James R. Kincaid, "Tennyson's Mariners and Spenser's Despair: The Argument of 'The Lotos-Eaters,'" *Papers on Language and Literature* 5 (1969): 273–81. In all, we have of late been occupied most with Milton's Spenserian links; see: Kathleen Williams, "Milton, Greatest Spenserian," in *Milton and the Line of Vision,* ed. Joseph Wittreich (Madison, 1975), pp. 25–55; Maureen Quilligan, *Milton's Spenser: The Politics of Reading* (Ithaca, N.Y., 1983); Richard Helgerson, *Self-Crowned Laureates: Spenser, Jonson, Milton, and the Literary System* (Berkeley, 1983); and John Guillory, *Poetic Authority: Spenser, Milton, and Literary History* (New York, 1983).
13. *Leigh Hunt's Literary Criticism,* ed. Lawrence H. and Carolyn W. Houtchens (New York, 1956), p. 446.
14. In *Edmund Spenser,* ed. Alpers, p. 79.
15. *Discoveries,* in *Ben Jonson,* ed. C. H. Herford, Percy and Evelyn Simpson (Oxford, 1947), 8:618. Ennius' *Annales* would have been useful to Virgil—so Jonson evidently implies—rather for its comprehensively historical tableaux than for its poetry. But the parallelism with Spenser has been rejected by all poets since Jonson.
16. Peter Bayley, *Edmund Spenser: Prince of Poets* (London, 1971), pp. 32, 181, 153.
17. "We hate poetry that has a palpable design upon us" (from Keats's letter to John Hamilton Reynolds, February 3, 1818).
18. In *Edmund Spenser,* ed. Alpers, pp. 55–56. But there have been those who, like the Viscount Preston in 1670, thought Spenser "blameable . . . in too much, on the whole, countenancing Knight-errantry"; while William Webbe in 1586 hinted darkly that the sixth eclogue encompasses homosexuality—

"scant allowable to English ears," he said, though proper enough for Italian ones!
19. In *Edmund Spenser,* ed. Alpers, p. 74.
20. First published in the *Edinburgh Review* (1830); partially reprinted in *Bunyan: "The Pilgrim's Progress"—A Casebook,* ed. Roger Sharrock (London, 1976), p. 66.
21. Harry Berger, in *Edmund Spenser,* ed. Alpers, p. 265; and Paul J. Alpers, *The Poetry of "The Faerie Queene"* (Princeton, 1967), p. 333.
22. Thomas P. Roche, Jr., *The Kindly Flame* (Princeton, 1964), p. 51, in *The Prince of Poets,* ed. Elliott, pp. 281–82; Williams, *Spenser's "Faerie Queene,"* p. 117; Alastair Fowler, *Edmund Spenser* (Writers and Their Work [London, 1977]), p. 41; and Williams again, p. 32.
23. See especially Lewis H. Miller, Jr., "Arthur, Maleger, and History in the Allegorical Context," *UTQ* 35 (1966): 176–87, and Maurice Evans, "The Fall of Guyon," in *Critical Essays on Spenser from "ELH"* (Baltimore, 1970), notably pp. 181f.
24. As James Russell Lowell observed in 1875; in *Edmund Spenser,* ed. Alpers, p. 157.
25. Cf. "No poet is so splendidly superfluous as he" (Lowell in *Edmund Spenser,* ed. Alpers, p. 158).
26. In *Edmund Spenser,* ed. Alpers, p. 74. Jonson is also reported by William Drummond to have said that "Spencers stanzaes pleased him not" (*Ben Jonson,* ed. Herford and Simpson, 1:132).
27. Alpers, *The Poetry of "The Faerie Queene,"* p. 98.
28. In *Edmund Spenser,* ed. Alpers, p. 62.
29. *An Apologie for Poetrie,* in *Criticism,* ed. Mark Schorer et al. (New York, 1948), p. 426.
30. From the prefatory essay to *Poems of Spenser.* The best essay I know on Spenser's language is by A. C. Hamilton, in *A Theatre for Spenserians,* ed. Judith M. Kennedy and James A. Reither (Toronto, 1973), pp. 101–23. See also Martha Craig, "The Secret Wit of Spenser's Language," in *Elizabethan Poetry,* ed. Paul J. Alpers (New York, 1967), pp. 447–72.
31. Humphrey Tonkin, *Spenser's Courteous Pastoral* (Oxford, 1972).
32. *Film Form,* trans. Jay Leda (New York, 1949; 1951), pp. 64–71. On the relationship between the cinema and modern literature, see the introduction to *Aspects of Time,* ed. C. A. Patrides (Toronto, 1976).
33. *Lectures and Notes on Shakspere,* ed. T. Ashe (1885), p. 514; also in *Edmund Spenser,* ed. Alpers, p. 144.
34. Northrop Frye, in *Edmund Spenser,* ed. Alpers, pp. 277ff., and C. S. Lewis, in *Edmund Spenser,* ed. Alpers, p. 243; respectively.
35. Aspiring numerologists should not fail to read William Nelson's indispensable review of Alastair Fowler's *Spenser and the Numbers of Time* (London, 1964), in *Renaissance News* 18 (1965): 52–57. See also p. 171.
36. S. K. Heninger, Jr., "The Aesthetic Experience of Reading Spenser," in *Contemporary Thought on Edmund Spenser,* ed. Richard C. Frushell and Bernard J. Vondersmith (Carbondale, Ill., 1975), p. 95.
37. It is clear that I agree with C. S. Lewis's contention that the letter to Ralegh is "a very careless blurb" on the poem (*Spenser's Images of Life* [Cambridge,

1967], pp. 137ff.). On the other hand, A. C. Hamilton sees "no divergencies" between the letter and the poem (*MLN* 73 [1958]: 481–85), while W. J. B. Owen claims that the letter concerns a version of the poem planned but never executed (*ELH* 19 [1952]: 165–72).

38. The recognition of Spenser's "comedy" is certainly the happiest of recent developments. See especially W. B. C. Watkins, "Spenser's High Comedy," in his *Shakespeare and Spenser* (Princeton, 1950), app. 1; Robert O. Evans, "Spenserian Humor: *Faerie Queene* III and IV," *Neuphilologische Mitteilungen* 60 (1959): 288–99; John M. Hill, "Braggadocchio and Spenser's Golden World Concept: The Function of Unregenerative Comedy," *ELH* 37 (1970): 315–24; James V. Holleran, "A View of Comedy in *The Faerie Queene*," in *Essays in Honor of E. L. Marilla*, ed. W. J. Olive and T. A. Kirby (Baton Rouge, 1970), pp. 101–14; Clyde G. Wade, "Comedy in Book VI of *The Faerie Queene*," *Arlington Quarterly* 2.4 (1970): 90–104; Linwood E. Orange, "'All Bent to Mirth': Spenser's Humorous Wordplay," *SAQ* 71 (1972): 539–47; William Nelson, "Spenser ludens," in *A Theatre for Spenserians*, ed. Kennedy and Reither, pp. 83–100; John D. Bernard, "Pastoral and Comedy in Book III of *The Faerie Queene*," *SEL* 23 (1983): 5–20; and my own remarks in "Spenser: The Contours of Allegorical Theology," *Centennial Review* 26 (1982): especially 29ff. The background to Spenser's tactics in *The Faerie Queene* is to be sought in his delightful *Muiopotmos*. See the studies by Franklin E. Court, "The Theme and Structure of Spenser's *Muiopotmos*," *SEL* 10 (1970): 1–15; Judith M. Anderson, "'Nat worth a boterflye': *Muiopotmos* and *The Nun's Priest's Tale*," *JMRS* 1 (1971): 89–106; Judith Dundas, "*Muiopotmos*: A World of Art," *YES* 5 (1975): 30–38; Robert A. Brinkley, "Spenser's *Muiopotmos* and the Politics of Metamorphoses," *ELH* 48 (1981): 668–76; and Andrew D. Weiner, "Spenser's *Muiopotmos* and the Fates of Butterflies and Men," *JEGP* 84 (1985): 203–20.

39. The statement is quoted by Walter F. Otto, *Dionysus*, trans. Robert B. Palmer (Bloomington, 1965), p. 75.

40. *Essays and Introductions*, p. 359.

41. *Essays and Introductions*, p. 383.

42. *Essays and Introductions*, p. 379.

Shakespeare: The Comedy beyond Comedy

> Foolery, sir, does walk about the orb like the sun, it shines every where.
> —*Twelfth Night*
>
> Dost thou call me fool, boy?
> —*King Lear*

I. "The real state of sublunary nature"

Shakespeare is often a stumbling block and, not infrequently, foolishness or *moria*. We like to think, for example, that he wrote comedies, histories, and tragedies; yet our neat categories are abrogated—not by himself, it should be emphasized, but by those who superintended his plays for publication—in that *Richard II* is described in the first quarto of 1597 not as history but as "tragedie," while *Troilus and Cressida* is designated "history" in the quarto of 1609, "comedy" in the address to the reader added in the second state, and "tragedy" in the First Folio.[1] True, the critical nomenclature of the Elizabethans and the Jacobeans was by any civilized standard crude at best and, at worst, barbarous;[2] and our own talents being far more creative, we have invented still other categories, notably that of "dark comedies" or, more generally still, of "problem plays." Polonius would not have disapproved.

What transpires within the plays, however, is not very reassuring. We are certainly concerned because in several plays that ought to have been comedies, some of the principal characters—Portia, Helen, Vincentio, Prospero—rely on "devious and astonishing methods"[3] of sufficiently grave implications to stretch even comedy's permissiveness. We are also concerned because the harrowing tragedy of *Titus Andronicus*—admittedly Shakespeare's first attempt in that direction (1592?)[4]—is possessed of a "grisly humor" whose presence we tend to justify, nervously, as part of the play's affirmation of the collapse of moral order and the eventual emergence of "a hierarchy of awareness."[5] Beyond, we are concerned too because Shakespeare's progress toward plays of the order of *Hamlet, Othello, King Lear, Macbeth,* and *Antony and Cleopatra,* appears increasingly to have involved a deliberate—a consistently deliberate—absorption of comic elements within the nominal tragic texture. *Romeo and Juliet* (1594?) was in all likelihood a major turning point, for the delineation of the star-crossed lovers against the well-nigh farcical background of their embattled families intimates the appearance if not the fact of a sustained, even massive, effort to conflate modes of expression traditionally apportioned to tragedy and comedy respectively.⁶ By the time of *Othello* (1604) Shakespeare felt secure enough boldly to resort to a plainly comic structure derived from the *commedia dell'arte*,⁷ even if the extant tradition was adjusted so that Iago is conceived this side of Zanni-Arlecchino-Brighella, and the "noble Moor" this side of the conventional cuckold presented mainly for our amusement.⁸ The approach increasingly perfected, there followed three years later *Antony and Cleopatra* (1607), not coincidentally described by one reader as "the most comic of Shakespeare's tragedies."⁹

Once with *Antony and Cleopatra*, we are not only spatially far removed from the "grisly humor" within *Titus Andronicus*; we are also distant from the categories dictated by our obsession with genres. "Problem plays," that is to say, may not be confined to comedies that partake of the tragic when they can as readily encompass tragedies that partake of the comic. By the same token, "comedy" and "tragedy" are as critical terms likely to mislead, indicative as both are of an approach not congruent with Shakespeare's actual practice. After all, even Coleridge was deflected into a condemnation of "the low porter soliloquy" in *Macbeth*, venturing the suggestion that it was perhaps "an interpolation of the actors," possibly "written for the mob by some other hand."¹⁰ Parallel arguments, emerging from similar premises, bedevil us still and they affect our judgment of the equally "low" scenes in plays as diverse as *Measure for Measure*, *Hamlet*, and *Pericles*.

The coexistence of comedy and tragedy in Shakespeare has of course been justified, definitively, by Samuel Johnson. His celebrated statement is sufficiently well-known to have lost its force. It deserves to be quoted at some length:

> Shakespeare's plays are not in the rigorous and critical sense either tragedies or comedies, but compositions of a distinct kind; exhibiting the real state of sublunary nature, which partakes of good and evil, joy and sorrow, mingled with endless variety of proportion and innumerable modes of combination; and expressing the course of the world, in which the loss of one is the gain of another; in which, at the same time, the reveller is hasting to his wine, and the mourner burying his friend; in which the malignity of one is sometimes defeated by the frolic of another; and many mischiefs and many benefits are done and hindered without design.
>
> Out of this chaos of mingled purposes and casualties the ancient poets, according to the laws which custom had prescribed, selected some the crimes of men, and some their absurdities; some the momentous vicissitudes of life, and some the lighter occurrences; some the terrours of distress, and some the gayeties of prosperity. Thus rose the two modes of imitation, known by the names of tragedy and

comedy, compositions intended to promote different ends by contrary means, and considered as so little allied, that I do not recollect among the Greeks or Romans a single writer who attempted both.

Shakespeare has united the powers of exciting laughter and sorrow not only in one mind but in one composition. Almost all his plays are divided between serious and ludicrous characters, and, in the successive evolutions of the design, sometimes produce seriousness and sorrow, and sometimes levity and laughter.

That this is a practice contrary to the rules of criticism will be readily allowed; but there is always an appeal open from criticism to nature. . . .[11]

Johnson's defense of Shakespeare may be annotated in terms of an essay he published in *The Rambler* in 1751. In appearance a complaint because "our greatest poets," as Johnson said, "unhappily confounded tragick with comick sentiments," the essay is actually a careful analysis of the perils inherent in the conflation of tragedy and comedy. Shakespeare is on this occasion not included among "our greatest poets." Dryden, however, is; and he should *inter alia* have considered, proclaimed Johnson, "that thoughts or incidents in themselves ridiculous, grow still more grotesque by the sublimity of such characters"; "that the most important affairs, by an intermixture of an unseasonable levity, may be made contemptible; and that the robes of royalty can give no dignity to nonsense or to folly."[12] Johnson's view of Shakespeare was clearly other.

The Johnsonian thesis may also be approached from a different perspective, and in different terms, by way of an opportunity provided by Pirandello in *L'umorismo* (1908, revised 1920). "All abstractions are necessarily rooted in a concrete fact," wrote Pirandello. He added, possibly with a conscious recollection of Shakespeare: "What existed, therefore, was tears *and* laughter, not tears *or* laughter. . . ."[13] The pattern here intimated was detailed for the first time by Shakespeare's early-nineteenth-century editor, Edmund Malone. ("There is, I believe, no image which our poet more delighted in than this".)[14] It occurs twice in *Richard II*. The first occasion is on Richard's return to England, when he greets her soil with intense devotion:

> Dear earth, I do salute thee with my hand,
> Though rebels wound thee with their horses' hoofs:
> As a long-parted mother with her child
> Plays fondly with her tears and smiles in meeting,
> So weeping, smiling, greet I thee, my earth.
>
> (III.ii.6–10)

The second occasion forms part of York's moving report on Richard after his forced abdication:

> No joyful tongue gave him his welcome home:
> But dust was thrown upon his sacred head;
> Which with such gentle sorrow he shook off,
> His face still combating with tears and smiles,
> The badges of his grief and patience . . . .
>
> (V.ii.29–33)

The pattern reappears next in *King Lear,* where it also occurs twice. Initially affirmed by the Fool, it is in the form of a ditty so characteristic of his inverted mode of discourse. Crudely assuring Lear of having lowered his breeches to be spanked by Goneril and Regan, he sings:

> Then they for sudden joy did weep,
>   And I for sorrow sung,
> That such a king should play bo-peep,
>   And go the fools among.
>
> (I.iv.191–94)

The pattern's second occurrence in *King Lear* is lucidly direct. It is significantly connected with Cordelia's imminent return to her father's ravaged kingdom:

>   patience and sorrow strove
> Who should express her goodliest. You have seen
> Sunshine and rain at once: her smiles and tears
> Were like a better way: those happy smilets,
> That play'd on her ripe lip, seem'd not to know
> What guests were in her eyes; which, parted thence,
> As pearls from diamonds dropp'd.
>
> (IV.iii.18–24)

Four subsequent uses of the pattern affect as many different situations. One, invested with oppressive dramatic irony, is Duncan's statement in *Macbeth*: "My plenteous joys, / Wanton in fulness, seek to hide themselves / In drops of sorrow" (I.iv.33–35). Another, in *Coriolanus,* involves Cominius' promise to report the protagonist's victories "Where senators shall mingle tears with smiles" (I.ix.3). A third, in *The Tempest,* is allotted to Miranda in conversation with Ferdinand: "I am a fool / To weep at what I am glad of" (III.i.73–74). The last, in *Cymbeline,* is a sustained description of Imogen, at the time in disguise as a youth:

> Nobly he yokes
> A smiling with a sigh, as if the sigh
> Was that it was, for not being such a smile;
> The smile mocking the sigh, that it would fly
> From so divine a temple, to commix
> With winds that sailors rail at.
>
> (IV.ii.51–56)

But the pattern also partakes of the attitude which in *Twelfth Night* is summarily said to be "Smiling at grief" (II.iv.118), in itself representative of that play's double vision, its smiles and its tears inseparable.[15]

My intent is clear. The convergence in Shakespeare of the comic and the tragic exhibits, as Johnson rightly claimed, "the real state of sublunary nature"; but it exhibits, too, an aspiration after the aesthetic apprehension of a unified vision whose dimensions, not confined to the merely sublunar, intimate a context veritably cosmic. A remark by the playwright Dürrenmatt guides us part of the way. Sketching the opportunities still available to the dramatist ("the tragic is still possible even if pure tragedy is not"), Dürrenmatt urged: "We can achieve the tragic out of comedy. We can bring it forth as a frightening moment, as an abyss that opens suddenly; indeed, many of Shakespeare's comedies are already really comedies out of which the tragic arises."[16] But the converse, I would plead, also obtains: the comic may be achieved—and, in Shakespeare's case, was achieved—out of tragedy; it was often brought forth as an exhilarating moment, as an apocalypse that is revealed suddenly; for, indeed, many of his tragedies are really tragedies out of which the comic arises.

Comedy, tragedy, and—as a last resort—tragicomedy: where the first two fail to serve, might we usefully invoke the third? But care must be had lest we equate "tragicomedy" with the particular genre that was much in evidence, no less in theory than in practice, by the time Shakespeare wrote his reputed "new kind of play" represented by *Pericles, Cymbeline, The Winter's Tale,* and *The Tempest.*[17] In theory, the term had figured centrally in Giambattista Guarini's sustained exposition in *Il compendio della poesia tragicomica* (1601), its burden carried in England somewhat later (ca. 1609) by the brief comments in John Fletcher's prefatory address to *The Faithfull Shepheardesse*; while in practice, developments ever since Giraldi Cinthio embarked on his "tragedies with a happy ending" were increasingly heralding the dramatic productions of Shakespeare's successors.[18] Yet the relevance of Cinthio's practice or Guarini's theory to Shakespeare's art is open to question, partly because Shakespeare appears to have been largely indifferent to Continental precedents of any kind, but also because Guarini's espousal of a new genre distinct from comedy and tragedy alike contradicts Shakespeare's manifest tendency so to borrow from both that his plays normally depend on an adjustment of elements—the same elements—that actually or potentially had been within his province from the outset. Plays like *Cymbeline* or *The Tempest,* in other words, do not constitute "a new kind of play markedly different from the other genres in which he had achieved success."[19] The just description of *Cymbeline* by one reader as comprised of experiences at once "good and evil, grave and gay, momentous and trivial,"[20] will upon consideration be seen to apply to earlier "comedies" like *Twelfth Night* and *All's Well* as much as to the major "tragedies" inclusive of *Hamlet* and *King Lear.* So, too, with *The Tempest,* whose designation as "divine comedy" in spite of its potentially explosive motifs—the usurpation of authority, the abuse of power, the scheme of assassination, the advent of lust so habitually associated by Shakespeare with upheavals in the body politic—corresponds to the same designation applied to *King Lear* where those motifs are actualized.[21] Nor is it an accident that still other readers have perceived affinities between *King Lear* on the one hand and *Twelfth Night* and *As You Like It* on the other, however drastically the same elements were adjusted to the requirements of the given "real state of sublunary nature."[22] We need not be surprised, indeed, that even Shakespeare's very first play, *The Comedy of Errors* (1591–92), has been observed to possess elements which, jointly considered, "might easily have worked out as a tragedy."[23] Shakespeare's vision involves not tears or laughter so much as tears and laughter inseparable.

But it is time to take a closer look, primarily at the major history tetralogy in the first instance, and at *King Lear* in the second.

II. "I am not what I am"

The major history tetralogy comprised of *Richard II,* the two parts of *Henry IV,* and *Henry V* (1595–96), is like the earlier tetralogy—the three parts of *Henry VI,* and *Richard III* (1591–93)—in that each play may variously be designated after the fashion of *Troilus and Cressida* as "history," "comedy," and "tragedy." The earlier tetralogy demonstrably escalates from the knockabout farce of the first part of *Henry VI* to the grotesque comedy of its third part; while *Richard III,* presided over by a demonic gargoyle—"comic in his grotesqueness, diabolic in his leer"—modulates eventually into "a kind of Divine Comedy."[24] A comic history, *Richard III* nevertheless directs our gaze toward tragedy, "Look the right way through the cruel-comic side of Richard," it has been suggested, "and you glimpse Iago."[25]

The materials of the earlier tetralogy once hammered into dramatic shape, Shakespeare approached the rise of the Lancastrians with evidently increased subtlety. His realistic assessment of political opportunism remained essentially unchanged; but his aggressiveness was tempered greatly, his taste for melodrama reduced markedly, and his sympathetic response to the human predicament qualified substantially. It is indicative, certainly, that the initial portrait of Richard II—irresolute in his response to the conflict between Bolingbroke and Mowbray, insensitive to the perils confronting his kingdom and his throne, and reprehensible in his decision "to farm our royal realm" (I.iv.45)—yields to a steadily increased sympathy for the sovereign once fallen. In theory, of course, Richard was always possessed of the qualities that surface after he is dethroned. Granted, it may not be particularly significant that the pattern of smiles and tears inseparable figures in this play twice, as we have seen; but it is scarcely insignificant that the first occasion ("Dear earth, I do salute thee with my hand") is not only correlated with the second but is voiced as if in response to John of Gaunt's prophecy of imminent catastrophes which, we know, are realized during the reign not so much of Richard as of his successor. Richard's better self is displayed, ironically enough, as a direct result of the opportunity provided by the usurper Bolingbroke, much as Marvell's "Horatian Ode" suggests with equal irony that Charles I was unintentionally assisted to his greatness by Cromwell (see p. 276). Also like Marvell's Cromwell, Bolingbroke develops into a highly complex figure whose ambition heralds the emergence of a theme variously central to Shakespeare's plays from *The Comedy of Errors* to *The Tempest*.

The dimensions of this theme may be said to expand outwardly from four utterances in as many plays, thus:

> I cannot flatter and speak fair,
> Smile in men's faces, smooth, deceive and cog
> . . . .
> Oh, what may man within him hide
> Though angel on the outward side!
> . . . .
>   the devil hath power
> To assume a pleasing shape
> . . . .
>   I am not what I am

The first speaker, claimant to a natural incapacity either to smile in men's faces or to smooth and to deceive, is that authority in the exquisite art of dissimulation, Richard III, who at other times is not unprepared to acknowledge that he can "add colours to the chameleon, / Change shapes with Proteus for advantages, / And set the murderous Machiavel to school" (*R3* I.iii.47–48, and *3H6* III.ii.191–93, respectively). The second speaker is Duke Vincentio, his remarkable perception of Angelo's criminal conduct not matched by any awareness that his words are scarcely less relevant to himself (*MM* III.ii.285–86). Next, Hamlet contemplates the implications of the appearance of the Ghost (II.ii.628–29), resolved though he has already been to assume a particular "shape" himself, the notorious "antic disposition" (I.v.172). The last speaker ("I am not what I am") might have been Richard III or Vincentio or Hamlet but is in fact Viola (*TN* III.i.153), attesting yet again to the presence within the "comedies" of those methods—"devious and astonishing methods"—already noted in connection with other "comic" protagonists such as Portia, Helena, and Prospero. Viola's "I am not what I am" is repeated, not coincidentally I am inclined to believe, by a very different individual within a rather different context:

>   when my outward action doth demonstrate
> The native act and figure of my heart
> In compliment extern, 'tis not long after
> But I will wear my heart upon my sleeve
> For daws to peck at: I am not what I am . . . .

Thus none other than Iago (*Oth.* I.i.61–65). No less intriguing, however, is the fact that Iago's statement in turn possesses "a certain resemblance"—as W. H. Auden noted with characteristic reserve[26]—to the soliloquy by Prince Hal early in the first part of *Henry IV*:

>   when this loose behaviour I throw off
> And pay the debt I never promised,
> By how much better than my word I am . . .
> I'll so offend, to make offence a skill;
> Redeeming time when men think least I will.
>   (I.ii.231–40)

Dissimulation, hypocrisy, deception: the concern—"the dominant concern"—not only of late "tragicomedies" like *Cymbeline*[27] but of comedies and tragedies late or early and dark or otherwise, it reaches one of its several apogees in the morally compromising soliloquy by Prince Hal.

Dr. Johnson was of a different opinion, true. But his valiant defense of the Prince was not devoid of an instinctive awareness that something is amiss after all:

> This speech is very artfully introduced to keep the Prince from appearing vile in the opinion of the audience; it prepares them for his

future reformation, and, what is yet more valuable, exhibits a natural picture of a great mind offering excuses to itself, and palliating those follies which it can neither justify nor forsake.[28]

"To keep the Prince from appearing vile"! It is, I think, quite unnecessary to aver that Hal is even remotely like Iago or any other demonic personality from Angelo ("this outwardly-sainted . . . devil" [*MM* III.i.89–92]) to Richard III ("[I] seem a saint when most I play the devil" [*R3* I.iii.338]). But it is imperative to accept that, family relations in Shakespeare invariably fraught with import as they are, Prince Hal is very much a son worthy of Henry Bolingbroke. Falstaff's belated recognition of "the cold blood" that the Prince "did naturally inherit of his father" (*2H4* IV.iii.127–28) is symptomatic of familial links by no means restricted to coldness of blood.

The inauguration of the Lancastrian dispensation is marked in the tetralogy by two victims in particular. One, on the national plane, is displaced by the first Lancastrian sovereign; the other, on the expressly human level, is displaced by the second. The methods on which Bolingbroke relies are specified well enough by himself in conversation with his worthy heir apparent: "God knows, my son, / By what by-paths and indirect crook'd ways / I met this crown" (*2H4* IV.v.184–86). His foremost self-justification, "necessity" (*2H4* III.i.73), did not have to wait on Milton to be specified as "the tyrant's plea" (*Paradise Lost* IV.393). It is writ large in the new dispensation, from the ruthlessness endorsed by the gardener ("Cut off the heads of too fast growing sprays" [*R2* III.iv.29ff.]) to the brutal conduct of another worthy member of the House of Lancaster, Prince John (*2H4* IV.ii.116–23), as he suppresses civil insurrections after a fashion quite unlike anything that obtained during the reign of Richard II. The methods on which Prince Hal also relies—"devious and astonishing methods" as before—are more specifically connected with his hypocrisy-laden relations with Falstaff until the fat knight is renounced publicly (*2H4* V.v.51–75). "In terms of Policy," we have been told, "Falstaff must go. He is a demon of jest, subversive to the State. No custom, no institution is safe from him. He will absorb or undermine all."[29] Who would have thought the old man had so much power in him! It rather appears, however, that the timing of Falstaff's rejection, and the harsh language used on the occasion, suggest a calculated gesture for "maximum political effect," to quote Auden once more.[30] In retrospect, even Prince Hal's earlier "playful" censure of Falstaff distresses because no one, Falstaff least of all, could possibly have penetrated the flawless royal disguise. Hal has just decided to "play" his own father reproaching the heir apparent; but the comic extravaganza is also prologue to the omen coming on:

> There is a devil haunts thee in the likeness of an old fat man; a tun of man is thy companion. Why dost thou converse with that trunk of humours, that bolting-hutch of beastliness, that swollen parcel of dropsies, that huge bombard of sack, that stuffed cloak-bag of guts, that roasted Manningtree ox with the pudding in his belly, that reverend vice, that grey iniquity, that father ruffian, that vanity in years? . . . Falstaff, that old white-bearded Satan.
>
> (*1H4* II.iv.492–509)

Hal's role-within-a-role inverts the motif of "I am not what I am" to provide us with a chilling instance of Lancastrian duplicity. When Policy eventually triumphs, it triumphs at the expense of humanity. Shakespeare has after all forcefully impressed on us that Falstaff has eyes, hands, organs, dimensions, senses, affections, passions; is fed with the same food, hurt with the same weapons, subject to the same diseases, healed by the same means, warmed and cooled by the same winter and summer, as the Lancastrian is. But the Lancastrian's response we know; and it lessens him much.

The major history tetralogy is not necessarily an epic *Henriad*. Its last member, *Henry V,* may possess the external signs of an unqualified paean to a thoroughly "reformed" sovereign, but is in fact concerned with the development of a king in search of the humanity he has so coldly denied. Within that framework, the play emerges as yet another "comic history," displaying for one reader a gaiety, "a legerity of spirit"; for another, a satire grounded in irony "gently sympathetic and covertly hilarious"; and for a third, a decisive convergence of its protagonist on Richard III—no less!—as fellow-trickster.[31] Adverse notes, hardly "comic," are also sounded throughout, from the moment that "the mirror for Christian kings" is poised apocalyptically to unleash famine, sword, and fire (Prol. 5–8) to the actual conduct of the barbarous campaign inclusive of the execution of prisoners of war (IV.vii.9–11). The "reformation" of Bolingbroke's son hardly predates events of the play; it occurs within their course, as a result of experience, until the address at Agincourt enlists the high and the low within one "band of brothers" (IV.iii.60), be they "ne'er so vile" or even—so one is led to credit—reverend vices, grey iniquities, fathers ruffian, white-bearded Satans. Not at all coincidentally that address is not undermined by any parody, in telling opposition to the earlier address at Harfleur ("Once more unto the breach, dear friends, once more") and its prompt deflation by Bardolph ("On, on, on, on, on! To the breach, to the breach!" [III.i.1ff., and ii.1ff.]).

Henry V may well be a "divine comedy" in the suggestive sense that *King Lear* and *The Tempest* have also been so designated. Otherwise, however, it defies categorization, since it is not "history" as that genre is properly understood, nor "comedy" strictly so conceived, nor "tragedy" save in a very spasmodic sense. If "epic," finally, it also qualifies that genre to such an extent that it can even be seen as an antiepic, partaking of the overtones of *Troilus and Cressida*.[32] It is obvious that, at times, Shakespeare's *moria* can drive one to distraction.

III. "Wise enough to play the fool"

If like so many other plays *Henry V* cannot be categorized, we expect *King Lear* (1605-6) to be the tragedy that it so clearly is. It is a play of intense and, it would appear, unjustifiable suffering. The storm which at the outset hovers menacingly over Lear's kingdom explodes with a viciousness beyond one's worst expectations. The stars are put out altogether; and by the end, even Edgar is driven darkly to suspect that he is witnessing the "image" of history's final horrors (V.iii.264). Distant echoes of a redemptive pattern are heard, distantly; but the most sustained sound is of a demonic cacophony in a universe apparently beyond salvation. Lear's hysterical invocation of the elements to strike flat the thick rotundity of the world (III.ii.1-9) is well-nigh realized as his rhetoric of excess is confronted by the metallic language of cruelty:

> *Regan:* Hang him instantly.
> *Goneril:* Pluck out his eyes.
>
> (III.vii.4-5)

Yet for all that, as we noted earlier, *King Lear* has not infrequently been seen as a "divine comedy."

The designation of *King Lear* as a "divine comedy" appertains to thematic considerations, not to generic ones, it is true. On the other hand, the determination of genre depending as it does on the manner a given subject is presented, the designation responds at the very least to a part of the play's total effect. Much more to the point, the argument presented some decades ago that at the heart of *King Lear* resides a "comedy of the grotesque"[33] has by now been so refined that we accept as a matter of course that the play is a "less concentrated" genre than tragedy, that its numerous comic aspects are "outward signs" of the Shakespearean strategy of advancing through the comic to the tragic, and that its fusion of these creates a dislocation that terminates in a particularly devastating tragic effect.[34]

The congregated motifs that in *King Lear* partake of the comic in the midst of the tragic, and of the tragic in the midst of the comic, begin with a brief scene intended to deflate Lear's grandiose entrance immediately thereafter: Gloucester's report of the "good sport" he had in producing his "whoreson" Edmund, ventured with gross indifference before Kent, who remains neutral, and before Edmund, who remains silent. The scene evidently draws on materials common to the most common of comedies; yet later, as the subplot centered on Gloucester unfolds more fully, it becomes clear that it shares in an equally common theme, the swindling of the gullible *senex* by a clever and unprincipled son.[35] The play's subplot in general, and its first scene in particular, mark the consequences of Shakespeare's daring conflation of the tragic and the comic. Our potential laughter is stifled before it issues forth, aware as we are that the nominally "comic" episodes obscure—but obscure only in order to reveal more forcefully—the silence of an Edmund who in soliloquy will display a very different personality, the neutrality of a Kent who will eventually realize how imperative involvement is, and the insensitivity of a Gloucester who will see only when he is deprived of sight. With the primary plot once center-stage, connections multiply as the silence of Edmund appears alarmingly parallel to Cordelia's, the initial neutrality of Kent links with Lear's aloofness from his kingdom's "poor naked wretches," and the insensitivity of Gloucester reflects Lear's toward Cordelia—the folly of one father, that is to say, in massive juxtaposition with the folly of another.

Such responses to the world of *King Lear* are well attested. But should it be objected that my association of Edmund's silence with Cordelia's is extreme, I would argue that nothing in the play, and disguise least of all, is accidental. "I am not what I am" appertains to behavior we have considered in plays whether designated histories, comedies, or tragedies; and disguises, nominally "a convention of comedy," are in fact suggestive—invariably suggestive—of dissimulation, hypocrisy, deception.[36] In *King Lear,* of course, such behavior is characteristic in the first instance of Edmund, Goneril, and Regan. But once that satanic trinity assumes power, disguises become the exclusive province of others—Kent, Edgar, the utterly mysterious Fool—whose joint tendency is not infrequently to rely on those "devious and astonishing methods" we observed in plays far different from *King Lear.* It may well be that, for Kent and Edgar and the Fool, the end justifies the means; if so, they stand accused of endorsing the most sinister principle yet. I know that to claim as much about Cordelia may seem an outrage and, to those who have converted her into a symbol of the ultimate Christian verities, a blasphemy. After all, she does not assume a disguise, nor is she in consequence still another exemplar of the dissimulating personality represented by "I am not what I am." On the contrary, she is precisely what she is. At the same time, however, the absence of a disguise can be in itself a form of disguise, all the more onerous because it is not studied but spontaneous, even innate. Such a view need not imply that Cordelia is possessed of a latent evil. But it may—I would myself claim it must—suggest the play's affirmation of the "intermixt" nature of good and evil. To endorse "nothing" may seem, and perhaps is, admirable; but as it is hardly admirable in Edmund's similar insistence on "nothing" (I.i.89–92, and I.ii.29–31), it may on occasion become emblematic of the nature of evil, diametrically opposed as it is to God's dissemination of love and goodness during the act of creation, not through the silence of nothing ("Love and be silent" [I.i.631]), but through the sacrament of speech ("And God *said* . . ."). Equally, to be intolerant of the manifest folly of a father and a king may seem, and perhaps is, wise; but it partakes, too, of a different kind of folly: the intolerance of those who, fanatically secure in their goodness, fall into that most perilous of states, a pride in their own humility. The clash between Lear and Cordelia, in other words, is a clash between pride and pride, as always in line with the premise observed in connection with Bolingbroke and his heir apparent, that family relations in Shakespeare are invariably fraught with import. Whether for ill as the play's outset suggests, or for good as the final acts so clearly proclaim, Cordelia is very much a daughter worthy of her father.[37]

If in one respect Cordelia's behavior is connected with Edmund's and in another with Lear's, in a third it is related to that of the Fool. It has been remarked often that, since Cordelia and the Fool do not ever appear on the stage at one and the same time, a director could extend the Elizabethan practice of allotting both roles to one and the same actor. Yet Cordelia and the Fool are not interchangeable. Their methods though alike "devious and astonishing" are informed by very different motives; and their aims though eventually parallel are pursued diversely, in measure equal to the developing personality of the one and the static personality of the other. The most surprising figure within the canon of Shakespearean drama, the anonymous Fool is unchanging, fixed, the one steady factor in a world of flux. He is also, as noted in passing, quite mysterious.

Shakespeare had created several Fools and a number of clowns in advance of *King Lear* and, it is said, would do as much later, in *Antony and Cleopatra,* in the person of Enobarbus ("a cousin of Lear's Fool").[38] But care must be had not to enlist as Fools still other characters—Falstaff, for example, who has been seen as a masked "holy Fool" privy to the follies of the earth's mighty[39]—since Shakespeare's practice is not tolerant of overly ingenious theories. In advance of the creation of Lear's Fool, that practice centered primarily if not exclusively on Touchstone in *As You Like It* and Feste in *Twelfth Night,* with Lavache in *All's Well* hovering about them but peripherally. The lesser importance that attaches to Lavache is indicated by the minor role he is assigned, its relative lack of consequence confirmed by his deployment of wit for its own sake, largely for "the increase of laughter" as he himself remarks.[40] Touchstone and

Feste, on the contrary, advance the thematic preoccupations of *As You Like It* and *Twelfth Night* in material ways. Touchstone is in accordance with his name indispensable both to the play's vision and to the play's tone, his mode of expression always pointedly inverted. "He uses his folly like a stalking-horse," as Duke Senior observes, "and under the presentation of that he shoots his wit" (V.iv.111–12). If Jacques aspires after a parallel folly ("O that I were a fool! I am ambitious for a motley coat" [II.vii.42–43]), the ensuing achievement is radically different from Touchstone's, complementary though the two are as commentators on the world about them, "the one transparently foolish in his wisdom, the other opaquely wise in his fooling."[41] Touchstone's approach—"opaquely wise in his fooling," one must insist—is extended within a likewise inverted mode by Feste, the cumulative strains in both cases best sounded by Viola:

> This fellow is wise enough to play the fool;
> And to do what well craves a kind of wit:
> He must observe their mood on whom he jests,
> The quality of persons, and the time,
> And, like the haggard, check at every feather
> That comes before his eye. This is a practice
> As full of labour as a wise man's art;
> For folly that he wisely shows is fit,
> But wise men, folly-fall'n, quite taint their wit.
>
> (*TN* III.i.67–75)

"Wise enough to play the fool": Viola ("I am not what I am") is sufficiently well qualified to know that "play" partakes of the comic as of the tragic in that it embraces both "a legerity of spirit"—to quote the phrase used in connection with *Henry V*—and a predilection for dispositions antic or otherwise. But the lines of demarcation are not always clear, witness the way that Hamlet's simplistic account of the end of "playing"—"to hold, as it were, the mirror up to nature" (III.ii.22–23)—is dramatically qualified once the reputedly accurate mirror is observed to have distorted "nature" rather too grotesquely. If life is a play, therefore, it is a play in the ambivalent sense indicated; and if construed as a play of folly Erasmian in its dimensions and Pauline in its eventual premises, it should be understood to involve the projection of folly on a universal canvas that includes fools and Fools alike. Feste's celebrated adaptation of the Ciceronian "Stultorum plena sunt omnia" ("Foolery, sir, does walk about the orb like the sun, it shines everywhere" [III.i.42–43]) should in this respect be regarded as a comic version of a somberly conceived truth; for we might then appreciate the odd propriety of using phrases like "a constant spectacle of illusion and deception" or "the terror of nightmare" to describe the effect not of any tragedy but of a "comedy" such as *Twelfth Night*.[42]

That Feste and Touchstone are in the direct line of descent that focuses on the Fool in *King Lear* is no less well known than it is obvious. The antecedents of the Fool within the developing dramatic and intellectual tradition of England and the Continent have also been examined, and so have his links with the Pauline premises as well as their annotation by Erasmus.[43] Lear's Fool is certainly every way as "opaquely wise in his fooling" as either Touchstone or Feste; he is also given to a similarly inverted mode of discourse; and he is likewise instrumental in the creation of "comedy," most notably by obliging us to see Lear's aspirations after tragic grandeur within a context always about to collapse into farce.[44] His relations with his two predecessors may be said to be symbolized by his extension of the epilogue Feste sings in *Twelfth Night* ("When I was a little tiny boy, / With hey, ho, the wind and the rain . . .") with yet another stanza in the same vein of nominal nonsense verse:

> He that has and a little tiny wit,—
>   With heigh-ho, the wind and the rain,—
> Must make content with his fortunes fit,
>   For the rain it raineth every day.
>
>   (*Lr.* III.ii.74–77)

But the differences separating Lear's Fool from Touchstone and Feste should also be marked. For one, the Fool is much closer to his play's thematic center, voicing its capital motifs with a sustained pressure not exerted by anyone else to the same extent; for another, he is much more evidently cruel, venturing his commentary after an uncompromising fashion that often verges on a lack of sympathy; and for a third, he is much more obviously shrouded in mystery, insistently raising questions about his anonymity inclusive of his origins and mode of discourse. That mode, habitually inverted as it is, veers on occasion abruptly to display a language of unexpected directness, especially when his own role has been adopted by someone else:

> *Lear:* Is it the fashion, that discarded fathers
>   Should have thus little mercy on their flesh?
>   Judicious punishment! 'twas this flesh begot
>   Those pelican daughters.
> *Edgar:* Pillicock sat on Pillicock-hill:
>   Halloo, halloo, loo, loo!
> *Fool:* This cold night will turn us all to fools and madmen.
>
>   (III.iv.74–81)

Of the Fool's origins within the world of *King Lear* we know, needless to say, nothing whatsoever; and we are left to speculate whether he is but a primeval force, or perhaps an emissary of the just gods, or even a palpably demonic personality.

The Fool as primeval force is a possibility we entertain naturally, especially if we care to align him with the "sacred clowns" so important to the rituals of tribes whether primitive or sophisticated.[45] The Fool as an emissary of the just gods is an equally reasonable possibility, all the more so because of his undeniable function as a catalyst in Lear's eventual self-knowledge. But the Fool as a demonic personality is likely to be resisted, if only out of concern lest the "comedy" within *King Lear* is inadvertently construed as tainted by satanic malice. Yet we may not, I think, overlook the Fool's frequent cruelty, relentless as that cruelty can be in spite—and indeed because—of the nominal "comic" contexts. The ensuing exchange might have been penned by an advocate of *humour noir* precisely because it winds its comic way toward a passionate cry of anguish:

> *Fool:* The reason why the seven stars are no more than seven is a pretty reason.
> *Lear:* Because they are not eight?
> *Fool:* Yes, indeed: thou wouldst make a good fool.
> *Lear:* To take 't again perforce! Monster ingratitude!
> *Fool:* If thou wert my fool, nuncle, I'd have thee beaten for being old before thy time.
> *Lear:* How's that?
> *Fool:* Thou shouldst not have been old till thou hadst been wise.
> *Lear:* O, let me not be mad, not mad, sweet heaven! Keep me in temper: I would not be mad.
> (I.v.37–51)

Nor may we sidestep the Fool's relationship with the developing tradition that looms behind him, particularly his connections however distant with medieval grotesque figures—themselves often palpably satanic—and his much firmer connection with that "comic" representative of nihilism, the Lord of Misrule. We are inclined to refer these antecedents rather to Falstaff than to the Fool, true. But it is indicative of Shakespeare's actual intentions that while Falstaff was created as an irresistibly lovable human being, the Fool was conceived as a-personal, his humanity intentionally distanced; and while Falstaff is temperamentally incapable of any dissimulation, the Fool assumes the most impenetrable of disguises yet, a disguise sufficiently innate to have obliterated the person behind it. The implications might have been mapped by invoking any of Shakespeare's numerous other experts in deception. But Viola will do. "Disguise," she observes with a perceptiveness conveniently not applicable to herself,

> Disguise, I see, thou art a wickedness,
> Wherein the pregnant enemy does much.
> (*TN* II.ii.28–29)

The comedy of *King Lear* is quite as much "a constant spectacle of illusion and deception" as is the tragedy of *Twelfth Night*.

To recognize the Fool's demonic aspects is necessary; but to recognize only those aspects were injudicious. The medieval background helps us to relate him no less to the demonic than to the divine, in the latter case because, like his medieval predecessors, he adumbrates "the laughter of the Infinite about the Finite when it pretends to be absolute."[46] Such a vision suggests that the assumption by Lear's Fool of "the most impenetrable of disguises yet" is not exclusively satanic. His retreat into total anonymity may in itself be regarded as a premeditated removal from the evil-fraught phenomenal world, a sort of subsistence in a realm of Platonic ideas inverted in order to provide for detachment, the a-personal lack of humanity earlier seen as solely demonic. Under this dispensation, "I am not what I am" is so transmuted as to assert a sharp differentiation between consistently demonic fools like Iago or Richard III ("[I] seem a saint when most I play the devil") and Fools like the Fool in *King Lear* with his several extensions in Kent, in Edgar, and—to a preeminent degree—in Cordelia. The crucial factor in determining the nature of folly whether demonic or divine is not the extent to which one knows oneself; it is the extent to which self-knowledge directs one beyond oneself, to engage in action that terminates in tears or laughter or—given the nature of the human condition—tears and laughter inseparable. The challenge confronting Shakespeare's characters both comic and tragic is well enough articulated by Prince Hal: "We play the fools with the time, and the spirits of the wise sit in the clouds and mock us" (*2H4* II.ii.155–57).

IV. "Monstrous and deformed Notions of God"

"The spirits of the wise sit in the clouds and mock us" has the appearance of an affirmation definitive and absolute. Within its dramatic context, however, the statement is casual, delivered by Prince Hal to Poins in preparation of yet another game at the expense of Falstaff. The tactic is characteristic of Shakespearean drama at large: a passage quoted out of context may seem pregnant of meaning but, considered in relation to the speaker, proves otherwise. One assumes that in the meantime Shakespeare remains much like the ideal artist envisaged by Joyce's Stephen Dedalus: "invisible, refined out of existence, indifferent, paring his fingernails."[47]

But that would be to simplify grossly. Shakespeare's art does not unfold in a vacuum of indifference. It is on the contrary informed by a vision which, even though not grounded on expressly Christian dogmas,[48] appeals to the highest standards of a morality universal in its applicability. The claim may seem odd in the light of the casual nature of Prince Hal's allusion to "the spirits of the wise" above us. But Shakespeare's moral vision is not apprehensible through any single statement ventured by any single character. It is, rather, articulated in strictly dramatic terms, so that the significance of Prince Hal's allusion resides not in that he uttered it but in that he uttered it so casually. Placed within the broader framework of the major history tetralogy, that casualness becomes emblematic of the Lancastrian dispensation's immoral—or, better still, amoral—"by-paths and indirect crook'd ways" acknowledged as we have seen by Bolingbroke to his worthy heir apparent. Given such conduct on the human plane, the spirits of the wise might not only mock; they might even be convulsed with laughter—"the laughter of the Infinite about the Finite when it pretends to be absolute." Isabella's words in *Measure for Measure* are apposite:

>   man, proud man,
> Drest in a little brief authority,
> Most ignorant of what he's most assured,
>   His glassy essence, like an angry ape,
> Plays such fantastic tricks before high heaven
> As make the angels weep, who, with their spleen,
> Would all themselves laugh mortal.
>
>   (II.ii.117–23)

Conveniently for Isabella, the denunciation is not meant to include herself. We need not be surprised. As noted earlier, the demesne of folly is inhabited by fools as much as by Fools.

The moral dimension of *King Lear* may be gathered in analogous ways. The play has by some readers been christianized unduly, and by others dechristianized no less radically, since it can support whatever theory is pursued, with determination, eclectically. But the play as a unified dramatic entity must be regarded in terms neither of the statements made by its several characters nor of the patterns created in any single instance. The numerous references to "the gods" are in this respect instructive, in that Edgar's view ("The gods are just, and of our pleasant vices, / Make instruments to plague us") is but a reflection of strenuous belief in a predictable moral order; Kent's view ("It is the stars, / The stars above us, govern our conditions") is but a desperate effort to impose a comprehensible design on incomprehensible developments; while Gloucester's view ("As flies to wanton boys are we to the gods, / They kill us for their sport") is but a transmutation of his personal sufferings into a universal experience (*Lr.* V.iii.170–71; IV.iii.34–35; and IV.i.38–39). The dramatic context, however, suggests a different perspective, best appreciated if Gloucester's dark view of the gods' cruel "sport" is aligned with his insensitive amusement over the "good sport" he himself had in producing Edmund. It is I think evident that each character within *King Lear*—each character, indeed, in every other Shakespearean play as well—creates the gods after his own image. "Every one attributes to *God*," the Cambridge Platonists would later say, "what he finds in *Himself.*" Stated even more sharply, it could be said that "nothing is more ordinary, then for us to shape out monstrous and deformed Notions of God unto our selves, by looking upon him through the *coloured Medium* of our own corrupt hearts."[49]

As with "the gods," so with "nature." Persistently invoked in *King Lear* by nearly every character in both the primary and the secondary plots, "nature" is made to assume as many disguises as there are speakers determined to subordinate her to their given purposes. Pointedly, for example, Edmund's conception of nature as anarchic ("Thou, nature, art my goddess..." [I.ii.1ff.]) is only two scenes later transformed by Lear into an instrument of *his* personal vengefulness, even to the limit of using parallel terminology ("Hear, nature, hear; dear goddess, hear!..." [I.iv.297ff.]). The attitudes of Lear and Edmund, however, are diametrically opposed to the interpretation standard during the Renaissance that nature is not a variable "goddess" in her own right but strictly subordinate to the Divine Purpose, "nothing else but Gods instrument" according to Hooker, or—to use some of Donne's metaphors—"Gods immediate commissioner," "foreman," "Lieutenant," and "Vicegerent."[50] Explicitness of this order is of course entirely absent from *King Lear;* yet the dramatic context does induce a gathering sense that the events in Lear's kingdom advance, not without purpose, in a certain direction. The precise direction may elude us; but it suffices that it is other than that expected whether by Lear or by anyone else.

My intent is not triumphantly to conclude that *King Lear* unfolds this side of an optimistic "divine comedy." As observed earlier, even if echoes of a redemptive pattern are heard distantly, the predominant sound is of a demonic cacophony in a universe apparently beyond salvation. At the same time, a merely nihilistic view of the play would be less than just to its remarkable fusion of implausibly contradictory states. One must devise elaborate definitions in order to accommodate Edmund's zestful villainy as well as his resolution however belated to effect "some good... / Despite of mine own nature" (V.iii.242–43); Edgar's lethargic goodness no less than his unexpected leap into action; Gloucester's vulgar insensitivity but also his well-nigh heroic vow to bear affliction (IV.vi.75–76); the Fool's alienating cruelty as much as his manifest loyalty to his master; Lear's boundless egotism yet his transcendent humility too; and of course Cordelia's uncompromising pride no less than her eventual emergence as one who "redeems nature from the general curse" (IV.vi.210–11). The achievement that is the balance of these states in *King Lear* is also reflected in the style, especially the increasing modulation of Lear's rhetoric of excess into the rhythms of unadorned simplicity represented by his testament of yet another view of "the gods": "Upon such sacrifices, my Cordelia, / The gods themselves throw incense" (V.iii.20–21). The magnificent affirmation, in appearance yet again definitive and absolute, is promptly blasted, however, for Lear presently reenters the stage bearing Cordelia dead in his arms. The spirits of the wise are on that occasion silent, as if stunned by the obscenity of the evil before their eyes.

We are tempted to deny the relevance of those spirits to Shakespearean drama; but then we are so tempted whenever the inexplicable mystery of iniquity confronts us brutally. For Shakespeare, however, evil is an awesome reality precisely because it can be measured against the coexistent reality of goodness and of love. "The web of our life," someone observes in *All's Well* with almost Miltonic finality, "is of a mingled yarn, good and ill together" (IV.iii.83–84). It constitutes, in Dr. Johnson's phrase, "the real state of sublunary nature"; but it constitutes also, as I said earlier, the state of a unified vision whose dimensions, not confined to the merely sublunar, intimate a context veritably cosmic. I know that our sense of justice is outraged because Lear's punishment far exceeds his crimes. But in the light of a moral code that transcends ours, we are not invited to presume; for to presume would be to misunderstand the sense in which as there is a justice beyond justice, so there is a comedy beyond comedy. We may wish to recall that creators of literature have claimed as much instinctively, professing with Yeats that Lear was "gay" or averring with D. H. Lawrence that "Lear was essentially happy, even in his greatest misery."[51] It may be regarded as indicative that, within the play, it is reported that Cordelia mingled happy smiles with tears that dropped as pearls from diamonds.

NOTES

An earlier version of this chapter appeared in the *Kenyon Review*, n.s. 10, no. 2 (1988): 38–57. Copyright © 1988 by Kenyon College. Reprinted with permission of the author's estate and publisher. Shakespeare is here quoted from *The Complete Works of Shakespeare*, ed. Hardin Craig (Chicago, 1951).

1. Noted often, as by Brian Morris, "The Tragic Structure of *Troilus and Cressida*," *Shakespeare Quarterly* 10 (1959): 481–91. Morris himself, clearly unnerved, thinks that *Troilus and Cressida* has a tragic structure even though many of its features are "alien to the basic tragic effect."
2. Madeleine Doran has concluded authoritatively that the Elizabethan dramatists tended increasingly toward the separation of tragedy and comedy; but she has also observed the noteworthy phenomenon of "the continued resistance to complete separation" (*Endeavors of Art* [Madison, 1954], p. 102). Marvin T. Herrick has with equal authority remarked that, in Renaissance criticism, "the borderline between comedy and tragedy was always uncertain" (*Comic Theory in the Sixteenth Century* [Urbana, Ill., 1964], p. 70).
3. Leo Salingar, *Shakespeare and the Traditions of Comedy* (Cambridge, 1974), p. 20. Larry S. Champion, in *The Evolution of Shakespeare's Comedy* (Cambridge, Mass., 1970), p. 149, is even more uncompromising on Duke Vincentio ("utterly devious in his methods").
4. The dates provided throughout are but approximations of the dates of composition.
5. Richard T. Brucher, " 'Tragedy, Laugh On': Comic Violence in *Titus Andronicus*," *Renaissance Drama*, n.s. 10 (1979): 71–91.
6. On the play's comic aspects, see Susan Snyder's study from a different perspective in *The Comic Matrix of Shakespeare's Tragedies* (Princeton, 1979), pp. 57–70; Stanley Wells's more particularized remarks in "Juliet's Nurse: The Use of Inconsequentiality," in *Shakespeare's Styles*, ed. Philip Edwards et al. (Cambridge, 1980), pp. 51–66; and especially the substantial essay by Franklin L. Dickey, "The Comical Tragedy of *Romeo and Juliet*," in his *Not Wisely But Too Well* (San Marino, Calif., 1957), chap. 6.
7. See Barbara Heliodora C. de Mendonça, "*Othello*: A Tragedy Built on a Comic Structure," *Shakespeare Survey* 21 (1968): 31–38.
8. See Russ McDonald, "Othello, Thorello, and the Problem of the Foolish Hero," *Shakespeare Quarterly* 30 (1979): 51–67. Two other essays on the subject—by Ann Blake, "The Comedy of *Othello*," *Critical Review* (Melbourne) 15 (1972): 46–51, and Carolyn Herbert, "Comic Elements in *Othello*," *Renaissance Papers*, 1957, 32–38—are disappointingly superficial. But Robert A. Watts in "The Comic Scenes in *Othello*," *Shakespeare Quarterly* 19 (1968): 349–54, focuses perceptively on the implications for the play at large of the drinking scene in Act II (ii), where "the comedy borders on slapstick," and the scenes involving the two clowns in Act III (i and iv). See also the discussion by Susan Snyder, *The Comic Matrix*, pp. 70–90, and the essays by Allan Gilbert, "Comedy in *Othello*," in his *The Principles and Practice of Criticism* (Detroit, 1959), pp. 27–45; Martha T. Rozett, "*Othello, Otello*, and the Comic Tradition," *Bulletin of Research in the Humanities* 85 (1982): 386–411; and Douglas Stewart, "*Othello*: Roman Comedy as Nightmare," *Emory University Quarterly* 22 (1967): 252–76.
9. Margery M. Morgan, " 'Your Crown's Awry': *Antony and Cleopatra* in the Comic Tradition," *Komos* 1 (1968): 128–39. See also the equally excellent discussion by J. L. Simmons, "The Comic Pattern and Vision in *Antony and*

Cleopatra," *ELH* 36 (1969): 493–510. Consult too the essays by Walter C. Foreman, Jr., *The Music at the Close* (Lexington, Ky., 1978), pp. 178–94, and A. L. French, *Shakespeare and the Critics* (Cambridge, 1972), chap. 5.
10. *Coleridge's Writings on Shakespeare,* ed. Terence Hawkes (New York, 1959), pp. 188 and 195.
11. *The Yale Edition of the Works: Johnson on Shakespeare,* ed. Arthur Sherbo (New Haven, 1968), 7:66–67.
12. *The Yale Edition of the Works: The Rambler,* ed. W. J. Bate and Albrecht B. Strauss (New Haven, 1968), 4:299–305 (*Rambler* no. 125 for May 28, 1751). On the post-Johnson critical attitudes toward Shakespeare's "tragedies" by Schlegel, Hegel, and A. C. Bradley, consult Clayton Koelb, " 'Tragedy' and 'The Tragic': The Shakespearean Connection," *Genre* 13 (1980): 275–86.
13. *On Humor,* trans. Antonio Illiano and Daniel P. Testa (Chapel Hill, n.d.), p. 13.
14. In a note, annotating *Richard II,* in *The Plays and Poems of William Shakespeare,* ed. James Boswell the Younger (London, 1821), 16:147–48.
15. Consult Roger Warren, " 'Smiling at Grief': Some Techniques of Comedy in *Twelfth Night* and *Così fan Tutte,*" *Shakespeare Survey* 32 (1979): 79–84.
16. *Problems of the Theatre,* trans. Gerald Nellhaus (New York, 1964), p. 32.
17. Joan Hartwig, *Shakespeare's Tragicomic Vision* (Baton Rouge, 1972). Except for its theoretical framework, Hartwig's study is quite useful as an investigation of the four plays mentioned. However, I would much rather commend the study by Susan Snyder, *The Comic Matrix,* even though I think its emphasis on "conventions of comedy" is misleading (see note 36). Still another study, Thomas McFarland's *Shakespeare's Pastoral Comedy* (Chapel Hill, 1972), opens with a promising first sentence ("Comedy is at once the opposite and the complement of tragedy") but thereafter follows after gods quite different from my own.
18. See Madeleine Doran, *Endeavors of Art,* chap. 8; and on the dimension centered on Guarini: Eugene M. Waith, *The Pattern of Tragicomedy in Beaumont and Fletcher* (New Haven, 1952), chap. 2. The definitive work is by Marvin T. Herrick, *Tragicomedy* (Urbana, Ill., 1962).
19. Joan Hartwig, *Shakespeare's Tragicomic Vision,* p. 3.
20. J. M. Nosworthy, "Introduction" to his edition of *Cymbeline,* The Arden Shakespeare (London, 1955, repr. 1969), p. lxxix.
21. Harry Epstein, "The Divine Comedy of *The Tempest,*" *Shakespeare Studies* 8 (1976): 279–96, and Morris H. Partee, "The Divine Comedy of *King Lear,*" *Genre* 4 (1971): 60–75. But consult also Russell A. Fraser's thesis that the play is "a kind of *Commedia*" (*Shakespeare's Poetics in Relation to "King Lear"* [London, 1962], p. 131). For the association of still another play with the Dantesque "comedy," consult Nevil Coghill's study of "comic form" in *Measure for Measure* (*Shakespeare Survey* 8 [1955]: 14–27). Elsewhere, Coghill again posits Shakespeare's Dantesque vision ("The Basis of Shakespearean Comedy," *Essays and Studies,* n.s. 3 [1950]: 1–28); but his concurrent emphasis on a single-minded notion of "comedy" is, I think, flawed. In general, I would rather endorse the thoughtful study by Astrid Kirchheim, *Tragik und Komik in Shakespeares "Troilus and Cressida," "Measure for Measure" und "All's Well that Ends Well"* (Frankfurt, 1971).

22. See Julian Markels, "Shakespeare's Confluence of Tragedy and Comedy: *Twelfth Night* and *King Lear,*" *Shakespeare Quarterly* 15 (1964): 75–88; and on *Lear* and *As You Like It:* Maynard Mack, *"King Lear" in Our Time* (Berkeley, 1965), pp. 63–66. On *Hamlet*, see Kathleen Latimer, " 'Tragical-comical-historical-pastoral': Generic Patterns in Shakespeare's *Hamlet,*" in *Legacy of Thespis,* ed. Karelisa V. Hartigan (Lanham, Md., 1984), pp. 43–52; and further: Edward Tomarkin, "The Comedy of the Graveyard Scene in *Hamlet:* Samuel Johnson Mediates between the Eighteenth and Twentieth Centuries," *Eighteenth-Century Life* 8 (1983): 26–34.
23. Gwyn Williams, "*The Comedy of Errors* Rescued from Tragedy," *Review of English Literature* 5.4 (1964): 63–71. Leo Salingar, *Shakespeare and the Traditions of Comedy,* pp. 59–61, observes of the same play that its very opening has "a tone of stage heroics, the rhythm and almost the ring of *Tamburlaine,*" while the ensuing allusions to strife and calamity "would not be out of place in a tragedy." Salingar attributes this oddity to the play's affinities with romance; but one ought to consider, too, the dramatic effect of sounding a tragic note within a comedy, especially a comedy of "errors."
24. Donald G. Watson, "The Dark Comedy of the Henry VI Plays," *Thalia* 1.1 (1978): 11–21, and William E. Sheriff, "The Grotesque Comedy of *Richard III,*" *Studies in the Literary Imagination* 5.1 (1972): 51–64.
25. A. P. Rossiter, *Angel with Horns* (London, 1961), p. 15.
26. See the essay by W. H. Auden, "The Prince's Dog," in *King Henry IV Parts 1 and 2: A Casebook,* ed. G. K. Hunter (London, 1970), pp. 187–211.
27. As even Joan Hartwig is obliged to acknowledge (*Shakespeare's Tragicomic Vision*, p. 63). Larry S. Champion, *The Evolution of Shakespeare's Comedy,* also grants that the experiences of, say, Leontes in *The Winter's Tale* are "hardly the normal material for comedy," but insists that the play's primary tone remains "comic." So, too, Ruth Nevo, who marks the "incipient tragic possibility" in *Twelfth Night,* the "fracture" in *The Tempest,* and the like, yet refuses to abandon the traditional critical taxonomies (*Comic Transformations in Shakespeare* [London, 1980], pp. 122 and 212). Equally representative of this reluctance is Clifford Leech in *"Twelfth Night" and Shakespearean Comedy* (Toronto, 1965). Not inclined crudely to expostulate on "comedy," Leech prefers to emphasize "the rarification of Shakespearian comedy." Within that context, he reproaches another critic for leaving "no room for laughter," yet himself mentions the presence of "appreciative laughter" only accidentally (pp. 33, 39, 76). The oversight is telling, concerned as Leech is to establish that, ever since the introduction into *Love's Labour's Lost* of a "disturbing quality," Shakespeare's recognition of "an imperfection that is not easily faced" increased so that, thereafter, "we are sometimes not sure whether the picture of the world is any longer truly, or at least wholly, comic" (p. 25). Precisely.
28. *Johnson on Shakespeare,* ed. Sherbo, 7:458.
29. Ruth Nevo, *Comic Transformations,* p. 153.
30. W. H. Auden, "The Prince's Dog," p. 194. For a particularly energetic censure of the Lancastrians' Machiavellian duplicity, see Thomas McFarland, *Shakespeare's Pastoral Comedy,* pp. 177–211.
31. Charles Williams, *"Henry V,"* in *Shakespeare Criticism 1919–35,* ed. Anne Ridler (London, 1936), pp. 187–88; Roy W. Battenhouse, *"Henry V* as Heroic Com-

edy," in *Essays on Shakespeare and Elizabethan Drama,* ed. Richard Hosley (London, 1963), pp. 163–82, and Phillip Mallett, "Shakespeare's Trickster Kings: Richard III and Henry V," in *The Fool and the Trickster,* ed. Paul V. A. Williams (Cambridge, 1979), chap. 1, respectively. Consult also the essay by Helen J. Schwartz, "The Comic Scenes in *Henry V,*" *Hebrew University Studies in Literature* 4 (1976): 18–26; the broader survey by S. L. Bethel, "The Comic Element in Shakespeare's Histories," *Anglia* 71(1952): 82–101; and the investigation of background materials by Anne Barton, "The King Disguised: Shakespeare's *Henry V* and the Comical History," in *The Triple Bond,* ed. Joseph G. Price (University Park, Pa., 1975), pp. 92–117.
32. As H. M. Richmond points out in *Shakespeare's Political Plays* (New York, 1967), pp. 175ff. Richmond's discussion of the entire tetralogy (in Part III) is first-rate; my indebtedness to it, in fundamental ways, should be obvious.
33. Consult G. Wilson Knight, "*King Lear* and the Comedy of the Grotesque," in his *The Wheel of Fire,* 4th rev. ed. (London, 1949), chap. 8. See also the exposition of the play's "undercurrent of fierce comedy" by Clifford Leech in *Shakespeare's Tragedies* (London, 1950), pp. 76–81; the persuasive discussion by Katherine Stockholder in "The Multiple Genres of *King Lear,*" *Bucknell Review* 16 (1968): 40–63: the assessments by Peter L. McNamara, "*King Lear* and Comic Acceptance," *Erasmus Review* 1 (1971): 95–105, and Paul M. Cubeta, "Lear's Comic Vision," in *Teaching Shakespeare,* ed. Walter Edens (Princeton, 1977), pp. 138–52; the intriguing essay by Russell A. Peck, "Edgar's Pilgrimage: High Comedy in *King Lear,*" *SEL* 7 (1967): 219–37; and—in opposition—the thesis by John Bayley, *Shakespeare and Tragedy* (London, 1981), pp. 28ff.
34. Morris H. Partee, "The Divine Comedy of *King Lear,*" p. 60; Ronald F. Miller, "*King Lear* and the Comic Form" *Genre* 8 (1975): 3; and Susan Snyder, *The Comic Matrix,* p. 137, respectively. A particularly illuminating essay in this respect is A. P. Rossiter's delineation of the nature of "comic relief" (*Angel with Horns,* chap. 14).
35. As Northrop Frye observes in *Anatomy of Criticism* (Princeton, 1957), p. 175. Tolstoy, who did not like Shakespeare much, liked the opening lines of *Lear* even less: he objected to Gloucester's "coarseness" as "out of place in the mouth of a person intended to represent a noble character" (*Tolstoy on Shakespeare,* trans. V. Tchertkoff and I.F.M. [New York, 1906], pp. 10–11). But that is precisely the point: the coarseness is intended as a measure of Gloucester's "nobility." On the consequences of this "nobility," see Claude J. Summers, " 'Stand Up for Bastards!': Shakespeare's Edmund and Love's Failure," *College Literature* 4 (1977): 225–31.
36. Susan Snyder argues that a given character's assumption of another identity is a convention of comedy; and when it appears in, say, Lear or Hamlet, it is meant to remind us of comedy (*The Comic Matrix,* pp. 23–24 and *passim*). True enough, in one sense; but I would also argue that in Shakespeare the "convention" partook, *from the outset,* of both the comic and the tragic. Disguise is disguise, whatever the play; and Shakespeare always meant it to set off unpleasant reverberations, however distant in Viola's case, for example, and however immediate in Hamlet's.
37. The importance I attach to familial links in Shakespearean drama includes, in

the case of Cordelia, her connections with Goneril and Regan suggested early in the play. The point is made metaphorically: in expressing their love for Lear, Goneril's first line ("Since I love you more than word can *wield* the matter . . .") connects not only with Regan's first line ("I am made of that self *metal* as my sister . . .") but also with Cordelia's aside ("I am sure my love's / More *ponderous* than my tongue . . ." [I.i.56, 71, and 80]). My case rests on the reading rather of the Folio ("ponderous") than of the Quarto ("richer").

38. Elkin C. Wilson, *Shakespeare, Santayana, and the Comic* (University, Ala., 1973), p. 145.
39. See Roy W. Battenhouse, "Falstaff as Parodist and Perhaps Holy Fool," *PMLA* 90 (1975): 32–52 and 919–22. Far more responsible is Walter Kaiser's extended treatment in his chapter on "Falstaff the Fool" in *Praisers of Folly* (Cambridge, Mass., 1963).
40. To Parolles' observation that "thou are a witty fool, I have found thee," Lavache replies: "Did you find me in yourself, sir, or were you taught to find me? The search, sir, was profitable, and much fool may you find in you, even to the world's pleasure and the increase of laughter" (II.iv.32–37).
41. D. J. Palmer, "*As You Like It* and the Idea of Play," *Critical Quarterly* 13 (1971): 243.
42. The phrases are borrowed from the brilliant essay by F. B. Tromly, "*Twelfth Night:* Folly's Talents and the Ethics of Shakespearean Comedy," *Mosaic* 7.3 (1974): 53–68. The extravagantly popular Ciceronian phrase occurs in *Epistulae ad familiares,* IX.xxii.4. The Pauline premises are of course set forth in I Corinthians 1:21ff.; the echo in Feste's epilogue of a later portion of the same epistle ("When I was a child, I spake as a child . . .: but when I became a man, I put away childish things" [13.11]) has been noted often, as by Barbara K. Lewalski in "Thematic Patterns in *Twelfth Night,*" *Shakespeare Studies* 1 (1965): 168–81, and earlier still by Richmond Noble in *Shakespeare's Biblical Knowledge* (London, 1935), pp. 212–13. The play's Erasmian burden has been argued most convincingly by F. B. Tromly; but see also the "significant connections" claimed by Thelma N. Greenfield between *The Praise of Folly* and *A Midsummer Night's Dream* (in *Comparative Literature* 20 [1968]: 236–44) and by Frank McCombie between *The Praise of Folly* and *Hamlet* (in *Shakespeare Survey* 27 [1974], 59–69). R. Chris Hassel, Jr., has proposed in *Faith and Folly in Shakespeare's Romantic Comedies* (Athens, Ga., 1980) that "the familiar Pauline and Erasmian paradoxes concerning the reversals of folly and wisdom inform a number of plays from *Love's Labour's Lost* through *Twelfth Night.* For a different approach to the earliest of these plays, see the lively discourse by Louis A. Montrose, " 'Folly, in wisdome hatch'd': The Exemplary Comedy of *Love's Labour's Lost,*" *Comparative Drama* 11 (1977): 147–70.
43. In addition to the studies by G. Wilson Knight and others cited earlier (notes 33 and 34), consult also the essays by Gareth Lloyd Evans, "Shakespeare's Fools: The Shadow and the Substance of Drama," in *Shakespearian Comedy,* ed. Malcolm Bradbury and David Palmer (London, 1972), chap. 7; Carolyn F. French, "Shakespeare's Folly: *King Lear,*" *Shakespeare Quarterly* 10 (1959): 523–29; Robert H. Goldsmith, *Wise Fools in Shakespeare* (East Lansing, Mich., 1963), especially pp. 60ff., 95ff.; Annemarie Schöne, "Shakespeares weise Narren und ihre Vorfahren," *Jahrbuch für Ästhetik und allgemeine Kunstwis-

senschaft 5 (1960): 202–45; Melvin Seiden, "The Fool and Edmund: Kin and Kind," *SEL* 19 (1979): 194–214; Glena D. Wood, "The Tragi-Comic Dimensions of Lear's Fool," *Costerus* 5 (1972): 197–226; Susan Snyder, *The Comic Matrix,* chap. 4; and William Willeford, "The Sovereign Fool: *The Tragedy of King Lear,"* in his *The Fool and His Sceptre* (London, 1969), chap. 12. Enid Welsford's study of *The Fool* (London, 1935) remains the best investigation of the background.

44. Ronald F. Miller, *"King Lear* and the Comic Form," p. 20; also Katherine Stockholder, "The Multiple Genres of *King Lear."* Cf. G. Wilson Knight: "Herein lies the profound insight of the Fool: he sees the potentialities of comedy in Lear's behavior" (*"King Lear* and the Comedy of the Grotesque," p. 164).

45. See, for example, Elsie C. Parsons and Ralph L. Beals, "The Sacred Clowns of the Pueblo and Mayo-Yaqui Indians," *American Anthropologist,* n.s. 36 (1934): 451–514.

46. Wolfgang M. Zucher, "The Clown as the Lord of Disorder," in *Holy Laughter,* ed. M. Conrad Hyers (New York, 1969), p. 316.

47. *A Portrait of the Artist as a Young Man* (New York, 1964), p. 215. W. H. Auden phrased the same conviction somewhat less memorably: "The artist is the person who stands outside and looks, stands even outside himself and looks at his daydreams" (*The English Auden,* ed. Edward Mendelson [New York, 1977], p. 359).

48. As Roland M. Frye has conclusively argued in *Shakespeare and Christian Doctrine* (Princeton, 1963).

49. Benjamin Whichcote and Ralph Cudworth, respectively; in *The Cambridge Platonists,* ed. C. A. Patrides (London, 1969), pp. 100 and 131n. Also John Smith: "That *Idea* which men generally have of God is nothing else but the picture of their Corruption" (*The Cambridge Platonists,* pp. 131–32).

50. Donne and Hooker are cited within a general exposition of "the nature of nature" in my study of *Milton and the Christian Tradition* (Oxford, 1966), chap. 3.

51. Yeats in "Lapis Lazuli," 1.16, and Lawrence in "John Galsworthy" (1928), in his *Selected Literary Criticism,* ed. Anthony Beal (London, 1955), p. 123, respectively.

Ben Jonson: A Poet Nearly Anonymous

> o'er-step not the modesty of nature
> —*Hamlet*

I. "Guides, not Commanders"

Poetry, wrote Jonson in *Discoveries,* is "the Queene of Arts: which had her originall from heaven, received thence from the *'Ebrewes,* and had in prime estimation with the Greeks, transmitted to the *Latines,* and all Nations, that profess'd Civility."[1] To grant poetry's divine origin and civilizing mission is of course to grant that poets must necessarily moralize. The notion, here crudely stated, was twice during the Renaissance in England predicated with passionate conviction and in memorable terms. One formulation was Milton's in *The Reason of Church-Government* (1642):

> These abilities [of a poet], wheresoever they be found, are the inspired guift of God rarely bestow'd, but yet to some (though most abuse) in every Nation: and are of power beside the office of a pulpit to inbreed and cherish in a great people the seeds of vertu, and publick civility, to allay the perturbations of the mind, and set the affections in right tune, to celebrate in glorious and lofty Hymns the throne and equipage of Gods Almightiness, and what he works, and what he suffers to be wrought with high providence in his Church, to sing the victorious agonies of Martyrs and Saints, the deeds and triumphs of just and pious Nations doing valiantly through faith against the enemies of Christ, to deplore the general relapses of Kingdoms and States from justice and Gods true worship. Lastly, whatsoever in religion is holy and sublime, in vertu amiable, or grave, whatsoever hath passion or admiration in all the changes of that which is call'd fortune from without, or the wily suttleties and refluxes of mans thoughts from within, all these things with a solid and treatable smoothnesse to paint out and describe. Teaching over the whole book of sanctity and vertu through all the instances of example with such delight to those especially of soft and delicious temper who will not so much as look upon Truth herselfe, unlesse they see her elegantly drest, that whereas the paths of honesty and good life appear now rugged and difficult, though they be indeed easy and pleasant, they would then appear to all men both easy and pleasant though they were rugged and difficult indeed.[2]

The other formulation was Jonson's in *Discoveries,* its rhetoric no less passionate—even if it is so much more obviously restrained—than Milton's:

> I could never thinke the study of *Wisdome* confin'd only to the Philosopher: or of *Piety* to the *Divine*: or of *State* to the *Politicke*. But that he which can faine a *Common-wealth* (which is the *Poet*) can governe it with *Counsels,* strengthen it with *Lawes,* correct it with *Iudgements,* informe it with *Religion,* and *Morals*; is all these. Wee do not require in him meere *Elocution*; or an excellent faculty in verse; but the exact knowledge of all vertues, and their Contraries; with ability to render the one lov'd, the other hated, by his proper embattaling them.[3]

If Jonson for the sake of emphasis here subordinates manner to matter or style to content, he had adequate warrant in Horace:

> The very root of writing well, and spring
> Is to be wise; thy matter first to know.[4]

Jonson was well enough aware that manner can hardly be divorced from matter. Wedded, however, they are not interchangeable since it is manner that pierces the otherwise inert matter and animates it. "Language," as Jonson remarked in *Discoveries,* "most shewes a man: speake that I may see thee."[5] Adapting a phrase from the first of his sequence of ten lyrics on Charis, it could be said that the poet's progress is not from the truth to the language but from the language to the truth; so much so, that language frequently—and in Jonson habitually—itself constitutes the "truth." Style, in other words, is fundamental—and, in Jonson's case, imperative.

Jonson spoke about style on several occasions, and definitively on one. His single most important statement does not only present an argument, however. It enacts the argument, so that the language used confirms as usual the "truth" propounded:

> *For* a man to write well, there are required three Necessaries. To read the best Authors, observe the best Speakers: and much exercise of his owne style. In style to consider, what ought to be written; and after what manner; Hee must first thinke, and excogitate his matter; then choose his words, and examine the weight of either. Then take care in placing, and ranking both matter, and words, that the composition be comely; and to doe this with diligence, and often. No matter how slow the style be at first, so it be labour'd, and

accurate: seeke the best, and be not glad of the forward conceipts, or first words, that offer themselves to us, but judge of what wee invent; and order what wee approve. Repeat often, what wee have formerly written. So that the summe of all is: Ready writing makes not good writing; but good writing brings on ready writing.[6]

As advice to aspiring authors, the statement is remarkably unexceptional. No less naïve in its generalizations than conservative in its emphases, it is also likely to mislead by the apparently mechanical approach to "good writing." But Jonson is dispensing advice not *in* so many words as *through* so many words. Positively, I am suggesting, the statement endorses solely the self-same virtue it demonstrates: the virtue of economy that terminates in clarity.

Jonson's partiality to "plainness" is writ as large in his poetry as it is in his prose, and has been studied within the context of parallel tendencies in his age.[7] But the frame of reference I would regard as crucial for his style—and through his particular style to his particular "truth"—is that of the classical tradition. For Jonson truly inhabits the centuries of Greece and Rome, more than any other poet of the English Renaissance save Milton; and attests that fact, again like Milton, on countless occasions. It is of course an understatement to aver that Jonson had much Greek and even more Latin. The evidence of the well-studied volumes surviving from his library—but the evidence also of his learned annotations and most particularly of his poetry—suffice to confirm his proud claim, recorded by William Drummond of Hawthornden, that he was "better Versed & knew more in Greek and Latin, than all the Poets in England."[8] He himself declared in the prefatory note to *Hymenæi* that he was ever "grounded upon *antiquitie,* and solide *learnings,*" yet in *Discoveries* warned with equal force that the Graeco-Roman heritage should not be permitted to enslave:

> I know *Nothing* can conduce more to letters, then to examine the writings of the *Ancients,* and not to rest in their sole Authority. . . . For to all the observations of the *Ancients,* wee have our owne experience: which, if wee will use, and apply, wee have better meanes to pronounce. It is true they open'd the gates, and made the way, that went before us; but as Guides, not Commanders.[9]

The statement is immediately relevant to matter not to manner; yet it is no less applicable to questions of style, witness the extent to which Jonson's comedies unfold—freely—under the formidable influence of Aristophanes.[10] So far as his nondramatic poetry is concerned, the contours of the classical tradition are equally clear. Jonson himself indicated that in some of his odes he put on "the wings of Pindars Muse" ("An Ode to James Earle of Desmond," l. 3). He elsewhere named Pindar yet again but in the company of three other poets who also constitute Jonson's major predecessors in lyric poetry:

> take th' Alcaike Lute;
> Or thine owne Horace, or Anacreon's Lyre;
> Warme thee by Pindars fire.
> ("Ode to Himselfe," ll. 42–44)

Still another poem invokes the seven poets from ancient Rome to Renaissance England who immortalized as many ladies and thereby established the tradition that encompasses Jonson's Celia and Charis: Catullus's Lesbia, Tibullus's Delia, Propertius's Cynthia, Ovid's Corinna, Petrarch's Laura, Ronsard's Cassandra, and Sidney's Stella (enumerated in "An Ode: Helen, did Homer never see").

II. "Readily, and fully, not profusely"

Jonson's affinities with the classical tradition are impressed upon any number of his poems, among them the well-known song to Celia. First used as part of *Volpone* (III.vii.166ff.) and next significantly published as one of the lyrics within *The Forrest,* the poem is a free adaptation of the celebrated fifth song of Catullus, "Vivamus, mea Lesbia":

> Come my *Celia,* let us prove,
> While we may, the sports of love;
> Time will not be ours, for ever:
> He, at length, our good will sever.
> Spend not then his guifts in vaine.
> Sunnes, that set, may rise againe:
> But if once we loose this light,
> 'Tis, with us, perpetuall night.
> Why should we deferre our joyes?
> Fame, and rumor are but toyes.
> Cannot we delude the eyes
> Of a few poore household spyes?
> Or his easier eares beguile,
> So removed by our wile?
> 'Tis no sinne, loves fruit to steale,
> But the sweet theft to reveale:
> To be taken, to be seene,
> These have crimes accounted beene.

The Forrest provides after the song to Celia another poem "To the same." It is manifestly closer to the spirit, and in part even to the phrasing, of the Catullan original:

> Kisse me, sweet: The warie lover
> Can your favours keepe, and cover,
> When the common courting jay
> All your bounties will betray.
> Kisse againe: no creature comes.
> Kisse, and score up wealthy summes
> On my lips, thus hardly sundred,
> While you breath. First give a hundred,
> Then a thousand, then another
> Hundred, then unto the tother
> Adde a thousand, and so more:
> Till you equall with the store,
> All the grasse that *Rumney* yeelds,
> Or the sands in *Chelsey* fields,
> Or the drops in silver *Thames,*
> Or the starres, that guild his streames,
> In the silent sommer-nights,
> When youths ply their stolne delights.
> That the curious may not know
> How to tell 'hem, as they flow,
> And the envious, when they find
> What their number is, be pin'd.

Familiar though these rhythms are to us, they were for their time utterly and intentionally subversive of the predominant modes of articulation. For Jonson's accommodation of the spirit of the classical lyric to English poetry vastly enriched the latter's potential; and if his efforts are seen as no more vital than Donne's were in another direction, his influence must certainly be judged as infinitely more lasting. In immediate relation to Jonson's diverse responses to "Vivamus, mea Lesbia," it should be insisted that its imitations during the Renaissance were so far from being confined to his practice that they embrace an impressive number of other poets too.[11] Yet Jonson's example remains crucial, arguably instrumental as it was in conditioning the response of still another poet who never figures in the roll-calls of "the sons of Ben." We expect the poet in question to have been Lovelace or, most likely, Suckling. But he is in fact Richard Crashaw, whose version of the Catullan poem echoes the distinctly Jonsonian rhythms both in the overall movement and in the particular sound patterns created. The achievement is self-evidently superior to, say, Coleridge's parallel effort in "To Lesbia":

> Come and let us live my Deare,
> Let us love and never feare,
> What the sowrest Fathers say:
> Brightest *Sol* that dyes to day
> Lives againe as blith to morrow,
> But if we darke sons of sorrow
> Set; ô then, how long a Night
> Shuts the Eyes of our short light!
> Then let amorous kisses dwell
> On our lips, begin and tell
> A Thousand, and a Hundred Score
> An Hundred, and a Thousand more,
> Till another Thousand smother
> That, and that wipe of another.
> Thus at last when we have numbred
> Many a Thousand, many a Hundred;
> Wee'l confound the reckoning quite,
> And lose our selves in wild delight:
> While our joyes so multiply,
> As shall mocke the envious eye.[12]

If Crashaw would later be observed to have been affianced rather to Herbert than to Jonson, we may consider that Herbert's own debt to Jonson was not—as we shall note presently—of slight consequence. The sons of Ben are clearly a variegated tribe indeed.

The achievement of Ben Jonson centers on his full cognizance that, in the classical lyric, matter depends entirely on manner. Style, that is to say, is paramount. We might consider, in the first instance negatively, that the classical lyric is not intent on elevating an exclusive image into an argument after the fashion of Ezra Pound's "In a Station of the Metro":

> The apparition of these faces in the crowd;
> Petals on a wet, black bough.[13]

Nor is the classical lyric concerned, as its Hellenistic counterpart is, to indulge in sensationalism deriving from potentially uncontrolled excess of emotion as in most of the poems in *The Greek Anthology* inclusive of the verses by the third-century Peloponnesian poet Mnasalkes:

Aristocrateia,
You've crossed the dark stream
Young and unwed, alas!
Your mother's left with just
The tears she sheds, when
Often now she weeping lies
Prostrate upon your tomb.[14]

The contrast with an earlier metrical inscription on a tomb is instructive:

Ἦ καλὸν τὸ μνῆμα [πα]τὴρ ἔστησε θανούσ[ηι]
Λεαρέτηι οὐ γὰρ [ἔτ]ι ζῶσανἐσοψόμ[εθα].

[When Learete died her father set up a monument
  which was beauty. But we shall nevermore see her alive.][15]

The contrast, one might venture to propose, is between those exclusive modes of articulation evident also in Greek sculpture: on the one hand, the severity of the classical period that in its aspiration after an ethically oriented idealism terminates in the frieze of the Parthenon, the Apollo of Phidias, the discuss thrower of Myron, and—however suggestive of the incoming novel dispensation—the Hermes of Praxiteles; and on the other, the subsequently wayward laxity that in its pursuit of "realism" encompasses the increasing turbulence so noticeable as we pass from the Aphrodite of Milos to the Victory of Samothrace and thence to the Laöcoön group. In espousing the former attitude, the classical lyric best defines its nature through any sequent provision of representative examples we may care to invoke. The ensuing eight instances, from the work of four lyric poets, might have been multiplied by drawing as well on the choric songs of Attic tragedy and, indeed, the comedies of Aristophanes. But the representative suggestiveness had been much the same, as it is in the poetry of the earliest Greek lyric poet, Archilochus:

ἔχουσα θαλλὸν μυρσίνης ἐτέρπετο
ῥοδῆς τε καλὸν ἄνθος,
    ἡ δέ οἱ κόμη
ὤμους κατεσκίαζε καὶ μετάφρενα.

[A spray of myrtle and beauty of a rose
were happiness in her hands, and her hair
fell as darkness on her back and shoulders.][16]

Again from Archilochus, with an even more impressive sense of economy:

εἰ γὰρ ὣς ἐμοὶ γένοιτο χεῖρα Νεοβούλης θιγεῖν.

[If it only were my fortune just to touch Neoboule's hand.][17]

Sappho wrote:

Μνάσεσθαί τινά φαιμ' ὕστερον ἀμμέων

[You may forget but

Let me tell you
this: someone in
some future time
will think of us.][18]

Next:

ψαύην δ'οὐ δοκίμοιμ' ὀράνω ἔσσα διπάχεα.

[I could not hope
to touch the sky
with my two arms.][19]

Also:

τοῦτο δ' ἴσθι, διπλασίαν
κήναν νύκτ' ἄρασθαί μ' ἄμμι γένεσθαι.

[All the while, believe me, I prayed
our night would last twice as long.][20]

Pindar, ever advancing from the exquisitely crafted detail to the intimation of states of mind, wrote:

ἐγκωμίων γὰρ ἄωτος ὕμνων
ἐπ' ἄλλοτ' ἄλλων ὧτε μέλισσα θύνει λόγον.

[The light of the holiday-song
Darts from one thought to another like a bee!][21]

Also:

> τὸν μὲν ἀγάλλων θεός
> ἔδωκεν δίφρον τε χρύσεον πτεροῖσίν τ' ἀκάμαντας ἵππους.
>
> [The God glorified him, and gave him a chariot of gold
> And winged horses that never tired.]²²

Finally, Socrates is thus said by Plato to have spoken of his lover:

> Τὴν ψυχὴν 'Αγάθωνα φιλῶν ἐπὶ χείλεσιν ἔσχον
> ἦλθε γὰρ ἡ τλήμων ὡς διαβησομένη.
>
> [As I kissed Agathon my soul swelled to my lips,
> where it hangs, pitiful, hoping to leap across.]²³

Veritable "touchstones" of the classical lyric, these eight poems suggest but do not pronounce, and intimate but do not exhaust. Their apparent qualities are economy to the point of telegraphic brevity, clarity to the point of obviousness, and restraint to the point of indifference. Yet economy conceals potential fullness; the clarity, a complexity of attitudes; and the restraint, total commitment. Greek poets like Archilochus or Sappho, and Roman ones like Catullus, would have agreed with Jonson's categoric judgment in *Discoveries* that "Wee must expresse readily, and fully, not profusely."²⁴ Profusion limits—and, worse, it corrupts.

I say "corrupts" advisedly; for the moral tenor of classical lyric poetry depends on much the same ambition which underlines Jonson's poems and was to have informed his proposed grammar: "To teach . . . The puritie of Language" ("An Execration upon Vulcan," ll. 92–93). A statement in *Discoveries* makes the point with exceptional brilliance in that the style once again confirms the argument:

> Many Writers perplexe their Readers, and Hearers with meere *Nonsense*. Their writings need sunshine. Pure and neat Language I love, yet plaine and customary. A barbarous Phrase hath often made mee out of love with a good sense; and doubtfull writing hath wrackt mee beyond my patience.²⁵

Jonson's endorsement of "plainness" is by no means primarily a reflection of contemporary interests in the "plain style." His own remarks on style diverge dramatically in that they are, in theory as in practice, moral judgments. In theory, even his nefarious wish that Shakespeare might have "blotted" a thousand lines is a reproach to be understood—if it can be understood at all—strictly in the light of the classical tradition. Hence Jonson's own practice, where "good sense" persuades not by its inherent goodness so much as by the firm clarity of its expression. For example:

> Not to know vice at all, and keepe true state,
>   Is vertue, and not *Fate*:
> Next, to that vertue, is to know vice well,
>   And her blacke spight expell.
>
> ("Epode," ll. 1–4)

The contrary is evident in Shakespeare—so Jonson was presumably inclined to argue—in that profusion encloses the potential to overwhelm the "good sense" or, *in extremis,* annihilate it altogether. If eventually Jonson in his munificent elegy on the "Soule of the Age" was to recognize Shakespeare's supremacy, something of his earlier attitude lingered in the barbed reference to the other's "small *Latine,* and lesse *Greeke.*" At issue in any case is not Shakespeare's misunderstood practice but Jonson's actual one; and in the latter, the corruption attending the profusion of language is stamped not only on his epigrams but often on his plays too, for example *Volpone,* where the exhilarating hyperboles of the opening speech are meaningfully conflated with the cacophonous sounds of Nano, Androgyno, and Castrone:

> Now, room for fresh gamesters, who do will you to know,
> They do bring you neither play nor university show;
> And therfore do entreat you that whatsoever they rehearse,
> May not fare a whit the worse, for the false pace of the verse. . . .
>
> (I.ii.1ff.)

Donne's response was positive. His commendatory verses on *Volpone*—pointedly phrased in Latin ("Amicissimo, et meritissimo Ben. Jonson. *In Vulponem.*")—hail Jonson not generally because of his adherence to the cumulative wisdom of the ancients but expressly because that adherence promised to stem the perfidious influences emanating from other quarters. The perception is vital, all the more because Donne himself remained distant from the classical tradition in poetry but saw clearly enough how Jonson's talents might, and did, use that tradition's moral authority to great advantage.

The authority is most evident, we may now maintain, where Jonson's restraint is most palpably present. His natural predilection was for the particulars within—the monosyllabic word strategically placed, the comma intended to guide the voice, the "plain" expression calculated to suggest, the rhythm aimed to elicit a specific response—which in accumulation argue on the technical level an awesome, almost Pindaric commitment to the expertly attended detail, and on the thematic level a confirmation of a manifest order or, in its absence, the intimation of that same order all the more urgently precisely because it is absent. To be sure, not all of Jonson's efforts were perfectly wrought. The elegy on the Marchioness of Winchester, for instance, extends to one hundred lines, and is one hundred lines too long. The version of Horace's *Art of Poetry,* also unsatisfactory, may charitably be described as versified journalism, all the more dispiriting because it is the labor of a poet otherwise fully conversant with classical poetry. But where Jonson succeeds—and he succeeds gratifyingly often—he exerts his individual talent in the direction of the classical tradition to attain the level of the nearly anonymous poet.[26]

Nearly anonymous: for Jonson temperamentally could not, and in any case should not, have obliterated his self altogether. But this is not to say that the display of self is marked in Jonson to the same degree that it is in Donne. In terms of the language each poet used—and language, Jonson reminded us, "most shewes a man"—the "masculine expression" which Carew noted in Donne is no less apparent in Jonson. The two poets shared a partiality for "strong lines."[27] Jonson could be fully as irreverent as Donne, and so he was (for example in the poem of *The Forrest* beginning "And must I sing? what subject shall I chuse?"). He could also be uneconomic in utterance and splenetic in tone, and so he was (in "A Speech according to Horace" and, far more virulently because much more personally engaged, in "An Expostulation with Inigo Jones"). He could also write "elegies" not only in Donne's sense of the term but in close emulation of Donne's particular manner, witness the four such poems included in *Under-wood* (nos. 38–41), of which one is so far from being Jonson's that it may well be Donne's.[28] Yet in spite of the several affiliations between the two poets, the norm in Jonson's poetry resides in its discretion. The few religious poems he wrote are particularly delicate exemplars of this discretion, in that restraint and clarity and economy—the qualities already commended—yield rhythms quite unlike anything in Donne:

> I Sing the birth, was borne to night,
> The Author both of Life, and light. . . .
> ("A Hymne on the Nativitie of My Saviour," ll. 1–2)

Only Herbert was eventually to appreciate the Jonsonian approach to religious poetry,[29] especially the stunning "simplicity" of

> Heare mee, O God!
> A broken heart,
> Is my best part:
> Use still thy rod,
> That I may prove
> Therein, thy Love.
>
> ("A Hymne to God the Father," ll. 1–6)

Jonson's discretion was reinforced, in his secular poems, by his habitual fondness for firmly ordered stanzaic patterns and carefully measured single lines which themselves control the centrifugal tendencies of the given emotion. The technique appears to negate the self but in a very particular sense asserts it all the more decisively. It is Jonson's way of confirming the circle of the classical tradition through, not against, his individual talent.

III. "The puritie of Language"

But to conclude where a conclusion may be—and, I hope, is—singularly irrelevant: where the poets' poet is normally said to be Spenser, the same appellation should be recognized as equally merited by Jonson. Spenser's poetic practice has of course been utterly crucial for the development of English poetry; but as it is a practice representative of a particular mode of articulation, it made Jonson's contribution all the more necessary. Individually, Spenser and Jonson had a decisive impact on numerous other poets; jointly, they affected English poetry at large.

Spenser's influence is readily identifiable because of its particularity. But Jonson's influence cannot be defined categorically, nor detailed unequivocally. Our task would have been very easy had we wished solely to trace Jonson's distinct rhythms in, say, Crashaw, or to observe the way Jonson's dramatic lyric "A Nymphs Passion" was transformed into Coleridge's "Mutual Passion" with an embarrassing minimum of amendments. Our task is on the contrary very difficult because Jonson's influence, extending far beyond the mundane details just enumerated, is almost—but certainly not quite—impersonal. His near anonymity was ideally suited to his ambition to accommodate the spirit of the classical lyric to English poetry; and en route, juxtaposing "solide *learnings*" and "our owne experience," he created sound patterns violent enough to have impressed Donne, "simple" enough to have attracted Herbert, urbane enough to have allured Marvell, and variable enough to have commanded the respect of Milton. Upon consideration, I believe, Jonson's multiform poetry will also be observed to have affected Pope as much as Blake, Coleridge as much as Tennyson, and Yeats as much as T. S. Eliot. My large claims will astonish only those who are yet to discern that Jonson is to English poetry as Erasmus is to the civilization of the Renaissance: a formidable talent in himself, but also the cause why talent is in others.

NOTES

An earlier version of this chapter appeared in *Classic and Cavalier: Essays on Jonson and the Sons of Ben,* ed. Claude J. Summers and Ted-Larry Pebworth (Pittsburgh: University of Pittsburgh Press, 1982), pp. 3–16. Copyright 1982 by the University of Pittsburgh Press. Reprinted by permission. Jonson's poetry is here quoted from *The Complete Poetry of Ben Jonson,* ed. William B. Hunter, Jr. (New York, 1963).

1. *Ben Jonson,* ed. C. H. Herford, and Percy and Evelyn Simpson (Oxford, 1925–52), 8:636. One of the most discriminating studies of Jonson's premises is by Anthony Mortimer, "The Feigned Commonwealth in the Poetry of Ben Jonson," *SEL* 13 (1973): 69–79.
2. *Selected Prose,* ed. C. A. Patrides, rev. ed. (Columbia, Mo., 1985), p. 57.
3. *Ben Jonson,* ed. Herford and Simpson, 8:595.
4. *The Art of Poetrie,* trans. Ben Jonson (revised version), ll. 440–41.
5. *Ben Jonson,* ed. Herford and Simpson, 8:625.
6. *Ben Jonson,* ed. Herford and Simpson, 8:615–16.
7. See especially Wesley Trimpi, *Ben Jonson's Poems: A Study of the Plain Style* (Stanford, 1962).
8. *Conversations with William Drummond of Hawthornden,* in *Ben Jonson,* ed. Herford and Simpson, 1:149. The list of Greek and Roman writers represented in Jonson's library (*Ben Jonson,* ed. Herford and Simpson, 11:598–600) has been dramatically expanded by David McPherson in "Ben Jonson's Library and Marginalia: An Annotated Catalogue" (*SP* 71 [1974], Appendix), which cites editions from the Geneva Greek grammar to editions of Aristophanes, scholia on Euripides, *The Greek Anthology* (not the much fuller *Palatine Anthology* which was published, of course, long after Jonson), and especially the two volumes that between them print "virtually all ancient Greek words in verse": the editions by J. Lectius and P. de la Roviere (Geneva, 1606 and 1614).
9. *Ben Jonson,* ed. Herford and Simpson, 7:209 and 8:567, respectively. See further the detailed study by Katharine E. Maus, *Ben Jonson and the Roman Frame of Mind* (Princeton, 1985).
10. See Coburn Gum, *The Aristophanic Comedies of Ben Jonson* (The Hague, 1969), and Aliki L. Dick, *Paedeia through Laughter* (The Hague, 1974).
11. See James A. S. McPeek, *Catullus in Strange and Distant Britain* (Cambridge, Mass., 1939), pp. 110–26, and Gordon Braden, "*Viuamus, mea Lesbia* in the English Renaissance," *ELR* 9 (1979): 199–24. It may be that Milton also resorted to the Catullan poem—in *Lycidas* no less! See Robert E. Jungman, "Milton's Use of Catullus in *Lycidas,*" *Classical Folia* 32 (1978): 90–92.

12. "Out of Catullus," in *The Complete Poetry of Richard Crashaw,* ed. George W. Williams (New York, 1970), pp. 523–25.
13. *Personae* (London, 1952), p. 119.
14. Trans. Edward Lucie-Smith, in *The Greek Anthology,* ed. Peter Jay (London, 1973), p. 109 (no. 201).
15. Paul Friedländer with Herbert B. Hoffleit, *Epigrammata: Greek Inscriptions in Verse* (Berkeley, 1948), p. 71 (no. 60); trans. Richmond Lattimore, *Greek Lyrics,* 2nd rev. ed. (Chicago, 1960), p. 32.
16. Ernst Diehl, ed., *Anthologia lyrica graeca,* (Leipzig, 1925), 1:218 (no. 25); Willis Barnstone, trans., *Greek Lyric Poetry* (1962; reprint New York, 1972), p. 29.
17. Diehl, *Anthologia lyrica graeca,* 1:231 (no. 71); trans. Lattimore, *Greek Lyrics,* p. 5.
18. J. M. Edmonds, ed. and trans., *Lyra graeca* (New York, 1922–24), 1:236 (no. 76); *Sappho,* trans. Mary Barnard (Berkeley, 1958), no. 60. The expansion in translation of Sappho's highly compressed single line is visible proof of one's difficulties in suggesting to the Greekless reader what "economy" actually means in Greek poetry. In his literal translation, Edmonds renders the line: "Somebody, I tell you, will remember us hereafter."
19. Edmonds, *Lyra graeca,* 1:222 (no. 53); Barnstone, *Greek Lyric Poetry,* p. 68.
20. Edmonds, *Lyra graeca,* 1:244 (no. 84a); Barnstone, *Greek Lyric Poetry,* p. 79.
21. *Pythian* 10.53–54, in *Pindari Carmina,* ed. Otto Schroeder (Leipzig and Berlin, 1923), p. 260; *The Odes of Pindar,* trans. C. M. Bowra (Harmondsworth, England, 1969), p. 23.
22. *Olympian* 1.87–88, in *Pindari Carmina,* ed. Schroeder, p. 87, and in *The Odes of Pindar,* trans. Bowra, p. 67.
23. Diehl, *Anthologia lyrica graeca,* 1:87 (no. 1); Barnstone, *Greek Lyric Poetry,* p. 179.
24. *Ben Jonson,* ed. Herford and Simpson, 8:623.
25. *Ben Jonson,* ed. Herford and Simpson, 8:620.
26. I adopt the phrase, but not its implications, from John Crowe Ransom's memorable essay on *Lycidas* as "A Poem Nearly Anonymous," in *The World's Body* (New York, 1938), pp. 1–28. My own emphasis partakes far more of the comment by L. C. Knights, ventured but in passing, that in Jonson "classical" simplicity and restraint are married to "the tones and rhythms of personal feeling" ("Ben Jonson: Public Attitudes and Social Poetry," in *A Celebration of Ben Jonson,* ed. William Blissett et al. [Toronto, 1973], p. 181). On Jonson's classicism as ethical, social, and individual expression, see also Claude J. Summers and Ted-Larry Pebworth, *Ben Jonson* (Boston, 1979), especially pp. 37–41 and 134–35.
27. Carew's poem on Donne is quoted on p. 90. See also George Williamson, "Strong Lines," in his *Seventeenth Century Contexts* (London, 1960), chap. 5.
28. The poem "probably" written by Donne is his fifteenth elegy, "The Expostulation" (no. 39 in *Under-wood*). Consult Evelyn Simpson, "Jonson and Donne: A Problem of Authorship," *RES* 15 (1939): 274–82, and, in support of its thesis, the "internal structural evidence" provided by D. Heyward Brock, "Jonson and Donne: Structural Fingerprinting and the Attribution of Elegies

XXXVIII–XLI," *PBSA* 72 (1978), 519–27. I am grateful to Ted-Larry Pebworth and Claude J. Summers for assistance with this as with other matters.

29. For an attempt to argue Herbert's indebtedness to Jonson, see Ilona Bell, "Circular Strategies and Structures in Jonson and Herbert," in *Classic and Cavalier: Essays on Jonson and the Sons of Ben,* ed. Claude J. Summers and Ted-Larry Pebworth (Pittsburgh, 1982), pp. 157–70.

John Donne: The Aesthetics of Morality

> Framed in the prodigality of nature
> —*Richard III*

I. "The first poet . . . in some things"

Donne is in the first instance coarse. The judgment is ventured in earnest, and meant not in denigration but in praise. In extreme reaction to the mellifluous verses of his immediate predecessors and contemporaries, he deployed extreme means in order to focus attention on neglected dimensions of human experience. We may with Ben Jonson sever the means deployed from the experience illumined, offended by the one ("Done for not keeping of accent deserved hanging") yet appreciative of the other ("Done [is] the first poet in the World in some things").[1] We may also, with Henry Hallam, scan only the means, and thereby conclude—as conclude we must—that "Donne is the most inharmonious of our versifiers, if he can be said to have deserved such a name by lines too rugged to seem metre."[2] On the face of it, certainly, Donne's violation of "accent"— "the chiefe Lord and grave Governour of Numbers" or meter, according to Samuel Daniel[3]—appears very nearly to have wrecked poetry, much as Joyce's deviant tactics seem to have dismantled the novel. But in Donne as in Joyce manner aspires to an engagement with matter, and the mode of articulation with that which is articulated. The risks taken were manifestly grave; but we may consider that English poetry since Donne could not—and, demonstrably, did not—confine itself to the range that obtained before his advent. His patterns of thought were, as patterns of thought, not unique; but the frequent harshness surrounding those patterns, the intentionally *bent* sounds, pierced realms no poet had yet attempted to explore. In this respect it is an understatement even to claim as I claimed, that Donne is in the first instance coarse.

II. "The highest technical expertness"

Francis Thompson in 1899 commended Donne as "pungent, clever, with metre like a rope all hanks and knots."[4] Thompson is in the direct line of descent from Thomas Carew who in his elegy on Donne—itself a sharply perceptive exercise in literary criticism—praised the "masculine expression," the robust metrical and linguistic calisthenics:

> Our stubborn language bends, made only fit
> With her tough-thick-rib'd hoopes to gird about
> Thy Giant phansie. . . .
>
> ("An Elegie upon the Death of the Deane
> of Pauls, Dr John Donne," ll. 50–52)

Yet this is exactly what Dryden disapproved when he wished that Donne "had taken care of his words, and of his numbers," eschewing in particular his habitual "rough cadence."[5] Those antagonistic to Donne, in other words, condemn precisely what his partisans approve. What does the practice of Donne suggest?

Two widely loved poems point the way. The first is the song beginning "Sweetest love, I do not goe"; the other, "A Valediction forbidding mourning." The song expresses a single mood in very simple terms. Its tone is essentially melodious, gentle, serene:

> Sweetest love, I do not goe,
>   For wearinesse of thee,
> Nor in hope the world can show
>   A fitter Love for mee . . .

and so on for some thirty-five more lines in perfectly modulated iambic rhythm. It is of course obvious that the song is considerably different from the poems usually regarded as characteristically Donne's.[6] Did he write it to proclaim his competence in a mode the other poems reject? But I submit that it was also meant as a norm—a metrical norm—we should recall whenever the slightest deviation is detected elsewhere. In "A Valediction forbidding mourning," for instance, the nominal argument is that lovers may without alarm be parted physically since they are joined spiritually; yet the comforting thought is phrased rather oddly:

> Dull sublunary lovers love
>   (Whose soule is sence) cannot admit
> Absence, because it doth remove
>   Those things which elemented it.
>
> But we by a love, so much refin'd,
>   That our selves know not what it is,
> Inter-assured of the mind,
>   Care lesse, eyes, lips, hands to misse.
>
>   (ll. 13–20)

The oddity is in the last line, which in accordance with the norm should have had only four stresses but has six:

Cáre lésse, eýes, líps, hánds to mísse.

In traditionally idealistic visions, we may remind ourselves, the rhythm adheres to the basic iambic pattern. Shakespeare, for instance, wrote of

>   sweet beauty's best,
> Of hánd, of fóot, of líp, of eýe, of brów ....
> (Sonnet CVI, ll. 5-6)

Donne could be just as regular when the occasion demanded:

>   the great soule which here amongst us now
> Doth dwell, and moves that hánd, and tóngue, and brów ....
> (*Metempsychosis,* ll. 61-62)

Where he wished to be emphatic, however, he deviated from the norm as in the arrangement of the crucial words in a strongly accented sequence:

> Hath my náme, wórds, hánd, féet, héart, mínde and wít;
> ("To Mr R. W.: If, as mine is," l. 6)

or, much more relevant thematically:

> I never stoop'd so low, as they
> Which on an eýe, cheéke, líp, can prey ....
> ("Negative Love," ll. 1-2)

By the same token, the departure from the iambic pattern in the line already quoted:

Cáre lésse, eýes, líps, hánds to mísse

joins the intentionally reduced syllables[7] to affirm through the disturbed rhythm what the sense expressly denies. In short, the nominal argument in the "Valediction" is nominal only so far as the narrator is concerned; for the actual argument—consciously on the part of the poet, "unconsciously" on the part of the narrator—is that the physical separation of the lovers will matter very much, as matter very much it must. The detail may or may not persuade. But if we care to lavish on Donne's poetry the close study it demands, even a mere detail will alert us to the presence of a "counter-movement" which, present in his best poems, is here confirmed through the sexual orientation of his celebrated analogy of the two souls to "stiffe" compasses:

> Thy soule the fixt foot, makes no show
>   To move, but doth, if th'other doe.
>
> And though it in the center sit,
>   Yet when the other far doth rome,
> It leanes, and hearkens after it,
>   And growes erect, as that comes home.
>
> (ll. 27–32)

The conflation of the spiritual and the physical in the "Valediction" is commensurate to a like emphasis in the poems we shall examine later. In advance, however, it is well to understand in what sense Donne had— *pace* Dryden—"taken care of his words, and of his numbers." The generalization of that elegant poet and critic, John Crowe Ransom, still obtains: "Donne's skill is of the highest technical expertness in English poetry."[8]

The skill is disclosed variously and, at its best, in direct relation to the unfolding sense. Where the skill coincides with the sense only fitfully, the weaknesses of Donne are exhibited with impressive clarity. Lines often hesitate between prose and poetry, for instance:

> Let us love nobly, and live, and adde againe
> Yeares and yeares unto yeares,
>
> ("The Anniversarie," ll. 28–29)

or:

> For ill is ill, and good good still,
>
> ("Communitie," l. 2)

and again:

> If we love things long sought, *Age* is a thing
>   Which we are fifty yeares in compassing.
>
> (Elegy IX, ll. 33–34)

Equally, we expect a poet to improve on the vapid supposition that "some man, unworthy to be possessor of old or new love, himself being false or weak, thought his pain and shame would be lesser if on womankind he might his anger wreak"; and we are unnerved when we read precisely that:

> Some man unworthy to be possessor
> Of old or new love, himselfe being false or weake,
>   Thought his paine and shame would be lesser,
> If on womankind he might his anger wreake. . . .
> ("Confined Love," ll. 1–4)

Where the skill is commensurate to the sense, however, Donne persuades fully. The grammar and the punctuation are on such occasions wont to be tortuous in the extreme, broken in order forcefully to make a point as in "The Canonization":

> And wee in us finde the 'Eagle and the dove,
>   The Phœnix ridle hath more wit
>   By us, we two being one, are it.
> (ll. 22–24)

Or syncopated in order to suggest the lover's agony as in "The Legacie":

> When I dyed last, and Deare, I dye
>   As often as from thee I goe,
>   Though it be but an houre agoe,
> And Lovers houres be full eternity,
> I can remember yet, that I . . .
> (ll. 1ff.)

—and so on. But the lines are also wont to respond to the demands of the sense, expanding in one instance, contracting in the next, and sometimes compacted within two monosyllables which herald the imminent change in the argument:

> Though shee were true, when you met her,
> And last, till you write your letter,
>   Yet shee
>   Will bee
> False, ere I come, to two, or three.
> ("Song: Goe, and catche," ll. 23–27)

or:

> when thou
> Art in anguish
> And dost languish
> For some one
> That will none,
> Or prove as false as thou art now.
>
> ("The Message," ll. 19–24)

It may also be that the external form of Donne's poems is not casually conceived since four-fifths of the poems he cast in stanzas appear to employ patterns he did not repeat. But to what extent there is a conjunction of the form without and the argument within, must be left to the judgment—and possibly to the ingenuity—of the given reader.

My emphasis on Donne's attention to "accent" is meant to balance the praise commonly bestowed on his language. Donne's originality does not reside in his linguistic pyrotechnics, however "colloquial" their nature and surprising their effects. It resides in his manipulation of meter—"metre like a rope all hanks and knots"—which alone is capable of conveying his stupendous range of tone. Granted that the satirists of the late sixteenth century display an equally "astonishing roughness";[9] granted also that the Elizabethan dramatists provided Donne with numerous instances of variable cadences;[10] and granted, too, that nondramatic poets at home and abroad had already exploited some of his more celebrated images, even the image of the compasses in the "Valediction."[11] These contexts are indispensable for a full appreciation of "the moment," and could profitably be amplified by studies of the dramatic element inherent in "dialogues" Platonic as well as Neoplatonic (Bembo, Leone Ebreo, Castiglione, et al.) but also Augustinian (in the *Confessions*) and eventually scientific too (in Giordano Bruno's *On the Infinite Universe* [1584] and in Galileo's *Dialogues on the Two Great Systems of the World* [1632]). But details appertaining to the background do not necessarily clarify Donne's achievement in the foreground, *id est*, his introduction into lyric poetry of elements innate to dramatic literature, his boldness in adjusting those elements to his immediate purposes, his use of variable cadences to evoke diverse emotional states. Within English poetry Donne's metrical innovations are comparable only to those of Hopkins, save that the influence of Hopkins was limited while Donne's was extensive. Mindful but of Donne's striking opening lines, we identify readily the progeny of the equally dramatic starting points in Pope or in Browning:

> Shut, shut the door, good John! fatigu'd I said,
> Tye up the knocker, say I'm sick, I'm dead ...
> *(Epistle to Dr. Arbuthnot)*
> Now, don't sir! Don't expose me! Just this once!
> This was the first and only time, I'll swear....
> *(Mr. Sludge, "the Medium")*

Donne's "rough cadence" taught generations of poets to look with their ears.

III. "Forget the Hee and Shee"

We accept that Donne's poems are dramatic, and more specifically dramatic monologues presupposing a listener. Each has in consequence a distinct narrator; and each, its own "theatrical" language.

The theatrical language includes the conceits, that is to say elaborate comparisons, extended analogies, or (in T. S. Eliot's phrase) "distended metaphors and similes."[12] The operative words here are not the nouns but the adjectives ("elaborate," "extended," "distended") which suggest a range beyond mere similitudes. As Eliot further explained, a conceit is "the elaboration (contrasted with the condensation) of a figure of speech to the farthest stage to which ingenuity can carry it."[13] Not designed for dull sublunary minds, it was often abused during the Renaissance; and aspiring writers were therefore frequently warned that conceits, and even the less hazardous similitudes, "are not to be taken from things altogether different."[14] One might after all leap over the decorous into the risible, as did the preacher heard by Du Perron: "Lord, wipe my beak clean with the napkin of thy love." In Donne's case, of course, there is always "The Flea."

"The Flea" was a very popular poem, and surprisingly traditional; for many poets had already pined to be fleas, hoping to land on the bosom of their beloved and even (the ultimate felicity this) to be slapped to death.[15] Donne's version is certainly erotic, possibly to the point of vulgarity; but it is also highly ingenious, certainly to the point of exhilaration. The argument, such as it is, entails the transmutation of the amorous insect into a symbol of the desired union.[16] But it is the technique that impresses, involving as it does a conceit elaborated "to the farthest stage to which ingenuity can carry it." Dr. Johnson would not have approved, and did not; yet he might have said of "The Flea" what he remarked of another whimsical work, Sir Thomas Browne's *Garden of Cyrus*, that it is "a perpetual triumph of fancy to expand a scanty theme" (see p. 170). And "The Flea" is of the scantiest.

96 / Figures in a Renaissance Context

Conceits elaborated through an entire poem are most unusual in Donne. So far, "The Flea" is an exception; and so is "The good-morrow":

> I wonder by my troth, what thou, and I
> Did, till we lov'd? were we not wean'd till then?
> But suck'd on countrey pleasures, childishly?
> Or snorted we in the seaven sleepers den?
> T'was so; But this, all pleasures fancies bee
> If ever any beauty I did see,
> Which I desir'd, and got, t'was but a dreame of thee.
>
> And now good morrow to our waking soules,
> Which watch not one another out of feare;
> For love, all love of other sights controules,
> And makes one little roome an every where.
> Let sea-discoverers to new worlds have gone,
> Let Maps to other, worlds on worlds have showne,
> Let us possesse one world, each hath one, and is one.
>
> My face in thine eye, thine in mine appeares,
> And true plaine hearts doe in the faces rest,
> Where can we finde two better hemispheares
> Without sharpe North, without declining West?
> What ever dyes, was not mixt equally;
> If our two loves be one, or, thou and I
> Love so alike, that none doe slacken, none can die.

The conceit in "The good-morrow," initiated in the wide-ranging allusions of the first stanza, surfaces in the reference to newly discovered lands in the second, advances promptly to new maps superimposed upon the old, links them with the hemispheric faces of the two lovers, suggests that the hemispheres of the world are to those of the faces as both are to the eyeballs, and affirms at last the annihilation of the external globe by the self-sufficient lovers, their hemispheric entities now fused into one perfect sphere. The idealistic vision charms; but realistic as Donne was, he could not utterly forego the past when the lovers "suck'd on countrey pleasures, childishly." "The good-morrow" is committed to an aspiration, not an accomplished fact. The imperative is clear enough: "*Let* us possesse our world . . ." So is "the modest tentativeness" of the concluding lines where two propositions are alike based upon an *if*:[17]

> If our two loves be one, or, thou and I
> Love so alike, that none doe slacken, none can die.

Donne's poetry, it is clear, endures an expansion.

The expansion is also evident in Donne's use of several distinct narrators who not only include more than one woman but represent various and often conflicting attitudes. These attitudes do not cohere into a vision of "the softness of love," as Dryden wished they might have done.[18] They cohere in terms of reality embodied not only in softness but in violent passion, tenderness as well as cynicism, restraint and frenzy, joy and unqualified hate. In Donne's words,

> To Love, and Griefe tribute of Verse belongs,
> But not of such as pleases when 'tis read.
> ("The Triple Fool," ll. 17–18)

Extreme emotions, passionately felt, are conveyed in appropriately extreme terms. Love—"*all* love"—is "fever." It includes "fire of Passion, sighes of ayre, / Water of teares, and earthly sad despaire." It induces misery, for it is a "spider . . . which transubstantiates all, / And can convert Manna to gall." Rebuffed, love can lead to hate; and indulged in strictly for sexual gratification—"the tillage of a harsh rough man"—it can yield chillingly clinical epigrams on the male animal ("Men leave behind them that which their sin showes, / And are, as theeves trac'd, which rob when it snows") or repulsive lines on the bestiality of woman:

> Thine's like the dread mouth of a fired gunne,
> Or like the hot liquid metalls newly runne
> Into clay moulds, or like to that Ætna
> Where round about the grasse is burnt away.
> Are not your kisses then as filthy, and more,
> As a worme sucking an invenom'd sore?

Lines of this order, it must be emphasized, are not only directed outwardly in furious denunciation of their recipient. Given the omnipresent dramatic context, they are also directed inwardly against the speaker in oblique condemnation of his obsessions.

The point is of some moment since we could be tempted to attribute to Donne attitudes characteristic of his narrators. We may scarcely deny the frequent cynicism of the *Songs and Sonnets,* and especially the ultimate cynicism in "Communitie":

> Chang'd loves are but chang'd sorts of meat,
> And when hee hath the kernel eate,
>   Who doth not fling away the shell?
> (ll. 22–24)

Nor may we deny the explicit endorsement of promiscuity in several poems, whether in "The Indifferent" ("I can love both faire and browne") or in one of the elegies:

> all beasts change when they please,
> Shall women, more hot, wily, wild then these,
> Be bound to one man . . .?
>
> (Elegy III, ll. 11–13)

The ascription of such attitudes to Donne could lead us—and has led us—to reproach him as a "lascivious prig."[19] Granted, the women who flap their wings about his narrators appear to be there primarily in order to flap. Granted also that the contempt is consequently total:

> Women are all like Angels; the faire be
> Like those which fell to worse;
>
> (Elegy II, ll. 29–30)

or:

> Hope not for minde in women; at their best,
> Sweetnesse, and wit they'are, but *Mummy,* possest.
>
> ("Loves Alchymie," ll. 23–24)

Women's constant inconstancy, moreover, appears to elicit Donne's approval in line with the categorical manner of another poet:

> We had need to goe borrow that fantastique glasse
> Invented by *Galileo* the Florentine,
> To view another spacious world i' th' Moone,
> And looke to find a constant woman there.

But this sentiment, voiced by the Cardinal in *The Duchess of Malfi* (II.iv.24–27), can hardly be said to reflect Webster's own convictions. Can it be said to reflect Donne's, the dramatic nature of his poems notwithstanding?

"Passion," says D. H. Lawrence's Ursula, "is only part of love. And it seems so much because it can't last. That is why passion is never happy" (*The Rainbow,* chap. 13). The experience she seeks, and eventually gains, does not negate passion but places it within an apocalyptic reality—itself passionately apprehended—which stands on earth yet is fitted to the overarching heaven. Donne's experience inclined him to a parallel balance. The fever of love is not love itself. It is but the passion of love: the spider that converts manna to gall, the self-centered gratification of the senses, the promiscuity, the lasciviousness. True, most of Donne's narrators are, even at the best of times, egocentric. But are not lovers by definition egocentric, self-regarding and self-sufficient, turned inwardly upon themselves? As "The Sunne Rising" proclaims,

> She'is all States, and all Princes, I,
>   Nothing else is.
> (ll. 21-22)

"Nothing else is" because love—not the raging fever but the sustained joy—can possess a world where time and place are annihilated:

> Love, all alike, no season knowes, nor clyme,
> Nor houres, dayes, moneths, which are the rags of time.
> (ibid., ll. 9-10)

>   our love hath no decay;
> This, no to morrow hath, nor yesterday,
> ("The Anniversarie," ll. 7-8)

>   though thy heart depart,
>   It stayes at home,
> ("Loves infinitenesse," ll. 29-30)

or, more expansively, from the memorable peroration in one of the elegies (XII: "His parting from her"):

>   when I change my Love, I'll change my heart;
> Nay, if I wax but cold in my desire,
> Think, heaven hath motion lost, and the world, fire:
> Much more I could, but many words have made
> That, oft, suspected which men would perswade;
> Take therefore all in this: I love so true,
> As I will never look for less in you.

Such reflections persuade not only experientially. They persuade aesthetically too, because in accordance with the norm—the metrical norm as before stated—their rhythm confirms what their sense expressly claims.

Love in Donne's poetry is not etherealized out of existence. As he once wrote to Sir Henry Wotton, "You (I think) and I am much of one sect in the Philosophy of love; which though it be directed upon the minde, doth inhere in the body, and find piety entertainment there."[20] Some poems, "The Canonization" for example, scale upwardly: "Beg from above / A patterne of our love!"[21] But the common preference is for the middle regions mapped in "Aire and Angels": "Love must not be, but take a body too" (l. 10). As the second of the verse letters to the Countess of Huntington likewise maintains, "The soule with body, is a heaven combin'd / With earth, and for mans ease, but nearer joyn'd" (ll. 97–98). Statements of this order echo not the nominal but the actual argument of "A Valediction forbidding mourning" (as above), itself linked to the emphatic declaration in the elegy already quoted:

> Rend us in sunder, thou canst not divide
> Our bodies so, but that our souls are ty'd.
>
> (Elegy XII, ll. 69–70)

"Loves growth" assents, all the more because it offers a context for the reference in the "Valediction" to earth-bound, "elemented" love:

> Love's not so pure, and abstract, as they use
> To say, which have no Mistresse but their Muse,
> But as all else, being elemented too,
> Love sometimes would contemplate, sometimes do.
>
> (ll. 11–14)

Love is not *agape* or *eros*; it is both. Nor is it monomaniacally Platonic or exclusively Petrarchan since it qualifies the one tradition in the light of the other, and both in terms of experience. According to a reiterated word, love is a "mixture"; and according to a recurring image, a circle ("perfect motions are all circular" ["To the Lady Bedford," l. 31]). It involves when all is said the invitation extended by the narrator of "The undertaking": "forget the Hee and Shee" (l. 20).

"The Extasie" tries to forget, and fails brilliantly. The title raises expectations of the suspension of the physical in a riotous display of religious masochism, or (if we are mindful of primitive pathology) any of the morbid states of unconsciousness inclusive of catalepsy. But Donne would not have been Donne had he met our expectations. The first surprise generated by "The Extasie" is its external appearance. It should have been promiscuous in its deviation from the norm, the stanzas disordered and the lines disarrayed; but it is in fact quite temperate, the stanzas ordered and the lines highly controlled. Within, the argument advances with a serenity to the point of detachment. The basic premise, we have been assured, occurs also in Giordano Bruno:

> Fascination by love takes place when owing to very frequent looking or to an intense, though instantaneous, look, one eye meets another, and two eyebeams reciprocally encounter, and light couples together

with light. Then spirit joins with spirit; and the superior light informing the inferior one, they come to sparkle through the eyes, rushing to, and penetrating, the inner spirit which is rooted in the heart; and in this manner they kindle erotic fire.[22]

But the "erotic fire" in Donne's poem is not particularly erotic, or even a fire. The act of consummation may be presumed to have already taken place when the poem begins; if so, the ensuing reflections are about the implications of that act. There are no surprises: the "mixture" here as elsewhere is comprised of an upward aspiration as well as the acceptance of the "elemented" nature of love. But the complexities are infinite, aimed as they are at validating the incomprehensible mystery succinctly stated in another poem: "All love is wonder" (Elegy II, l. 25). The brilliance is palpable. It depends on the use of metrically significant words which call attention to themselves, as in the case of the etymologically pregnant "interinanimates" (l. 42), and also highly sophisticated adjustments to the syntax in order to qualify the nominal argument:

> But O alas, so long, so farre
> Our bodies why doe wee forebeare?
> They'are ours, though not wee, Wee are
> The intelligences, they the spheares.
>
> We owe them thankes, because they thus,
> Did us, to us, at first convay,
> Yielded their senses force to us,
> Nor are drosse to us, but allay.
>
> (ll. 49–56)

"I should never find fault with metaphysical poems," said Coleridge, "were they all like this, or but half as excellent."[23]

IV. "Dishes for Death to eate"

Donne's concern with love is so ample that before it all else appears to buckle. But Donne is in fact the foremost English poet—as well as the greatest English prose-writer—of death.

Death was for Donne an obsession. While his love of love was mutable though all-pervasive, and ephemeral though spacious, his love of death was undeviating, constant, permanent, fixed. He did not maintain death only metaphorically, in the sense that the separation of lovers is a type of the dissolution to come. He maintained it literally, as a dissolution at once expected and presently present. Confined to a body prone to illness—"an infirme and valetudinary body" he called it in one of his letters[24]—he reported to his friend Sir Henry Goodyer in about 1608:

> I have contracted a sicknesse which I cannot name nor describe. For it hath so much of a continual Cramp, that it wrests the sinews, so much of a Tetane, that it withdraws and puls the mouth, and so much of the Gout, (which they whose counsell I use, say it is) that it is not like to be cured....[25]

Another letter of the same period exhibits the consequences:

> The pleasantnesse of the season displeases me. Every thing refreshes and I wither, and I grow older and not better, my strength diminishes, and my load growes, and being to passe more and more stormes, I finde that I have not only cast out all my ballast which nature and time gives, Reason and discretion, and so am as empty and light as Vanity can make me; but I have over fraught my self with Vice....[26]

More than twenty years later, at the apex of his fame but deprived of his beloved wife Anne and ever tormented by ill health, he told his sister, "I have never good temper, nor good pulse, nor good appetite, nor good sleep." He added:

> I am afraid that Death will play with me so long, as he will forget to kill me; and suffer me to live in a languishing and uselesse age, A life, that is rather a forgetting that I am dead, then of living.[27]

The burden of the letters is borne even more compulsively by the poems. The infrequently read elegiac tribute to Cecilia Bulstrode, for instance, explicitly demonstrates how a conventional lament in conventional clichés is transformed as Donne forgoes the occasion and the departed lady in favor of a paean to death:

> Th'earths face is but thy Table; there are set
>   Plants, cattell, men, dishes for Death to eate.
> In a rude hunger now hee millions drawes
>   Into his bloody, or plaguy, or sterv'd jawes.
> Now hee will seeme to spare, and doth more wast,
>   Eating the best first, well preserv'd to last.
> Now wantonly he spoiles, and eates us not,
>   But breakes off friends, and lets us peecemeale rot ...
> How could I thinke thee nothing, that see now
>   In all this All, nothing else is, but thou ...

> And though thou beest, O mighty bird of prey,
>   So much reclaim'd by God, that thou must lay
> All that thou kill'st at his feet, yet doth hee
>   Reserve but few, and leaves the most to thee.
>   ("Elegie on Mistris Boulstred," ll. 5-34)

Death—"the whirle-poole death"—is present not only in elegiac poems, however. Death is also present where he seems to have been virtually stilled into extinction. Thus one of the most famous of the *Holy Sonnets* nominally advances from the loftiness of the octave's sweeping movement to the meekness of the sestet's threnodic rhythms:

> At the round earths imagin'd corners, blow
> Your trumpets, Angells, and arise, arise
> From death, you numberlesse infinities
> Of soules, and to your scattred bodies goe,
> All whom the flood did, and fire shall o'erthrow,
> All whom warre, dearth, age, agues, tyrannies,
> Despaire, law, chance, hath slaine, and you whose eyes,
> Shall behold God, and never tast deaths woe,
> But let them sleepe, O Lord, and mee mourne a space,
> For, if above all these, my sinnes abound,
> 'Tis late to aske abundance of thy grace,
> When wee are there; here on this lowly ground,
> Teach mee how to repent; for that's as good
> As if thou'hadst seal'd my pardon, with thy blood.

But to invoke the metrical norm as before is to realize that the departure from the basic iambic beat in the octave induces a countermovement, affirming through the disturbed rhythm what the sweeping movement endeavors to bypass:

> Áll whóm the flóod díd, and fíre shall o'erthrów,
> Áll whóm wárre, déarth, áge, águes, týrannies,
> Despaíre, láw, chánce....

The same pattern surfaces in another celebrated sonnet, "Death be not proud," where the congregation of three strongly accented words—"Fate, Chance, kings" (l. 9)—calls attention to the masters not of death but of ourselves.

Multiform death also provided Donne with a vocabulary to reinforce his canescent vision of the world and man's state within it. The lines

> Whilst in our soules sinne bred and pamper'd is,
> Our soules become wormeaten carkases
>
> ("On himself," ll. 15–16)

are not at all unusual. The imagery of decay, decomposition, dissolution, pervades the secular and the sacred poems alike, sustaining *inter alia* the survey of the universe in a verse letter of 1614:

> all is withered, shrunke, and dri'd,
> All Vertues ebb'd out to a dead low tyde,
> All the worlds frame being crumbled into sand,
> Where every man thinks by himselfe to stand,
> Integritie, friendship, and confidence,
> (Ciments of greatnes) being vapor'd hence ....
>
> ("To the Countesse of Salisbury," ll. 9–14)

Donne's fear of death was probably minimal; but his fear of that fear was all-encompassing.

V. "The poyson'is gone through all"

The *Songs and Sonnets* are commonly read to the exclusion of Donne's other poems: the verse letters, the satires, the elegies, the two *Anniversaries*. The verse letters to his friends and patrons were dismissed by Donne himself as "the sallads and onions of *Micham*,"[28] yet he must have known they were not necessarily the one, and much less the other. In their nature essentially dramatic, they are based on the principle that "more then kisses, letters mingle Soules";[29] and they include poems in which the syntax may often be impossible but the diction is quite agreeable, the rhymes are generally certain, and the numbers painless. Of the many which may be commended, the several letters addressed to the Countess of Bedford are particularly noteworthy in that their poetic quality is sustained and their thematic interests jointly disclose "the Idea of a Woman" as claimed on behalf of the two *Anniversaries* (see below). The second of these letters ("You have refin'd mee") is a provident achievement which redeems even the uncertainties spasmodically evident elsewhere.

Donne's five satires were like his elegies written periodically from the early 1590s. Their tone and argument are summarily indicated in the comment of one speaker in particular: "I do hate / Perfectly all this towne" (II.1–2). But the hate is Swiftian, and rises to the level of great art. The first satire is concerned with the abuses of opportunists and lechers; the second, of lawyers; the fourth, of courtiers; the fifth, of officers and suitors; while the third satire—"central in both position and theme"—is an idealistic soliloquy on the spiritual values which the narrator sees everywhere perverted.[30] Eminently moral, the five satires aim in the direction pointed by Izaak Walton's rhetorical question:

> Was every sinne,
> Character'd in his *Satyres*? made so foule
> That some have fear'd their shapes, and kept their soule
> Freer by reading verse?[31]

The poems are attended by the triumvirate of Roman satirists, bearing the mark of the stinging mockery of Horace, the premeditated roughness of Persius, and the intentional hyperboles of Juvenal. They are "satirique fyres," as Donne said, "writt / In skorne of all" ("To Mr. R.W.: Kindly I envy," ll. 7-8). Their language, images, syntax, meter are violent, tortuous, contorted, brilliantly conveying the scorching indignation, the burning hatred. But towering above the negative tableaux stands the positive image of truth:

> on a huge hill,
> Cragg'd, and steep, Truth stands, and hee that will
> Reach her, about must, and about must goe . . . .
> (Satire III, ll. 79ff.)

Donne does not pretend that the ascent is easy. The pilgrim's progress— a "progress of self-discovery," it has been accurately said[32]—is along a narrow path fraught with obstacles, witness the laborious punctuation and the repetition of "about must, and about must goe." One is reminded of Satan's ascent toward light in *Paradise Lost:*

> So hee with difficulty and labour hard
> Moved on, with difficulty and labour hee.
> (II.1021-22)

Individually, Donne's satires are among his most successful productions; and jointly, his most perfectly orchestrated cluster of poems. In time they were to impress themselves upon a greater poet, Pope, who versified two of them, the second and the fourth. Donne, wrote Pope in 1706, "has infinitely more wit than he wanted versification; for the great dealers in wit, like those in trade, take least pains to set off their goods, while the haberdashers of small wit spare for no decorations or ornaments."[33] The validity of Donne's versification, we observe, is not denied; and though Pope shaped it to his own aims, he remained fully aware of Donne's versatile use of the dramatic voice and his impressive correlation of sense and rhythm. The awareness is apparent not in the juvenile pompousness of *An Essay on Man* or the sparkling frivolities of *The Rape of the Lock* but in the consummate discriminations of *The Dunciad* generally and of the epistles in particular. The line of descent, I am suggesting, leads from Donne's merciless portrait of the parasitic courtier—the "thing" of his fourth satire (ll. 18ff.)—through Pope's version of it (ll. 24ff.) to the crushing portrait of Sporus in the *Epistle to Dr. Arbuthnot* (ll. 305ff.).

Donne's elegies borrow their general designation from Ovid's *Amores,* which the Elizabethans commonly termed "elegies." Strikingly uneven, they have irritated so many readers so much that one of them renounced even one of the best, the ninth elegy known as "The Autumnall" ("The poem is a mess").[34] More charitably it might be submitted that the elegies provoke what a novelist is said to have said of the productions of a fellow craftsman, "inconceivable boredom associated with the most extreme ecstasy which it is possible to imagine."[35] In part at least, the boredom sets in especially when Donne tries to impress us with his originality as a thinker. For his ideas are on the whole simple; and though they dazzle if phrased vigorously, they only embarrass if not. The following lines are a fair measure of political astuteness misplaced intellectually if not dramatically too:

> Sick Ireland is with a strange warr possest
> Like to an Ague; now raging, now at rest;
> Which time will cure: yet it must doe her good
> If she were purg'd, and her head vayne let blood.
> (Elegy XX, ll. 13–16)

We need not passionately anathematize Donne's "convulvulus-growth of intellectual whim-whams."[36] Suffice it that on occasions such as the one cited, the schism between the matter and the manner, or the sense and its poetic articulation, terminates in what may fairly be described as obscenity. The judgment is not moral because the elegies happen to be preoccupied with "fairely irrelevant nastiness";[37] it is, rather, aesthetic— or, better still, it is moral *because* it is aesthetic. Thus "The Perfume" (IV) is obscene because its basic idea and the supporting language are vicious to excess, unredeemed even by the dramatic context:

> Base excrement of earth, which dost confound
> Sense, from distinguishing the sicke from sound;
> By thee the seely Amorous sucks his death
> By drawing in a leprous harlots breath;
> By thee, the greatest staine to mans estate

Falls on us, to be call'd effeminate;

(ll. 57ff.)

and the like. Also aesthetically obscene is "The Comparison" (VIII) because it multiplies a few powerful lines (ll. 39–44) without any sense of economy; "Julia" (XIII), because it revisits the obsessive interest in vomit; the so-called "Variety" (XVII), because it admits embarrassing clichés and perfunctory rhymes; and "Loves Progress" (XVIII), because a promising journey across the female body founders in risibly excessive analogies:

> The Nose (like to the first Meridian) runs
> Not 'twixt an East and West, but 'twixt two suns;
> It leaves a Cheek, a rosie Hemisphere
> On either side, and then directs us where
> Upon the Islands fortunate we fall,
> Not faynte *Canaries* but *Ambrosiall*,
> Her swelling lips . . .
> These, and the glorious Promontory, her Chin
> Ore past; and the streight *Hellespont* between
> The *Sestos* and *Abydos* of her breasts . . .
>
> (ll. 47ff.)

and so on. Against these failures in discernment, however, is "the most extreme ecstasy which it is possible to imagine." Such ecstasy centers on "The Dreame" (X), where an uncommon serenity is mirrored in the exceptional stanzaic form; "The Bracelet" (XI)—so much admired by Ben Jonson that he had it "by heart"—where an inauspicious subject is transmuted by a superbly dramatic tone; "His parting from her" (XII), where sense coincides with skill "of the highest technical expertness"; "The Expostulation" (XV)—also attributed to Jonson (*Under-wood*, no. 39)—where the rampant antifeminism is dexterously related to the narrator's oscillating emotions ("Now have I curst, let us our love revive"); and "On his Mistris" (XVI), where the Miltonic sweep of the first sentence heralds a dramatic situation upheld with passionate energy to the very end. Donne's elegies often ascend to greatness; yet it is telling that they also descend to aesthetic grossness.

The two *Anniversaries* are the only substantial poems published in Donne's lifetime. Their given subject, the fourteen-year-old Elizabeth Drury, who died in 1610, was less than intimately known by Donne ("I never saw the Gentlewoman").[38] A funeral elegy he wrote at the time claimed that "shee / Being spent, the world must needes decrepit bee" (ll. 29–30)—a notion judged sufficiently attractive to have been multiplied by nearly five hundred lines on the first anniversary of her death

(*An Anatomy of the World,* 1611), and by as many on the second (*Of the Progres of the Soule,* 1612). Approached theoretically, the two *Anniversaries* have afforded opportunities for the display of much scholarly ingenuity. They have been seen to manifest the direct or indirect influence of the meditative tradition associated with St. Ignatius Loyola on the one hand and of the tradition of the mixed genre—instruction, meditation, and praise—developed by Protestants on the other.[39] They have also been seen to belong to a qualified tradition of the funeral elegy, else to the traditions variously centered on *sapientia creata,* St. Lucy, and Petrarch's *Trionfi;* yet because their "oppositions and contradictions" linger stubbornly, they have also been triumphantly designated "paradoxical poems."[40] As regards their structure, the two poems are sometimes said to be "a single poem";[41] but if indeed two, then they are companion pieces closely related through a series of antitheses. The "anatomy" in the first *Anniversary* is largely negative, but in the second positive. The first is a descent into sin, but the second an ascent to virtue. The setting of the one is time, earth, the sublunar world generally; but that of the second is space, heaven, the supernatural regions. The *Anniversaries* oppose "doubt and faith, despair and hope, death and the triumph of immortality."[42]

Not everyone will confuse the background with the foreground, however. It could be argued that, regarded as poems, the two *Anniversaries* have their great moments—but they are only moments. It could even be maintained that the first poem is bombastic in tone and opaque in aim, while the second is no less marred in phraseology than it is precarious in orientation. True, Donne himself is reported to have said of the first what is also applicable to the second, that "he described the Idea of a Woman and not as she was." But the remark does not answer Jonson's strictures of the *style,* namely, that as the poems were not written in celebration of the Virgin Mary, they are "profane and full of Blasphemies."[43] At issue, in other words, is Donne's lack of economy, made worse by his inability to feel Elizabeth Drury's death upon his pulses (as Keats would have said). The result is a fabricated hysteria which impels Donne to several infelicities, for instance the apotheosis of the girl at the expense of hapless Eve *and* the sum of her descendants:

> One woman at one blow, then kill'd us all,
> And singly, one by one, they kill us now.
>
> (I, ll. 106–7)

The lack of moderation disconcerts. Donne was perfectly free to associate the girl's death with the widespread belief in the decline of man's stature, but he was not at liberty to do so in casual lines such as:

>   in length is man
> Contracted to an inch, who was a span.
> For had a man at first, in Forrests stray'd,
> Or shipwrack'd in the Sea, one would have laid
> A wager that an Elephant, or Whale
> That met him, would not hastily assaile
> A thing so equall to him . . . .
>
> (I, ll. 135–41)

The exaggerations mar even the much-praised second *Anniversary*. The hysteria continues, attended as usual by immoderate dicta about "this deluge, grosse and generall," "this rotten world," and the like; by the questionable realism of "the putrid stuff, which thou dost spit" (l. 273); and by the linguistic crudity in the description of the effects of sin:

> The poyson'is gone through all, poysons affect
> Chiefly the cheefest parts, but some effect
> In Nails, and Haires, yea excrements, will show.
>
> (II, ll. 335–37)

Hyperbole also generates at times unintended amusement, as in the earnest plea to the "immortall" girl:

>   though thou wouldst refuse
> The name of Mother, be unto my Muse,
> A Father.
>
> (II, ll. 33–35)

But there is not much evidence that the Father responded.

Positively, the *Anniversaries* are useful in that they confirm Donne's engagement with multiform death; and negatively, in that they chart the limits of his originality as a thinker and evince the perils attendant upon his flirtation with hyperbole. The poems are, like a particular category of sins, splendid.

VI. "Open to most men"

In 1619, some ten years after he wrote his prose extravaganza *Biathanatos,* Donne proposed that it was "a Book written by *Jack Donne,* and not by D[octor] *Donne.*"[44] The claim that his life was neatly divided into two periods, the secular and the sacred, may or may not be credited; but that his poetry was likewise divided, is not open to question. For one, several of his divine poems—*The Litanie* for instance, but also some of the *Holy*

Sonnets—were written before his ordination; and for another, his secular poems frequently partake of the sacred dimension, and indeed vice versa. The interpenetration of the two realms has distressed a number of readers, one of whom marks "the drastic impropriety of the theological conceits" in "The Canonization" and protests because Donne is "impertinently confounding mere carnality with a prime mystery of religion."[45] But are not lovers wont to describe their experiences in language borrowed from theology? And have not some of the most moving expressions of divine love been set forth in explicitly secular terms? Love, as I said earlier, is both *agape* and *eros*. The formidable tradition centered on the Song of Solomon is otherwise an impertinence; and so, among other testaments, is the striking summary of Christian experience by St. Ignatius of Antioch: "my love (*eros*) is crucified."[46]

Donne's divine poems include "To Mr Tilman after he had taken orders," which is less than divine, and hardly a poem; "The Crosse," which is so ingenious that its stated aims are misplaced en route; and the seven interlocking "holy sonnets" comprising *La Corona,* which in offering a "crown of prayer and praise" invite comparison with Herbert's deftly economic "A Wreath." But the divine poems also include "Goodfriday, 1613. Riding Westward," whose cosmic sweep involves an eschatological journey toward the Last Judgment in the West, correlated with Christ's first advent in the East;[47] "A Hymne to God the Father," whose lyrical complexity depends on the impressive coincidence of the form without and the argument within, impacted to assert the endless restlessness of man; and *The Litanie,* where the underestimated argument comprehends touchstone lines such as:

> Oh, to some
> Not to be Martyrs, is a martyrdome.
>
> (ll. 89–90)

The *Holy Sonnets* designated "Divine Meditations" reflect the varieties of religious experience in the Psalms, reenacted in the light of the cosmic patterns of the Christian view of history.[48] The influence of the Psalms—"formes of joy and art," according to Donne's evaluation ("Upon the Translation of the Psalmes," l. 34)—can hardly be denied. But the pressure exerted by the Book of Lamentations was even more decisive. Its characteristic mood of black despair could not have escaped Donne, especially once he versified its passionate cries of agony:

> I am the man which hath affliction seene,
>   Under the rod of Gods wrath having beene,
>   He hath led mee to darknesse, not to light,
>   And against mee all day, his hand doth fight . . .

>   . . . .
> His hand hath of my sinnes framed a yoake
>   Which wreath'd, and cast upon my neck, hath broke
> My strength . . .
>   . . . .
> . . . oughtest thou, O Lord, despise us thus
>   And to be utterly enrag'd at us?
>   (*The Lamentations of Jeremy,* ll. 177–80, 53–55, 389–90)

The violent imagery here as in the *Holy Sonnets* discloses how intermittent the sense of God's favor is, and how impossible readily to attain "the peace that passeth understanding." On the other hand, Donne controlled the potential hysteria by resorting in his version of the Lamentations to rhyme, and in the *Holy Sonnets* to the mold of the sonnet.

The sonnet as form tempers, moderates, restrains. So far, it may even be said to intimate a terminal Order which the *Holy Sonnets* never directly assert, and sometimes even question. As an organizational principle, the sonnet afforded Donne opportunities to provide for a nominal division after the Shakespearean model (three quatrains and a couplet), yet an actual one after the Italian pattern (an octave and a sestet). But the most impressive aspect of Donne's use of the sonnet is that he appears not to use the form at all. So swift is the flow of the given movement, and so overpowering are the punctuation and the imagery, that the rhymed lines are submerged until we are, abruptly, stopped. Always excepting Hopkins, I am not aware of any English poet who has so thoroughly obliterated the sonnet form even as he was demonstrating its immense powers.

The *Holy Sonnets* share with other poems Donne's obsession with death. They also share his obsession with love, often explicitly physical love, as in the imagery of the sonnets beginning "Batter my heart" and "As due by many titles," but especially in the audacious plea that Christ's spouse may be "open to most men" (in "Show me deare Christ"). The tonal range is well-nigh boundless. As the opening lines of several sonnets indicate, it encompasses the moving acceptance of

> Since she whom I lov'd hath payd her last debt . . .

the reflective amazement of

> I am a little world made cunningly . . .

the passionate anxiety of

> Show me deare Christ, thy Spouse, so bright and clear . . .

the triumphant vision of

> At the round earths imagin'd corners, blow
> Your trumpets, Angells . . .

or the sheer terror of

> What if this present were the worlds last night?

Donne mounts in the dramatically variable *Songs and Sonnets,* the perfectly orchestrated satires, the fitfully great elegies, and even the amiable verse letters. But the summit of his art is in the *Holy Sonnets.*

VII. "Thy strict lawes will be / Too hard"

Donne was much praised in his lifetime, underpraised thereafter, and overpraised earlier in our century. The lowest point of his reputation was during the Augustan period, in spite—and doubtless because—of the revision of his satires by Pope. At the outset of the nineteenth century, however, Donne was inching forward; by the end of it, he was rising meteorically; and three decades later he was stepping gingerly into the throne rumored to have been vacated by Milton. T. S. Eliot's judgment was crucial. Donne, he proclaimed in 1921, is distinguished by "a direct sensuous apprehension of thought or a recreation of thought into feeling," whereas poets like Milton and Dryden are merely responsible for a "dissociation of sensibility."[49] In retrospect, it is not easy to decide which was admired most, Donne's poetry or Eliot's apocalyptic theory. In time, of course, the theory was challenged with some zest; yet it was already undercut by Eliot himself when he proposed as an afterthought that Donne displays "a manifest fissure between thought and sensibility." "His learning," added Eliot rather unkindly, "is just information suffused with emotion, or combined with emotion not essentially relevant to it."[50]

Donne would have had a wry comment or two to make about his undulating fortunes, possibly borrowing a parallel from a familiar field: "the Astronomers of the world are not so much exercised, about all the Constellations, and their motions, formerly apprehended and beleeved, as when there arises a new, and irregular meteor."[51] Donne's irregularity persists. But indispensable as it was to his patterns of thought, it sounds his uniqueness; and inimitable, it thunders his greatness. Carew rightly perceived that

> thy strict lawes will be
> Too hard for Libertines in Poetrie . . . .
> ("An Elegie upon . . . Donne," ll. 61–62)

Donne founded no "school" because he was, like all major poets, unrepeatable. Some minor talents waited on him, as minor talents do; but those who are often said to constitute "the school of Donne"—Herbert, Vaughan, Crashaw, Marvell—absorbed the example and rejected the overpowering voice. They would have said of Donne much as Keats was later to say of Milton: "Life to him would be death to me."[52] For Donne entices the most unsympathetic, captures the most hostile, subdues the most antagonistic; and by tomorrow we may think so too.

NOTES

An earlier version of this chapter, entitled " 'Extreme, and Scattring Bright': The Poetry of John Donne," appeared as the introduction to *The Complete English Poems of John Donne,* ed. C. A. Patrides, Everyman's Library (London: Dent, 1985), pp. 14-45. Copyright 1985 by J. M. Dent and Sons Ltd. Reprinted by permission. Donne's poetry is here quoted from this edition.

1. As reported by William Drummond of Hawthornden (in *Ben Jonson,* ed. C. H. Herford and Percy Simpson [Oxford, 1925], 1:133 and 135).
2. In his *Introduction to the Literature of Europe* (1837-39), quoted by Kathleen Tillotson, "Donne's Poetry in the Nineteenth Century," in *Elizabethan and Jacobean Studies Presented to F. P. Wilson* (Oxford, 1959), p. 316.
3. *A Defence of Rhyme* (1603?), in *Elizabethan Critical Essays,* ed. G. Gregory Smith (Oxford, 1904), 2:379.
4. *Literary Criticism,* ed. Terence L. Connolly (New York, 1948), p. 251.
5. *A Discourse concerning the Original and Progress of Satire* (1693) and *An Essay of Dramatic Poesy* (1668), respectively; in *Essays of John Dryden,* ed. W. P. Ker (Oxford, 1900), 1:52, and 2:102.
6. For a different reading of the poem, the emphasis on Donne's "disjunction of argument" however muted, see Murray Roston, *The Soul of Wit* (Oxford, 1974), chap. 2.
7. To seven, if one follows the text of 1633 as I do in opposition to the increased regularity of eight syllables endorsed by the manuscripts.
8. *The World's Body* (New York, 1938), p. 286.
9. George Saintsbury, in *John Donne: A Collection of Critical Essays,* ed. Helen Gardner (Englewood Cliffs, N.J., 1962), p. 15.
10. It is reported that Donne was "a great frequenter of Playes" (Sir Richard Baker, *A Chronicle of the Kings of England* [London, 1643], p. 156). But Donne's modern biographer oddly counters that "the drama seems to have left surprisingly few traces on Donne's work" (R. C. Bald, *John Donne: A Life* [Oxford, 1970], p. 72). Surely the *dramatic* nature of Donne's poetry is trace enough?
11. Its use by Guarini in Italy and Joseph Hall in England is noted by Mario Praz and F. P. Wilson, both cited by J. B. Leishman, *The Monarch of Wit,* 4th ed. (London, 1959), p. 231. But see also the material collected by Stanton J.

Linden, "Compasses and Cartography," *John Donne Journal* 3 (1984): 23-34, and the pertinent studies by Rosemary Freeman, *English Emblem Books* (London, 1948), and Josef Lederer, "John Donne and the Emblematic Practice," in *Essential Articles for the Study of John Donne's Poetry,* ed. John R. Roberts (Hamden, Conn., 1975), pp. 107-21.
12. "Andrew Marvell" (1921), in his *Selected Essays* (London, 1932), p. 262.
13. "The Metaphysical Poets" (1921), in his *Selected Essays,* p. 242.
14. John Weemes, *The Christian Synagogue* (London, 1623), p. 281.
15. The tradition, centered on the late medieval *Carmen de pulice* ascribed to Ovid (translated by H. David Brumble in *Critical Quarterly* 15 [1973]: 148-49), issued in a collection of over fifty poems in several languages gathered for Etienne Pasquier's *La Puce de Madame des Roches* (1582; see the essay by Marcel Françon in *PMLA* 56 [1941]: 307-36, and the commentary by Helen Gardner in *The Elegies and The Songs and Sonnets* [Oxford, 1965]).
16. As Gardner notes in *The Elegies and The Songs and Sonnets,* p. 174. Murray Roston detects in the poem "an intellectual and emotional energy that belies its apparently casual tone" (*The Soul of Wit,* chap. 2).
17. As Arnold Stein observed in *John Donne's Lyrics: The Eloquence of Action* (Minneapolis, 1962), p. 73. Louis L. Martz also argued, in a lecture, that Donne frequently resorted to "the conditional *if*" in order to qualify his seemingly unqualified claims.
18. Donne, said Dryden, "perplexes the minds of the fair sex with nice speculations of philosophy, when he should engage their hearts, and entertain them with the softness of love" (*A Discourse* . . . , in *Essays of John Dryden,* ed. Ker, 2:19).
19. J. E. V. Crofts, "John Donne: A Reconsideration," in *John Donne,* ed. Gardner, p. 81.
20. *Letters to Severall Persons of Honour* (London, 1651), p. 121.
21. The "patterne" suggests not only the ideal realm of Platonic Forms but the relations within the Trinity, reinforced by the distinctly theological images of the dove, the phoenix, and the eagle. But the same images are also secular in orientation, and even erotic. See the excellent essay by Albert C. Labriola, "Donne's 'The Canonization': Its Theological and Religious Imagery," *HLQ* 36 (1973): 327-39.
22. *Candelaio* I.10; quoted by Mario Praz, "Donne's Relation to the Poetry of His Time," in *John Donne,* ed. Gardner, p. 70.
23. *Coleridge on the Seventeenth Century,* ed. Roberta F. Brinkley (Durham, N.C., 1955), p. 524.
24. *Letters to Severall Persons,* p. 174. Among the several available studies of Donne's obsession with death, consult Bettie Anne Doebler, *The Quickening Seed: Death in the Sermons of John Donne* (Salzburg, 1974), and Arnold Stein, "Handling Death: John Donne in Public Meditation," *ELH* 48 (1981): 496-515, but especially John Carey's chapter on Death in his *John Donne: Life, Mind and Art* (London, 1981).
25. *Letters to Severall Persons,* pp. 31-32.
26. *Letters to Severall Persons,* pp. 78-79.

27. *Letters to Severall Persons*, p. 316, and *A Collection of Letters, made by Sir Tobie Mathews* (London, 1660), p. 351; respectively.
28. *Letters to Severall Persons*, p. 63. Mitcham in Surrey was Donne's residence for some five years.
29. From the opening line of "To Sir Henry Wotton: Sir, more then kisses" etc. On the epistolary exchanges between Donne and Wotton, see in particular the essay by Ted-Larry Pebworth and Claude J. Summers, " 'Thus Friends Absent Speake': The Exchange of Verse Letters between John Donne and Henry Wotton," *MP* 81 (1984): 361–77.
30. See N. J. C. Andreasen, "Theme and Structure in Donne's *Satyres*," *SEL* 3 (1963): 59–75. The most sustained study of the *Satires* is by M. Thomas Hester, *"Kinde Pitty and Brave Scorn": John Donne's "Satyres"* (Durham, N.C., 1982).
31. "An Elegie upon Dr Donne," in the 1633 edition of Donne's *Poems*; in *John Donne: The Critical Heritage*, ed. A. J. Smith (London, 1975), p. 92.
32. John R. Lauritsen, "Donne's *Satyres*: The Drama of Self-Discovery," *SEL* 16 (1976): 120.
33. Letter to Wycherley, April 10, 1706; in *Literary Criticism of Alexander Pope*, ed. Bertrand A. Goldgar (Lincoln, Neb., 1955), p. 29. Pope versified Donne's second satire in 1713 (revised in 1735), and his fourth in 1733. They are ably discussed by Addison C. Bross in *Xavier University Studies* 5 (1966): 133–52; Ian Jack in *Essential Articles for the Study of Alexander Pope*, ed. Maynard Mack, rev. ed. (Hamden, Conn., 1968), pp. 420–38; Howard Erskine-Hill in *John Donne: Essays in Celebration*, ed. A. J. Smith (London, 1972), chap. 10; and Aubrey L. Williams in *A Provision of Human Nature*, ed. Donald Kay (University, Ala., 1977), pp. 111–19.
34. T. J. Kelly, "Donne's 'Firme Substantial Love,' " *Critical Review* 13 (1970): 104.
35. The source is no longer within my ken. I used to think that the remark was made by Henry James about Proust; but it appears I was far too optimistic! Professor Leon Edel assures me that the attribution of the remark to James is inaccurate.
36. J. E. V. Crofts, "John Donne: A Reconsideration," p. 89. "Though interested in thought," Mario Praz has more judiciously observed, Donne "was no original thinker himself. . . . He was like a lawyer choosing the fittest arguments for a case in hand, not like a searcher after universally valid truth" ("Donne's Relation," p. 68).
37. Roma Gill, "*Musa Iocosa Mea*: Thoughts on the *Elegies*," in *Essays in Celebration*, ed. Smith, p. 57.
38. *Letters to Severall Persons*, p. 239.
39. Louis L. Martz, *The Poetry of Meditation* (New Haven, 1964), and Barbara K. Lewalski, *Protestant Poetics and the Seventeenth-Century Religious Lyric* (Princeton, 1979); respectively. See further the latter's *Donne's "Anniversaries" and the Poetry of Praise* (Providence, R.I., 1973).
40. W. M. Lebans, "Donne's *Anniversaries* and the Tradition of Funeral Elegy," *ELH* 39 (1972): 545–59; Frank Manley in his edition of *The Anniversaries* (Baltimore, 1963); Richard E. Hughes, "The Woman in Donne's *Anniversa-*

ries," *ELH* 34 (1967): 307–26; Silvia Ruffo-Fiore, *Donne's Petrarchism* (Florence, 1979), p. 81; and Rosalie L. Colie, "'All in Peeces': Problems of Interpretation in Donne's Anniversary Poems," in *Just So Much Honor*, ed. Peter A. Fiore (University Park, Pa., 1972), pp. 189–218, and especially her *Paradoxia Epidemica* (Princeton, 1966), pp. 412–29.
41. Carol M. Sicherman, "Donne's Timeless *Anniversaries*," in *Essential Articles*, ed. Roberts, p. 375.
42. Marjorie H. Nicolson, "The Death of a World," in her *The Breaking of the Circle*, rev. ed. (New York, 1960), p. 82. Patrick Mahony in "The *Anniversaries*: Donne's Rhetorical Approach to Evil," in *Essential Articles*, ed. Roberts, pp. 363–67, quotes Nicolson's antitheses and cites the others mentioned from Louis L. Martz, George Williamson, et al., as well as from his own storehouse.
43. *Ben Jonson*, ed. Herford and Simpson, 1:133. Elsewhere Donne wrote of Elizabeth Drury, "I took such a person, as might be capable of all that I could say" (*Letters to Severall Persons*, p. 239).
44. *Letters to Severall Persons*, p. 22.
45. Wilbur Sanders, *John Donne's Poetry* (Cambridge, 1971), pp. 22, 51. Brian Vickers defends the poem's hyperboles as rhetorically appropriate, in *Essays in Celebration*, ed. Smith, pp. 164–73.
46. ὁ ἐμός ἔρως ἐσταύρωται (*Epistola ad Romanos*, VII.2; quoted by "Dionysius the Areopagite," *De divinis nominibus*, IV.12). On the tradition centered on the Song of Solomon, see Stanley Stewart, *The Enclosed Garden* (Madison, 1966). In fact, as Donne reminds us, the Scriptures "abound with the notions of *Love*, of *Spouse*, and *Husband*, and *Marriadge Songs*, and *Marriadge Supper*, and *Marriadge-Bedde*" (in *Sermons*, ed. G. R. Potter and E. M. Simpson [Berkeley, 1953–62], 7:87).
47. See the discussion by A. B. Chambers, "'Goodfriday, 1613. Riding Westward': The Poem and the Tradition," in *Essential Articles*, ed. Roberts, pp. 333–48.
48. See John N. Wall, Jr., "Donne's Wit of Redemption: The Drama of Prayer in the *Holy Sonnets*," *SP* 73 (1976): 189–203; and on the general background, my exposition in *"The Grand Design of God": The Literary Form of the Christian View of History* (London, 1972).
49. "The Metaphysical Poets," in *Selected Essays*, pp. 246–47. On Donne's fluctuating reputation, see the study of his "critical heritage" by A. J. Smith, as well as Arthur H. Nethercot's three essays on the fortunes of the "metaphysical" poets to the early nineteenth century in *JEGP* 23 (1924): 173–98; *PQ* 4 (1925): 161–79; and *SP* 22 (1925): 81–132.
50. "Donne in Our Time," in *A Garland for John Donne*, ed. Theodore Spencer (Cambridge, Mass., 1931), p. 8.
51. From the Domestic State Papers; in *The Complete Poetry and Selected Prose of John Donne*, ed. Charles M. Coffin (New York, 1952), p. 392.
52. Letter to George and Georgiana Keats, September 21, 1819.

George Herbert:
The Transfiguration of Plainness

> A combination and a form indeed,
> Where every god did seem to set his seal
>
> —*Hamlet*

I. "Marked out for piety"

On first looking into Herbert's poetry we note the grace, the artlessness, the self-conscious plainness. Recalling the ecstatic sentences in Izaak Walton's hagiography ("he seem'd to be marked out for piety, and to become the care of Heaven"),[1] we may also be persuaded of Herbert's seraphic reverence and steadfast holiness. But so far we would err.

The piety, the reverence, and the holiness are never absent from Herbert. But they are aspects of his religious experience which transform themselves when judged within the controlled turbulence of his larger utterance. The extent to which Walton remained a stranger to this quality need not surprise us: the exigencies of his art demanded a particular point of view, and he elected to observe in Herbert the self-abnegation of a pious individual, not the agony of a poet for whom humility was unattainable precisely because he was a great poet.

The grace, the artlessness, and the plainness are by the same token responses which Herbert's poetry does initially elicit. But they are also responses in constant need of qualification. The grace will on reflection appear to be something more than a monotone, for Herbert's articulation invariably testifies to his spacious tonal range. The artlessness will similarly emerge as less than artless in that Herbert's poetry possesses a dormant complexity not unlike Marvell's or Milton's. The self-conscious plainness, finally, will be observed to comprehend an all-pervasive consciousness of self that negates even the nominal "plainness."

The claims are large. Can they be substantiated?

II. "Setting a just price of your qualities"

"Thus he liv'd, and thus he dy'd like a Saint, unspotted of the World, full of Alms-deeds, full of Humility, and all the examples of a vertuous life."[2] The conclusion of Walton's life of Herbert is by no means unique. Nicholas Ferrar's preface to *The Temple* in 1633 had already described Herbert as "a companion to the primitive Saints"; Vaughan's *Mount of Olives* in 1652 had canonized him even more enthusiastically as "a most glorious true Saint"; while the rambling first hagiography of Herbert by Barnabas Oley in the same year set the stage for Walton's definitive performance in 1670. To deny Herbert's holiness is obviously impossible, and in any case pointless. But holiness, we should remind ourselves, does not necessarily exclude violent upheavals in the saint's private universe. Quite the contrary indeed! Even Walton was obliged to report that the saintly Herbert, when young, "kept himself too much retir'd, and at too great distance with all his inferiours: and his cloaths seem'd to prove, that he put too great a value on his parts and Parentage."[3] In providing this report, Walton obviously meant to emphasize Herbert's subsequent and reputedly total conversion. But did the poet ever fully subordinate the way of the world to his spiritual aspirations? Did he absolutely deny his parts and parentage which, alike impressive, appeared to promise a public career considerably different from his eventual translation to Bemerton's "pittifull little chappell"?[4]

George Herbert belonged to an aristocratic family whose head, after the death of his father, was his brother Edward, himself a poet, an influential philosopher, and a public servant eventually elevated to the peerage as Lord Herbert of Cherbury. Their mother Magdalen was equally estimable. One of the great ladies of the late Elizabethan and early Stuart period—"Beauty's vision to the world, the glass of God," Herbert called her later[5]—she had chosen as her second husband the wealthy Lord Danvers who was over two decades her junior. Her house in Chelsea soon became one of the foremost centers of intellectual activity: "a *Court,* in the conversation of the best," to quote Donne's judgment.[6] Emerging from such a context, Herbert naturally strove after knowledge and, beyond knowledge, position. "I want Books extremely," he wrote to his young stepfather in 1618.[7] But books and his generous education at Cambridge were means to that end which his election a year later as the University's Public Orator appeared to foreshadow. The Orator, he pointedly informed his stepfather, "takes place next the Doctors, is at all their Assemblies, and Meetings, and sits above the Proctors, is Regent or Nonregent at his pleasure, and such like Gaynesses, which will please a young man well." The post is "the finest place in the University, though not the gain-fullest."[8] The great expectations are patently obvious. Had not his predecessors attained high political office, two of them—Sir Robert Naunton and Francis Nethersole—having risen to become Secretaries of State? After all, the king's favor had also been secured, especially after Herbert had praised an oration by James I as superior to whatever Greek and Roman "hirelings" may have ventured.[9] The flattered monarch returned the extravagant compliment by describing Herbert as the University's "Jewel."[10] No wonder that later, in 1675, Charles Cotton suspected that Herbert was "deeply tainted with Ambition"![11]

Yet Cotton's suspicion was extreme. To ask whether Herbert's ambition like his pride was justified is to strike a less censorious note; for we would then appreciate that Herbert impressed himself not merely on a flattered king but on men of far greater perception, notably the saintly Lancelot Andrewes on the one hand, and the worldly Bacon on the other.[12] As Herbert counselled his younger brother Henry in 1618, "be proud, not with a foolish vanting of yourself when there is no caus, but by setting a just price of your qualities: and it is the part of a poor spirit to undervalue himself and blush."[13] Herbert's progress, I am suggesting, was rather cumulative than strictly linear, not because he was ever totally self-centered but because he was not. It is for this reason that he experienced, as he said, "such spiritual Conflicts, as none can think, but only those that ever endur'd them."[14] How different was Donne's experience! For Donne would rear his mighty ego in order to exorcise it before his angry God. Not so Herbert, whose spiritual conflicts were all the more shattering in that they did not involve pride. They involved humility and *therefore* pride, to the extent that the practice of humility can be the most sinister form of pride. Donne displays pride in his highly personal diction, phrasing, and tone; yet Herbert in electing a plainer diction, simpler phrasing, and far more subdued tone, displays not humility but pride still. *The Temple* is the work of a humble man devoid of humility only because a great poet must necessarily set a "just price" on his qualities.

III. "In a vulgar and illustrative way"

On the face of it, Herbert's foremost quality is certainly his plainness, even his simplicity. But simplicity as such cannot account for Herbert's influence immediately on Crashaw and Vaughan, and later on such diverse poets as Hopkins and Emily Dickinson; nor does it explain either Coleridge's acclaim of "the great general merit of his Poems, which are for the most part exquisite in their kind," or T. S. Eliot's judgment that Herbert "may justly be called a major poet."[15] Herbert's simplicity, it is clear, needs must be modified considerably.

But Herbert's approach to poetry, it may be objected, is plainly analogous to the parson's approach to the sermon as lucidly delineated in *A Priest to the Temple*:

> The Parsons Method in handling of a text consists of two parts; first, a plain and evident declaration of the meaning of the text; and secondly, some choyce Observations drawn out of the whole text, as it lyes entire, and unbroken in the Scripture it self. This he thinks naturall, and sweet, and grave. Whereas the other way of crumbling a text into small parts, as the Person speaking, or spoken to, the subject, and object, and the like, hath neither in it sweetnesse, nor

gravity, nor variety, since the words apart are not Scripture, but a dictionary, and may be considered alike in all the Scripture.[16]

But opposition to a given practice—the practice of Lancelot Andrewes among others—need not enlist Herbert among those who preferred rather Senecan brevity than Ciceronian expansiveness, much less among those who endorsed mathematical plainness so that (as Hobbes said of Thucydides) "the number of his sentences [i.e., thoughts] doth almost reach to the number of his words."[17] Herbert's opposition is grounded on a decisive partiality not so much to any particular style as to Biblical precedents.

Herbert looked beyond the Bible firstly for parodic purposes, next for the surprisingly numerous classical allusions which he promptly christianized, and lastly for the opportunities that the emblematic tradition afforded to render his poetry "at once visual and intellectual."[18] Otherwise, almost every aspect of Herbert's poetry is traceable to the Bible. The evident lucidity—the "terrifying lucidity," as one critic remarks with understandable awe[19]—is Biblical. So is the omnipresent propensity toward understatement. Even more important, however, is the palpable influence of wisdom literature, of the Psalter, and of the parables embedded in the Gospels.

Herbert's interest in wisdom literature, especially the Book of Proverbs, is reflected in his own extensive collection of proverbial utterances. Simple in themselves, they prove less than simple on reflection, witness:

254. Providence is better then a rent.
381. We are fooles one to another.
462. To weepe for joy is a kinde of Manna.
540. Love is the true price of love.
792. Service is no Inheritance.[20]

Thematically, the sanctified worldliness of wisdom literature affected Herbert's poetry rather adversely, if not in "Charms and Knots" where the limit of sequentially arranged proverbs is reached expeditiously, then certainly in "The Church-porch," the unduly long introductory poem to *The Temple,* where the versified morality often contains excellent advice ("Never exceed thy income"!) but questionable poetry. Stylistically, on the other hand, Herbert's emulation of the Book of Proverbs afforded him the opportunity to indulge in that highly compressed, economic phrasing whose precise impact on his poems we are yet to study fully. It is far otherwise with the Book of Psalms, not only because we are aware how crucial for Herbert were the translations by his relative Sir Philip Sidney,[21] but because we know how often adaptations from the Psalter were the first fruits of poets who then proceeded, like Milton, to far more substantial harvests. Herbert himself, it will be noted, "imitated" only one psalm, even though it is the celebrated twenty-third, "The Lord is my shepherd." Yet so profoundly was Herbert engaged with the Psalter that its echoes reverberate across his poetry, to an extent unmatched by any other poet in English literature. The primary attraction of the Psalms was, of course, that devotional nature which Herbert celebrated in one of his Latin poems:

> O holy banquets! O soothing
> Oil of the spirit! Flakes of heaven, falling
> Droplets of a better world![22]

But Herbert was equally impressed by the Psalter as poetry. It is not unwarranted to assume that he joined his contemporaries in regarding David, to whose pen the Psalms were traditionally ascribed, as a great poet—"a better *Poet* than *Virgil*," as Donne proclaimed with assurance.[23]

The parables also exerted a strong influence on Herbert, not least because they are, like his poetry, "the natural expression of a mind that sees truth in concrete pictures rather than conceives it in abstractions."[24] We are reminded of the interest taken by Nicholas Ferrar and his band of dedicated souls at Little Gidding in stories, those "divine interludes, dialogues and discourses in the Platonic way" which eventually yielded the "short moral histories" incorporated into the community's *Story Books*.[25] Herbert perceived their uses readily enough. As he asserts in *A Priest to the Temple* of the parson's instruction of his parishioners,

> Sometimes he tells them stories, and sayings of others, according as his text invites him; for them also men heed, and remember better then exhortations.[26]

True, the literary dimension of the parables is severely circumscribed: their claim as art cannot be pressed very hard. In *The Temple*, however, parabolic teaching appears in many forms. It is by no means confined to poems like "Redemption," "Christmas," "Peace," or "Love III." Infinitely pliable in Herbert's hands, it reinforces all the poems which involve stories, among them "Time" and "Love unknown." Moreover, given the dramatic nature of Herbert's verse, the parable will be perceived to have been significantly extended in poems of dialogue or exchanges, for instance "The Pulley," itself foremost among the productions whose apparent naïvete is wont to elicit our condescending smiles. But Herbert's method is the method of the Gospels in particular, and of the Bible generally: "unspeakable mysteries in the Scriptures," according to Sir Thomas Browne's apposite reminder, "are often delivered in a vulgar and illustrative way, not as they truely are, but as they may be understood."[27] Prompt understanding of the central point is essential; but because the parable is fundamentally an indirect discourse, full understanding is reserved for those qualified to respond. It might therefore be said of Herbert's poetry what a Biblical scholar has asserted of parabolic teaching, that it possesses a complexity dormant within apparent simplicity.[28] As much is suggested by the New Testament in exclusively theological terms:

> Unto you it is given to know the mystery of the kingdom of God: but unto them that are without, all these things are done in parables (ἐν παραβολαῖς); that seeing they may see, and not perceive; and hearing they may hear, and not understand.
> (Mark 4.11–12)

In like fashion parables are related in the Psalter to the "dark sayings of old" (78.2), and in the apocryphal Ecclesiasticus to "the secrets of grave sentences" (39.3). The metaphysical justification was best formulated by St. Paul: "now we see through a glass, darkly" (1 Corinthians 13.12).

The parabolic approach, then, represents tendencies in Herbert which argue his indebtedness to Biblical precedents. But as much might be said of his tonal range, his polymorphic vocabulary, and his architectonic imagery, however pronounced the adjustment of each may have been under the impact of other influences. Herbert's tonal range, for instance, is the direct result of his training as an orator even while it is, demonstrably, the legacy of Donne. Yet it is no less the legacy of the Bible, especially in the studied understatement of a verse such as:

> My God, thou art all love.
> ("Even-song," l. 29)

There is no "final" way of reading such a verse. Is it a contrite confession, or an exultant prayer? Does it involve passionate longing, absolute assurance, or profound amazement? The justly celebrated last lines of Herbert's poems often have the same effect. "Redemption," for example, ends:

> Who straight, *Your suit is granted,* said, & died.

which induces astonishment precisely because of its nominal simplicity, much as Milton's elaborate patterns in *Paradise Regained* are finally suspended with:

> Tempt not the Lord thy God; he said and stood.
> (IV.561)

We observe elsewhere the significant extensions of the "simple" Biblical language. The detected principle that "the dominant emotion of each poem dictates its rhythmic form"[29] is all too often not the rule but the exception. An emotion apparently dominant is likely to prove of secondary importance as the tone veers, sometimes abruptly, to accommodate even childish delight:

> He will be pleased with that dittie;
> And if I please him, I write fine and wittie.
> ("The Forerunners," ll. 11–12)

The technique of "Deniall" and especially of "The Collar" is more noteworthy still, for the violent spasms in the internal arguments and external forms of both poems terminate in lines which, in their restored order, provide at last the neglected norm. We are again put in mind of Milton, this time *Lycidas,* where the concluding *ottava rima* cancels the disorder of the casual rhymes, the half lines, the broken rhythm.

Herbert clearly belongs with Milton in manipulating the verse to reflect the thematic patterns. Yet in other poems he also belongs with Marvell in suggesting much more than the lucid texture seems to posit. The suggestiveness depends on a vocabulary which, in appearance limited and even "simple," expands outwardly in accordance with the given context. Just as the Bible qualifies familiar words, so Herbert is wont to amend the meaning of a word dramatically—as in "winding" or "twist,"[30] but especially in the omnipresent "rest" which appears with marked ingenuity as part of the serial (and heavily ironic) imagery of gaming in "The Church-porch" (ll. 227 and 297), with calculated ambiguity in the last line of "The Answer," with suggestive orchestration in the rhyme scheme of "Aaron," and with exceptional brilliance in the five instances of "The Pulley," two of them almost totally submerged. We need only compare the argument of "The Pulley" with the meditation on "rest" by Sir John Hayward in 1623, to appreciate how a commonplace theme and even strikingly similar language were improved by Herbert. Hayward had thus urged his soul to cleave to God:

> Thou doest naturally desire nothing but him; the desire of worldly things is but a disease. Goe too then, tumble upon the bed of honour, riches, or pleasure; thou shalt never find rest, because thou cariest thy disease within thee: ridde thee of thy sicknesse, and thou shalt finde reste only in GOD. The reason is plaine. GOD made thee only for himselfe; and therefore being thy last end, thou canst not find quiet, but onely in him. . . .[31]

Herbert's expression of the same theme is not only more economic; it is also more elliptical, in line with his frequent indulgence in word-play which accepts that verbal connections never look inwardly upon themselves. Herbert himself furnishes one lucid example, the traditional pun Son/sun: "we give one onely name / To parents issue and the sunnes bright starre" ("The Sunne," ll. 5–6). Once juxtaposed, connections of this order intimate transcendent relationships best represented in the interlocked terms deployed in "A Wreath," else the reiterated pattern of thine/mine in "Clasping of Hands," and even the significant if apparently naïve rhyme schemes of "Paradise" and "Heaven" which alike uphold—as in delight/light and persever/ever—the mystery veiled by familiarity.[32] Herbert did not indulge in several pyrotechnics that "burnish, sprout, and swell" ("Jordan II," l. 4) because, as he remarks in *A Priest to the Temple*, Jesus also confined himself to homely language, "that by familiar things hee might make his Doctrine slip the more easily into the hearts even of the meanest."[33]

"Familiar things" also inform Herbert's imagery, for its clusters are manifestly if not primarily Biblical. One notable exception is the imagery derived from music—"in which heavenly Art," Walton emphasizes, Herbert was "a most excellent Master."[34] The deployment of musical imagery is, of course, a commonplace of literature generally as of Renaissance thought in particular: to quote Sir Thomas Browne again, "there is musicke where-ever there is a harmony, order, or proportion" (*Religio Medici* II.9). Yet it is a commonplace that Herbert's fertile imagination again transformed into a novelty. His frequent boldness is noteworthy, as when he remarks of Christ, "His stretched sinews taught all strings, what key / Is best to celebrate this most high day" ("Easter," ll. 11–12)—a forceful reminder that Christ has not merely taught us to sound the appropriate music but offered us the instrument too: himself. Often, a musical image marks a transition in the tone. In the sonnet "Prayer I," for instance, the initially elaborate endeavors to understand the nature of prayer yield to a musical reference that promptly affects the rhythm:

> A kind of tune, which all things heare and fear;
> Softnesse, and peace, and joy, and love, and blisse,
>   Exalted Manna . . . .

In "Sunday," on the other hand, the joyful rhythm reflects the exuberance not of a child as of the man reborn into the kingdom of the Christ:

> O let me take thee at the bound,
> Leaping with thee from sev'n to sev'n,
> Till that we both, being toss'd from earth,
>   Flie hand in hand to heav'n!

(ll. 60–63)

The Biblical burden of Herbert's other images is manifest in the light of the Christ's habitual resort to "the familiar things of daily life"—the moon and the stars, birds and sheep and fish, flowers and the vine, bread and water, door and keys.[35] In Herbert, accordingly, one group of pervasive images derives from the natural order. It marks the labors of the bee and next the flight of the dove, even as it measures the effect of dew and frost and rain and snow on fruit such as grapes, grain such as corn, and flowers like the rose. Man's life within the garden of the world—"Gods rich garden" ("Sunday," l. 27)—buds with joy, else withers in despair, and finally blooms again under the influence of implanted Grace. But other images expressly reminiscent of St. Paul are also present, for example images of warfare as in "Artillerie," and especially images derived in the first instance from commercial and legal activities, and in the second from architecture. The relations between Redeemer and redeemed are most often set forth in commercial terms. The Christ is said to have been "sold" for us ("Antiphon II," l. 12; "The H. Communion," l. 3; etc.), or to have taken "the debt upon him" ("Love unknown," l. 61)—and so on through a vocabulary involving gain and loss, sales and bargains, rent and lease, bills and interest and the like. It sounds odd, not to say singularly inappropriate, until we recognize not only the Pauline terminology of Romans 3.21–26 but the forensic language characteristic of the classic Protestant theory of the Atonement. In time that theory was to be enshrined in *Paradise Lost* (III.80–415); but it had been formulated any number of times by major and minor theologians in statements of this order:

> Wee must then know that Christ is our Surety: and looke, as the debter is discharged by the payment performed by the Surety, and such payment made, is imputed to the Debtor, and reckoned as if hee had payed it himselfe: So God in sentence giving, imputeth unto us that which our Surety hath done or suffered for us, and (whatsoever we are in our selves) respecteth us as if it had beene done by us, and so dischargeth us.[36]

The uniqueness of Herbert's adaptation of the commonly held view resides not in that view but in its adaptation. One result is the sonnet "Redemption"; another, the triumphant proclamation of the Christ's sacrifice

> Whose drops of blood paid the full price,
> That was required to make us gay
>
> ("Sunday," ll. 54–55)

where the first line is a concession to tradition-bound thought, but the second marks Herbert's particular sensibility.

The last notable cluster of images favored by Herbert is drawn from architecture. Generously used by St. Paul, architectural imagery is also basic to the fabric of the Bible at large. As Donne reflected in one of his sermons,

> The Holy Ghost seemes to have delighted in the Metaphore of *Building.* I know no figurative speech so often iterated in the Scriptures, as the name of a *House*; Heaven and Earth are called by that name, and wee, who being upon earth, have our conversation in heaven, are called so too, (*Christ hath a House, which House wee are*). And as God builds his House, (*The Lord builds up Jerusalem,* saith *David*) so hee furnishes it, he plants Vineyards, Gardens, and Orchards about it, He layes out a way to it, (*Christ is the way*) He opens a gate into it, (*Christ is the gate*) And when hee hath done all this, ... then he keepes house, as well as builds a house, he feeds us, and feasts us in his house, as well as he lodges us, and places us in it.[37]

The image is fundamental to several of Herbert's poems, for instance "The World," "Man," and "Sion." But it also sustains their collective title, *The Temple.*

IV. "Proporcioned ... with a certain order"

"*The Temple* is, in fact, a structure." One tends to agree with T. S. Eliot's generalization[38] only to disagree about its precise import. The constituent poems of *The Temple* have been observed to link in diverse ways, so that sequentially arranged poems (for instance "Nature," "Sinne I," "Affliction I," "Repentance," and "Faith") intimate both in their titles and arguments the progress of the soul.[39] But is the total structure meant to symbolize a pilgrim's progress under the care of the Church, or possibly the divine order as reflected in the life of man within the Church?[40] Is it perhaps based on the analogy between man's religious and aesthetic activities, themselves patterned after the activities of the Creator?[41] Even more elaborately, does the threefold division of *The Temple* into "The Church-porch," "The Church," and "The Church Militant" correspond to the tripartite division of the Hebraic temple into porch, holy place, and holy of holies, else to the three regions of the universe—the earth, the heavens, and the abode of God?[42] To compound our difficulties, the first and the third of the collection's divisions—alike brutally moralistic—have not met with wide approbation: "The Church-porch" is occasionally dismissed as dull, while "The Church Militant" is generally regarded with stony silence. As a poem evidently predating the rest of *The Temple,* "The Church

Militant" has even been said not to form an integral part of the collection.[43] But it refuses to go away, stubbornly.

One analogy at least could not have been absent from Herbert's mind, for it was no less sanctified by tradition than it is implicit throughout *The Temple*: the analogy between Creator and poet. As George Puttenham (?) wrote at the outset of *The Arte of English Poesie* (1589):

> A poet is as much to say as a maker. And our English name well conformes with the Greeke word, for of ποιεῖν, to make, they call a maker *Poeta*. Such as (by way of resemblance and reverently) we may say of God; who without any travell to his divine imagination made all the world of nought.[44]

A popular collection of commonplaces pronounced God a poet in even more sweeping terms:

> The begynner of meter was God, whych proporcioned the world, with all the contentes of the same, with a certain order, as it were a meter, for there is none (as *Pythagoras* taughte) that douteth, but that there is in thynges hevenly and earthely a kynde of harmonye, and onless it were governed, wyth a formall concorde and dyscribed nomber, howe could it longe continue?[45]

On the widely accepted metaphor of God the poet was often superimposed the metaphor of God the architect. The Biblical text usually cited was invoked from the apocryphal Wisdom of Solomon: "thou hast ordered all things in measure and number and weight" (11.20). The creative method evident in the universe at large was also said to have been applied within history when the divine architect instructed Noah on the proportions of the Ark, Moses on those of the Tabernacle, and Solomon on those of the Temple. In time the Solomonic Temple became the foremost precedent for many medieval churches. As late as 1535 Francesco Giorgi could write of the projected church of S. Francesco della Vigna in Venice:

> We, being desirous of building the church, have thought it necessary, and most appropriate, to follow that order of which God, the greatest architect, is the master and author. When God wished to instruct Moses concerning the form and proportion of the tabernacle which he had to build, He gave him as model the fabric of the world [Exodus 25.8ff.]. . . . And rightly so, because it was necessary that the particular place should resemble His universe . . . in proportion, which He wills should be not only in the material places, in which He dwells, but particularly in us of whom Paul says, writing to the

Corinthians: "ye are the Temple of God" [1 Corinthians 2.16]. Pondering on this mystery, Solomon the Wise gave the same proportions as those of the Mosaic tabernacle to the famous Temple he erected.[46]

The argument is clear in the extreme: all artistic endeavors rest on a metaphysical foundation according to the precedent established by God himself. Sir Thomas Browne once again provides the appropriate generalization. "In brief," he wrote, "all things are artificiall, for nature is the Art of God" (*Religio Medici* I.16). Obviously shared by Herbert, the assumption is most emphatically evident in the poet's mimesis of the orderly pattern of words emanating from God, the archetypal Logos or Word.[47] But the apprehension is not merely external. It is also an experience within, in line with the several meanings that the Biblical witness attaches to "temple."

The term, in the first and most obvious sense, designates the house of the Lord—"an house of prayer for all people" (Isaiah 56.7). On other occasions, however, "temple" is sharply differentiated from any particular edifice: "God that made the world and all things therein, seeing that he is Lord of heaven and earth, dwelleth not in temples made with hands" (Acts 17.24; cf. Matthew 12.6, Acts 7.48). Metaphorically the term also appears as the natural order in general (Psalms 29.9), more emphatically as the body of Christ (Matthew 26.61, Mark 14.58, John 2.19), and by extension as the body of man: "ye are the temple of the living God" (2 Corinthians 6.16). By the early seventeenth century, moreover, tradition had endorsed the application of "temple" to the Church at large. Donne explained in a sermon delivered in 1619 that the early Christians as well as "all the *Fathers*" were wont to specify the Church by various terms, for instance *ecclesia* ("a company, a Congregation") and *dominicum* ("The Lords possession"). He added:

> But for all Names, which were then usually given to the Church, the name of *Temple* seems to be most large, and significant, as they derive it *à Tuendo*; for *Tueri* signifies both our beholding, and contemplating *God* in the Church: and it signifies Gods protecting, and defending those that are his, in his Church: *Tueri* embraces both.[48]

The correspondent relationship between God and man stressed by Donne appears in Herbert through the communal sacramentalism of all his poems of dialogue, if more particularly of the two poems alike entitled "Antiphon." But communal sacramentalism should not be mistaken for an act of worship performed solely in a given place at a given time. It is on the contrary the essence of things, the very nature of nature, in that it reflects the activities of the divine architect-poet both during his initial act of creation and his subsequent preservation of the world. "Preservation," Herbert asserts in *A Priest to the Temple,* "is a Creation; and more, it is a continued Creation, and a creation every moment."[49] However traditional the basic concept,[50] its application by Herbert suggests the way the activities of the imitating poet are sanctified, the way language and even individual words look beyond themselves, the way the archetypal "temple"— and each derivative "temple" inclusive of structures like poems—possesses an external form even though it is fundamentally an internal experience: the "frame and fabric," in his words, "is within" ("Sion," l. 12). These various strands merge in Herbert's thought because they depend on a singular reality, the immanence of God in history through the sacrament of the Lord's Supper, the Eucharist.

V. "All things are bigge with jest"

The Eucharist is the marrow of Herbert's sensibility. Far more important than baptism, the only other sacrament recognized by Protestants, it had elicited ever since the Reformation acrimonious disagreements as to the precise nature of the Christ's "presence" during its celebration. While Calvinists claimed that the Christ is present solely through the communicant's faith, Roman Catholics asserted (as a rather crude formulation had it) that he is present "not only to fayth, but also to the mouth, to the tongue, to the lips, to the flesh, to the bowells of all Communicants."[51] Characteristically eschewing both extremes, Anglicans maintained in flexible if vague fashion that "the Body and Blood of Christ are really and actually and substantially present and taken in the Eucharist, but in a way which the human mind cannot understand and much more beyond the power of man to express."[52] Herbert agreed, but only after he had eradicated the partisan zeal he had once displayed in a harsh tirade against a Puritan, to understand at last the advantage of an irenic temper in the midst of his contemporaries' "private Enthusiasmes."[53] The Anglican formulation of the Eucharist's *modus operandi*—"mystical, heavenly, and spiritual," the elements present but "figuratively and sacramentally"[54]—became increasingly acceptable to Herbert, obliging him to exclude from *The Temple* a rather militant meditation on "The H. Communion" ("O gratious Lord how shall I know") in favor of a version far less explicitly theological ("Not in rich furniture, or fine aray"). The larger consequence was poetry replete with words reminiscent in their literal dimension of Roman Catholic claims—*altar, table, board, repast, banquet, feast, store, bread, meat, wine,* and especially *blood,* no less than the reiterated verbs *taste* and *eat*—yet aspiring to intimate the mystery of "the pattern, the shadow, the type" of the ultimate reality.[55] It is of course hardly accidental that the central division of *The Temple,* "The Church," is preceded by the invitation of the

"Superliminare"—i.e., the lintel over the entrance to the church—to "approach, and taste / The churches mystical repast." Within "The Church" proper, moreover, the first poem is "The Altar," promptly and significantly followed by the sixty-three stanzas of "The Sacrifice" whose liturgical rhythms reenact *and* commemorate the original historical event, even as they suggest the ideal response demanded of man. That response is also specified, at the other end of "The Church," as the third of the poems entitled "Love" concludes with:

> You must sit down, sayes Love, and taste my meat:
> So I did sit and eat.

If *The Temple* is indeed a "structure," it is a eucharistic one. In form as in content it is itself a "eucharist," a εὐχαριστία or "thanksgiving": the crown of praise offered, humbly, by "A Wreath."

The sacraments of the Eucharist and baptism were commonly said to be "visible signs of invisible Grace."[56] Herbert's understanding of the nature of Grace involves in the first instance a full awareness of the chaotic state of fallen man. All too often dismissed as mere dust, fallen man—man literally in-dependent of God—is variously termed "a poore clod of earth," "a foolish thing," "a brittle crazie glasse," "an intangled, hamper'd thing," a "sick toss'd vessel," "a rotten tree," even "a silly flie." But in the divine scheme of the world's preservation ("a creation every moment"), Grace is not so much present as omnipresent. Herbert would have agreed with the categorical statement of one of his contemporaries that God "giveth *Grace* freely, conserveth *Grace* given, multiplieth *Grace* conserved, and rewardeth *Grace* multiplied."[57] But he would have added that Grace is above all "prevenient," anticipatory of man's behavior by virtue of the Christ's presence in history. As much is attested by the position of "The Sacrifice" within *The Temple*, for its liturgical stanzas "prevent" (anticipate) the complaints to be heard in later poems by placing them in advance of their articulation within the context of the Christ's Passion. To juxtapose "The Sacrifice" and, say, "The Collar" is to realize how indirectly Herbert is deploying his devastating irony. The convulsions in "The Collar" appear to refer solely to the agony of the individual speaker:

> Is the year only lost to me?
> Have I no bayes to crown it?

And:

> Have I no harvest but a thorn
> To let me bloud, and not restore
> What I have lost with cordiall fruit?

But the same language was already used by the Christ in the vastly different context of "The Sacrifice":

> on my head a crown of thorns I wear . . .

and especially:

> my blood [is] the onely way
> And cordiall left to repair mans decay. . . .

The Christ's words in "The Sacrifice" are significantly transferred to the predicament of the individual sinner in the poem immediately following, "The Thanksgiving," which also anticipates (prevents) "The Collar" in its use of words like *store* and *restore, thorns* and *flower, hand* and *blood*. The principle is stated with characteristic clarity:

> Oh King of wounds! how shall I grieve for thee,
>   Who in all grief preventest me?
> Shall I weep bloud? why, thou hast wept such store
>   That all thy body was one doore.
> Shall I be scourged, flouted, boxed, sold?
>   'Tis but to tell the tale is told.
>   ("The Thanksgiving," ll. 2–8)

Prevenient Grace in *The Temple* assumes numerous other forms too. Visually, it extends to the enactment of its dispensation in "Easter-wings"; thematically, it embraces the recurrent prayers that link verse to verse in a chain of pleas:

> O let thy graces without cease
>   Drop from above! . . .
>   ("Grace," ll. 3–4)

> Lord, hunt me not . . .
>   ("Affliction IV," l. 2)

> O my God,
> My God, relieve me!
>   ("Sighs and Grones," ll. 29–30)

> Throw away thy rod . . .
>   ("Discipline," l. 1)

> Lord restore thine image, heare my call . . .
>   ("The Sinner," l. 12)

"prevented" pleas all, answered by Grace even before they are voiced by man:

> Lord heare! *Shall he that made the eare,*
> *Not heare?*
>
> ("Longing," ll. 35–36)

The "structure" of *The Temple* may be eucharistic, as claimed, but it is more generally charitological, centered on Grace—the invisible reality of which the Eucharist is the visible sign. Jointly central to Herbert's poetry, Grace and the Eucharist aver—to quote T. S. Eliot—"the absolute paternal care / That will not leave us, but prevents us everywhere" ("East Coker," ll. 160–61).

Herbert's poetry celebrates the grace of Grace but is dominated by the love of Love. Crashaw, who was not altogether unaware of the love that moves the sun and the other stars, rightly proclaimed of *The Temple*: "Divinest love lyes in this booke."[58] For Herbert, however, love was not the exuberant, inflammatory, even hysterical experience it proved for Crashaw. On the contrary, love is a rationally apprehended obligation imposed by the very nature of love; for as St. Paul had long since recognized, love "constrains" (2 Corinthians 5.14)—or to use Herbert's telling word, it "entices" ("Affliction I," l. 1), and more eloquently: it constitutes a "crosse-bias" (ibid., l. 53). While Donne thrived on contrary states, Herbert transcended them under the impact of irresistible love. "I am he / On whom thy tempests fell all night" bears the unmistakable imprint of the self-centered elder poet; but Herbert wrote:

> O my onely light,
> It cannot be
> That I am he
> On whom thy tempests fell all night.
>
> ("The Flower," ll. 38–42)

So, too, the numerous allusions in *The Temple* to history's *eschata*—"the four last things": death, judgment, heaven, hell—consistently avoid detailed references to "the day of great vengeance" when the Christ was traditionally expected to return "in strength as a storme of haile, & as a whirlwinde breaking and throwing downe whatsoever standeth in his way, as a rage of many waters that flow and rush together...."[59] Herbert composed merely two exclusively eschatological poems, "Dooms-day" and "Judgement," but they are alike arranged in low key as fourth and third from the end of the central division of *The Temple*. They are immediately followed by two parabolic visions, delivered as usual "in a vulgar and illustrative way ... as they may be understood": first a pointedly naïve glimpse of "Heaven," and next the eucharistic banquet of "Love III" we noted earlier:

> You must sit down, sayes Love, and taste my meat:
>   So I did sit and eat.

Hell as the future abode of the damned, so thunderously present in the consciousness of Herbert's contemporaries, is completely bypassed in *The Temple*. The reality of its experience at any given time is not denied; but in the end, Herbert suggests, Divine Love overwhelms the terrors of history with mirth. The final realization is that "All things are bigge with jest" ("The Church-porch," ll. 239–40).[60]

VI. "A verse is not a crown"

For the modern reader the exclusively sacred burden of *The Temple* is a serious stumbling block. "We hate poetry that has a palpable design upon us" is a remark by Keats quoted earlier[61] and not altogether inapposite to Herbert's poetry too. How is it possible to respond to *The Temple* when its final aim is made so embarrassingly clear in the first stanza of "The Church-porch"?

> A verse may finde him, who a sermon flies,
> And turn delight into a sacrifice.

It were relatively easy to dismiss the problem by reminding ourselves that Herbert shares the widespread Renaissance assumption that poetry teaches (as Milton wrote) "the whole book of sanctity and vertu through all the instances of example."[62] Can an appeal to traditional modes of thought allay our suspicions that Herbert's poetry is less insistently propagandistic than it appears to be?

Hardly. On the other hand, what is the nature of Herbert's "palpable design"? It is certainly explicit—militantly explicit—in his Latin poetry, as in his vision of the Anglican Church under James I:

>   See how
> The lovely Church outspreads its wings and sheds
> Its radiance as far as heaven. Far and wide
> The neighbour nations wonder, and, their minds adazzle,
> Want to learn a ritual in harmony with ours. . . .[63]

Vestiges of such explicitness linger in both "The Church-porch" and "The Church Militant." But in so far as *The Temple* eschews the declamatory for the dramatic, the impression is conveyed of the presence in it of several voices and experiences so that the reader finds himself—often to his surprise—at the very center of the given situation. Herbert's poetry, in other words, does indeed have "a palpable design upon us"; but it is a design woven aesthetically.

The presence in *The Temple* of several voices and experiences can scarcely be missed: the speakers range from the Christ in "The Sacrifice" to a courtier in "The Pearl," and from the narrator as detached storyteller in "The Pulley" to the narrator as participant in "The Collar." The poems of *The Temple* could still be said to emanate from a single if infinitely varied consciousness, yet they may not be regarded as so many forays into autobiography. Composed at a time when dramatic literature had extended far beyond drama properly so called, they share with the poems of many other creators a natural inclination to dramatize in order to achieve an optimum of tonal range. Each poem is an invitation to us to differentiate between the creating artist and the created artifact; for to be cognizant of the total control that the poet exerted over his poetry is to appreciate how far "simplicity" conceals complexity, and apparent artlessness the highest reaches of art. Herbert, who had known "such spiritual Conflicts, as none can think, but only those that have endur'd them," impresses not because he evinces those conflicts in his poetry but because, all too often, he transcends them. The experience he had as man of "the sicknesse that destroyeth at noone day (Ghostly pride and self-conceite),"[64] could not have been carried into his poetry unqualified; for that poetry were else partial, incapable of displaying that controlled turbulence which is among Herbert's foremost characteristics. Marvell, who was to share with Herbert a similar quality—turbulence so far controlled in his case as to be subterranean!—discloses it both in "Bermudas" where nature's loveliness is qualified by the presence of huge monsters within the roaring seas, and in "To his Coy Mistress" where a mere game is transformed into a nightmarish vision of the passage of time (see pp. 282ff.).

I invoke Marvell when I might have invoked Donne. But we have heard so much of Donne's decisive influence on Herbert—and much more of "the school of Donne" with its several obedient students—that it may prove worthwhile to ascertain the individual talent where earlier readers were content to seek the common denominator. The generalization once confidently made that Herbert is "a metaphysical poet of the school of Donne with the same undivided consciousness of his tribe"[65] will no longer serve; while the oracular pronouncement of T. S. Eliot that the peculiar characteristic of the "metaphysical" strain is "a direct apprehension of thought or a recreation of thought into feeling" (as above, p. 112) will mislead as often as it could be said to enlighten. For how might either claim apply to a poet whose self-effacement obliges us to discourse rather in negative than in positive terms, much as he himself does?

> My God, a verse is not a crown,
> No point of honour, or gay suit.
> No hawk, or banquet, or renown,
> Nor a good sword, nor yet a lute....
>
> ("The Quidditie," ll. 1–4)

A "metaphysical" Herbert might have shared Donne's fondness for cerebral pyrotechnics, Vaughan's pursuit of the single effect, Crashaw's display of uninhibited explosiveness, and Traherne's indulgence in torrential lyricism. But he elected not to speak out loud and bold, aware that the range of experience incorporated in *The Temple* could best be attained by eschewing every given "tribe."

And the range was vital; for Herbert was much possessed with life.

NOTES

An earlier version of this chapter, entitled *"A Crown of Praise*: The Poetry of Herbert," appeared as the introduction to *The English Poems of George Herbert,* ed. C. A. Patrides, Everyman's Library (London: Dent, 1974), pp. 6–25. Copyright 1974 by J. M. Dent and Sons Ltd. Reprinted by permission. Herbert's poetry is here quoted from this edition.

1. "The Life of Mr. George Herbert" (1670, rev. 1675), in *George Herbert: The Critical Heritage,* ed. C. A. Patrides (London, 1983), p. 93.
2. "The Life of Herbert," p. 130.
3. "The Life of Herbert," p. 98.
4. Aubrey, *Brief Lives,* ed. Oliver L. Dick, 3d ed. (London, 1958), p. 137. Charles I with his customary perception thought it "a very neate Curious Chappell" (C. Leslie Craig, *Nicholas Ferrar Junior* [London, 1950], p. 50).
5. *The Latin Poetry of George Herbert,* trans. Mark McCloskey and Paul R. Murphy (Athens, Ohio, 1965), p. 153.
6. *Sermons,* ed. E. M. Simpson and G. R. Potter (Berkeley, 1953–62), 8:89. Lady Danvers was the recipient of Donne's sequence of sonnets *La Corona,* together with their prefatory sonnet "To the Lady Magdalen Herbert, of St. Mary Magdalen"; see further the verse letter "To Mrs M. H. (Mad paper stay...)." Her definitive portrait is given by Walton ("Life of Herbert," pp. 94ff.); but see also Herbert's elegy in Latin and Greek, *Memoriae matris sacrum* (*Latin Poetry,* pp. 122–55); and for two accounts of her relationship with Donne: H. W. Garrod, "Donne and Mrs. Herbert," *RES* 21 (1945): 161–73; and Helen Gardner, ed., *The Elegies and the Songs and Sonnets* (Oxford, 1965), pp. 251–58.
7. *The Works of George Herbert,* ed. F. E. Hutchinson (Oxford, 1941), p. 364.
8. *Works,* pp. 369–70.
9. *Works,* p. xxvii.
10. Walton, "Life of Herbert," p. 99.

11. In *George Herbert: The Critical Heritage,* p. 133. Herbert's ambition may also have prompted his poem(s) to the Queen of Bohemia. See Ted-Larry Pebworth, "George Herbert's Poems to the Queen of Bohemia: A Rediscovered Text and a New Edition," *ELR* 9 (1979): 108–120.
12. See *George Herbert: The Critical Heritage,* p. 100. Herbert addressed Latin poems to Andrewes and especially to Bacon (*Latin Poetry,* pp. 4–5 and 166–73). The poem to Bacon has also been spiritedly translated by Edmund Blunden in *Essays and Studies* 19 (1933): 35–36. The best study to date of Herbert's relationship to Bacon is William A. Sessions, "Bacon and Herbert and an Image of Chalk," in *Too Rich to Clothe the Sunne: Essays on George Herbert,* ed. Claude J. Summers and Ted-Larry Pebworth (Pittsburgh, 1980), pp. 165–78.
13. *Works,* p. 366.
14. Walton, "Life of Herbert," p. 287.
15. *Coleridge on the Seventeenth Century,* ed. Roberta F. Brinkley (Durham, N.C., 1955), pp. 533–40, and T. S. Eliot, *George Herbert,* Writers and their Work, no. 152 (London, 1962), p. 17. Eliot's increasingly favorable regard of Herbert is detailed in *George Herbert: The Critical Heritage,* pp. 32–33 and 332–36.
16. *Works,* pp. 234–35.
17. The statement, borrowed from Cicero's *De oratore* (II.xiii.56), is quoted by George Williamson, *The Senecan Amble* (London, 1951), p. 215.
18. On Herbert's fondness for parody, see Rosemond Tuve, "Sacred 'Parody' of Love Poetry, and Herbert," in her *Essays* (Princeton, 1970), pp. 207–51; on his classical allusions: Mary E. Rickey, *Utmost Art* (Lexington, Ky., 1966); and on his emblematic predilections: Rosemary Freeman, *English Emblem Books* (London, 1948), chap. 6; and Joseph H. Summers, *George Herbert: His Religion and His Art* (Cambridge, Mass., 1954), chap. 6.
19. Robert Ellrodt, "George Herbert and the Religious Lyric," in *English Poetry and Prose 1540–1674,* ed. Christopher Ricks (London, 1970), chap. 8. See also the recent ambitious study by Chana Bloch, *Spelling the Word: Herbert and the Bible* (Berkeley, 1985).
20. *Works,* pp. 323ff.
21. See Louis L. Martz, *The Poetry of Meditation* (New Haven, 1954), chap. 7; and consult further: Hallett Smith, "English Metrical Psalms in the Sixteenth Century and their Literary Significance," *HLQ* 9 (1946): 249–71, and Coburn Freer, *Music for a King: George Herbert's Style and the Metrical Psalms* (Baltimore, 1972).
22. *Latin Poetry,* p. 35.
23. *Sermons,* 4:167.
24. C. H. Dodd, *The Parable of the Kingdom* (London, 1935), pp. 15–16.
25. From John Ferrar's biography of his brother Nicholas, quoted by Alan L. Maycock, *Nicholas Ferrar of Little Gidding* (London, 1938).
26. *Works,* p. 233.
27. *Religio Medici,* I.45. The theory of "accommodation" endorsed by Browne and operative in Herbert is extensively deployed in Renaissance theology and literature. See my remarks in *Bright Essence,* by William B. Hunter, J. H. Adamson, and myself (Salt Lake City, 1971), pp. 159ff.
28. "Simple as most of the parables seem to be, and easy to understand, when

first read, there are many which are seen to be very difficult as soon as they are pondered over" (W. O. E. Oesterley, *The Gospel Parables in the Light of their Jewish Background* [London, 1936], p. 13).
29. Margaret Bottrall, *George Herbert* (London, 1954), chap. 4.
30. "Winding" describes in one poem the "fashion / Of adoration" ("The Starre," l.27), yet in another is qualified as "winding stair" ("Jordan I," l.3) and in a third as "winding sheets" ("Mortification," l.5). "Twist" appears in one instance as "a twist checker'd with night and day" ("Providence," l.58), in another as "twist a song / Pleasant and long" ("Easter," ll.13–14), and in a third as "with my yeares sorrow did twist and grow" ("Affliction I," l.23). The sense of both words, moreover, is enacted in "A Wreath."
31. *Davids Teares* (London, 1623), pp. 298–99.
32. See M. M. Mahood, "Something Understood: The Nature of Herbert's Wit," in *Metaphysical Poetry,* ed. Malcolm Bradbury and David Palmer (London, 1970), chap. 5.
33. *Works,* p. 261.
34. "Life of Herbert," p. 119.
35. Stephen J. Brown, *Image and Truth: Studies in the Imagery of the Bible* (Rome, 1955), p. 86. This is the most convenient summary I know of the metaphors in the Gospels and St. Paul's epistles.
36. Elnathan Parr, *The Grounds of Divinitie,* 2d ed. (London, 1615), p. 213. See also my studies of "Milton and the Protestant Theory of the Atonement," *PMLA* 74 (1959): 7–13, and *Milton and the Christian Tradition* (Oxford, 1966), chap. 5.
37. *Sermons,* 7:302–3. The Biblical quotations are Hebrews 3.6, Psalms 147.2, John 14.6, and Matthew 7.13; respectively.
38. *George Herbert,* p. 17.
39. See Martz, *Poetry of Meditation,* chap. 8; and John R. Mulder, "George Herbert's *The Temple*: Design and Methodology," *Seventeenth-Century News,* 31 (1973): 37–45.
40. See Charles A. Pennell and William P Williams, "The Unity of *The Temple,*" *Xavier University Studies* 5 (1966): 37–45; and Joseph Summers, *George Herbert,* chap. 4; respectively.
41. See Valerie Carnes, "The Unity of George Herbert's *The Temple*: A Reconsideration," *ELH* 35 (1968): 505–26.
42. See John W. Walker, "The Architectonics of George Herbert's *The Temple,*" *ELH* 29 (1962): 289–305.
43. See Annabel M. Endicott, "The Structure of George Herbert's *The Temple*: A Reconsideration," *UTQ* 34 (1965): 226–37; and Lee A. Johnson, "The Relationship of 'The Church Militant' to *The Temple,*" *SP* 68 (1971): 200–206. So far, the best studies of the opening and closing poems of *The Temple* are by Robert B. Hinman, "The 'Verser' at *The Temple* Door: Herbert's 'The Church-porch,' " in *Too Rich to Clothe the Sunne,* ed. Summers and Pebworth, pp. 55–75, and Raymond A. Anselment, " 'The Church Militant': George Herbert and the Metamorphoses of Christian History," *HLQ* 41 (1978): 299–316.
44. *Elizabethan Critical Essays,* ed. G. Gregory Smith (Oxford, 1904), 2:3. The etymology is also noted by Sir Philip Sidney in his *Apology for Poetry.*

45. Polydore Vergil, *An abridgement of the notable worke . . . conteygnyng the devisers . . . of Artes, Ministeries* etc., abridged by Thomas Langley (London, 1546), fols. 17–17v.
46. Translated by Rudolf Wittkower, *Architectural Principles in the Age of Humanism*, 2d ed. (London, 1952), p. 136.
47. See Rosalie L. Colie, "Logos in *The Temple*," in her *Paradoxia Epidemica* (Princeton, 1966), chap. 6.
48. *Sermons*, 2:221. One of Herbert's Latin poems suggests the broad circumference of "temple" by asserting its transformation by Christ into a world: "non urbem . . . sed Orbem" (*Latin Poetry*, pp. 76–77). For Milton's use of "temple," see William G. Riggs, *The Christian Poet in "Paradise Lost"* (Berkeley, 1972), pp. 42ff., 164ff.
49. *Works*, p. 281.
50. Cf. Peter Sterry: "Learned men and Divines teach us; that the Preservation of the world is *continuata Creatio*, a continued Creation. In every moment of Time from the Beginning of the world to the end, the Divine Act of Preserving . . . is entirely the same with the Act of Creation" (*The Kingdom of God in the Soul of Man* [London, 1683], pp. 409–10).
51. Sylvester Norris, *An Antidote or Treatise of Thirty Controversies* (1622), quoted by C. W. Dugmore, *Eucharistic Doctrine in England* (London, 1942), pp. 28–29.
52. William Forbes, in a treatise published posthumously in 1658; in *Anglicanism*, ed. Paul E. More and Frank L. Cross (London, 1935), p. 471. On the developing interpretations of the Lord's Supper, consult the magisterial survey by Darwell Stone, *A History of the Doctrine of the Holy Eucharist* (London, 1909), 2 vols., which expounds views common from the outset of the Reformation in chap. 9 et seq.
53. From his "Brief Notes" on *The Hundred and Ten Considerations* of Juán de Valdés (Italian version, 1550; English translation by Nicholas Ferrar, 1638), in *Works*, p. 308. The Puritan in question was Andrew Melville; the tirade: *Musae Responsoriae* (in *Latin Poetry*, pp. 2–61). On Herbert's continuing anti-Puritanism in matters of church ceremony and governance, see Claude J. Summers and Ted-Larry Pebworth, "The Politics of *The Temple*: 'The British Church' and 'The Familie,' " *George Herbert Journal* 8 (Fall 1984): 1–14.
54. Bishop Overall and Archbishop Ussher, respectively; in Dugmore, *Eucharistic Doctrine*, pp. 40 and 54.
55. From Edward Reynolds' definition of sacraments (1638), in *Anglicanism*, ed. More and Cross, p. 411.
56. I quote from the great Anglican apologist Richard Hooker (in *Anglicanism*, ed. More and Cross, p. 407). But the phrase is a commonplace of Protestant theology, derived from Augustine.
57. Daniel Price, *The Creation of the Prince* (London, 1610), sig. C4v.
58. "On Mr G. Herberts booke intituled The Temple," l.2; in *Steps to the Temple* (1646).
59. George Hakewill, *An Apologie* (Oxford, 1627), p. 458.
60. See Sterne's use of these lines in *Tristram Shandy* ("Everything in this world, said my father, is big with jest,—and has wit in it, and instruction too,—if we can but find it out" [bk. 5, chap. 32]), as noted by Herbert Rauter, "Eine Anleihe Sternes bei George Herbert," *Anglia* 80 (1962): 290–94.

61. From a letter to John Hamilton Reynolds, February 3, 1818; quoted above, p. 34.
62. See above, p. 73.
63. *Latin Poetry,* p. 57.
64. *Works,* p. 238.
65. Helen C. White, *The Metaphysical Poets* (1936; reprint New York, 1962), chaps. 6–7.

Richard Crashaw:
The Merging of Contrarieties

> The imaginary relish is so sweet
> That it enchants my sense
> —*Troilus and Cressida*

I. "A bleeding Heart that gaspes for blood"

Crashaw is a poet in search of readers. We need but instance the acknowledgment by one of his foremost champions that several of his poems are "the very model of bad taste in poetry."[1] In case we missed the point, the same critic adds that the poems in question "comprehend passages of the worst taste, not merely in rhetoric but in spirit, to be found in the whole range of English poetry."[2]

Crashaw's taste is not merely bad, however. At times, it is also quite mean. A particularly harrowing example is the notorious epigram entitled "Luke 11. Blessed be the paps which Thou hast sucked." It reads:

> Suppose he had been Tabled at thy Teates,
>   Thy hunger feels not what he eats:
> Hee'l have his Teat e're long (a bloody one)
>   The Mother then must suck the Son.

Reprehensible as theology and intolerable as poetry, the lines astonish by Crashaw's evident insensitivity to their odious implications. Yet it may be that, here as elsewhere, the usual canons of poetry do not obtain. If, as I am prepared to argue, Crashaw's ultimate purpose was far more ambitious than we have credited, we may discern that behind the frequent lapses in taste hovers an earnest endeavor to reform poetry in emulation of his *miglior fabbro,* Herbert. An understanding of the nature of that endeavor will not necessarily promote Crashaw to the level of Herbert; but it should provide a context within which the enthusiasm of a limited poet can be appreciated, and perhaps even be sanctioned.

Crashaw's enthusiasm, deeply engraven on all his poems, should not be confused with the torrent of mere feeling so often denounced during the Renaissance. Its peculiar quality may best be gathered comparatively, through the versions of St. Thomas Aquinas' hymn "Adoro te" made on the one hand by Crashaw, and on the other by a later Catholic poet,

Hopkins. The version by Hopkins evinces even in part the presence of his powerful intellect actively imposing a decisively ordered rhythm:

> Bring the tender tale of the Pelican;
> Bathe me, Jesu Lord, in what thy bosom ran—
> Blood that but one drop of has the world to win
> All the world forgiveness of its world of sin.
> ("S. Thomae Aquinatis Rhythmus ad
> SS. Sacramentum," ll. 21–24)

Crashaw rendered the same lines thus:

>   O soft self-wounding Pelican!
> Whose brest weepes Balm for wounded man.
> Ah this way bend thy benign floud
> To'a bleeding Heart that gaspes for blood.
> That blood, whose least drops soveraign be
> To wash my worlds of sins from me.
> Come love! Come LORD! . . .
> ("The Hymn of Sainte Thomas in Adoration of
> the Blessed Sacrament" [1652], ll. 45ff.)

and so on. But the pattern is much the same if we mark the way that Psalm 23 was versified by Crashaw and, before him, by Herbert. The opening lines of the psalm in the King James version are familiar enough:

> The Lord is my shepherd; I shall not want.
> He maketh me to lie down in green pastures:
> He leadeth me beside the still waters . . . .

Herbert doubled the number of words but with an unerring sense of decorous economy retained the argument of the original while suggesting the eucharistic implications ever-present in his poetry:

> The God of love my shepherd is,
>   And he that doth me feed:
> While he is mine, and I am his,
>   What can I want or need?
>
> He leads me to the tender grasse,
>   Where I both feed and rest;
> Then to the streams that gently passe:
>   In both I have the best.

Crashaw's version defines the nature of his winging enthusiasm:

> Happy me! ô happy sheepe!
> Whom my God vouchsafes to keepe
> Even my God, even he it is,
> That points me to these wayes of blisse;
> On whose pastures cheerefull spring,
> All the yeare doth sit and sing,
> And rejoycing smiles to see
> Their greene backs were his liverie:
> Pleasure sings my soule to rest,
> Plenty weares me at her brest,
> Whose sweet temper teaches me
> Nor wanton, nor in want to be.

Crashaw's adaptation of Psalm 23 is numbered among his earliest productions; and while his version of the "Adoro te" is a much later effort, it is apparent that the chromatic differences between the two poems are minimal. We may in other words accept that his poetry is in its totality homogeneous—"homogeneous to an extraordinary degree"[3]—in that his development as a poet advanced rather by a process of exclusion than by any notable effort to embark in novel directions. This process involved especially the conscious renunciation of a variety of metrical forms, for instance the qualified tetrameters of his version of Psalm 23 or, earlier still, the couplets he had used with considerable promise in his three youthful poems on the Gunpowder Plot. We need not exaggerate our sense of deprivation over the abandoned metrical forms, since their pursuit might have led Crashaw to multiply lines such as the two he composed in an uncertain elegiac strain on William Herrys:

> The rush of Death's unruly wave,
> Swept him off into his Grave.
>
> ("His Epitaph," ll. 47–48)

The achievement here is not unlike to that memorable epitaph on Queen Victoria:

> Dust to dust,
> Ashes to ashes,
> Into her grave,
> The old Queen dashes.

Yet Crashaw's renunciation of several tried forms is significant all the same, indicative as it is of his ambition from the outset to develop the mode of articulation which was to inform his more substantive poems. This mode was to center on a particular tone dependent upon a particular sentence structure and a particular vocabulary. The sentence structure is displayed in his version of Psalm 23 where the restraining rhyme scheme is transcended in order to permit the argument to flow unimpeded, partly as Milton's verse paragraphs do, but also somewhat after the fashion of free verse. The vocabulary, on the other hand, appears increasingly to animate the very rhymes which the sentence structures seem to nullify. As Crashaw's total output demonstrates and his successive revisions confirm, he remained fully conscious of the patterns created by rhyme.[4] His given predilections are to be observed in one of his earliest poems, "Upon the Kings Coronation," which, probably written as early as 1626 in honor of Charles I when Crashaw was but fourteen years old, anticipates the subsequent regard for certain words and phrases in particular, among them the "heart burning in love" and especially the "radiant darts" (ll. 35, 37). Transferred in time from the secular domain to the sacred, these words and phrases engendered reiterated rhymes such as heart/dart, and eventually blood/flood, breath/death, and breast/rest or breast/nest.[5] The effect is inescapable, witness the cluster of sounds generated in a passage which among other things constitutes the most distinct echo of Herbert anywhere in Crashaw's poetry. The passage occurs in the second of the two poems addressed to Mrs. M.R., and involves the promise that God's "heavnly art"

>   might tosse you
>   And strike your troubled heart
> Home to himself; to hide it in his breast
>   The bright ambrosiall nest,
> Of love, of life, and everlasting rest.
>   ("To the Same Party Councel concerning
>   her Choice," ll. 45–52)

We may note in passing that Crashaw does not share Herbert's interest in revealing significant implications in rhymed words. Even where we obtain telling rhymes such as lust/dust or desire/fire, and especially the recurring dove/love, the juxtaposition is in each case probably accidental. Words in Crashaw, intentionally reiterated so as to become familiar, are signposts en route to that polyphonic lyricism which is his most estimable contribution to English poetry.

The route followed is best discerned in the collection of sacred epigrams in Latin published in 1634.[6] Said to be "the best Latin epigrams written by an Englishman,"[7] they are beyond competition largely because the Latin epigram never flourished in England as it did on the Continent. Crashaw's efforts are in fact mostly exercises laboriously bent after a predetermined effect; and so far one would not have wished them to be more numerous than they are. But they alert us to preoccupations which thereafter were to loom very large indeed, notably the impelling concern with the physical as in Mary's "love-lost heart" hungrily longing for her son's "hungry kisses" (in the extended English version of "Luc. 2. Quærit Jesum suum beata Virgo"); the fascination with the paradoxical as in the proposition that Christ's burden presses one down to the highest heavens (in "Matth. 11. Onus meum leve est"); and especially the sustained interest in the impact of theological issues at the noteworthy expense of the theology involved. But the epigrams also alert us to the unfolding "process of exclusion" noted earlier. The numerous classical allusions, for one, were in time mercilessly reduced. Moreover, the metrical variety of the English adaptations of the Latin epigrams highlights a deliberate series of experiments with diverse metrical forms later abandoned altogether or made subordinate to the desired effect. No less obviously, the economy of utterance in nearly all the Latin epigrams, and in several of the English, was consciously forfeited for the sake of the freely flowing verse. The Latin poems are in this respect best represented by the brilliantly compressed epigram on the cure of the centurion's son:

> Quàm tacitis inopina salus illabitur alis!
>   Alis, quas illi vox tua, Christe, dedit.
>
> Quàm longas vox ista manus habet! hæc medicina
>   *Absens, & præsens* hæc madicina fuit.[8]

The most succinct epigram in English, on the other hand, reads:

> *Upon the Sepulchre of our Lord.*
> Here, where our Lord once laid his Head,
>   Now the Grave lies buried.

The same spirit informs the motto prefixed to his first collection of poems, the *Steps to the Temple:*

> Live Jesus, Live, and let it bee
> My life to dye, for love of thee.[9]

Crashaw's journey from the restrained utterances of his youth to the rapturous rhythms of his maturity may be measured in terms of two early secular poems in particular. The one is in Latin, the engagingly sparse "Pulchra non diuturna"; the other is in English, the carefully wrought "Upon the death of a freind":

Hee's dead: Oh what harsh musicks there
Unto a choyce, and curious eare!
Wee must that Discord surely call,
Since sighs doe rise, and teares doe fall.
Teares fall too low, sighes rise too high,
How then can there be Harmony?
But who is he? him may wee know,
That jarres, and spoiles sweet consort soe?
O Death, 'tis thou: you false time keepe,
And stretch'st thy dismall voice too deepe.
Long time to Quavering age you give,
But to Large youth short time to live.
You take upon you too much,
In striking where you should not touch.
How out of tune the world now lies,
Since youth must fall, when it should rise!
Gone be all Consort, since alone
He, that once bore the best part, 's gone.
Whose whole life Musick was; wherein
Each vertue for a part came in.
And though that Musick of his life be still
The Musick of his name yett soundeth shrill.

Not all of Crashaw's early poems are opposed to his later mode, however. Some of his epigrams already attain that mode by displaying his characteristically spiralling lyricism:

O Frontis, lateris, manuúmque pedúmque cruores!
    O quæ purpureo flumina fonte patent![10]

I quote from the epigram "In vulnera Dei pendentis," where the singular voice continues in like fashion for an additional seven couplets. Freely rendered into English by Crashaw, the result was not one version but two, alike beginning with the familiar stanza:

Jesu, no more, it is but full tide
    From thy hands and from thy feet,
From thy head, and from thy side,
    All thy *Purple Rivers* meet.
            ("On the bleeding wounds of our crucified Lord"
            [1646] and "Upon the bleeding crucifix" [1648, 1652])

The nine stanzas which follow in the one version, and the eight which follow in the other, leap from hyperbole to hyperbole with mounting enthusiasm until the pointedly restrained couplet at the end stills the turbulent emotions even as it justifies the momentary explosiveness:

> Nere was't thou in a sence so sadly true,
> The well of living Waters, Lord, till now.

We are not far removed from a proper understanding of what I described as Crashaw's polyphonic lyricism. But as his epigrams are only prefatory to the subsequent performances, it is necessary to consider his major poems in greater detail before venturing to be absolute about Crashaw and the love he experienced so passionately.

II. "Love's delicious Fire"

Crashaw's major poems are contained in three collections: *Steps to the Temple. Sacred Poems with other Delights of the Muses*, published in 1646; the amended edition of the same, issued two years later; and *Carmen Deo Nostro* ("Hymn to our God"), published posthumously in Paris in 1652. Sometime before any of these collections appeared, but certainly not in advance of 1643, Crashaw was converted to Roman Catholicism. His brief life thereafter unfolded all too expeditiously. Ejected from his fellowship at Peterhouse, Cambridge, by the victorious parliamentary army (1644), he departed initially for Leyden and later for Paris (1645), secured through the intercession of Queen Henrietta Maria an appointment with Cardinal Palotta in Rome (1646), and died a month or so after he moved to Loretto to serve in a minor post at the Cathedral of the Santa Casa (1649).[11]

We expect Crashaw's conversion to have been an event of crucial importance, yet it was the most inevitable decision he ever made. A Catholic in spirit long before he abandoned Protestantism, he exposed his innate inclinations not only in the devotional burden of his epigrams—published, as we have seen, in 1634—but in his activities at Peterhouse. It is of course commonplace knowledge that Peterhouse was at the time the center of high-church Anglicanism, committed to opulent traditionalism with an enthusiasm equal to that which Emmanuel College manifested in the opposite direction. The most obvious representative of the commitments of Peterhouse was the new chapel which, consecrated the year Crashaw published his epigrams, proclaimed in its ornate decoration and prodigal ritual loyalties no less congenial to the young poet than utterly pernicious to Emmanuel's zealous reformers. A parliamentary committee appointed in 1641 to investigate the situation reported a number of serious "antichristian" practices (see p. 314). Crashaw was singled out for rebuke:

His practises in little S^ت Maryes where he is Curat are superstitious. On every sunday & on many holy dayes he hath a Communion . . . what this Implyes those know who are not ignorant of the popish doctrine of private masses. The Church plate he hath exchanged for a covered bowle made after his owne devising, on the cup is the full portrature of Christ wth these words, This is my blood indeede. Soe likewise on the lipp of ye Cover are these words, This is my body indeed, on the top of ye Cover is a Crosse. Before he officiates at ye Communion he washeth his hands in ye vestry where is a table set Altarwise towards the East. . . . All the remainder of wyne after he hath made his low incurvation he drinks off & picks vp the crummes wch remaine of the bread. . . .[12]

Indulgence in these practices may not have been "superstitious" but was certainly "popish" in spirit and not infrequently in fact.

Crashaw's decision to embrace the Catholic Church was not determined either by the luxuriance of Catholic ritual or the devotional nature of Catholic poetry, each of which could also be found within the circumference of high-church Anglicanism. Crashaw was attracted to the Catholic Church, I am inclined to hold, especially because he responded to the confluence within its tradition of normally exclusive states such as the mystical and the rational. Our credulity is taxed, I know, by the mere possibility that Crashaw, inclined toward the mystical as he was, might have been no less committed to the rational. After all, where other poets think, Crashaw appears primarily to acclaim, to venerate, to adore; and where they are temperate, he abounds, he revels, he soars. But two considerations press themselves upon us here. One emerges from the nature of the man himself, whose well-attested interests include expert knowledge of the sacred and secular literature not only of English but of Hebrew, Greek, Latin, French, Italian, and Spanish; and we will presently note how he placed one of these traditions—the Greek—at the service of his poetry and his faith. The other consideration emerges from the nature of Catholic mysticism, which ascends beyond the literal in terms of the literal, and wings above the physical by means of the physical. The experiences of St. Teresa of Avila are here particularly representative in the matter-of-fact way she relates visions we are invited to accept as "natural" occurrences (see pp. 303–4). Crashaw's three attempts to versify those experiences[13] are not very highly regarded; and indeed, save for the lyrical lines added to "The Flaming Heart" in *Carmen Deo Nostro* (ll. 85ff.), none of the poems emit the fire they intimate. Yet his intention is unmistakable all the same, in that the three poems evolve from the statement at the outset of the first poem ("Love, thou art Absolute sole lord / OF LIFE and DEATH") to the ensuing conversational tone in order to assert the "natural" dimension of the events depicted. All appearances to the contrary, moreover, the three poems confirm that Crashaw did not soar with Icarian abandon. Earnestly seeking to correlate form and content, he strove to align the individual word within the given vision, ever intent after an unremitting lyricism in spite (and often because) of the extreme reaches of the sonic patterns created.

Thus defined, Crashaw's achievement in his greater hymns and a handful of other odes may still not persuade since he appears solely to "sing / And be All Wing" ("To the Name of Jesus," ll. 15–16). Yet he sings, and is all wing, within that Catholic tradition which as already indicated conflates states customarily regarded as mutually exclusive. An impressive instance of such conflation is afforded by the refusal to establish sharp lines of demarcation between the sacred love of *agape* and the secular love of *eros*. The refusal is characteristic of the Christian tradition at large, but has most often been accommodated within Catholic theology and Catholic worship. True, Crashaw behaves at times as if the sublunar world is nought else but "the lower sphear / Of froth and bubbles," and man but a "Hyperbolized NOTHING!"[14] The bleak assessment impels us to question whether Crashaw's feet ever touched our planet; and so far we could be tempted to conclude with T. S. Eliot that he is "deficient in humanity":

> We feel at times that his passion for heavenly objects is imperfect because it is partly a substitute for human passion. It is not impure, but it is imperfect.[15]

The dichotomy posited by Eliot is not warranted by Crashaw's poetry at large, however. *Eros,* in particular, was not beyond the range of his committed fervor. Strictly secular poems abound among his early productions—"Loves Horoscope," "Epithalamion," and "Wishes to his (supposed) Mistresse" are among the most successfully articulated efforts—even as his translation of Moschus' paean to Eros attests to a disposition not altogether impersonal:

>   ô what place,
> What farthest nooke of lowest Hell
> Feeles not the strength, the reaching spell
> Of his small hand? Yet not so small
> As 'tis powerfull therewithall.
> Though bare his skin, his mind hee covers,
> And like a saucy Bird he hovers
> With wanton wing, now here, now there,
> 'Bout men and women, nor will spare

Till at length he perching rest,
In the closet of their brest.
> ("Out of the Greeke *Cupid's* Cryer," ll. 34–44)

Crashaw was disinclined to suspend *eros* in favor of *agape* (cf. p. 100). Once his reading and his personal experience indicated that *eros* has much the same cosmic impact as *agape*, he determined to resort to a vocabulary appropriate to both equally, witness the elevation of the concluding rhyme here into one of the most recurrent in his sacred poetry too. However much expanded in time, Crashaw's vocabulary remained palpably physical in a concerted attempt to demonstrate that the thrust of divine love is *agape* manifested through *eros*. The ever-present burning sensation of "love's delicious Fire," the sheer intoxication of the "pure inebriating pleasures," the erotic surrender to "love's souldiers"[16]—and, not least, the meaningfully ambiguous "death"—are so many testimonies that Grace and nature constitute a single interpenetrating order. One poem in particular, gathering within its confines terms we have noted in a variety of different contexts, exhibits Crashaw's bold application of the language commonly reserved for *eros* to the case of the God-man. The subject is the familiar one of the wounds of the Christ:

> Come, brave soldjers, come, & see
> Mighty love's Artillery.
> This was his conquering dart; & loe
> There shines his quiver, there his bow
> These the passive weapons are,
> That made great Love a man of warre.
> The quiver, that he bore, did bide
> Soe neare, it prov'd his very side.
> In it there sate but one sole dart;
> A peircing one his peirced heart.
> His weapons were nor steele, nor brasse:
> The weapon, that he wore, he was.
> > ("In cicatrices Domini Jesu" [MS.]; cf. "Luc. 24.
> > In cicatrices Domini adhunc superstites" [1634])

Crashaw understood much more literally a later visionary's claim that eternity is in love with the productions of time.

The proliferation of mutually exclusive states—*agape* and *eros*, Grace and nature, eternity and time—centered for Crashaw on the one theological dogma which is also a historical reality, the Incarnation. Every way as crucial to his poetry as the Eucharist is to Herbert's, the Incarnation is insistently celebrated by Crashaw precisely because it is the ultimate paradox:

> Æternity shutt in a span.
> Sommer in Winter. Day in Night.
> Heaven in earth, & GOD in MAN.
> ("In the Holy Nativity," ll. 80–82)

Exploding outwardly from this point, Crashaw repeatedly joys over the "sweet sad mirth" ("To the Name of Jesus," l. 62) generated by the prospect of the sacrifice on the Cross:

> O sad, sweet TREE!
> Wofull & joyfull we
> Both weep & sing in shade of thee.
> ("Office of the Holy Cross": Evensong)

"The Weeper" endorses a parallel outlook:

> O sweet Contest; of woes
> With loves, of teares with smiles disputing!
> O fair, & Freindly Foes,
> Each other kissing & confuting!
> While rain & sunshine, Cheekes & Eyes
> Close in kind contrarietyes.
> ("The Weeper" [1652], st. 16)

The same poem attributes the "contrarictyes" to the divine "wit of love" (st. 15), just as the hymn to St. Teresa asserts that "Love's noble history" is dictated by the "witt" of God (ll. 155–57). The claims, not casually voiced, are tantamount to a theory of poetry which eventually appeals to the precedent of Herbert.

III. "Love is eloquence"

Herbert was essential to Crashaw. Their links are declared both in the title of Crashaw's *Steps to the Temple* and in the claim of its preface that Crashaw is "*Herbert's* second, but equall, who hath retriv'd Poetry of late, and return'd it up to its Primitive use; Let it bound back to heaven gates, whence it came." Some twenty years later David Lloyd confirmed that Crashaw while at Peterhouse was "esteemed the other *Herbert* of our Church, for making Poetry, as Divine in its object, as in its Original."[17]

Yet it were a mistake to speak dogmatically of the affinities between the two poets. Thematically, after all, Crashaw depended on Herbert less than often, while poetically he emulated his predecessor on very rare occasions, sometimes by adapting a Herbertian phrase or short line[18] and once by aspiring after Herbert's simplicity of utterance in "Charitas Nimia." Crashaw's primary debt to Herbert may be said to reside in his respect for Herbert's pioneering efforts to reform English poetry by dedicating it to the service of God. Thus in emulation of Herbert's habitual "sacred parody" of secular poetry, Crashaw borrowed the licentious language of a poem by Thomas Carew and transferred it to the argument of the ode "On a prayer booke sent to Mrs. M.R."[19]—itself reminiscent in some instances of Herbert's language, not least the language of "Prayer I." The rationale of such occasions was explored by Crashaw in a manner intended to remind us of Herbert. Just as Herbert inquired in "Jordan I,"

> Who sayes that fictions onely and false hair
> Become a verse? Is there in truth no beautie?

so Crashaw demands in one of his epigrams,

> Hath onely Anger an Omnipotence
>   In Eloquence?
> Within the lips of Love and Joy doth Dwell
>   No miracle?
>   ("Upon the Asse that bore our Saviour," ll. 1–4)

Another poem provides the answer all too categorically—"love is eloquence" ("An Apologie for the fore-going Hymne [on St. Teresa]," l. 8)—while the great hymn "To the Name of Jesus" defines, with at least one echo of Herbert's language, the ambition behind Crashaw's poetry:

> O you, my Soul's most certain Wings,
> Complaining Pipes, & prattling Strings,
>   Bring All the store
> Of SWEETS you have; And murmur that you have no more.
>   Come, nere to part,
>   NATURE & ART!
> . . . .
>   Powres of my Soul, be Proud!
>   And speake lowd
> To All the dear-bought Nations This Redeeming Name,
> And in the wealth of one Rich WORD proclaim
> New Similes to Nature.
>   (ll. 64–69, 92–96)

The "New Similes" include a phrase we have encountered before, now recast within a definitive framework: "the witt of love o'reflowd the Bounds / Of WRATH" (ll. 223-24).

Crashaw's discriminating response to Herbert parallels his response to some of his other predecessors, notably Spenser and Jonson. Spenser's evocative language notwithstanding, Crashaw forswore it once efforts such as the elegy on James Stanenough proved abortive. The resolution was made possible by the concurrent pressure exerted by Jonson, whose distinctive rhythms pervade so many of Crashaw's early poems inclusive of his exquisite version of the fifth song of Catullus (quoted on p. 78). At their best, the diverse voices of Spenser and Jonson were merged by Crashaw in another early poem, the one beginning "Though now 'tis neither May nor June." In the event, at any rate, Spenserian language and Jonsonian form were further qualified for Crashaw by the practice of still other poets, among them Southwell, Marino, and the neo-Latin epigrammatists.

Much has been said of the influence of these poets on Crashaw, and I do not propose here to rehearse the esoteric evidence.[20] The influence of the epigrammatists has in any case been much exaggerated since Crashaw normally adapted their poems only to reduce them, except that in his engaging "Musicks Duell"—based on a largely neolithic poem by the Jesuit Famianus Strada—the process was inverted. The influence of Marino may seem an altogether different matter since his "Sospetto d'Herode" ("The Suspicion of Herod"), the first of the four books comprising his sacred epic *La Strage degli Innocenti* ("The Slaughter of the Innocents," 1610), was translated by Crashaw with creditable bravura. Yet here too we must consider that Marino's epic is by no means his finest performance, that Crashaw pointedly refused to proceed beyond the poem's first book, and that so far as he went he kept his eye nominally on Marino but actually on Spenser. In all, I should have thought, the practice of Southwell was much more material. For unlike *La Strage degli Innocenti,* Southwell's lachrymose *Saint Peters Complaynt* (1595) anticipates on native soil and from a Catholic vantage point the winging ardor so characteristic of Crashaw.[21] The poem's opening line, threatening to "Launch forth my Soule into a maine of teares," adequately suggests the ensuing inundation. But Crashaw would have been especially interested in the attendant hyperboles, for example the abrupt transformation of the Christ's eyes from "blazing Comets" to

>   Pooles of Hesebon, the bathes of grace,
> Where happy spirits dive in sweet desires:
> Where Saints rejoyce to glasse their glorious face,
> Whose banks make Eccho to the Angels quires;
> An Eccho sweeter in the sole rebound;
> Then Angels musick in the fullest sound.[22]

Southwell's hyperboles could justly be said to anticipate Crashaw's own, much more so than the precedent set by Marino. But Southwell was also important to Crashaw by virtue of his thematic interests, especially as these derived from theology.

IV. "All Things . . . Are Musicall"

Most of Crashaw's poems, and particularly his great hymns, are securely grounded on a number of Catholic traditions, and not infrequently on specific dogmas. "The Weeper," for example, is nominally devoted to Mary Magdalene but actually to the Sacred heart of Jesus.[23] Three of Crashaw's more striking hymns—"On the Assumption," "Sancta Maria Dolorum," and "O Gloriosa Domina"—are concerned with Mariolatry. Four other hymns—"To the Name of Jesus," "In the Holy Nativity," "New Year's Day," and "In the Glorious Epiphanie"—appear to form "a sequence with a remarkable structural and progressive unity of themes" dependent on the Christian view of time by way of the Christ's three advents (past, present, and future).[24] Yet when all is said such poems are rather lyrical meditations on, than substantial expositions of, their given theological patterns. The Incarnation as before noted remains of central importance; but it is an importance vested not so much in that dogma's dogmatism as in its diffusive impact.

Crashaw's approach to theology strains one's ability precisely to measure the contours of his thought. Perhaps the best method at our disposal is the negative one, parallel to "the frugal negative light" of the "rightey'd Areopagite" which informs the splendid hymn on the Epiphany. Like Herbert, Sir Thomas Browne, and the Cambridge Platonists, Crashaw is not inclined to engage in controversial subjects. Also like the Cambridge Platonists, he does not display any pronounced sense of sin; and like Herbert, he is entirely absent-minded about Hell. Uniquely, Crashaw is not ever hounded by the terrors of death, nor is he concerned either with the crushing majesty of God or the awe-inspiring divine wrath—save that in the epigram on "Our Lord in his Circumcision to his Father" the heavy burden of God's wrath imposed on the Christ is protested in a manner quite unthinkable by other poets, notably Milton. In all, Crashaw's thought is essentially Christocentric, not theocentric. Yet omnipresent though the God-man is in Crashaw's poetry, the emphasis falls rather on the Christ's divine nature than on his human, and far less on the implied theological dogma than on its impact on the earth-bound lives of Jesus and his mother and the saints who followed in their footsteps. The consequence is not analysis. It is celebration terminating in lyricism.

The lyricism peculiar to Crashaw was best if unwittingly defined by a fellow Catholic poet, Pope. Obedient to the canons he was to exhibit in his own practice, Pope strained to discern the presence in Crashaw of "something of a neat cast of verse," especially in unexceptional poems like the version of Psalm 23 and the epitaph on Mr. Ashton with their ordered tetrameters, or the version of the "Dies Irae" with its equally ordered quatrains. Crashaw was otherwise deemed to have been careless:

> This author writ fast and set down what came uppermost. A reader may skim off the froth and use the clear underneath, but if he goes too deep will meet with a mouthful of dregs; either the top or bottom of him are good for little, but what he did in his own, middle way is best.

Pope's premises surface last. "To speak of his numbers," he added, "is a little difficult, they are so various and irregular and mostly Pindaric."[25]

Pope's predilections, however gently stated, are clearly to be marked; and once marked, call attention to Crashaw's claim to be not the poet of ordered tetrameters or quatrains as Pope would have it, but "the first English poet whom we honor chiefly as an ode writer."[26] Michael Drayton in the preface to his *Poemes Lyrick and Pastorall* (1606) conveniently reminds us of the meaning of the term "ode" and summarizes its two lines of descent from Pindar and Anacreon. In his words,

> an Ode is knowne to haue been properly a song modulled to the ancient harp, and neither too short breathed as hasting to the end, nor composed of longest verses as vnfitte for the suddaine turnes and lofty tricks with which *Apollo* vsed to menage it: They are (as the learned say) diuerse, some transcendently lofty and farre more high then the Epick (commonly called the Heroique Poeme) witnesse those of the Inimitable *Pindarus*, consecrated to the glory and renown of such as returned in triumph from *Olimpus, Elis, Isthmus* or the like: Others among the Greekes are amorous soft and made for chambers, as other for Theatres, as were *Anacreon's*.

Crashaw's practice is comprehensible, as Pope realized, mainly in connection with Pindar's "transcendently lofty" odes. Composed for ceremonial occasions like the Olympic and other games enumerated by Drayton, they were consistently impersonal and elevated in tone, marked by their extensive compass, their impressive opening lines, and their "cosmic" imagery. Elaborately constructed, they depended largely on the reiteration of a dance-like pattern of strophe, antistrophe, and epode. In time, the Pindaric ode was understood to be "irregular" despite its regularity, "free" despite its strict internal discipline, and always "lofty."

Crashaw with his expert knowledge of Greek was hardly unaware of the constituent elements of the Pindaric ode. Save for his displacement of its impersonal tone by the devotional nature characteristic of Catholic poetry, he adapted Pindar's practice to the purposes of the Christian faith so brilliantly that he could fairly be said to have christianized the "irregular" ode. Had the achievement been solely in terms of the subject matter, we might not have been impressed. But it was in terms of the very fabric of the Pindaric ode, in that Crashaw welded, especially in his greater hymns, loftiness of themes with a versatile manner commensurate to the emotions aroused. Complaining in an early secular poem because his fancy had not yet found "wings," Crashaw maintained that his aim was a "rapture" of that order which

> starts to Heaven and brings
> *Enthusiasticke* flames, such as can give
> Marrow to my plumpe *Genius,* make it live
> Drest in the glorious madnesse of a Muse,
> Whose feet can walke the milky way, and chuse
> Her starry Throne; whose holy heats can warme
> The Grave, and hold up an exalted arme
> To lift me from my lazy Urne, to climbe
> Upon the stooped shoulders of old Time;
> And trace Eternity—
>
> ("To the Morning," ll. 20–29)

Several of Crashaw's poems exhibit the obstacles that confronted him. Thus the hymn on New Year's Day suggests in its controlled external form and sparse internal argument how severely Crashaw's flight could be checked; the version of the "Dies Irae," how an excessively personal involvement could impoverish the original's somber rhythms; the liturgical "Office of the Holy Cross," how musical lines could if unduly multiplied tax the reader's patience to the utmost; and the hymn on the Nativity, how drastic revisions could yield not an enriched meaning but a different poem.[27] "The Weeper," revised no less drastically, also suggests in its transposed proliferating stanzas "little more than a rosary of epigrams or madrigals clumsily linked together, without progression," to quote a celebrated judgment.[28] By way of contrast, Crashaw's greater hymns—specifically those "To the Name of Jesus," "In the Glorious Epiphanie," "On the Assumption," "Sancta Maria Dolorum," and "O Gloriosa Domina"— assert that he did not rhapsodize indiscriminately. As the tone veers, so does the argument; which is to say that Crashaw's carefully controlled sound patterns, especially the consonantal ones, ratify the given themes as the verse swerves to intimate a variety of emotional states. The resultant polyphonic lyricism was not inappropriate to a poet who held that

> All Things that Are,
> Or, what's the same,
> Are Musicall....
> ("To the Name of Jesus," ll. 56–58)

V. "Love lights the Fire"

Crashaw's reputation and influence appear to have been alike minimal. Immediately, he may have contributed to the fervent tone of *Psyche* (1648), an allegorical poem which his friend Joseph Beaumont extended intolerably to well over thirty thousand lines. Judgments on Crashaw himself have been ventured in terms extreme enough to correspond to his own practice. Hazlitt, for one, described him with contemptuous brevity as "a hectic enthusiast in religion and in poetry, and erroneous in both." At the other end of the spectrum we have the equally uncritical opinion of the writer who in 1657 inquired rhetorically, "What nation can shew more refined witts then those of our Ben, our Shakespeare, our Baumont, our Fletcher, our Dunn, our Randol, our Crashaw, our Cleveland, our Sidney, our Bacon, &c."[29]

It is at the same time possible to speak of Crashaw's influence in another key. Milton, for instance, may have been aware of Crashaw, less in relation to the representation of Hell in Marino's "Sospetto d'Herode" as sometimes claimed, and more in relation to Crashaw's skillful handling of the ode which together with Cowley's subsequent "pindariques" (1656) appear to have affected the "irregular" verse of *Samson Agonistes*.[30] Far more explicitly, Coleridge who in one instance was unfavorably disposed ("Crashaw is far too apt to weary out a Thought"), in another singled out the ode "On a prayer booke sent to Mrs. M.R." for unqualified praise ("I recollect few Poems of equal length so perfect in suo genere, so passionately supported, & closing with so grand a Swell"). Additionally, some twenty lines central to the hymn to St. Teresa (ll. 43–64) were, said Coleridge, "ever present to my mind whilst writing the second part of Christabel; if, indeed, by some subtle process of the mind they did not suggest the first thought of the whole poem."[31]

Crashaw is not a poet for all seasons. But where his technical brilliance is recognized, it may be possible to prize even the angelic wings beating about him. So his friend Cowley commended what we might have expected him to censure. As he wrote in his epitaph on Crashaw, "A *Fever* burns thee, and *Love* lights the *Fire*" (l. 42).

NOTES

Crashaw's poetry is here quoted from *The Complete Poetry of Richard Crashaw*, ed. George W. Williams (Garden City, N.Y., 1970).
1. Ruth C. Wallerstein, *Richard Crashaw* (Madison, 1935, reprint 1962), p. 10.
2. Wallerstein, p. 112.
3. Helen C. White, *The Metaphysical Poets* (1936, reprint New York, 1962), p. 215.
4. As Mary E. Rickey conclusively maintains in *Rhyme and Meaning in Richard Crashaw* (Lexington, Ky., 1961).
5. "Nest" is itself one of Crashaw's favorite words, usually deployed in connection with Jesus ("warm Nest," "Rosy Nest," "baulmy Nest," "Royall Phoenix' nest," etc.)—or, joined to a predictable rhyme: "that full nest / Of loves, thy lord's too liberall brest" ("Vexilla Regis," ll. 7–8). The earliest use of the rhyme breast/nest is in his version of Psalm 23, quoted above.
6. *Epigrammatum sacrorum liber* (Cambridge, 1634). Crashaw provided English adaptations of nearly fifty of these epigrams in *Steps to the Temple* (1646) and translated a number of them into Greek (first published in the 1670 edition of his poems). Some forty of the Latin epigrams were also reprinted, with translations into English, by Clement Barksdale in *Epigrammata sacra* (1682).
7. Austin Warren, *Richard Crashaw: A Study in Baroque Sensibility* (Ann Arbor, Mich., 1939, reprint 1957), p. 89.
8. "Matth. 8:13. Absenti Centurionis filio Dominus absens medetur," trans. Phyllis S. Bowman in the Williams edition, p. 320:
   What unexpected health glides in on silent wings!
   On wings which your voice gave it, Christ.
   What long hands your voice has! This voice
   was the cure, *absent and present* it was the cure.
9. The couplet adapts a statement by St. François de Sales, *Traité de l'amour de Dieu*, XII.13. On the impact of the Salesian spirit, see A. F. Allison, "Crashaw and St. Francis de Sales," *RES* 24 (1948): 295–302, and Marc F. Bertonasco, *Crashaw and the Baroque* (University, Ala., 1971), Chap. 2.
10. "O streams of blood from head, side, hands, and feet! / O what rivers rise from the purple fountain!" (trans. Phyllis S. Bowman in the Williams edition, p. 390).
11. The standard biographical account in L. C. Martin's edition of *The Poems, English, Latin, and Greek, of Richard Crashaw*, 2d ed. (Oxford, 1957), pp. xv–xlii, has been supplemented by P. G. Stanwood, "Crashaw at Rome," *N&Q* 211 (1966): 256–57, and Kenneth J. Larsen, "Some Light on Richard Crashaw's Final years in Rome," *MLR* 66 (1971): 492–96.
12. Allan Pritchard, "Puritan Charges against Crashaw and Beaumont," *TLS*, July 2, 1964, p. 578. The placement of the communion table "Altarwise" was a Laudian practice.
13. "A Hymn to Sainte Teresa," "An Apologie for the fore-going Hymne," and "The Flaming Heart." The first two were initially published in 1646; the third appeared in 1648; and all three were reprinted in 1652 with the addition of the twenty-four lines at the end of "The Flaming Heart."

14. "To the Same Party [Mrs. M.R.] Councel concerning her Choice," ll. 8–9, and "Death's Lecture," l. 11; respectively. Thomas Car, in "The Anagramme" prefixed to *Carmen Deo Nostro*, remarks more crudely of Crashaw that "No care / Had he of earthly trash."
15. "A Note on Richard Crashaw," in his *For Lancelot Andrewes* (London, 1928), p. 125.
16. "A Song: Lord, when the sense," l. 4; "On a Prayer Booke sent to Mrs. M.R.," l. 120; and "A Hymn to Sainte Teresa," l. 95; respectively. On the physical sensation of heat among mystics, cf. the well-attested experiences of St. Philip Neri (d. 1595), in Meriol Trevor, *Apostle of Rome* (London, 1966), chap. 3, "The Divine Fire." On death through "the kiss of the Lord," consult Nicolas J. Perella, *The Kiss Sacred and Profane* (Berkeley, 1969), pp. 69–70.
17. *Memoires of the Lives . . . of those . . . that suffered . . . in our late Intestine Wars* (London, 1668), p. 619. On Herbert's influence on Crashaw, see especially Hamish Swanston, "The Second *Temple*," *Durham University Journal* 55 (1963): 14–22.
18. Cf. phrases such as "the curl'd Waves work and wind" or "has the Year no Spring for you?" (both in the verse letter to the Countess of Denbigh, ll. 38 and 41), and "A nest of new-born sweets," etc. (in "On a Prayer Booke," l. 2). Herbert's short lines are imitated most successfully in the hymn "To the Name of Jesus," all the more because they alternate with Crashaw's habitually lengthy lines to create the latter's polyphonic lyricism.
19. The borrowing from Carew's poem "A Rapture" is noted by A. F. Allison, "Some Influences in Crashaw's Poem 'On a Prayer Booke . . .' " *RES* 23 (1947): 41–42.
20. On the epigrammatists and Marino, see especially Wallerstein, chaps. 3 and 4, and Warren, pp. 119ff. Marino is discussed in depth by James V. Mirollo, *The Poet of the Marvellous* (New York, 1963). Consult also Claes Schaar, *Marino and Crashaw: "Sospetto d'Herode"—A Commentary* (Lund, 1971).
21. *Saint Peters Complaynt* is the English counterpart to another Italian work, Luigi Tansillo's unfinished *Le Lagrime di San Pietro*, 1585 (see Pierre Janelle, *Robert Southwell* [London, 1935], chap. 8, and Mario Praz, *The Flaming Heart* [New York, 1958]). But Southwell's poem is far superior to Tansillo's and, for Crashaw, the only major precedent in English.
22. From the 1595 edition of the poem, p. 17.
23. See Leland Chambers, "In Defense of 'The Weeper,' " *Papers on Language and Literature* 3 (1967): 111–21. A commendable defense of the poem as a poem is by Paul A. Parrish, "Crashaw's Two Weepers," *Concerning Poetry* 10.2 (1977): 47–59.
24. See Albert R. Cirillo, "Crashaw's 'Epiphany Hymn': The Dawn of Christian Time," *SP* 67 (1970): 67–88.
25. Letter to Henry Cromwell, December 17, 1710; in *Literary Criticism of Alexander Pope*, ed. Bertrand A. Goldgar (Lincoln, Nebr., 1965), pp. 35–37.
26. Carol Maddison, *Apollo and the Nine: A History of the Ode* (New York, 1960), pp. 336–61. Cf. Robert Shafer, *The English Ode to 1660* (Princeton, 1918), pp. 145–49.
27. See Kerby Neill, "Structure and Symbol in Crashaw's 'Hymn in the Nativity,' " *PMLA* 63 (1948): 101–13.

28. Praz, *The Flaming Heart*, p. 218.
29. Quoted in Martin's edition, p. xl. Hazlitt's remark is quoted by Austin Warren, "Crashaw's Reputation in the Nineteenth Century," *PMLA* 51 (1936): 769–85; but see further Warren's supplementary studies in *SP* 31 (1934): 385–407, and in his *Crashaw*, chap. 5. Expressly Catholic estimates should be approached with caution, especially if they are like the attempt of R. A. Knox (in his *Literary Distractions* [London, 1958], chap. 4) to commend the "fully integrated" Crashaw at the expense of both Donne ("morbidly preoccupied with sex") and Herbert ("a moderate poet").
30. See Edward Weismiller, "The 'Dry' and 'Rugged' Verse," in *The Lyric and Dramatic Milton*, ed. Joseph H. Summers (New York, 1965), especially pp. 137ff.
31. *Coleridge on the Seventeenth Century*, ed. Roberta F. Brinkley (Durham, N.C., 1955), pp. 613–14.

Sir Thomas Browne: The Strategy of Indirection

> his delights
> Were dolphin-like, they show'd his back above
> The elements they lived in
> —*Antony and Cleopatra*

I. "The Logos on high plays"

The creative mind can be perverse. It introduces exceptions when we labor to study an artist's work *in toto,* and embarrassments when we fabricate schemes to accommodate the given vision. In the case of T. S. Eliot, for example, while we endeavor to align *The Waste Land* with the *Four Quartets,* he confronts us with his performance in that improbable cluster of poems, *Old Possum's Book of Practical Cats.* In the case of Browne, while we strive to unravel the oddities of *Religio Medici* or *The Garden of Cyrus,* he provides us with the ultimate oddity, the short piece entitled *Musæum Clausum, or Bibliotheca Abscondita: containing some remarkable Books, Antiquities, Pictures and Rarities of several kinds, scarce or never seen by any man now living.*[1]

Not many have read the piece; and those who have, behave as if they have not. *Musæum Clausum* is but an inventory of a collection, its three parts devoted to rare books, rare paintings, and rare items "of several sorts." At the outset of the inventory we are informed that the collection is not readily accessible ("I may justly say you have not seen [it] before"); and at the end, that its location is unknown ("He who knows where all this Treasure now is, is a great Apollo. I'm sure I am not He"). In point of fact, the collection is inaccessible, and its location unknown, for one very good reason: it has never existed.

The farcical situation is ill-concealed. True, a number of the items enumerated might have belonged to an actual collection, however odd the description of each ("A *Sub Marine* Herbal, describing the several Vegetables found on the Rocks, Hills, Valleys, Meadows at the bottom of the Sea"). Most of the items, however, are so utterly and absurdly unlikely that it is positively impossible to mistake their burden. It is more probable, indeed, that Browne endeavored not to obscure but actually to underline the inherent absurdity. In this respect, the context he provides for the collection ("There are many Collections of this kind in Europe") argues an effort to call attention to yet another "vulgar error" of his time, the indiscriminate accumulation of "rarities" by scientists who should have displayed not so much virtuosity as judgment. One of several such collections in England was gathered by the Tradescants, father and son, and exhibited at the Ashmolean Museum in Oxford; another was detailed by Nehemiah Grew, F.R.S., in *Musæum Regalis Societatis: Or a Catalogue of Description of the Natural and Artificial Rarities belonging to the Royal Society and preserved at Gresham Colledge* (1681), and contained, side by side with eminently respectable items, objects that ranged from the tears of a stag to an unspecified stone "anomalously shaped" and the like.[2] Browne's inventory parallels such standard collections by citing *inter alia* "A Ring found in a Fishes Belly taken about Gorro," its potential utility promptly undercut by the added supposition that it is "conceived to be the same wherewith the Duke of Venice had wedded the Sea." The evident restraint here is in other instances so delivered as to intimate a sense of veritably black humor, especially when the given item is visualized. Thus of several paintings mentioned by Browne, one is "of Tamerlane ascending his Horse from the Neck of Bajazet"; another, "of Œdipus when he first came to know that he had killed his Father, and married his own Mother"; and a third—the most deliciously gruesome of all—"of Thyestes when he was told at the Table that he had eaten a piece of his own Son"!

The humorous dimension of *Musæum Clausum* is inescapable; but so is the serious one. As much can certainly be said of a parallel compilation in England, Donne's *Catalogus Librorum Aulicorum incomparabilium et non vendibilium* (ca. 1603–11), which ascribes thirty-four imaginary books to real authors.[3] Elaborate jokes of this order, in fact, were rather widely disseminated, their format—the inventory as inventory—determined largely by the example of Rabelais. Accordingly, just as Donne's ambition was to satirize the extravagant labors of some of his predecessors and contemporaries, and Browne's was to parody the indiscriminate collection of "rarities" by scientists in the seventeenth century, the ambition of Rabelais had been to lampoon the equally indiscriminate books written by authorities in his time. In listing the contents of the Library of St. Victor where Pantagruel was to expand his educational horizons (Bk. II, Chap. VII), Rabelais augmented the credible volumes by adding others, whether on jurisprudence ("The Flimflams of the Law"), pharmacy ("The Bumsquibcracker of Apothecaries"), or social activities ("The Trictrac of the Knocking Friars").[4] Still another title is mentioned by Browne himself, in the course of his castigation within *Religio Medici* of that

> bundle of curiosities, not onely in Philosophy but in Divinity, proposed and discussed by men of most supposed abilities, which indeed are not worthy our vacant hours, much lesse our serious study; Pieces onely fit to be placed in *Pantagruels* Library, or bound up with *Tartaretus de modo Cacandi*. (P. 88)

Tartaretus was real enough, an authority of the Sorbonne much given to esoteric elaborations of medieval arcana; but I need hardly insist that the book ascribed to him by Rabelais could scarcely have existed! Its admission by Browne into *Religio Medici* is the closest he ever came to a scatological reference.

Browne's seriousness of purpose, it is clear, is bisected by "a most uncanonical levity" (to borrow the phrase that Emerson applied to Montaigne).[5] The strategy was described best in Coleridge's commendation of "that grave Humour that renders Sir T. B. so delightful to a learned Reader."[6] Placed within a broader context, this "grave Humour" attests to Browne's affiliation with that Greek tradition for which the ideally balanced man is σπουδαιογέλοιος or "grave-merry," his life fully responsive to the Platonic precept that "fun and gravity"—or indeed comedy and tragedy—"are sisters." Peculiarly relevant to Christianity's paradoxical affirmation of the joy that emanates from the tragedy of the Crucifixion, the tradition evolved in time into a *theologia ludens* that posited not only a Church that "plays" (*ludet in pace / omnis Ecclesia*) but also a *Deus ludens:* "the Logos on high plays (παίζει), stirring the whole cosmos back and forth, as he wills, into shapes of every kind," to quote a hymn by St. Gregory of Nazianzus.[7] Such, in very broad terms, is the background to Browne's "grave Humour"; and in mentioning it here at all I mean not to prescribe but to suggest that the three works we are to consider next form part of the inurement of the Renaissance to "art as play,"[8] but part, too, of a more comprehensive *philologia ludens* that derives its orientation from the Logos that plays on high.

And so to that improbable discourse, *Hydriotaphia*.

II. "A vanity almost out of date"

The immediate occasion of *Hydriotaphia* was the discovery in Norfolk of some forty or fifty urns, thought by Browne to have been Roman even as he recognized that some individuals "might somewhat doubt" whether they were not of a later provenance (p. 281). Connected with funerary rites as these "sad and sepulchral Pitchers" were, they incited Browne to examine in detail a prodigious number of obsequial traditions drawn from his considerable experience and polymorphic reading. A treatise devoted largely to funerary habits is likely, I should have thought, to arouse at best expectations of a rebarbative dissertation, at worst suspicions of a rather necrological obsession. Oddly enough, the tone of *Hydriotaphia* is not even remotely lugubrious, nor even—if one dares to use the word in this context—grave. The convergence of the lusory and the solemn is indeed an elemental aspect of Browne's rhetorical tactics, sustaining his argument in providential ways.

The argument unfolds in proportions directly inverse to the occasion of the discovery of the urns. In spite of the work's specific title—"A Discourse of the Sepulchrall Urnes lately found in Norfolk"—Browne focuses on the discovered objects but once, at the outset of chapter II. The treatise otherwise advances in a variety of directions, immediately to consider funerary customs across time and space, but mediately to place them within a distinct moral framework. The pattern is first sounded within range of the opening paragraph, in a sentence that forms part of a larger structural unit, to the effect that "men have been most phantasticall in the singular contrivances of their corporall dissolution" (p. 268). Thus discreetly announced, the pattern is orchestrated thereafter fully. It reaches a resonant pitch at the ingress to the centrally placed chapter III:

> Playstered and whited Sepulchres, were anciently affected in cadaverous, and corruptive Burials; And the rigid Jews were wont to garnish the Sepulchres of the righteous; *Ulysses* in *Hecuba* cared not how meanly he lived, so he might finde a noble Tombe after his death. Great Princes affected great Monuments, And the fair and larger Urnes contained no vulgar ashes, which makes that disparity in those which time discovereth among us. (P. 284)

The pattern peals last in the final pages of *Hydriotaphia,* during that sonorous peroration generally regarded as Browne's ultimate achievement in the modulation of auditory cadences: "Man is a Noble Animal, splended in ashes, and pompous in the grave, solemnizing Nativities and Deaths with equall lustre, nor omitting Ceremonies of bravery, in the infamy of his nature" (p. 313).

Within the unfolding argument, the quotation from chapter III cited above includes *inter alia* two features that invite further comment. The first involves the apparent reappearance of the urns as urns; the other, the casual reference to "time." The urns are indeed the actual "Sepulchrall Urnes lately found in Norfolk"; concurrently, however, they have been transmuted by Browne into symbolic entities that elicit a diversity of fully premeditated responses. The transmutation is evident as early as the opening paragraph of *Hydriotaphia,* where the urns—again in conjunction with "time"—are said to symbolize man's ignorance of the very world he inhabits:

> The treasures of time lie high, in Urnes, Coynes, and Monuments, scarce below the roots of some vegetables. Time hath endlesse rarities, and shows of all varieties; which reveals old things in heaven, makes new discoveries in earth, and even earth it selfe a discovery. That great Antiquity *America* lay buried for a thousand years; and a large part of the earth is still in the Urne unto us. (P. 267)

Other urns attest other attitudes, like the interment of ashes in silver urns (p. 269)—indicative yet again, of course, of man's propensity ever to be "splendid in ashes, and pompous in the grave." Jointly, it is clear, the absurd customs enumerated by Browne argue the absurdity of man. They argue more particularly folly, recurrently if diversely emphasized as "vanity, feeding the winde, and folly" (p. 312), "a vanity almost out of date, and superanuated peece of folly" (p. 308).

As with the urns, so with time: the spiriform pattern woven by Browne depends on such a multiplicity of references to time that they may fairly be said to embrace his main argument. These references, inaugurated in the opening paragraphs of *Hydriotaphia* as we have observed, proliferate most persistently in his fifth and final chapter. Their admonitory role is clear: time resists us, misleads us, defeats us. It resists us where we endeavor to establish the time of the urns, only to discover "nothing of more uncertainty" (p. 279); it misleads us where we hope "to subsist in bones, and be but Pyramidally extant," only to be confronted by "a fallacy in duration" (p. 308); and it defeats us where we entertain great expectations, only to realize that time itself is far from timeless: "The great mutations of the world are acted, or time may be too short for our designes" (p. 309). The ultimate irony is that time becomes most meaningful when it ceases to exist, its mission accomplished precisely when it ushers in that "day" which according to "the decretory term of the world" is to be history's last (p. 313). Not in time but beyond time is time finally comprehensible, in the "infallible perpetuity" espoused by the Christian faith (p. 314). Hence that polyphonic peroration which, quoted earlier but in part, in full display conjoins Browne's variegated sounds inclusive of "folly" and "duration":

> There is nothing strictly immortall, but immortality; whatever hath no beginning may be confident of no end. All others have a dependent being, and within the reach of destruction, which is the peculiar of that necessary essence that cannot destroy it self; And the highest strain of omnipotency to be so powerfully constituted, as not to suffer even from the power of it self. But the sufficiency of Christian Immortality frustrates all earthly glory, and the quality of either state after death, makes a folly of posthumous memory. God who can only [i.e., alone] destroy our souls, and hath assured our resurrection, either of our bodies or names hath directly promised no duration. Wherein there is so much of chance that the boldest Expectants have found unhappy frustration; and to hold long subsistence, seems but a scape in oblivion. But man is a Noble Animal, splendid in ashes, and pompous in the grave, solemnizing Nativities and Deaths with equall lustre, nor omitting Ceremonies of bravery, in the infamy of his nature. (Pp. 312–13)

The solemnity of the argument is beyond dispute. Yet it is a measure of Browne's complexity that the solemnity is pervaded by a playfulness of considerable latitude, its purpose as much to deride the funerary customs he records as to subvert his own prodigal ostentatiousness. We have already noted the oddity of a treatise which, nominally devoted to "Sepulchrall Urnes lately found in Norfolk," attends to those urns but once, and even then all too laconically; and we have noted, too, the unexpectedness of a work of scholarship that marshals countless details concerning funerary rites primarily in order to render them equally absurd. The mode of thought witnessed by these tactics is amply confirmed by the use of a telling phrase or even a word, and often by an abrupt change in the tone, to remind us of Browne's unflagging amusement over man's boundless capacity for folly. To be informed of the cremation of a hero, for instance, disposes us one way; but to be told of his "solemn combustion," quite another (p. 268). Our response is similarly qualified when faced by "the *Ichthyophagi* or fish-eating Nations about Ægypt" (p. 271), especially if we recall—as recall we might—Othello's equally pompous "Anthropophagi, and men whose heads / Do grow beneath their shoulders" (I.iii.144–45). The impact of several other references is measurably more substantial if each is visualized: the corpse of Pyrrhus cremated successfully enough save for his toe, which could not be burnt (p. 291); the Balearians bruising the flesh and bones of their dead in order to crowd them into urns (p. 271); the Hebrew patriarchs insisting that they be buried in Canaan so as to be among the very first to be resurrected (p. 297); or the numerous pagans, Jews, Christians, and Muhammadans who dispatch their remains into the grave sometimes feet first, sometimes head first, and who position each cadaver supine or prone or pendulous or indeed erect (p. 300). As Browne noted drily, "Men have lost their reason in nothing so much as their religion" (p. 299).

The conflation of the serious and the lusory in *Hydriotaphia* is most evident in the relentless roll call of individuals, tribes, nations, and sects that cumulatively testify to the awesome extent of human desipience. Cosmic as it is in its compass, the strategy is reminiscent of the procession of the demonic agents in *Paradise Lost*. However, Browne's most noteworthy effects are achieved after the fashion not so much of Milton as of Erasmus, Rabelais, and Shakespeare. *Hydriotaphia* is like the *Moriae encomium* in that both deploy a serrated irony that with sustained gaiety discloses the reality beneath the appearance. *Hydriotaphia* is at the same time like the Rabelaisian magnum opus in that both attend through playfulness to the regression of credulity into fanaticism. And it is like *King Lear* in that both resort to a purgatorial "comedy" that inverts wisdom to behave as if it were folly in order to expose the turpitude pretending to be rectitude. In short, *Hydriotaphia* enacts the principle sanctioned by the playful Logos on high: "God hath chosen the foolish things of the world to confound the wise" (1 Corinthians 1.27).

III. "A perpetual triumph of fancy"

Hydriotaphia is an entity unto itself that attains its maximal significance beyond itself, in the treatise with which it was jointly published in 1658, *The Garden of Cyrus*. The two works are intimately related in accordance with the principle of "nexus through contrast" claimed to be operative throughout.[9] The principle as a principle is the most meridian of oddities yet, for it aspires to link the mutually exclusive and to connect the strictly incompatible: death and life, mutability and immutability, darkness and light. But it is in the nature of *Hydriotaphia* and *The Garden of Cyrus* to be in terms of their unity dependently independent of one another, and in terms of their strategy exclusively inclusive, incompatibly compatible, and indeed negatively positive. In the face of such tonitruous ingenuity, Browne's reader is likely to be rather concerned, perhaps apprehensive, and possibly even vexed. But in due course concern yields to delight, apprehension to exhilaration, and vexation to a palpable joy.

Delight, exhilaration, and joy are the unmistakable effects of *The Garden of Cyrus*. One must be constantly alert, however, since the tone is likely to change ever so imperceptibly in order to betoken attitudes substantially more ambiguous than the stated ones. The epistle dedicatory to Nicholas Bacon is in this respect characteristic of the entire work:

> You have been so long out of trite learning, that 'tis hard to finde a subject proper for you; and if you have met with a Sheet upon this, we have missed our intention. In this multiplicity of writing, bye and barren Themes are best fitted for invention; Subjects so often discoursed confine the Imagination, and fix our conceptions unto the notions of fore-writers. Beside, such Discourses allow excursions, and venially admit of collaterall truths, though at some distance from their principals. Wherein if we sometimes take wide liberty, we are not single, but erre by great example. (Pp. 319–20)

We note that the passage on the one hand refers pejoratively to the "trite learning" about to be ventilated by Browne and on the other speaks favorably of his "invention"—a term which in the vocabulary of Renaissance rhetoric was pregnant with laudative implications (cf. p. 18). We note also the description of his approach by way of "excursions . . . at some distance from their principals," which we later find are not excursions so much as errant perambulations, nor "at some distance" so much as at distances quite beyond our wildest expectations. We note finally—that is, if we remember to consult Browne's marginal clarification—that the "great example" he invokes as precedent for his own "wide liberty" is Hippocrates, who digressed in one work on tonsillitis, and in another on sexual intercourse. Improving even on such an authority, however, Browne did not provide digressions from his nominal subject: he provided a nominal subject for his digressions.

The stage of *Hydriotaphia* is the world; that of *The Garden of Cyrus* is the universe. Browne's range, appropriately cosmic, draws freely on any number of his manifold interests such as Biblical scholarship, astronomy, zoology, archaeology, history, and literature. But his primary concern is with botany, in keeping both with his nominal subject of gardens and with his ambition to ascend by means of those gardens to the Creator, "that eminent Botanologer" (p. 333). There is certainly no lack of gardens in *The Garden of Cyrus,* ranging as they do from the grove of Abraham through the hanging gardens of Babylon to the gardens variously of Solomon and of Homer's Alcinous. But as gardens have a certain shape, not infrequently rhomboidal, Browne's fecund imagination explodes in search of rhombi throughout the created order. Within his gardens, moreover, Browne discerns further evidence of "the higher Geometry of nature" (pp. 353–54) in the proliferation of figures such as the circle, the ellipse, the cone, the rectangle, the isosceles triangle—and, the most remarkable figure of all, the quincunx.

It would be a gross understatement to propose that the quincunx fascinated Browne. It propelled him, rather, into ecstasy—yet an oddly *controlled* ecstasy that allowed him to delineate nature's geometric disposition after an orderly fashion, advancing eventually to suggestions of its "mystical" import in the last two of his inevitably five chapters. "The greatest mystery of Religion," we are informed, "is expressed by adumbration" (p. 376), and it is by adumbration—the "wide liberty" sanctioned in the epistle dedicatory, the "soft and flexible sense" endorsed in the preface to *Religio Medici* (p. 60)—that the quincunx can be understood best. The fugatious figure is, as it were, the capital ideogram within "the great Volume of nature" (p. 374), tolerant even of that saltatorial excursion into "the Emphaticall decussation, or fundamental figure," that is to say, the first letter of Christ's name in Greek—the letter *chi* (X)—formed whenever the five points said to constitute the basic design of all gardens are intersected (✕), also whenever the Roman numeral five is "doubled at the angle" to produce a like effect (> and < = X), and especially whenever the circle is observed to be but the figure X turned about on its axis (pp. 328, 378). A cardinal lesson in "Christian signality," the decussation is also the cardinal symbol within "the orderly book of nature" (pp. 330, 360).

But the delight, exhilaration, and joy generated by *The Garden of Cyrus* are not the consequences merely of ingenuity. They depend in particular on the "signality" of Browne's creativity in maintaining a fimbriated discourse with boundless zest. It is nevertheless true that while we are transported by the wittily extravagant first and fourth chapters, and by the extravagantly witty second and fifth, we may not be entirely patient with the third chapter, which is both the longest and the most specifically botanical one. If so, we have not fully discerned that Browne's intent in that chapter, like Milton's in the equally underestimated account of creation in Book VII of *Paradise Lost,* was not only to celebrate God's creative prowess but also to enact it through a disclosure of Browne's own talents at "invention." The details so dazzlingly flaunted by Browne do not of themselves attest much more than his prodigal knowledge; but animated imaginatively, they proclaim the fecundity of Providence, and urged creatively, they assert the harmony of the cosmic order. To cite two examples where any would have served as well, first:

> The exiguity and smallnesse of some seeds extending to large productions is one of the magnalities of nature, somewhat illustrating the work of the Creation, and vast production from nothing. The true seeds of Cypresse and Rampions are indistinguishable by old eyes. Of the seeds of Tobacco a thousand make not one grain.... From such undiscernable seminalities arise spontaneous productions. He that would discern the rudimentall streak of a plant, may behold it in the Originall of Duckweed, at the bignesse of a pins point, from convenient water in glasses, wherein a watchfull eye may also discover the puncticular Originals of Periwincles and Gnats. (Pp. 351–52)

And next:

> The *Arbustetum* or Thicket on the head of the Teazell, may be observed in this order: And he that considereth that fabrick so regularly palisadoed, and stemm'd with flowers of the royall colour; in the house of the solitary maggot, may finde the Seraglio of *Solomon,* And contemplating the calicular shafts, and uncous disposure of their extremities, so accommodable unto the office of abstertion, not condemne as wholly improbable the conceit of those who accept it, for the herbe *Borith*. (pp. 344–45)

The two passages define Browne's creative language at the service of his art: the unfamiliar words about to emerge into our understanding, the improbable connections galloping in search of compaction, the underlying nervous rhythm suggestive of the effort, the onward movement expressive of the eventual resolution. More critically still, the solemnity is ingested by the creator's sheer delight in words and their potential concent. So throughout *The Garden of Cyrus* the sounds support the argument in a sustained playfulness that terminates in joy.

Dr. Johnson—not a man easily impressed—was quite enchanted. He aligned *The Garden of Cyrus* with the *Muiopotmos* of Spenser as well as with *The Battle of the Frogs and the Mice* and the *Culex* formerly attributed to Homer and Virgil respectively in that all four demonstrate to what extent "it is a perpetual triumph of fancy to expand a scanty theme, to raise glittering ideas from obscure properties, and to produce to the world an object of wonder to which nature had contributed little."[10] No less appropriately, however, one could apply to Browne's strategies in *The Garden of Cyrus* the claim advanced by Erasmus on behalf of the *Moriae encomium,* that "just as nothing is more trivial than to treat serious matters in a trivial way, so too nothing is more delightful than to treat trifles in such a way that you do not seem to be trifling at all" (see p. 12). The finality of the claim is itself qualified, of course, by the elastic nature of the "trifles" at the heart of the *Moriae encomium.*

As with Erasmus in one respect and with Dr. Johnson in a second, so with the invariably perceptive Coleridge in a third: in Browne, he said, "the Humorist [is] constantly mingling with and flashing across the Philosopher."[11] Such flashing is most often immediate, sometimes prolonged and not infrequently "at some distance from [its] principals." Immediate where the effect depends primarily on Browne's creative language, it is prolonged where the given pattern is articulated incrementally after the fashion of "the Emphaticall decussation" or, even more spectacularly, after the fashion of that spirited discourse in chapter II that ranges through rectangular patterns from bricks and beds and windows to the Macedonian phalanx, the shape of Nineveh, and the Ark of the Covenant—but mercifully *not* the Tables of the Law since Browne was, he tells us, "unwilling to load the shoulders of *Moses* with such massive stones" (p. 342). The flashing is "at some distance" where Browne derives much of his gardenist lore from treatises like Benoît Court's *Horti* (1560) or Giambattista della Porta's *Villa* (1592),[12] which are indeed quite relevant, but also excruciatingly dull. More to the point, Browne's reiterated unwillingness to record any more material than absolutely necessary—an unwillingness invariably beginning with "We shall not call in . . ." or "we shall not insist . . ." or "to omit . . ." (pp. 330, 335, 336, and elsewhere)—is always followed by a detailed list of the items he has vowed to bypass. The most delightful example of this tactic is the entire last chapter, which begins with a ringing declaration of his refusal to indulge in Pythagorean speculations on the number five, yet promptly overtakes every numerologist ambling along:

> To enlarge this contemplation unto all the mysteries and secrets, accommodable unto this number, were inexcusable Pythagorisme, yet cannot omit the ancient conceit of five surnamed the number of justice; as justly dividing between the digits, and hanging in the centre of Nine, described by square numeration, which angularly divided will make the decussated number; and so agreeable unto the Quincunciall Ordination, and rowes divided by Equality, and just *decorum,* in the whole com-plantation; And might be the Originall of that common game among us, wherein. . . .

and so on to the end of *The Garden of Cyrus* (pp. 379ff.). Coleridge, for one, was overjoyed: "Quincunxes in Heaven above," he exclaimed, "Quincunxes in Earth below, & Quincunxes in the water beneath the Earth; Quincunxes in Deity, Quincunxes in the mind of man, Quincunxes in optic nerves, in Roots of Trees, in leaves, in petals, in every thing!"[13] Yet numerologists dare not enlist Browne as an ally since his enthusiasm for "inexcusable Pythagorisme" is, like so much else in *The Garden of Cyrus,* turned upside down. After all, where they favored numbers like three and seven—each diversely regarded as "a most holy and potent number," "a most powerfull number," "an universall & absolute number," "the nombre of fulnes," "the most sacred of Numbers," and the like[14]—Browne focused with an optimum of eccentricity on five; and in "proving" its truth, he disproved both his case and theirs. The approach appears to be nihilistic, and in a sense it is. But in a much more fundamental sense it is mimetic of the Creator's "vast production from nothing" (see p. 169), while in the last analysis it reflects too the fondness of the *Deus ludens* for inversion which proscribes the folly that passes for wisdom and commends the folly that is wisdom.

The penultimate paragraph of *The Garden of Cyrus* translates the "wide liberty" Browne has taken up to that point into a refulgent statement of his major motif: "All things began in order, so shall they end, and so shall they begin again; according to the ordainer of order and the mystical Mathematicks of the City of Heaven." But the final paragraph is much more representative in its relaxation of the erstwhile somber tone into a conspicuously whimsical one:

> Though *Somnus* in *Homer* be sent to rowse up *Agamemnon,* I finde no such effects in these drowsy approaches of sleep. To keep our eyes open longer were but to act our *Antipodes.* The Huntsmen are up in *America,* and they are already past their first sleep in *Persia.*

But who can be drowsie at that hour which freed us from everlasting sleep? or have slumbring thoughts at that time, when sleep it self must end, and as some conjecture all shall awake again? (Pp. 387–88)

Philologia ludens has not often scaled higher.

IV. "The best part of nothing"

To consider *Religio Medici* third and last when it was the very first of Browne's works to be published (1643) might be construed as a tactic pregnant with numerological import or, worse still, as a distant reflection of Browne's own predilection for inversion. But such ambitions, I should insist, would have been far less tolerable had they been far more modest. *Religio Medici* is here placed after *Hydriotaphia* and *The Garden of Cyrus* strictly because it anticipates those symbiotic works in some respects and, just as strictly, because it does not.

It does not anticipate the other two in its carefully designed title page, for example. Frontispieces to Renaissance books were, we know, rarely if ever merely decorative. As they were also frequently wrought under the supervision of the given author—the elaborate title page for Sir Walter Ralegh's *The History of the World* (1614) is an extravagantly eloquent case in point[15]—we could accept that Browne was not altogether averse to the design prefixed to *Religio Medici;* indeed, as that design was the same for both the authorized edition and for the earlier, pirated version, it could even appear that the unauthorized edition was not entirely unauthorized. At any rate, in displaying the hand of God arresting a man's fall into the sea (p. 55), the design invites attention to a pattern iterated within *Religio Medici* with such frequency as to coincide with the axis of Browne's argument. The first reference, fully congruent with God's "cryptick and involved method," is obliquely to a Spanish salute—"bezo las manos": "I kiss the hands"—which is presently transposed from its naturalistic context to suggest with ironic understatement "the meere hand of God" (pp. 81–82). Expansively applied thereafter, the pattern includes references to secondary causes as the "visible hands of God" (p. 84) and to the Primary Cause as "that invisible hand" or "that hand which doth uphold [our] natures" (pp. 102, 152). Moreover, the intervention of the divine through miracles is described as "the extraordinary effect of the hand of God" (p. 95), while a normal disclosure of the divine is said to be simply "the hand of God," more expressly his "hand or providence," and lastly "the finger of God"—or, more adventurously, "the little finger of the Almighty" (pp. 114, 161, 126, 87). In brief, *Religio Medici* is concerned with Providence in general while *Hydriotaphia* and *The Garden of Cyrus* attend to its manifestation through order in particular.

Religio Medici anticipates the other two works in several illuminating ways, each apocalyptic of Browne's evolving thought and artistry. Order, certainly, is already a major preoccupation. But not yet articulated with the ardent commitment to the fecundity of Providence so clearly impressed upon *The Garden of Cyrus,* it is still confined to mere affirmations of hierarchy in the universe as in society (pp. 101, 134), and especially to several invocations of the commonplace parallelism between the macrocosm of the universe and the microcosm of man, for example, "every man is a *Microcosme,* and carries the whole world about him" (p. 152). The exception is that sustained paean to cosmic hierarchy in part II:

> There is a musicke where-ever there is harmony, order of proportion; and thus farre we may maintain the musick of the spheares; for those well ordered motions, and regular paces, though they give no sound unto the eare, yet to the understanding they strike a note most full of harmony. Whatsoever is harmonically composed, delights in harmony; which makes me much distrust the symmetry of those heads which declaime against all Church musicke. For my selfe, not only from my obedience but my particular genius, I doe embrace it; for even that vulgar and Taverne Musicke, which makes one man merry, another mad, strikes in mee a deepe fit of devotion, and a profound contemplation of the first Composer, there is something in it of Divinity more than the eare discovers. It is an Hieroglyphicall and shadowed lesson of the whole world, and Creatures of God, such a melody to the eare, as the whole world well understood, would afford the understanding. In briefe, it is a sensible fit of that Harmony, which intellectually sounds in the eares of God. (Pp. 149–50)

Even more evidently anticipatory of *Hydriotaphia* and *The Garden of Cyrus* is Browne's fully evolved attitude toward time. The "day" that the later treatises proclaim in accordance with "the decretory term of the world" to be the last, already figures prominently in that magniloquent meditation on "the great Jubilee" of the Day of Judgment and the end of the time-bound world:

> This is the day that must make good that great attribute of God, his Justice, that must reconcile those unanswerable doubts that torment the wisest understandings, and reduce those seeming inequalities, and respective distributions in this world, to an equally and recompensive Justice in the next. This is that one day, that shall include

and comprehend all that went before it, wherein as in the last scene, all the Actors must enter to compleate and make up the Catastrophe of this great peece. This is the day whose memory hath onely power to make us honest in the darke, and to bee vertuous without a witnesse. (P. 119)

Even as time advances relentlessly toward timelessness, however, never does it exist in God save in a strictly metaphorical sense, in the manner of that "easie and Platonic description" or "easie Metaphor" commended in *Religio Medici* (p. 70; cf. p. 160). God may indeed be styled the Ancient of Days (Daniel 7.9), yet he "cannot receive the adjunct of antiquity, who was before the world, and shall be after it, yet is not older then it: for in his yeares there is no Climacter, his duration is eternity, and farre more venerable then antiquitie" (pp. 96–97). By the same token, the Biblical claim that in the sight of God a thousand years are only a day (2 Peter 3.8) is hazarded, we are told, rather too "modestly":

> For to speak like a Philosopher, those continued instances of time which flow into a thousand yeares, make not to him one moment; what to us is to come, to his Eternitie is present, his whole duration being but one permanent point without succession, parts, flux, or division. (P. 73)

But time may be annihilated even by the believer whose "memory" of the future permits him to recognize that he died before he was born and that the last trumpet heralding the end of history has already sounded (pp. 73, 132). Impelled by faith, one may nightly close his eyes in security, "content to take [his] leave of the Sunne, and sleepe unto the resurrection" (p. 157).

Religio Medici foreshadows the later treatises in still other respects that, not yet fully regulated by Browne, are conspicuous because of their distance from their later manifestations. Thus the hyperborean prospect of *The Garden of Cyrus* may in *Religio Medici* be scanned solely through the analogy of God to "a skilfull Geometrician" on the one hand, and the commendation of "the mysticall way of *Pythagoras* and the secret Magicke of numbers" on the other (pp. 73, 80), insofar as Browne had not yet mounted an effort to elevate the former into a cosmic principle or to depress the latter into an inversion of its essential truth. Thus, too, the placement in *Hydriotaphia* of men's aspirations after temporal perpetuity merits in *Religio Medici* but a passing reference devoid of the later sonority:

> This conceit and counterfeit subsisting in our progenies seems to mee a meere fallacy, unworthy the desires of a man, that can but

conceive a thought of the next world; who, in a nobler ambition, should desire to live in his substance in Heaven rather than his name and shadow in the earth.

Nor is folly mentioned in *Religio Medici* except within the conventional framework of objurgations whether directed passionately against our prejudices ("folly and madness" [p. 140]), uncharitably against the multitude ("fooles" [p. 134]), or amusingly against sexual intercourse ("an odde and unworthy piece of folly" [p. 149]). One other manifestation of folly is said to be man's frequent indulgence in activities of scant consequence:

> What a Βατραχομυομαχία [*Batrachomyomachia* or *The Battle of the Frogs and the Mice*], and hot skirmish is betwixt *S*. and *I*. in *Lucian?* How doth Grammarians hack and flash for the Genitive case in *Jupiter?* How doe they breake their owne pates to salve that of *Priscian?* (P. 138)

In time, of course, Browne would indulge in a scanty excursion of his own. But in *Religio Medici* the mental disposition that was to create the quincunx is evident only tangentially.

As it is in the nature of a tangent to meet a curved surface, however, so *Religio Medici* touches the later treatises at a specific point, the point of indirection implicit in Browne's espousal of a "soft and flexible sense" (p. 60). Particularly apposite in this respect are the principles of organization upon which *Religio Medici* rests—the "order or œconomy" Browne acknowledges in another context (p. 69)—and the tonal range of seriousness not exclusive of playfulness, and of gravity not devoid of "a most uncanonical levity." The principles of organization are accessible though oblique, and apprehensible though abaxial. The division of *Religio Medici* into two parts, for example, revolves about the three cardinal virtues, with Faith and Hope apportioned to part I and Charity to part II. At the same time, the two parts unfold with an unremitting commitment to the vertical dimension that links man to God, even as the first part advances more specifically along a horizontal line that in coincidence with the Christian view of history extends from the initial act of Creation to the last scene of the Day of Judgment. Correspondences, moreover, are well-nigh numberless, informed throughout by the seminal parallelism between the macrocosm and the microcosm already noted and reinforced persistently by several "easie" metaphors: manuscripts, books, registers, letters, characters, figures, abbreviations, hieroglyphs, and the like. The elaborate structure is intended to uphold unity against plurality and congruence against dissonance. Nominal dichotomies, whether of reason versus faith or of philosophy versus divinity, are only nominal; the actual opposition is rather of truth against its perversion: "the right rule and law of reason" in agreement with divine precepts against "insolent" or "arrogant" reason (p. 127), and "mysterious Philosophy" in alliance with divinity against "the rules of our Philosophy," "common Philosophy," "meere Philosophy" (pp. 107, 123, 101, 120). Browne's emphatic partiality to "mysterious Philosophy"—"such," he adds, "as reduced the very Heathens to Divinity"—accounts also for his seduction by all manner of "*Ænigmaes*, mysteries and riddles" finally dependent on "the mysticall method of *Moses* bred up in the Hieroglyphicall Schooles of the Egyptians," *id est,* those supposed Egyptians who like the legendary Hermes Trismegistus were regarded as "addicted" to "abstruse and mysticall sciences" (pp. 143, 104, 136). The approach was eminently suitable to Browne, temperamentally inclined as he was to favor indirection or—to use the term deployed in both *Religio Medici* and *The Garden of Cyrus* (pp. 71, 376)—"adumbration." It will be observed that Browne's repeated description of himself as "irregular" (pp. 66, 132) describes his method too, which is at once entirely singular to him and yet comfortable to God's prototypically "cryptick and involved method" (see p. 172).

Indirection is also fundamental to Browne's eagerness to inosculate the serious and the playful. The diverse manifestations of his "grave Humour"—to quote Coleridge's apt phrase yet again—are wont in some instances to take the form of an expeditious passage from analogy to analogy, so that the implicit parallel between the creator of *Religio Medici* and the Creator of the world—himself "an excellent Artist," we are reminded (p. 79)—involves also relationships between the book that is *Religio Medici* and the books of nature and of God. In other instances Browne toys so extravagantly that we behold him as his friends did, "but in a cloud" (p. 140). Thus a celebrated metaphor in Isaiah (40.6) occasions a discourse that confirms Browne's pursuit of unity in a characteristically paradoxical way:

> *All fleshe is grasse,* is not onely metaphorically, but literally true, for all those creatures we behold, are but the hearbs of the field, digested into flesh in them, or more remotely carnified in our selves. Nay further, we are what we all abhorre, *Anthropophagi* and Cannibals, devourers not onely of men, but of our selves; and that not in an allegory, but a positive truth; for all this masse of flesh which wee behold, came in at our mouths: this frame we looke upon, hath beene upon our trenchers; In briefe, we have devoured our selves. (P. 107)

Even more arresting is the serious yet playful pirouette danced about the doctrine of creation *ex nihilo* or that "vast production from nothing" (see p. 169). First, the angels are wittily described as "the best part of nothing"

(p. 103); and two pages later Browne returns to elaborate on a related oddity: "God being all things is contrary unto nothing out of which were made all things, and so nothing became something, and *Omneity* informed *Nullity* into an essence." Coleridge's response was, for once, rather scalene: "An excellent *Burlesque* on some parts of the Schoolmen, tho' I fear an unintentional one."[16] It is more likely, however, that Browne aspired not so much after any outward-looking burlesque as after an inwardly directed gaiety over the surprising ways of God. Only four lines later, after all, God is said to have "played the sensible operator" in creating man (p. 105), which in turn echoes the assertion a few pages earlier that the Divine Spirit "playes within us" (p. 99). The implications of "playing" are of course suggestive of doing or acting no less than of toying and sporting, and certainly of performing on the stage as well as on a musical instrument.

But when all is said indirection as a strategy is most impressively operative in the ever seasonable dimension of man's fallen state. True, *Religio Medici* appears on the face of it to be concerned with the Fall only spasmodically if not indeed almost accidentally. Such absentmindedness is peculiar rather to Browne's narrator than to Browne, however. Here more than anywhere else in *Religio Medici* the distance between the two is measurably spacious; for if Browne's narrator eschews the Fall with an almost religious zeal, Browne himself presses hard to bring its reality within range of our consciousness. The transition from the first part of *Religio Medici* to the second should in this respect be noted because it is a transition from an agreeably irenic voice to a frequently prejudiced one. In part I, Browne's narrator is of the commendable opinion that "It is the method of charity to suffer without reaction" (p. 65); but in part II—the part specifically devoted to Charity—we are confronted by a violent reaction against the multitude ("fooles"), supported by an unwarranted appeal to "canonical Scripture" (p. 134). A fundamental truth uttered subsequently—"all is but what we all condemne, self-love," that is to say, pride (p. 141)—leads to an equally firm declaration that "Pride [is] a vice whose name is comprehended in a Monosyllable, but in its nature not circumscribed with a world" (p. 146). Browne's narrator, obviously unaware that his tintinnabulary generalizations apply as much to himself as they are meant to do to others, hastens proudly to detail his understanding of "no less then six Languages" besides the chorography of several countries, the topography of their cities, the structure of their laws, and so on (p. 147). The ensuing tirade against sexual intercourse ("an odde and unworthy piece of folly") is a manifestation of another form of pride—the pride of prejudice—which is all the more eloquent because of its disclaimer ("I speak not in prejudice"). In like manner, we may wish to recall, the narrator of the *Moriae encomium* had inverted the attitude of Erasmus himself by asserting that "the human race is propagated by the part which is so foolish and funny that it cannot even be mentioned without a snicker."[17]

Browne's irony, like that of Erasmus, is unmistakable; yet it is published with gentle humor and an infinite good will, precisely because Browne was so unlike his narrator in his recognition that the dimensions of pride are indeed "not circumscribed with a world." The strategy of indirection has plainly illumined a vital issue yet again, especially in that its gravity is at once intensified and tempered by a playfulness assertive of a sympathetic response to the oddities of human behavior. To speak parabolically after Browne's own "soft and flexible sense," the discernment by Yeats noted on an earlier occasion (see p. 66) that at the heart of *Lear* as of *Hamlet* lies a "Gaiety transfiguring all that dread" is no more eccentric in itself than it is irrelevant to the vision of Sir Thomas Browne.

"The whole creation," Browne maintained in *Religio Medici*, "is a mystery" (p. 105). The unexceptionable subject is a variation of a theme sounded by St. Paul as by many others, that we now see God "through a glass, darkly." But Browne's idiomorphic formulation of the same premise is quite as solemn as it is witty: "we behold him," he wrote, "but asquint upon reflex or shadow" (pp. 74–75).

Dare one visualize "asquint"?

NOTES

An earlier version of this essay appeared as " 'The Best Part of Nothing': Sir Thomas Browne and the Strategy of Indirection," in *Approaches to Sir Thomas Browne: The Ann Arbor Tercentenary Lectures and Essays*, ed. C. A. Patrides (Columbia: University of Missouri Press, 1982), pp. 31–48. Copyright 1982 by the Curators of the University of Missouri. Reprinted with permission. Unless otherwise noted, Sir Thomas Browne is here quoted from *Sir Thomas Browne: The Major Works*, ed. C. A. Patrides (Harmondsworth, England, 1977).

1. In *The Works*, ed. Sir Geoffrey Keynes (London, 1964), 3:109–19.
2. In Grew's *Catalogue*, pp. 21, 189, etc. For the inventory of the Tradescant collection, see R. T. Gunther, *Early Science in Oxford* (Oxford, 1925), 3:200ff. and 391ff. I am grateful to Robin Robbins for directing me to these materials.
3. Donne, *The Courtier's Library, or Catalogus Librorum Aulicorum*, ed. and trans. Evelyn M. Simpson (London, 1930); first published with the *Poems* of 1650. One of the thirty-four imaginary works, for example, is ascribed to Pico della Mirandola ("The Judaeo-Christian Pythagoras, proving the Numbers 99 and 66 to be identical if you hold the leaf upside down"); another, to the celebrated Elizabethan *magus* John Dee ("On the Navigableness of the Waters above heaven; and whether a ship in the firmament will in the Day of Judgment land there or in our harbours"). The satiric intention is clearly apparent;

it partakes, as Evelyn Simpson rightly observes, of the impulse informing the *Satires* written some ten years earlier.
4. *The Complete Works of . . . Rabelais,* trans. Sir Thomas Urquhart and Peter Motteux (London, 1927), 1:257–83.
5. *Representative Men,* rev. ed. (Boston, 1888), p. 158. It should be pointed out that A. C. Howell has written persuasively on "Sir Thomas Browne as Wit and Humorist" (*SP* 42 [1945]: 564–77), but his exclusive concern with Browne's "peculiar sense of humor" is clearly only one aspect of the total vision examined here.
6. *Coleridge on the Seventeenth Century,* ed. Roberta F. Brinkley (Durham, N.C., 1955), p. 462.
7. The tradition is outlined in a most eloquent survey by Hugo Rahner, S.J., *Man at Play,* trans. Brian Battershaw and Edward Quinn (London, 1965); I have quoted especially from pp. 9, 23, and 51, where full documentation will be found. On the "grave-merry" disposition in classical literature, consult in the first instance Lawrence Giangrande, *The Use of Spoudaiogeloion in Greek and Roman Literature* (The Hague, 1972). It should be emphasized that Rahner's thesis—and by extension my own—is distinctly different from modern theories of "play" inclusive of Johan Huizinga's emphases in *Homo ludens* (English trans., London, 1949). These latter are rather superficially linked with Browne by Anna K. Nardo, "Sir Thomas Browne: *Sub specie ludi,*" *Centennial Review* 21 (1977): 311–20.
8. See Frank J. Warnke, "Art as Play," in his *Versions of Baroque: European Literature in the Seventeenth Century* (New Haven, 1972), chap. 5. Consult also Judith Dundas, "Levity and Grace: The Poetry of Sacred Wit," *The Yearbook of English Studies* 2 (1972): 93–102.
9. See Frank L. Huntley, "Sir Thomas Browne: The Relationship of the *Urn Burial* and *The Garden of Cyrus,*" *SP* 53 (1956): 204–19; revised in his *Sir Thomas Browne: A Biographical and Critical Study* (Ann Arbor, Mich., 1962), chap. 13: reprinted in *Seventeenth-Century Prose,* ed. Stanley Fish (New York, 1971), pp. 424–39. Other Renaissance works, also published jointly in spite of their differences, have been observed to be related too. On Spenser's *Amoretti* and *Epithalamion* (published together in 1595), see Richard Neuse, "The Triumph over Hasty Accidents: A Note on the Symbolic Mode of the *Epithalamion,*" in *Spenser: A Collection of Critical Essays,* ed. Harry Berger, Jr. (Englewood Cliffs, N.J., 1968), pp. 47–62; and on Milton's *Paradise Regained* and *Samson Agonistes* (published together in 1671), see Balachandra Rajan, " 'To which is added Samson Agonistes—'," in *The Prison and the Pinnacle,* ed. Rajan (Toronto, 1973), pp. 82–100.
10. *The Life of Sir Thomas Browne* (1756), in *Sir Thomas Browne: The Major Works,* ed. Patrides, p. 494.
11. *Coleridge on the Seventeenth Century,* p. 448.
12. See Jeremiah S. Finch, "Sir Thomas Browne and the Quincunx," *SP* 37 (1940): 274–82.
13. *Coleridge on the Seventeenth Century,* p. 439.
14. As claimed on behalf of the numbers three and seven by Thomas Tymme, *A Dialogue Philosophicall* (London, 1612), p. 38; Heinrich Cornelius Agrippa, *Three Books of Occult Philosophy,* trans. J. F. (London, 1651), p. 179; Pierre de

la Primaudaye, *The French Academie,* trans. T. B. (London, 1586), p. 563; Heinrich Bullinger, *A Hundred Sermons upon the Apocalips,* trans. John Daws (London, 1561), p. 165; and David Person, *Varieties* (London, 1635), V.10; respectively. On the limits of numerology's endorsement during the Renaissance, see my essay in *Premises and Motifs in Renaissance Thought and Literature* (Princeton, 1982), chap. 4. Consult also William Nelson's review of Fowler's *Spenser and the Numbers of Time* in *Renaissance News* 18 (1965): 52–57; and p. 45 in this volume.

15. Reproduced, and remarked upon, in my edition of *The History of the World* (London, 1971), pp. xv–xvi. But see especially the more comprehensive study by Margery Corbett and Ronald Lightbrown, *The Comely Frontispiece: The Emblematic Title-Page in England, 1550–1660* (London, 1979). On the Browne plate, consult especially Frank Ardolino, "The Saving Hand of God: The Significance of the Emblematic Frontispiece of the *Religio Medici,*" ELN 15 (1977): 19–23.
16. *Coleridge on the Seventeenth Century,* p. 442.
17. *The Praise of Folly,* trans. Clarence H. Miller (New Haven, 1979), p. 18.

Milton: Apocalyptic Configurations

> prophesying with accents terrible
> Of dire combustion and confused events
> New hatch'd to the woeful time
>
> —*Macbeth*

I. "History and Prophecy strangely shake hands"

"Creatures of an inferiour nature," said Donne in 1627, "are possest with the *present: Man* is a *future Creature.*"[1] Donne's immediate reference is to the Christian belief that man journeys along a path that is to terminate beyond the sublunary maze of the phenomenal world, in the world to come. Conscious as man is of the future, however, he tends to inquire into that future habitually and sometimes obsessively. For a committed Christian during the Renaissance, certainly, the focus of such an obsession was the Book of Revelation, its imposing contours studied by major theologians, its numerous complexities examined by formidable mathematicians from Napier to Newton, its arresting visions intoned in the characteristic activity attested by one delighted father: "John repeated the 12th, Eliezer the 10th of Revelation last night in bed, blessed be God."[2]

The Apocalypse was widely commended as indispensable. On the popular level, Arthur Dent averred that "this booke doth not only concerne preachers, and deep divines; but even all the Lords people whatsoever: for it doth minister great comfort and strength of faith to all the people of God."[3] But on a higher level, too, it was proclaimed by no less an authority than King James that "of all the scriptures, the buik of the Revelatioun is maist meit for this our last age."[4] The method of approach was deceptively simple. The "argument" that, inspired by Heinrich Bullinger, was prefixed to the annotated text of the Geneva Bible (1560), urged the faithful to "Read diligently: judge soberly, and call earnestly to God for the true understanding hereof." But "true understanding" was by no means readily forthcoming. The generalization by Thomas Brightman ("the Revelation doth still require necessarily a Revelation")[5] was shared by all commentators, responsible and otherwise. The Apocalypse, after all, is "carried along by Figurative expressions"; it is "involved with mystical allegories, and types"; it is "replenished with great secrets, types, and darke sentences"; it soars—to quote Milton—"to a Prophetick pitch in types, and Allegories."[6] The great commentator Joseph Mede called it a "holy *Labyrinth*"—holy indeed, but a labyrinth all the same.[7] The penetration of its innermost recesses, however, became the ultimate challenge; and George Sandys was not exceptional in his commendation of the prevailing ambition:

> This booke of the Apocalyps ... is by all men confessed to be full of mysteries, and that it is by reason thereof verie darke and obscure, is by manie affirmed: yet I see this hath neither disswaded the mindes, nor discouraged the industries of godly men in all ages from searching to find out the true sence and meaning thereof.[8]

The difficulties stalking all explicators of the Book of Revelation did not prevent their unanimous conclusion that it appertains, after one fashion or another, to "history" past and to "history" future. Mede, for example, was of the opinion that the Apocalypse delineates "a certain bare history of things done," while one of his more discriminating successors, William Hicks, thought it adequate enough to call it "a Book of History of memorable Acts and passages."[9] The intent is clear: the dimension so manifestly concerned with what Hicks termed "Prophetical Representations, and Hyerogliphique Figures"[10] had to be firmly connected to the historical process, not severed from it as a mere "prophecy" of the obscure future. Henry More was later to make the point with admirable clarity. "History and Prophecy," he wrote, "strangely shake hands together in these things."[11]

But the problem persisted stubbornly. In the case of Napier's superior effort to comprehend the Book of Revelation (1593), a series of parallel columns neatly place every episode within an immediately intelligible context "historicallie applyed." Clearly uneasy over the implications, however, Napier was also obliged to warn that many details are "not literallie to be taken, but after a propheticall and figurative maner of speach."[12] The qualification, of course, militates against the recurrent Protestant declaration that the Bible may be interpreted solely after one sense, the literal. As early as the dawn of Protestantism in England, William Tyndale had defined the standard opposition to the four senses traditionally endorsed by Catholicism—the literal, the analogical, the tropological, and the anagogical—by asserting categorically that "ye scripture hath but one sence w^c is the litterall sence. And the literall sence is ye rote & grounde of all...." But even Tyndale was compelled to pause, troubled, before the gates to the Book of Revelation. "The Apocalipse or revelacions of John," he acknowledged, "are allegories whose litterall sence is herde to finde in many places."[13]

The problem was not beyond resolution, however, much though that resolution required the talents rather of a poet than of a theologian. Tyndale provided the hint when he observed in passing that the spirit that is God discourses in words that are spiritual. "His litteral sence," in this respect, "is spiritual." Later, when the polymath Andrew Willet opposed yet again the Catholic claim that there are "divers senses and meanings" to the Bible, he voiced the fully formulated Protestant attitude thus:

> We affirme that of one place of scripture there can bee but one sense, which we call the literall sense, when as the wordes are either taken properly, or figuratively to express the thing which is meant: as in this place. *The seede of the woman shall breake the Serpents head* [Genesis 3.15]: the literall sense is of Christ, who should triumph over Sathan, though it be spoken in a borrowed and figurative speech. There can be therefore but one sense, which is the literall: as for those three kindes [i.e., the analogical, the tropological, and the anagogical], they are not divers senses, but divers applications onely and collections out of one and the same sense.[14]

The sense that is at once literal and figurative can be explicated best—and perhaps solely—by a poet. "The literall sense," Donne declared conventionally enough, "is always to be preserved." "But," he added in an arresting display of his poetic sensibility, "the literall sense of every place, is the principall intention of the Holy Ghost, in that place: And the principall intention in many places, is to express things by allegories, by figures; so that in many places in Scripture, the figurative sense is the literall sense."[15]

For poets in particular, it is evident, the handshake between history and prophecy was prefatory to an imaginative adaptation of the literal to the purposes of the spiritual. But the deployment of materials drawn from the Bible generally, and from the Apocalypse specifically, was not undertaken in a vacuum. It was affected positively no less than negatively by the indefatigable labors of Protestant commentators during the Renaissance.

II. "Encroachments on the consciences of mankind"

The Protestant commentaries on the Apocalypse seem at first glance to partake of the nocturnal demesne of Nerval's *Aurélia,* as if they too inhabit a preternaturally dark planet of alarming shapes now stretched and now coiled, and of forms wild and forbidding against a universe of arid rocks. Unlike Nerval's shapes and forms, moreover, the commentaries do not suddenly change into visions of beauty, their erstwhile cacophonous sounds displaced by a celestial melody. Such, no doubt, was the aspiration; but the aridity lingers still, and the harsh sounds persist. In what sense, then, might one claim that commentaries so totally devoid of literary merit had an impact on literature?

We may consider by way of an example—an illuminating example precisely because it is nominally the least promising—the common Protestant identification of the Antichrist with the papacy. True, Sir Thomas Browne in *Religio Medici* irenically asserted his disinclination to bestow on the pope "the name of Antichrist, Man of sin, or whore of *Babylon*";[16] but Browne is the exception that proves the rule. For endorsed by both Luther and Calvin, codified in the marginal annotations to the Geneva Bible, and monotonously sanctioned in any number of treatises,[17] the conviction that the See of Rome is the Antichrist's "chiefe Kennell"—to quote Milton's phrase from *Of Reformation* (1641)[18]—assumed in Protestant commentaries on the Apocalypse proportions one may not unreasonably describe as hysterical. Express Biblical references to the Antichrist occur, in fact, solely beyond the Apocalypse, in a diversity of other contexts (1 John 2.18, 2 John 7; cf. 2 Thessalonians 2.3–9 and 1 Timothy 4.1); however, since the Apocalypse was widely regarded as the most sustained chronicle of the Antichrist's advent and progress to the end of time, the Protestant case was most often represented within its confines and in terms of its orotund language. That case depended, as one might expect, on interpretations not so much "historicallie applyed" as phrenetically distorted, the "proof" often encompassing such unpromising notions as the transposition of "666"—the number of the beast in Revelation 13.18—into letters that spelled, among other possibilities, ΛΑΤΕΙΝΟΣ (Latinus).[19] Improbabilities masked as the ultimate verities, joined to a tone of virulence unmatched even in that virulent age, finally obliged Catholic spokesmen to mount equally formidable efforts to prove that the pope is *not* the Antichrist[20]—itself, perhaps, the most astonishing development of all.

It was in the twilight of such a background that Milton studied, and responded to, the Book of Revelation. The wilder aspects of the polemic exchanges between Protestants and Catholics appear not to have affected him; but the common identification of the Antichrist with the pope was voiced in *Of Reformation* as already noted, while later, in *De doctrina christiana*, it was to be maintained with telling austerity that Antichrist is "a name given to the pope himself chiefly from his encroachments on the consciences of mankind."[21] Far more illuminating than these two instances, however, is the way Milton derived from the ongoing exchanges dimensions peculiarly suitable to his purposes both as polemicist in prose and as poet. In his prose, especially the antiprelatical tracts of the early 1640s, he repeatedly adopted the term "antichristian" not simply to argue the opposition of the episcopal form of ecclesiastical authority to the actual practice of "primitive" Christians but, more specifically, to suggest the distinctly apocalyptic notion that the prelates resemble in their "encroachments on the consciences of mankind" the activities of the Antichrist as intimated in the Apocalypse and practiced by the pope. The conviction that "Prelaty is Antichristian" was annotated in *The Reason of Church-Government* (1642) thus:

> If such like practises, and not many worse then these of our Prelats, in that great darknesse of the Roman Church, have not exempted both her and her present members from being judg'd to be Antichristian in all orthodoxall esteeme, I cannot think but that it is the absolute voice of truth and all her children to pronounce this Prelaty, and these her dark deeds in the midst of this great light wherein we live, to be more Antichristian then Antichrist himselfe.[22]

In his poetry, on the other hand, Milton adapted analogous materials after a fashion at once less predictable and more imaginative.

In advance of *Paradise Lost* there is but one poem that partakes of the controverted issues centered on the pope as the Antichrist: the sonnet composed in 1655 on the occasion of the massacre of the Piedmontese "Protestants," the so-called Waldensians, by Italian troops:

> Avenge O Lord thy slaughter'd Saints, whose bones
>   Lie scatter'd on the Alpine mountains cold,
>   Ev'n them who kept thy truth so pure of old
>   When all our Fathers worship't Stocks and Stones,
> Forget not: in thy book record their groanes
>   Who were thy Sheep and in their antient Fold
>   Slayn by the bloody *Piemontese* that roll'd
>   Mother with Infant down the Rocks. Their moans
> The Vales redoubl'd to the Hills, and they
>   To Heav'n. Their martyr'd blood and ashes sow
>   O're all th'*Italian* fields where still doth sway
> The triple Tyrant: that from these may grow
>   A hunderd-fold, who having learnt thy way
>   Early may fly the *Babylonian* woe.

Fully characteristic of the more passionate Protestant condemnations of the Roman Antichrist, the sonnet is a stunning explosion of scorching indignation that reflects the numinous wrath expected to be unsealed during the Second Advent. The language comprehends in the first instance an allusion to the cry of the martyrs in the Apocalypse, "How long, O Lord, holy and true, dost thou not judge and avenge our blood on them that dwell on the earth?" (6.10). But the language draws to an even more striking degree on the violent denunciations of evil by the great prophets as well as on the terms commonly used by Protestant expositors of the Apocalypse, most obviously in the persistent association of the pope—"the triple Tyrant" who presumes to hold the keys of Heaven, earth, and hell—with the diabolic Babylon in the Book of Revelation. The convulsions within the form that enact the argument would be recalled later, in *Paradise Lost,* when Milton was to attribute much the same zeal to the Son of God during the exorcism of the demonic forces from Heaven. The keynote on that occasion would be yet again the apocalyptic wrath of the numen.

Obviously cognizant of the Protestant expositions of the Apocalypse, Milton was also aware that while Catholics expected the Antichrist to materialize in a particular individual, Protestants insisted—to quote Willet once more—that "it is a meere fable, that Antichrist shall be one singular man."[23] The Protestant view once "historicallie applyed" tended in effect to regard the Antichrist as the cumulative mystery of iniquity rampant in the postlapsarian world, his diverse manifestations collectively including representatives of institutions like the papacy, national entities like the Ottoman Empire, extreme radicals like the millenarians at Münster, and individual persecutors of the elect whether like Antiochus IV Epiphanes—"he was," said the great Puritan Richard Sibbes, "a naughty man"[24]—or like Archbishop Laud, Charles I, Cromwell, and whoever else was judged by the given partisan to have been guilty of "encroachments on the consciences of mankind." The principle was, it appears, flexible.

It was also a principle that Milton used in *Paradise Lost* extensively if discreetly. Where Spenser in the first book of *The Faerie Queene* placed the "antichristian" activities of its demonic antagonists within an obviously apocalyptic framework, Milton in the first two books of *Paradise Lost* obscured their parallel burden in a premeditated effort to make Satan a nominally credible opponent of the Almighty. Yet Milton's Satan gathers in himself no fewer of the facets of the Antichrist that Spenser had diversely apportioned to Archimago or Duessa. For one, the designation of Satan as "great Sultan" (I.348) partakes of the medieval identification of the Antichrist with the Ottoman Empire, updated in the sixteenth century when "the scourge of the East" also became "the terror of the West" by advancing under Suleiman the Magnificent (1520-66) to the very gates of Vienna.[25] Still another facet, equally indirect but far more eloquent, is that other commonplace Milton adapted, the immemorial tradition of *diabolus simius Dei.*

The tradition in asserting Satan's parody of the activities of God reaches back to the New Testament, partly to St. Paul's prophecy of the advent of the Antichrist ("he as God sitteth in the temple of God, shewing himself that he is God" [2 Thessalonians 2.4]), but especially to the series of parodies enacted by the forces of darkness in the Book of Revelation: the dragon's bestowal of "great authority" in the style appropriate solely to Christ (13.2), the ominous figure seated on a white horse in imitation of Christ similarly astraddle (6.2, 19.11–13), and particularly the congregated essays of the demonic trinity—the dragon, the first beast, and the second beast—to be a false god, a false Christ, and a false prophet.[26] Generously extended thereafter, the tradition was reiterated with undeviating insistence whether by Calvin ("the Divell is always an Ape of God and a counterfeyter of his woorkes"), Sir Walter Ralegh ("the Divell changeth himself into an *Angell* of light: and imitateth in all he can the waies and workings of the most High"), or the eloquent Thomas Adams ("the Devill is Gods Ape, and strives to match and parallel him, both in his words and wonders").[27] The designation of Satan as "Gods Ape" was so common, indeed, as to have been reduced to a cliché;[28] but it was one that Spenser appears to have adapted to his purposes,[29] while Milton embedded it into the very fabric of *Paradise Lost*.

No reader of Milton's epic is likely to fail to observe either Satan's imitation of the form of angelic address common in Heaven or the way the fallen angels bow "prone" before Satan in hell as their counterparts do reverently before God in Heaven (II.477–78; III.349–50). In fact, however, the principle is operative in the poem at large, each of its revelations marking both the thrust of Satan's imitative ambitions and the impossibility of their realization beyond mere parody. Accordingly, the grandiose prospect of Satan seated on the throne of hell in plain emulation of the Most High—"shewing himself that he is God" or, in Milton's words, displaying a "God-like imitated State" (II.511; cf. VI.99)—is promptly undercut by its sheer vulgarity as much as by the narrator's massive sarcasm:

> High on a Throne of Royal State, which farr
> Outshon the wealth of *Ormus* and of *Ind*,
> Or where the gorgeous East with richest hand
> Showrs on her Kings *Barbaric* Pearl and Gold,
> Satan exalted sat, by merit rais'd
> To that bad eminence; and from despair
> Thus high uplifted beyond hope, aspires
> Beyond thus high, insatiat to persue
> Vain Warr with Heav'n.
>
> (II.1–9)

The word *"Barbaric"* explicates itself, diagnostic as it is of the nature of both the Antichrist and his agents like the Ottoman Empire or the papacy. Even more purposively, terms assertive of self-aggrandizement—"exalted," "rais'd," "high," "uplifted," "aspires"—explicate Satan's "merit" in relation to his misguided "sense of injur'd merit" that led to the war in Heaven. (I.98), to the same sense as gradually instilled in prelapsarian man (V.80), and to the correct pattern disclosed through the Son of God's reign "by Merit more then Birthright" (III.309; cf. VI.174–78).

The thematic pattern of "God's Ape" also operates within an apocalyptic context in the way that the parallelism between Satan's offer to destroy man, and the Son's to redeem him, is underlined by the moment of silence that precedes each (II.417–29; III.217–21). The silence would in both cases have been a nicely theatrical gesture had not the juxtaposed episodes invited us to recall that somber occasion in the Apocalypse, just after the opening of the seventh seal, when the "silence in heaven about the space of half an hour" (8.1) is followed by the blaring of the trumpets and the devastation of the created order. At that moment, in other words, the lines of demarcation between the Christ and the Antichrist are drawn firmly in the Apocalypse as they are in *Paradise Lost;* and the cosmic battle is joined in the one as it is in the other.

Diabolus simius Dei is no less an elemental aspect of the conception of Satan in *Paradise Lost* than it is of the vision of the Antichrist in the Book of Revelation. Placed within a broader context, the tradition also suggests that as the Apocalypse and *Paradise Lost* alike have a Christological dimension, so they also have an antichristological one. Innate to both works, in brief, is a sustained view of history.

III. "A gesture toward the Book of Revelation"

Milton's response to the Book of Revelation was ample and, because ample, could on occasion tempt us into a number of unwarranted claims. But the limits of his response are clearly inscribed and should be heeded. As if inclined to warn us, indeed, Milton went out of his way to avoid a specific detail within the Apocalypse: the shape of Heaven, conceived as a cube ("The length and the breadth and height of it are equal" [21.16]) in symbolic reflection of the sacrosanct nature not only of the square in prophetic literature (cf. Ezekiel 45.2) but especially of the cube that was the Holy of Holies. Several commentators on the Apocalypse pretended that the shape was "wonderful incredible."[30] Bunyan thought it represented "perfection," while Giovanni Diodati—the professor of theology at Geneva who was uncle to Milton's friend Charles Diodati and whom Milton visited in 1639—decided that as the cube is "the most stable and equal figure of all," it intimates necessarily "the perfect and everlasting stability of the Church in heaven."[31] But conditioned as they all were to favor not the square or the cube but the circle and the sphere, they should have wondered—as Napier was among the very few so to wonder—that the Holy Ghost had failed to resort to "the round figure, as of all solide bodies the most perfect figure."[32] Milton's resolution of the problem was to maintain in *Paradise Lost* that the shape of Heaven is neither square nor round but "undetermind square or round" (II, 1048). The authority of the Bible was not thereby negated; but neither was the cumulative witness of traditions beyond the Bible.

The detail is suggestive of Milton's habitual method of approach. It suggests that what inheres in the Bible and extra-scriptural traditions is jointly central to his poetry at large, but that claims we might advance about the exclusive impact of the Apocalypse on that poetry's structure, language, imagery, or tone, will in the end have to admit of substantial qualifications. The Apocalypse may or may not possess the "formal pattern" we have attributed to it.[33] But that Milton coincidentally discerned such a pattern and adapted it to his purposes, or that his major poems "take shape, substance, and strategies from the Revelation model,"[34] or that *Paradise Lost* is divisible—"plainly and most naturally divisible," it has been urged—into the same seven sections or visions said to comprise the Apocalypse which in this sense provided "the actual inner design, indeed the model for the poem":[35] these are claims we may accept only if we care to credit that any major poet has but a single "model" of rather remarkable exclusiveness.

Milton was certainly privy to the explication of the Apocalypse by David Pareus in terms of seven visions.[36] He mentions the theory twice, first in *The Reason of Church-Government* in 1642 ("the Apocalyps of Saint John is the majestick image of a high and stately Tragedy, shutting up and intermingling her Solemn Scenes and Acts with a sevenfold *Chorus* of halleluja's and harping symphonies: and this my opinion the grave authority of *Pareus* commenting that booke is sufficient to confirm") and lastly in the preface to *Samson Agonistes* in 1671 ("*Parœus* commenting on the *Revelation*, divides the whole Book as a Tragedy, into Acts distinguisht each by a Chorus of Heavenly Harpings and Song between").[37] The two statements are fully relevant to the "high and stately Tragedy" that is *Samson Agonistes* and have in fact resulted in a substantive study of its influence by the Apocalypse within the experiential and typological framework elucidated by Pareus and other commentators; but it was a case, we have been sagely assured, of simply "one influence" upon the play.[38] The larger claims involving the Apocalypse as an exclusive "model" are of a radically different order. Its numerological obsessions centered on seven— "this number seven," Diodati reasonably enough declared, "in Scripture signifieth perfection, or a compleat thing"[39]—are not in evidence in *Samson Agonistes*, much less in the two epics or the shorter poems. *Paradise Lost*, in particular, is "plainly and most naturally divisible" into seven visions only to the extent that it can also be apportioned into six parts in order to reflect the traditional division of universal history into Six Ages.⁴⁰ In short, predetermined theories often yield but predetermined results.

The range of Milton's allusions to the Book of Revelation should likewise not be overestimated. To tabulate his Biblical allusions, indeed, were to make the surprising discovery that the Apocalypse is invoked not more often than are the major prophetic utterances, the Pauline epistles, or the synoptic gospels.⁴¹ The apparently authoritative judgment that "Milton owed his greatest literary debts to the imagery of the Apocalypse" is, alas, a misrepresentation of the actual evidence.⁴² *Paradise Lost* may not be treated as if its comprehensive allusiveness coincides with the particularity of apocalyptic concerns so palpably evident whether in the first book of *The Faerie Queene*, in T. S. Eliot's "Journey of the Magi," or in Yeats's "The Second Coming." We but confine the epic by describing the Son of God as "the rider of the white horse" in order to align Milton's vision with that of the Apocalypse.⁴³ The Son of God astraddle a white horse is, in fact, quite alien to Milton's mode of conceptualization. But so are nearly all the great individual images of the Apocalypse inclusive of the visions of the seals or the vials, save only that there are adumbrations of its beasts in the portrayal of both Satan and Sin, and of its great whore in the portrayal again of Sin but also of Dalila in *Samson Agonistes*.

The language of the Apocalypse had no exclusive impact on Milton's poetry possibly because he was conscious that it is by no means the finest Greek of the New Testament; besides, its daedalian excesses severely circumscribed its compatibility with his intentions both linguistic and thematic. Thematically, we should remind ourselves, Milton went out of his way to oppose the relentless emphasis of the Apocalypse on implacable retribution by introducing into all the eschatological visions of *Paradise Lost* (III.323–38; X.635–39; XI.900–901; XII.458–65 and 545–51) a recurrent element of lenity. Where the tradition insisted that the Christ is to reappear "not as a Saviour or Mediator, but as a Judge,"⁴⁴ Milton on the contrary urged that the Christ at the end of time is to be as much judge as mediator and savior. This is not to say that *Paradise Lost* minimizes the Cimmerian shadow that evil casts on the sum of history. The vision of the future that Michael unfolds before the stricken Adam discloses that the world shall go on

> To good malignant, to bad men benigne,
> Under her own waight groaning.
>
> (XII.538–39)

The catalogue of woes that are to befall the human race (XI.477–90) was grim enough in the first edition of *Paradise Lost;* yet Milton amended it in the second edition by adding to the horrors detailed (ll. 485–87). Even so, the terminal point of history in the epic is not preceded by the devastating calamities set forth in the Apocalypse at such epidemic length and, it should be admitted, ever so lovingly. Not vengeance but the fulfillment of God's promises and the beatific vision beyond history are what appealed to Milton most: the prospect of the Second Advent when the Son of God is to

> raise
> From the conflagrant mass, purg'd and refin'd,
> New Heav'ns, new Earth, Ages of endless date,
> Founded in Righteousness and Peace and Love,
> To bring forth fruits Joy and eternal Bliss.
> (XII.547–51)

Whether in structure, language, imagery, or tone, Milton's response to the Apocalypse is not as if to an exclusive "model." It were best to say as has been said with caution due, that many elements in Milton's work "gesture toward the Book of Revelation."[45] The gesture, after all, is not insubstantial. It encompasses not only the antichristological dimension already noted but the spacious patterns we are to consider next.

IV. "To ordain wisely as in this world of evill"

The mighty line of the Nativity Ode, "The wakefull trump of doom must thunder through the deep" (156), heralds the emergence of a major poet with particular interests. Any number of other aspiring poets shared Milton's interests—but not, unfortunately, his talents, witness the versifier who ever so uncertainly looked ahead to

> the last Trump
> That up thou jump
> When all must rise and live again.[46]

Milton's version conflates the past and the future in order to rest on the present:

> to those ychain'd in sleep,
> The wakefull trump of doom must thunder through the deep.
>
> With such a horrid clang
> As on mount *Sinai* rang
>   While the red fire, and smouldring clouds out brake:

> The aged Earth agast
> With terrour of that blast,
>   Shall from the surface to the center shake:
> When at the worlds last session,
> The dreadfull Judge in middle Air shall spread his throne.
>
> And then at last our bliss
> Full and perfet is,
>   But now begins . . . .
>
>   (Nativity Ode, ll. 155–67)

The "now" marks Milton's primary commitment. However full the eventual bliss, and however perfect, it appertains to the future; and imperative though its study is to our direction and our conduct in the present, it should not be so exclusively contemplated as to displace the "now." That might partake in form if not in essence of those utopian schemes which in *Areopagitica* are renounced with specific reference to Sir Thomas More's *Utopia* and Bacon's *New Atlantis:* "To sequester out of the world into *Atlantick* and *Eutopian* polities, which never can be drawn into use, will not mend our condition; but to ordain wisely as in this world of evil, in the midd'st whereof God hath plac't us unavoidably."[47] Milton would have agreed with the insistence of the Cambridge Platonists that man is acknowledged by God only when he is "in motion" now, "upon Action" in the immediate present.[48] His endorsement of analogous premises is writ large in his early poetry, initially in the Nativity Ode as noted, and finally in both *Comus* and *Lycidas*.

The endorsement is involved with the declared ambition of the narrator in *Il Penseroso* after "Something like Prophetick strain" (l. 174). In that relatively early poem, probably written when Milton was twenty-three, the expectation is admittedly voiced by one who is far from identical with the poet and in any case refers to the distant future when "old experience" could realize the hope expressed. For Milton himself, however, the hope was to be realized all too soon. Once he reached his twenty-fourth year and dedicated himself to the Great Taskmaster in the sonnet beginning "How soon hath Time the suttle theef of youth," he penned also the exquisitely modulated poem "On Time" that wings beyond the "now" to a prospect of eternity fully anticipatory of the serenely apprehended beatific visions of *Paradise Lost*:

> Then long Eternity shall greet our bliss
> With an individual kiss;
> And Joy shall overtake us as a flood,
> When every thing that is sincerely good

> And perfetly divine,
> With Truth, and Peace, and Love shall ever shine
> About the supreme Throne
> Of him, t'whose happy-making sight alone,
> When once our heav'nly-guided soul shall clime,
> Then all this Earthy grosnes quit,
> Attir'd with Stars, we shall for ever sit,
>   Triumphing over Death, and Chance, and thee O Time.
>   ("On Time," ll. 11–22)

"On Time" is apocalyptic without recourse to the Apocalypse. But in a related poem of the same period, "At a Solemn Musick," Milton provided the first elaboration of the vision of the enthroned God so prominent in both the Apocalypse and *Paradise Lost*. "God which sitteth upon the throne" (Revelation 4.2ff., 20.11ff., but especially 7.10ff. in extension of Ezekiel 1.26) is envisaged with an optimum of musical imagery as the poet-prophet hears

> That undisturbed Song of pure concent,
> Ay sung before the saphire-colour'd throne
> To him that sits theron
> With Saintly shout, and solemn Jubily,
> Where the bright Seraphim in burning row
> Their loud up-lifted Angel trumpets blow,
> And the Cherubick host in thousand quires
> Touch their immortal Harps of golden wires,
> With those just Spirits that wear victorious Palms,
> Hymns devout and holy Psalms
> Singing everlastingly . . . .
>   ("At a Solemn Musick," ll. 6–16)

"At a Solemn Musick" advances next to the characteristic conflation of the past and the future—the time at the outset of time and the time beyond time—in order to pray for the immediate present: "O may we soon again renew that Song, / And keep in tune with Heav'n" (ll. 25–26). The prayer with its evident concern for the "now," and the poem's equally evident musical framework, inform also Milton's ensuing performance in the major achievement that is *Comus* (1634).

Like the poem "On Time," *Comus* is at once apocalyptic and distant from the Apocalypse. The apocalyptic dimension is measurable in terms of the pattern enacted initially through the mission of the Attendant Spirit to sustain those who "by due steps aspire / To lay their just hands on that Golden Key / That ope's the Palace of Eternity" (ll. 12–14), next through the expectations of the Lady that "the Supreme good . . . / Would send a glistring Guardian if need were / To keep my life and honour unassail'd" (ll. 217–20), and lastly through the advent of Sabrina "To help insnared chastity" (l. 909), in order to suggest that man's ascent through virtue is matched by Heaven's descent through Grace. The distance from the Apocalypse, on the other hand, is measurable in terms first of the antagonist's association with bestial forms to the conspicuous exclusion of the "antichristian" elements later to compass Satan in *Paradise Lost,* and secondly of the confinement of the pattern of *diabolus simius Dei* to but a single acknowledgment that Comus and his crew "Imitate the Starry Quire" (l. 112). Even more striking is the singular lack of interest in the eventual fate of Comus. He is certainly not punished. He simply disappears (l. 814); and the gathered protagonists, contemptuously silent about their antagonist, join by the end in a "victorious dance" (l. 974). The masque's "resolution," in short, is not deferred to any time or place attainable hereafter. It occurs "now," in the immediate present and within our own sublunary world. Evil may hover in the background, and does; but its potent weapons have been stilled in demonstration of the infinite capacity of good to overcome evil, precisely as the poem's concluding rhythms assimilate Comus' gay rhythms (ll. 93ff.) within a distinctly ethical context. The gaiety of Comus'

> Midnight shout, and revelry,
> Tipsie dance, and Jollity,

is merely derivative, a distant echo of the prototypical pattern that emerges with the invocation of Sabrina (ll. 867ff.) and ends with the proclamation of the joy inherent in virtue:

> Mortals that would follow me,
> Love vertue, she alone is free,
> She can teach ye how to clime
> Higher then the Spheary chime;
> Or if Vertue feeble were,
> Heav'n it self would stoop to her.

The orchestration in *Comus* of sounds attesting an ethical orientation became three years later, in *Lycidas,* a triumph of luminous suggestiveness. *Lycidas* is the first of Milton's poems to derive much of its power from a dialogue with the Apocalypse.[49] Most obviously, the final vision of "the blest Kingdoms meek of joy and love" (ll. 174–81) alludes through "the unexpressive nuptiall Song" to the marriage of the Lamb in the Apocalypse (19.7–9) and adapts, too, the celebrated promise that God shall eventually wipe away all tears from our eyes (7.17 and 21.4, in extension of Isaiah 25.8). Earlier in the poem, moreover, St. Peter's stern denunciation of the corruption within the Church (ll. 113ff.) is demonstrably responsive to the violent tone that attended similarly apocalyptic warnings in any number of Protestant commentaries. The ominous "two-handed engine at the door," in particular, is doubtless related to the "sharp two-edged sword" that, issuing according to the Apocalypse from the mouth of the Christ (1.16, 2.12), was usually interpreted as an image that "sheweth his wrath and indignation unto the enemies of his Church, and their destruction."[50] The position of the engine "at the door" is an explicit declaration of immediate expectations of the Christ's reappearance, as in the ensuing eloquent prayer:

> Thy Kingdome is now at hand, and thou standing at the dore. Come forth out of thy Royall Chambers, O Prince of all the Kings of the earth, put on the visible roabes of thy imperiall Majesty, take up that unlimited Scepter which thy Almighty Father hath bequeath'd thee; for now the voice of thy Bride calls thee, and all creatures sigh to be renew'd.

The prayer is Milton's, part of an extended plea uttered four years after the composition of *Lycidas*.[51] The poet's response to the Apocalypse and to apocalyptic modes of thought, it is clear, was by the late 1630s quite prominent and by the early 1640s fully conspicuous.

Notwithstanding, Milton's commitment to the "now" remained constant. The movement in *Lycidas* is not increasingly toward the vision of "the blest Kingdoms meek of joy and love"; it is, rather, an obliquation away from that vision toward the time and the place of our recognizable sublunar order:

> And now the Sun had stretch'd out all the hills,
> And now was dropt into the Western bay;
> At last he rose, and twitch'd his Mantle blew:
> To morrow to fresh Woods, and Pastures new.
>
> (*Lycidas*, ll. 190–94)

Within the poem, by the same token, the individual movements, whether centered on the reply of Phoebus (ll. 76–84) or the denunciation by St. Peter (ll. 113–31), are so inapposite to the urgent question of the premature death of young Lycidas that they are so many retrocessions from that question. The reply of Phoebus, for one, is couched in strictly pagan terms, within an exclusively mythological framework, and as such it "never can be drawn into use" (as Milton said of utopian schemes). The Petrine denunciation, by contrast, unfolds within a Christian context; yet its temper is so manifestly one-sided, so obsessed solely and merely with justice, that the dire warning about the "two-handed engine" awaiting to strike constitutes not a "vindication of God"[52] but—as the narrator specifically observes—a "dread voice" that has "shrunk" the very streams of Alpheus (ll. 132–33). Significantly, it is at this very point (ll. 134ff.) that Milton introduces the splendidly orchestrated rhythms of the flower passage. The urgent question at the heart of the poem can be answered, if at all, in terms of the natural order, the world as we know it. The search thus focused within history, the narrator advances expeditiously to the historical reality of the Christ who, as both man and God, connects the waves he once walked on and the "groves and other streams" beyond our planet (ll. 173–74). With supreme confidence, the poem's concluding *ottava rima* returns us to the "now" that we never really left.

V. "As an Eagle muing her mighty youth"

Milton's persuasion from the later 1630s through the early 1640s that the Last Judgment was imminent reflects an attitude widespread among his immediate contemporaries. "I cannot nor dare not prescribe," declared Bishop Godfrey Goodman in 1616, "the day and houre of that judgment, rather with patience I will waite on Gods leisure." He added:

> Yet sure I am, that the time cannot bee long absent, for all the signes of his comming doe already appeare: when the hangings and furniture are taken downe, it is a token that the King and the Court are remooving; nature now beginning to decay, seemes to hasten Christs comming.[53]

Nature's decay was in some accounts joined to "the vanity, decay, mortalitie, and marvellous abuse of the creatures." According to a lengthy tirade penned by a particularly pessimistic writer:

> The world waxeth old as a garment: it, and all the parts of it, fade, waste, consume, and draw toward their fatall period. All things (by sinfull, licentious, and rebellious man) are abused, perverted, misapplied (against the Creators scope, and the creatures desire) to unlawfull, or immoderate profite and pleasure: yea to revenge, and open persecution. The Sunne and Moone, those two great Eyes of heaven, are often darkened, and fearefully eclypsed, and (as learned Astronomers have observed) many thousand miles neerer the earth then in times past. The Planets and the other Starres, like so many Candles and Spangles in the heavens, are much decayed in their

vertues and operations. . . . In Plants, Hearbs, Trees, there is not the same vigor, efficacy, feeding, and medicinable vertue, which was in times past. Men are not so tall of stature, not so long lived, not so strong as in the daies of old: They are more fraile, feeble, mortall; and though they are more illumined, more witty, and learned, by many degrees, then in old time; yet they generally are more crafty, wicked, mischievous: they have science, but not so much conscience.[54]

But the imminence of the Last Judgment could be maintained even by the many who refused to profess the decay of nature and man. These would mount a judicious interpretation of the "signs" that the Book of Revelation details as prefatory to the end of history. The result was not unpredictable. Everyone by the later Renaissance had seen "with open eyes," it was contended, "the accomplishment of most of the Prophecies of this booke already."[55] Could the reappearance of Christ be far off? In vain did some writers cite in opposition the conclusive admonition by the Christ in Mark 13.32 as in Matthew 24.36 ("of that day and that hour knoweth no man, no, not the angels which are in heaven, neither the Son, but the Father"), and in vain also did Sir Thomas Browne entreat that "to determine the day and yeare of this inevitable time, is not onely convincible [i.e., convictable] and statute madnesse, but also manifest impiety."[56] The majority continued adamantly to believe that "the day draweth neer," that "this is even the last houre, the world cannot continue long."[57]

Milton was caught up in the rapture of the moment. He had been often, and was to be even more often, directly involved with partisans of the Apocalypse, among them Joseph Mede, author of the widely acclaimed *Clavis apocalyptica* (1627, translated into English in 1643), who was Milton's tutor at Cambridge and may have been the "old Damœtas" of *Lycidas* (l 36);[58] Stephen Marshall and Edmund Calamy, two of the combatants who comprised the "Smectymnuus" group defended by Milton in the *Animadversions* of 1642; and Samuel Hartlib, the recipient of Milton's treatise *Of Education* (1644), who was instrumental in securing the translation of Mede's great work. But Milton had in any case already entertained ambitions after "Something like Prophetick strain"; and as time appeared opportune to assume his prophetic mantle, he joined the embattled Presbyterians in their war against the latest manifestation of the Antichrist, the prelates of the established Church. The fourth of the five tracts he wrote to that purpose, *The Reason of Church-Government urg'd against Prelaty* (1642), articulates his ultimate aim, his sense of mission, and his foremost precedent, in a statement immemorially voiced by all aspirants after the office of the prophet:

> Surely to every good and peaceable man it must in nature needs be a hatefull thing to be the displeaser, and molester of thousands; much

> better would it like him doubtlesse to be the messenger of gladnes and contentment, which is his chief intended busines, to all mankind, but that they resist and oppose their own true happiness. But when God commands to take the trumpet and blow a dolorous or a jarring blast, it lies not in mans will what he shall say or what he shall conceal. If he shall think to be silent, as *Jeremiah* did, because of the reproach and derision he met with daily, and *all his familiar friends watcht for his halting* to be reveng'd on him for speaking the truth, he would be forc't to confess as he confest, *his word was in my heart as a burning fire shut up in my bones. I was weary with forbearing and could not stay.*[59]

Thus persuaded, Milton descended into battle armed with the prodigal vocabulary and the martial imagery of the great prophets and of St. John in the Apocalypse. The prelates—"a whippe of Scorpions"[60]—were associated with the dragon from the bottomless pit; but the Presbyterians in Parliament, with "our old patron Saint *George*":

> If our Princes and Knights will imitate the fame of that old champion, as by their order of Knighthood solemnly taken, they vow, farre be it that they should uphold and side with this English Dragon; but rather to doe as indeed their oath binds them, they should make it their Knightly adventure to pursue & vanquish this mighty sailewing'd monster that menaces to swallow up the Land, unlesse her bottomlesse gorge may be satisfi'd with the blood of the Kings daughter the Church; and may, as she was wont, fill her dark and infamous den with the bones of the Saints.[61]

"Apocalyptic thought," it has been said, "rarely throbbed with such baroque splendor."[62]

Of Milton's five antiprelatical tracts, however, it was the first and the third—*Of Reformation touching Church-Discipline* and *Animadversions,* both published in 1641—that reveal his apocalyptic predilections most lucidly. The two works contain lengthy prayers couched in unmistakably apocalyptic terms. Part of the prayer in *Animadversions* has been quoted already (see p. 195); the other, in *Of Reformation,* concludes the tract with a plea to the Trinity that is tantamount to an interpretation of history in full alignment with the common apocalyptic expectations within Protestantism. Accepting the standard view that the defeat of the Spanish Armada and the interception of "that horrible and damned blast"—the Gunpowder Plot of 1605—were alike displays of providential intervention, Milton prays for the continued support of Grace, vows himself to celebrate the divine favors hereafter, joys at the prospect of the rewards to be distributed by the "shortly-expected" Christ, and envisages with considerable pleasure the certain confinement of all "antichristian" forces within the dolorous regions. The prayer deserves to be quoted in full:

> Thou therefore that sits't in light & glory unapprochable, *Parent of Angels* and *Men!* next thee I implore Omnipotent King, Redeemer of that lost remnant whose nature thou didst assume, ineffable and everlasting *Love!* And thou the third subsistence of Divine infinitude, *illumining Spirit,* the joy and solace of created *Things!* one *Tri-personall* GODHEAD! looke upon this thy poore and almost spent, and expiring *Church,* leave her not thus a prey to these importunate *Wolves,* that wait and thinke long till they devoure thy tender *Flock,* these wilde *Boares* that have broke into thy *Vineyard,* and left the print of thir polluting hoofs on the Soules of thy Servants. O let them not bring about their damned *designes* that stand now at the entrance of the bottomlesse pit expecting the Watch-word to open and let out those dreadfull *Locusts* and *Scorpions,* to *re-involve* us in that pitchy *Cloud* of infernall darknes, where we shall never more see the *Sunne* of thy *Truth* againe, never hope for the cheerfull dawne, never more heare the *Bird of Morning* sing. Be mov'd with pitty at the afflicted state of this our shaken *Monarchy,* that now lies labouring under her throwes, and struggling against the grudges of more dreaded Calamities.
>
> O thou that after the impetuous rage of five bloody Inundations, and the succeeding Sword of intestine *Warre,* soaking the Land in her owne gore, didst pitty the sad and ceasles revolution of our swift and thick-comming sorrowes when wee were quite breathlesse, of thy *free grace* didst motion *Peace,* and termes of Cov'nant with us, & having first welnigh freed us from *Antichristian* thraldome, didst build up this *Britannick Empire* to a glorious and enviable heighth with all her Daughter Ilands about her, stay us in this felicitie, let not the obstinacy of our halfe Obedience and will-Worship bring forth that *Viper of Sedition,* that for these Fourescore Yeares hath been breeding to eat through the entrals of our *Peace;* but let her cast her Abortive Spawne without the danger of this travailling & throbbing *Kingdome.* That we may still remember in our *solemne Thanksgivings,* how for us the *Northren Ocean* even to the frozen *Thule* was scatter'd with the proud Ship-wracks of the *Spanish Armado,* and the very maw of Hell ransack't, and made to give up her conceal'd destruction, ere shee could vent it in that horrible and damned blast.
>
> O how much more glorious will those former Deliverances appeare, when we shall know them not onely to have sav'd us from greatest miseries past, but to have reserv'd us for greatest happinesse

to come. Hitherto thou hast but freed us, and that not fully, from the unjust and Tyrannous Claime of thy Foes, now unite us intirely, and appropriate us to thy selfe, tie us everlastingly in willing Homage to the *Prerogative* of thy eternall *Throne.*

And now wee knowe, O thou our most certain hope and defence, that thine enemies have been consulting all the Sorceries of the *great Whore,* and have joyn'd their Plots with that sad intelligencing Tyrant that mischiefes the World with his Mines of *Ophir,* and lies thirsting to revenge his Navall ruines that have larded our Seas; but let them all take Counsell together, and let it come to nought, let them Decree, and doe thou Cancell it, let them gather themselves, and bee scatter'd, let them embattell themselves and bee broken, let them imbattell, and be broken, for thou art with us.

Then amidst the *Hymns,* and *Halleluiahs* of *Saints* some one may perhaps bee heard offering at high *strains* in new and lofty *Measures* to sing and celebrate thy *divine Mercies,* and *marvelous judgements* in this Land throughout all AGES; whereby this great and Warlike Nation instructed and inur'd to the fervent and continuall practice of *Truth* and *Righteousnesse,* and casting farre from her the *rags* of her old *vice* may presse on hard to that *high* and *happy* emulation to be found the *soberest, wisest,* and *most Christian People* at that day when thou the Eternall and shortly-expected King shalt open the Clouds to judge the severall Kingdomes of the World, and distributing *Nationall Honours* and *Rewards* to Religious and just *Common-wealths,* shalt put an end to all Earthly *Tyrannies,* proclaiming thy universal and milde *Monarchy* through Heaven and Earth. Where they undoubtedly that by their *Labours, Counsels,* and *Prayers* have been earnest for the *Common good* of *Religion* and their *Countrey,* shall receive, above the inferiour *Orders* of the *Blessed,* the *Regall* addition of *Principalities, Legions,* and *Thrones* into their glorious Titles, and in supereminence of *beatifick Vision* progressing the *datelesse* and *irrevoluble* Circle of *Eternity* shall clasp inseparable Hands with *joy,* and *blisse* in over measure for ever.

But they contrary that by the impairing and diminution of the true *Faith,* the distresses and servitude of their *Countrey* aspire to high *Dignity, Rule* and *Promotion* here, after a shamefull end in this *Life* (which *God* grant them) shall be thrown downe eternally into the *darkest* and *deepest Gulfe* of HELL, where under the *despightfull controule,* the trample and spurne of all the other *Damned,* that in the anguish of their *Torture* shall have no other ease then to exercise a *Raving* and *Bestiall Tyranny* over them as their *Slaves* and *Negro's,* they shall remaine in that plight for ever, the *basest,* the *lowermost,* the *most dejected,* most underfoot and *downetrodden Vassals* of Perdition.[63]

The explicit conviction that God favors England above all nations, while by no means unique to Milton, fired his imagination and sustained his activities all too often. Its finest statement in prose—the very *locus classicus* of Milton's prophetic vision, we have been told[64]—was ventured on a particularly memorable occasion in *Areopagitica* (1644):

> Methinks I see in my mind a noble and puissant Nation rousing herself like a strong man after sleep, and shaking her invincible locks: Methinks I see her as an Eagle muing [i.e., moulting, renewing] her mighty youth, and kindling her undazl'd eyes at the full midday beam; purging and unscaling her long abused sight at the fountain it self of heav'nly radiance; while the whole noise of timorous and flocking birds, with those also that love the twilight, flutter about, amaz'd at what she means, and in their envious gabble would prognosticat a year of sects and schisms.[65]

Yet this conviction, together with every other precept embraced by the magniloquent prayer in *Of Reformation,* was in time to be reconsidered, on occasion drastically.

The reconsideration is in some respects readily to be marked. The prayer's monomaniacal emphasis on judgment, in particular, had been transcended in *Lycidas* before Milton was overwhelmed by the tide of apocalyptic expectations, and would be transcended again in *Paradise Lost* through the superimposed lenity already annotated (see p. 190). Equally, the nationalistic strain would eventually be qualified—some could justly say metamorphosed—into a cosmic vision distinctly more appropriate to a poet with stated prophetic aspirations. But such developments were in a sense inevitable in that Milton was temperamentally circumspect about the Apocalypse even during his most passionate apocalyptic moments. His disinclination to adapt most of the major images of the Apocalypse, noted earlier, corresponds to his equally evident reluctance to deviate from the mainstream of the Protestant apocalyptic tradition. Averse to the militantly apocalyptic theocracy of the Fifth Monarchists, for example, he was also indisposed even to mention the Joachimist surmises common in some quarters. Only about the vexing issue of the millennium postulated in the Apocalypse (20.1–6) did Milton prevaricate.

It was certainly an issue to prevaricate about. The experience of Luther and Calvin is indicative; for in spite of the Apocalypse's embarrassingly explicit reference to the Christ's earthbound reign of a thousand years, the two Reformers were so appalled by the violent consequences of its literal interpretation at Münster that thereafter they evinced but a "horror of apocalypticism."[66] Every form of chiliasm was as a result condemned by their followers as a "foolish error" at best or a "herisie" at worst,[67] while the "thousand years" specified by the Apocalypse were blandly annotated by Protestants and Catholics alike as "a long tyme" (thus Erasmus no less than Diodati), "a long time indefinitely" (Featley), "time without ende" (Marlorat), "æternitie" (Napier)—in brief, said Diodati, "the time that it shall please the Lord to suffer his Church to be at rest."[68]

By the early 1640s, however, presumptions about the imminence of a literally apprehended millennium had risen sharply, endorsed by one of the period's most eminent authorities, the Calvinist Johann Heinrich Alsted, professor of theology and twice rector of the University of Herborn.[69] The continuing opposition should not be underestimated;[70] yet when Milton hoped in *Of Reformation* that the "shortly-expected" Christ was about to inaugurate his "universal and milde *Monarchy*" through Heaven and Earth," he was very much on the side of the considerable majority of his contemporaries. All the same, given his temperamental circumspectness about the Apocalypse, he refused to specify the Christ's reign as a thousand years. In his vision, indeed, the millennial reign would seem to be the final event within time-bound history and yet coterminous with or protracted into eternity, *id est,* quite unlike the period precisely dated in the Apocalypse as scheduled to be followed by the loosing of Satan (20.7ff.). So far as the more esoteric aspects of millennial expectations are concerned, Milton appears to have agreed with Cromwell: "they are things I understand not."[71]

Milton's qualified response to the millennium was in time qualified still further by a decreasing emphasis on its imminence and an increasing emphasis on its spiritual aspects.[72] Some of the attitudes he espoused in the tracts of the early 1640s were in *Paradise Lost* to become explicit, most notably in connection with the transfer of the cosmic battle within the soul of man on the pattern of the "secret" deeds of Christ represented in *Paradise Regained* (I.15). On the other hand, Milton's theological treatise *De doctrina christiana* stands in diametric opposition not only to the two epics but to the antiprelatical tracts and the subsequent prose works. The treatise confirms Milton's ever more marked reluctance to credit the imminence of the Last Judgment, on this occasion with a suitable invocation of Matthew 24.36 as of Mark 13.32 ("The day and hour of Christ's coming are known to the Father only").[73] The millennial reign, however, is conceived literally as destined to occur "on earth" for the specified "thousand years," at the expiration of which Satan is to rage again.[74] The resolution is odd not because Milton could entertain it so late in life and so long after millennial expectations were fashionable but because he should expound it with such astonishing literalism. Unconfirmed as it is by *Paradise Lost,* however, one might argue that its presence in the treatise is further testimony that *De doctrina christiana* is "prosaic," indeed "a singularly gross expedition into theology."[75] Milton's prophetic soul, so often able resonantly to dream on things to come, dreamt in *De doctrina christiana* but vapidly.

VI. "From the first beginning to the last end"

Milton's gesture toward the Book of Revelation in *Paradise Lost* is comprised of many elements. There are the numerous echoes of the Apocalypse whether in the fallen Adam's plea to nature to hide him from the face of God[76] or in the association of Uriel with "the angel standing in the sun" as well as with the seven spirits before the throne of God.[77] There are also the poem's larger components that include the critical invocation of the Apocalypse at the outset of book IV, the entire account of the war in Heaven as we are to observe presently, and of course the proliferation of woes and the visions of the end in the last two books. There are in addition such comprehensive motifs as the antichristological pattern already noted and, attendant upon that, the bestial imagery that stalks Satan throughout the poem. And there are lastly the diverse general affinities that the poem shares with the Apocalypse, notably the theatrical configurations of their vision, the symmetrical parallelism of their structures, and the historically oriented burden of their thematic concerns.

The theatrical configurations of the Apocalypse and of *Paradise Lost* revolve about the widely held attitude that the Johannine vision is "the majestick image of a high and stately Tragedy," to quote Milton's summary statement of the conventional view (see p. 189). The numerous references in passing to "the last Act . . . of a most longe & dolefull Tragedy"[78] were not meant only metaphorically, it should be emphasized. They were on the contrary evidential of the belief that the Apocalypse constitutes an essentially dramatic form, even a "celestiall Theater"—to quote Joseph Mede—an "heavenly Theater" where events occur "as upon a Stage."[79] As David Pareus explained in his formulation,

> that which beginneth at the fourth Chapter (which is the first propheticall Vision) and the following unto the end, if you well observe them, have plainly a *Dramaticall* forme, hence the Revelation may truely be called a *Propheticall Drama,* show, or representation. For as in humane Tragedies, diverse persons one after another come vpon the Theater to represent things done, and so again depart: diverse Cho[i]res also or Companies of Musitians and Harpers distinguish the diversity of the *Acts,* and while the *Actors* hold vp, do with musicall accord sweeten the wearinesse of the Spectators, and keepe them in attention: so verily the thing it self speaketh that in this Heavenly interlude, by diverse *shewes* and *apparitions.*[80]

If Pareus' division of the Apocalypse into seven visions is not demonstrably applicable to *Paradise Lost,* his claim about its *"Dramaticall* forme" is not irrelevant to the songs of celebration interspersed "with musicall accord" within the poem's cosmic tableaux. The same "forme," however, could also be said to have had some influence on the poem's several perspicuously dramatic contours. But perhaps structurally, too, there is a relationship between the poem's tautly constructed parallels and the Apocalypse's predilection for a like symmetry, witness the latter's series of parodies noted already (see p. 187) but also its series of opposed parallels such as the mark of the Lamb and the mark of the beast (14.1, 13.16), the sacrificial mark on the Lamb and the maleficent mark on the beast (5.6, 13.1), or the bride of the Lamb and the whore of Babylon that is but a "counterfeit Lamb."[81] Given Milton's respect for Biblical precedents, he would have been sensible of these elements not as "models" to be followed submissively but as so many stimuli to his own inventiveness.

When all is said, however, it is the attitude of the Apocalypse toward the historical process that is most apposite to *Paradise Lost*. That attitude is a highly particular version of the view of history intrinsic to the Christian tradition at large. History, according to the Christian tradition, is essentially a unilinear movement in time distinguished by three interlocked acts—creation, redemption, and judgment—alike presided over by Christ. The central act is also history's central event: the advent of Christ at a specific moment in time, in "the reign of Tiberius Caesar, Pontius Pilate being governor of Judaea, and Herod being tetrarch of Galilee" (Luke 3.1). Eventually affirmed to have divided history into the periods respectively designated B.C., and A.D., the advent of Christ looks back upon the creation and ahead to its dissolution upon his reappearance at the end of time. In short, history is Christocentric.[82]

Like the tradition at the center, the Apocalypse is Christocentric, historically minded—"in the highest degree historically minded"[83]—and teleologically oriented. At the same time, the Apocalypse emphasizes eschatology relentlessly, upholds the sharp dichotomy between the Christ and the Antichrist rigidly, and asserts a fully deterministic viewpoint rigorously. "We may see by this [book]," wrote Richard Bernard in 1617, "all things falling out, in, with, or against the Church of Christ, from the day of the revelation thereof unto the worlds end, to have been by God fore-determined."[84] The pattern of the Apocalypse is begged strictly from above.

Yet it is a pattern that oddly delineates the future not at the expense of the past but in terms of that past. Here the fundamental presupposition is that the course of history can be accurately perceived solely from Heaven, for it is only from that vantage point that one can appreciate the eternal nature of God—"the first and the last" (1.11, 2.8), "Alpha and Omega, the beginning and the ending" (1.8), "which was, and is, and is to come" (4.8)—as against the transience of the futureless demonic powers, "the beast that was, and is not" (17.11). History's design thus apprehended, it will be recognized not only that the past and the present are anticipatory of the future but that the future is inherent in the past and that both are present in the present. In this respect the numerous allusions within the Apocalypse to times past as if they are times present or times future—the tree of life in Eden (2.7, 22.2), the plagues that befell Egypt (16.2ff.), the song of Moses (15.3), the manna (2.17), the several earthquakes so obviously reminiscent of the Crucifixion (6.12, 11.19, 16.18)—alike reinforce the Apocalypse's typological framework but proclaim, too, the concurrence of all events in the eyes of God. That "old Damœtas," Joseph Mede, happily termed this concurrence "synchronisme," characteristically observing its relevance whether he remarked on the flood caused by the dragon to overwhelm the woman clothed with the sun (12.15): "So also *Pharaoh* persecuted the people of *Israel* marching from under his dominion into the Wilderness, but with another floud," or argued that the mission of the two witnesses (11.13ff.) is "according to the pattern of those famous pairs under the Old Testament, *Moses* and *Aaron* in the wildernesse, *Elias* and *Elisæus* [i.e., Elijah and Elisha] under the Baaliticall apostasie, *Zorobabel* and *Jesua* under the Babylonian captivity,"[85] Mede's approach parallels Milton's, especially in the poet's like-minded preoccupation with typology but equally in his concern with the "synchronisme" of all events. We might have expected these strains to have been gathered in *Paradise Lost* within Michael's prophecy of the future in books XI and XII. In the event, however, they are gathered within another episode altogether, the war in Heaven.

The brief account of that war in the Apocalypse appears to be set in the future even though, somehow, it already "was" (12.7). Milton deliberately transferred it—"as divers Expositors doe," said Donne[86]—to the remote past, before even the foundation of the world and the outset of history, "on such day / As Heav'ns great Year brings forth" (V.582–83). Placed there, however, the war behaves most peculiarly as if it really belongs to the future. It is fraught with allusions to three historical events to come: first, Israel's redemption from Egypt and the annihilation of Pharaoh's might;[87] next, the redemption of the world by the Christ and his conquest of death on the third day of his Passion;[88] and finally, the Second Advent, intimated through the conduct of the Son of God when "full of wrauth bent on his Enemies" (VI.826) he adopts the style appropriate to the "wrath of the Lamb" detailed in the Apocalypse (6.16 and *passim*). Milton's vision of the war in Heaven, it has been asserted justly, "is a shadow of things to come, and more particularly a shadow of this last age of the world and of the Second Coming."[89]

It is also a war whose Christocentric emphasis is axiomatic. In the Apocalypse the protagonist of the war is, of course, Michael; and the commentators, embarrassed by the relegation of such an important role to a mere archangel, tried ever so valiantly to identify him with the Christ ("we affirme Christe to be figured and signified to us under the tipe of Michaell").[90] Milton, on the other hand, allotted the final victory not to Michael but to the Son of God, possibly on the authority of the Apocalypse that the dragon was ultimately overcome "by the blood of the Lamb" (12.11). The implications extend far beyond the poem's Christocentric argument. They encompass the suggestion that where anyone but God uses arms to attain a goal, the result will necessarily be the defeat that it is in Satan's case or, at best, the standstill that it is in Michael's. The farcical features of the war in Heaven are in this respect a commentary on the efforts as much of Satan as of Michael. In the light of the Apocalypse's display of the martial implements used—on the part of the demonic powers, armed warriors and horsemen and chariots; but on the part of the faithful, "the blood of the Lamb" and "the word of their testimony" (12.11)—one may presume that Milton's version was so structured as to commend the paradox and, equally, to deride the tactics of the satanic host. The classical allusions that escort those tactics are inverted not because Milton had turned against Græco-Roman civilization but because the powers of darkness imitate its external form without duplicating its ethical premises. Best expressive of Milton's attitude is that boldest of his gestures, the extension literally of the plea of the mighty of the earth in the Apocalypse that the mountains might fall on them (6.16). We have thought the corresponding episode in *Paradise Lost* to be merely risible when it is pregnant with Milton's contempt:

> [God's] mighty Angels . . .
> From thir foundation loosning to and fro
> They plucked the seated Hills with all thir load,
> Rocks, Waters, Woods, and by the shaggie tops
> Up lifting bore them in thir hands: Amaze,
> Be sure, and terrour seis'd the rebel Host,
> When coming towards them so dread they saw
> The bottom of the Mountains upward turnd,
> Till on those cursed Engins triple-row
> They saw them whelmed, and all thir confidence
> Under the weight of Mountains buried deep,
> Themselves invaded next, and on thir heads
> Main Promontories flung, which in the Air
> Came shadowing, and oppressed whole Legions armed . . . .
>   (VI.638–55)

Arguably, Milton's gesture toward the Book of Revelation in *Paradise Lost* is but a gesture. The historically oriented premises of both works, for example, need not argue the exclusive influence of the Apocalypse on the epic, so long as Milton might have been affected—and, demonstrably, was affected—by the collective interpretations of the historical process by Christian spokesmen. Equally, the obvious commitment of the Apocalypse to typology need not be regarded as the cardinal precedent for Milton's reading of history in terms of "types / And shadowes" (XII.232–33) so long as a similar strategy is common to the Christian tradition at large. All the same, both the Christian view of history and the typological patterns immemorially discerned in its course were materially advanced by the Apocalypse's espousal of the one as of the other. The Johannine vision, as Thomas Brightman observed in 1615, "sufficiently furnish[es] thee with the Historyes of the world from the first beginning of it to the last end."[91] Concurrently viewed as "the majestick image of a high and stately Tragedy," the Apocalypse displays within the context of a "celestiall Theater" the creative and redemptive thrusts of God in opposition to—and eventually in triumph over—the forces of the Antichrist defined as "the cumulative mystery of iniquity rampant in the postlapsarian world" (see p. 186). Placed centrally upon this mighty stage, man acts after a fashion suggestive of configurations at once literal and figurative: literal in that he adheres to a given mode of conduct, and figurative in that the mode intimates a spiritual reality. The approach is descriptive of the strategy at the heart of *Paradise Lost,* its imposing contours assertive of the epic nature of the engagement, its manifold complexities suggestive of the cosmic dimensions of "synchronisme," its arresting visions probative of the spiritual orientation characteristic of the sum of Milton's poetry.

The sum of Milton's poetry and, indeed, his prose: the Apocalypse, as we have had occasion to note, attends the ambition after "Something like Prophetick strain" that informs the Nativity Ode and "At a Solemn Musick," *Comus* and *Lycidas,* the antiprelatical tracts of the early 1640s, *Areopagitica,* the sonnet on the Piedmontese massacre, the two epics—and lastly both *Samson Agonistes* and, however odd its convolutions, *De doctrina christiana.* The impact of the Book of Revelation on Milton can be considerably exaggerated, and it has been. But it is also possible to underestimate it much.

NOTES

Earlier versions of this chapter appeared as " 'Something Like Prophetick Strain': Apocalyptic Configurations in Milton," first in *English Language Notes* 19 (1982): 193–207; and, then, in *The Apocalypse in English Renaissance Thought and Liter-*

ature, ed. C. A. Patrides and Joseph Wittreich (Manchester: Manchester University Press; Ithaca, N.Y.: Cornell University Press, 1984), pp. 207–37. Copyright 1984 by Manchester University Press. Reprinted by permission. Milton's poetry is here quoted from *The Poetical Works of John Milton,* ed. Helen Darbishire (Oxford, 1952–55), 2 vols.; and his prose, from *Complete Prose Works,* gen. ed. Don M. Wolfe (New Haven, 1953–82), 8 vols.

1. *Sermons,* ed. E. M. Simpson and G. R. Potter (Berkeley, 1953–62), 8:75.
2. Quoted by Kenneth Charlton, "The Educational Background," in *The Age of Milton,* ed. C. A. Patrides and Raymond B. Waddington (Manchester, 1980), p. 128. On Napier, see especially Katharine R. Firth, *The Apocalyptic Tradition in Reformation Britain 1530–1645* (Oxford, 1979), pp. 132–49. The broader background—early Christian, medieval, and Renaissance—is detailed in the essays by Bernard McGinn, Marjorie Reeves, Jaroslav Pelikan, Bernard Capp, and Michael Murrin, in *The Apocalypse in English Renaissance Thought and Literature,* ed. C. A. Patrides and Joseph Wittreich (Manchester, 1984), chaps. 1–5. On the period of the Renaissance consult (in addition to Firth's study): Paul Christianson, *Reformers and Babylon: English Apocalyptic Visions from the Reformation to the Eve of the Civil War* (Toronto, 1978).
3. *The Ruine of Rome: Or an Exposition upon the whole Revelation* (London, 1603), sig. aa2.
4. *Ane fruitfull Meditatioun . . . [on] Revelation in forme of ane sermone* (Edinburgh, 1588), sig. A3.
5. *A Revelation of the Revelation* (Amsterdam, 1615), sig. A2.
6. William Twisse, in his preface to Joseph Mede's *The Key of the Revelation,* trans. Richard More, 2d ed. (1650), sig. A4; Mede, 1:27; Pareus, *A Commentary upon the Divine Revelation,* trans. Elias Arnold (Amsterdam, 1644), p. 5; Milton, in *Animadversions, Prose Works,* 1:714; respectively.
7. *The Key of the Revelation,* sig. B1.
8. *Sacrae heptades* (London, 1626), p. 2.
9. Mede, *The Key of the Revelation,* 1:27, and Hicks, 'Αποκάλυψις 'Αποκαλύψεως, *or The Revelation Revealed* (London, 1659), sig. C1v.
10. *Revelation Revealed,* sig. A2.
11. *The Two Last Dialogues* (London, 1668), p. 148.
12. *A Plaine Discovery of the whole Revelation,* rev. ed. (London, 1611), p. 235.
13. "The iiii. senses of ye scripture," in *The Obedience of a Christian Man,* rev. ed. (Marburg, 1535), fols. 129–37.
14. *Synopsis Papismi, that is, A Generall Viewe of Papistrie,* 2d ed. (London, 1594), p. 43.
15. *Sermons,* 6:62; quoted, and discussed further on p. 308.
16. *Religio Medici,* I.5, in *The Major Works,* ed. C. A. Patrides (Harmondsworth, England, 1977), p. 65.
17. On Luther consult Warren A. Quanbeck, "Luther and Apocalyptic," in *Luther and Melanchthon,* ed. Vilmos Vajta (Göttingen, 1961), pp. 125f.; and on Calvin: Heinrich Quistorp, *Calvin's Doctrine of the Last Things,* trans. Harold Knight (Richmond, Va., 1955), pp. 118ff. In England the same cause was first espoused by John Bale, next writ large in the martyrology of his friend John

Foxe, and thereafter set forth in sustained treatises such as Thomas Becon's *The Actes of Christe and of Antichriste, concerning both their life and doctrine* (London, 1577) and George Downham's *Papa Antichristo* (London, 1620). On the background, consult Richard Bauckman, *Tudor Apocalypse* (London, 1978), chap. 5.
18. *Prose Works,* 1:590.
19. This particular exposition was endorsed by the Geneva Bible. Through even more specious "proofs," the number of the beast could also be made to yield phrases like "Ecclesia Italica" and even "Vicarius generalis dei in terris." See, for example, Henoch Clapham, *A Chronological Discourse* (London, 1609), sig. Llv; and John Hull, *Saint Peters Prophesie of these Last Daies* (London, 1610), p. 503. Later, Francis Potter wrote a treatise devoted entirely to *An Interpretation of the Number 666* (Oxford, 1642). It was commended by Mede, and regarded by Pepys as "mighty ingenious" (*The Diary of Samuel Pepys,* ed. Henry R. Wheatley [London, 1895], 6:58.
20. The foremost attempt in English was ventured by "Michael Christopherson" (i.e., Michael Walpole), S.J., *A Treatise of Antichrist, Conteyning the defence of Cardinall Bellarmines Arguments, which invincibly demonstrate, That the Pope is not Antichrist* (St. Omer, France, 1613). The treatise is mainly directed against Downham's *Papa Antichristo.*
21. *Prose Works,* 6:797–98. Cf. the analogous statement in *Of Civil Power* (1659): "Chiefly for this cause do all true Protestants account the pope antichrist, for that he assumes to himself this infallibilitie over both the conscience and the scripture."
22. *Prose Works,* 1:850. Thus, in consequence, evocative phrases like "Antichristian times" (2:439), "Antichristian rigor" (2:706), "Antichristian malice" (2:548), and the like.
23. *Synopsis Papismi,* p. 252.
24. *Bowels Opened* (London, 1641), p. 408. The persecutions by Antiochus (d. 163 B.C.) are related in 1 Maccabees 1.11–67, 2, 3, and 6.1–16 (cf. Daniel 11.11–45).
25. See the details I have provided in "'The Bloody and Cruell Turke': The Judgments of God in History," in *Premises and Motifs in Renaissance Thought and Literature* (Princeton, 1982), chap. 9. See further Samuel C. Chew, *The Crescent and the Rose* (New York, 1937), chap. 3; and on Luther's influential views: Dorothy M. Vaughan, *Europe and the Turk* (Liverpool, 1954), pp. 135ff., and Heinrich Bornkamm, *Luther's World of Thought,* trans. M. H. Bertram (St. Louis, 1958), pp. 195–217.
26. On the "demonic parody" at the heart of the Apocalypse, consult especially Austin Farrer, *A Rebirth of Images* (London, 1949), chap. 11.
27. Calvin, *Sermons . . . vpon the Booke of Job,* trans. Arthur Golding (London, 1574), p. 571; Ralegh, *The History of the World* (London, 1614), I.321 [II.6.7]; and Adams, *Workes* (London, 1629), p. 211. On the circumference of this tradition, see Maximilian Rudwin, *The Devil in Legend and Literature* (Chicago, 1931), chap. 12. Catholics accepted the tradition just as readily; Erasmus, for example, speaks of the devil as "a counterfetter of gods workes" (*The Second Tome or Volume of the Paraphrase of Erasmus upon the Newe Testament,* trans. Edmund Allen [London, 1549], fol. xi).

28. Thus, for example, Heinrich Bullinger, *A Hundred Sermons upon the Apocalips,* trans. John Daws (London, 1561), p. 148; Augustin Marlorat, *A Catholike Exposition upon the Revelation,* trans. Arthur Golding (London, 1574), fol. 200; Thomas Lodge, *Wits Miserie* (London, 1596), p. 2; Donne, *Sermons,* 3:148; William Narne, *Christs Starre* (London, 1625), p. 207; Daniel Dyke, *Two Treatises,* 5th impr. (London, 1631), p. 235; John Swan, *Profano-Mastix* (London, 1639), p. 38; Nicholas Billingsley, *A Treasury of Divine Raptures* (London, 1667), p. 23; among many others.
29. See Millar MacLure, "Nature and Art in *The Faerie Queene*," in *Critical Essays on Spenser from "ELH"* (Baltimore, 1970), pp. 143ff., who expands the seminal remarks by C. S. Lewis, *The Allegory of Love* (London, 1936), p. 326.
30. Richard Bernard, *A Key of Knowledge for the Opening of . . . Revelation* (London, 1617), p. 330.
31. Bunyan, *The Holy City* (London, 1665), in *Works,* ed. George Offor (Glasgow, 1859), 3:422, and Diodati, *Pious and Learned Annotations upon the Holy Bible,* 3d ed. (London, 1651), sig. Yyy3. Milton while in Geneva "saw Professor Diodati daily" (William R. Parker, *Milton: A Biography* [Oxford, 1968], 1:181).
32. *A Plaine Discovery,* p. 311. On the period's extreme partiality to the circle as reflected in literature, see Marjorie H. Nicolson, *The Breaking of the Circle,* rev. ed. (New York, 1962), chap. 2, and Frank L. Huntley, "Sir Thomas Browne and the Metaphor of the Circle," *Journal of the History of Ideas* 14 (1953): 353–64. On its wider manifestations in literature, consult Georges Poulet, *The Metamorphoses of the Circle,* trans. Carley Dawson and Elliott Coleman (Baltimore, 1966); and on its appearance in other disciplines—e.g., in architecture—observe the circular patterns of Bramante's Tempietto of S. Pietro in Montorio, discussed and illustrated by Paolo Portoghesi, *Rome of the Renaissance,* trans. Paul Sanders (London, 1972), pp. 53ff. and plates 17–20.
33. For a sophisticated endeavor to establish such a pattern, see Farrer, *A Rebirth of Images,* chaps. 2–3.
34. Joseph A. Wittreich, "'A Poet amongst Poets,'" in *Milton and the Line of Vision,* ed. Wittreich (Madison, Wis., 1975), pp. 97–142.
35. Michael Fixler, "The Apocalypse within *Paradise Lost*," in *New Essays on "Paradise Lost,"* ed. Thomas Kranidas (Berkeley, 1966), chap. 7. His theory is endorsed by Joseph Wittreich in *Visionary Poetics: Milton's Tradition and Its Legacy* (San Marino, Cal., 1979): "*Paradise Lost* is itself a sevenfold vision." Even more sweepingly, Austin C. Dobbins in *Milton and the Book of Revelation: The Heavenly Cycle* (University, Ala., 1975), p. 62, asserts that "the structure of *Paradise Lost*"—presumably the entire structure!—"Milton derived from the Book of Revelation."
36. *Commentary upon the Divine Revelation;* the relevant theory is initially proposed on p. 19 and detailed thereafter *passim.* The commentary was first published, in Latin, in Heidelberg (1618). On Pareus consult Joseph Wittreich, in *Visionary Poetics,* pp. 40ff. and *passim,* as well as the discussion by Michael Murrin in *The Apocalypse,* ed. Patrides and Wittreich.
37. The former quotation is in *Prose Works,* 1:815; the latter, in *Selected Prose,* ed. C. A. Patrides, rev. ed. (Columbia, Mo., 1985), p. 367. Fixler, in "The Apocalypse within *Paradise Lost,*" p. 146, rightly observes that the earlier statement represents a careless reading of Pareus who had referred not to "a seven-

fold Chorus" but—as the preface to *Samson Agonistes* correctly claims—to choruses in between the acts.
38. Consult Barbara K. Lewalski, "*Samson Agonistes* and the 'Tragedy' of the Apocalypse," *PMLA* 85 (1970): 1050–62.
39. *Pious and Learned Annotations,* sig. Xxxl.
40. This equally improbable theory is argued by George W. Whiting, *Milton and this Pendant World* (Austin, Tex., 1958), chap. 6.
41. Consult, among others, the index of Biblical references compiled by James H. Sims, *The Bible in Milton's Epics* (Gainesville, Fla., 1962), pp. 259–78. Professor Sims informs me that in fact "Milton's allusions to the major prophets and to Paul considerably outnumber his references to the Book of Revelation."
42. The judgment is ventured by Michael Fixler, *Milton and the Kingdoms of God* (London, 1964), pp. 71–72, who cites in support Theodore H. Banks, *Milton's Imagery* (New York, 1950), pp. 176–77. In fact, however, Banks asserts that Milton's most comprehensive debts are to the Apocalypse *and* the synoptic gospels.
43. Thus Dobbins, *Milton and the Book of Revelation,* p. 46. Dobbins usefully collects a number of "parallels" between the apocalyptic tradition and *Paradise Lost;* yet he appears on occasion to be unaware that parallels in poetry have a tendency to look in several directions at once, not solely toward the Apocalypse.
44. Samuel Smith, *The Great Assize . . . foure sermons, vpon the 20th Chap. of the Revel.,* 4th rev. impr. (London, 1628), p. 16. See further my study of "Renaissance and Modern Thought on the Last Things," *Harvard Theological Review* 51 (1958): 169–85.
45. Wittreich, *Visionary Poetics,* p. 89.
46. The lines were never published, which is probably just as well! They are quoted from a manuscript in the Bodleian Library, Edmund Spoure's *A Booke of Poems . . . transcrib'd. Anno Domini 1695* (M.S. Eng. poet. f. 52).
47. *Prose Works,* 2:526; also quoted on p. 279. Milton's statement is usefully annotated by G.R. Hibbard, "Sequestration into *Atlantic* and *Eutopian* Polities: Milton and More," *Renaissance and Reformation* 16 (1980): 209–25.
48. See the fuller details provided in the introduction to my edition of *The Cambridge Platonists* (London, 1969; reprint Cambridge, 1980).
49. *Most* of its power indeed, according to Wittreich in *Visionary Poetics.* As much cannot be claimed on behalf of *Comus,* however. The apocalyptic background sketched by Alice Lyle-Scoufos, "The Mysteries in Milton's Masque," *Milton Studies* 6 (1974): 113–42, is not evident in the foreground of the poem itself. On the other hand, the restrained observations of James H. Hanford on the impact of the Book of Revelation on Milton's shorter poems are entirely acceptable (see his sustained essay "The Youth of Milton: An Interpretation of his Early Literary Development," in his *John Milton: Poet and Humanist* [Cleveland, 1966], especially pp. 59–65).
50. Thomas Mason, *A Revelation of the Revelation* (London, 1619), p. 7. The Geneva Bible provides the equally standard identification of the sword with the word of God on the basis of Hebrews 4.12.
51. In *Animadversions, Prose Works,* 1:707.
52. Thus, Fixler, *Milton and the Kingdoms of God,* p. 61.

53. *The Fall of Man* (London, 1616), p. 383.
54. Thomas Draxe, *An Alarum to the Last Judgment* (London, 1615), pp. 43–45.
55. Henry Burton, *The Seven Vials* (London, 1628), p. 1.
56. *Religio Medici*, I.46; in *Major Works*, p. 118. For a typical discourse in agreement with Browne's thesis, see Samuel Gardiner, *Doomes-Day Booke* (London, 1606), pp. 15ff. Like everyone else, of course, Browne did accept that his age was history's last. "The great mutations of the world are acted," according to *Hydriotaphia*, "or time may be too short for our designes" (*Major Works*, p. 309).
57. Francis Rous, *The Diseases of the Time* (London, 1622), p. 324, and John Andrewes, *A Golden Trumpet* (London, 1648), sig. A5v.
58. As suggested by Marjorie H. Nicolson, "Milton's 'Old Damoetas,' " *MLN* 41 (1926): 293–300. On Mede consult especially Wittreich, *Visionary Poetics*, pp. 38–40, but also Firth, *The Apocalyptic Tradition*, pp. 213–28, as well as Christianson, *Reformers and Babylon*, pp. 124–29, and Ernest L. Tuveson, *Millennium and Utopia* (Berkeley, 1949), pp. 76–85.
59. *Prose Works*, 1:803. The Biblical reference is Jeremiah 20.8–10. Milton's statement—or indeed Jeremiah's—need not be construed as a negation of the prophet's personality. As John Smith the Cambridge Platonist remarked in his discourse on prophecy, "It may be considered that God made not use of Idiots or Fools to reveal his Will by, but such whose intellectuals were entire and perfect" (*Select Discourses* [London, 1660], facsimile ed. C. A. Patrides [Delmar, N.Y., 1979], p. 273).
60. *Of Reformation*, in *Prose Works*, 1:584.
61. *The Reason* etc., in *Prose Works*, 1:857.
62. Christianson, *Reformers and Babylon*, pp. 194–95.
63. *Prose Works*, 1:613–17.
64. By Wittreich, *Visionary Poetics*, p. 84.
65. *Prose Works*, 2:557–58.
66. Thus Quistorp, *Calvin's Doctrine*, p. 115. On Calvin's rejection of chiliasm, consult his *Institutes of the Christian Religion*, III.xxv.5, and Quistorp, pp. 158ff.
67. Dent, *The Ruine of Time*, p. 274, and Napier, *A Plaine Discovery*, p. 294. Thus also Pareus, *Commentary*, pp. 524ff., and Heinrich Bullinger's *Second Helvetic Confession* (1566), chap. 11: "We condemn the Jewish dreams, that before the day of judgment there shall be a golden age in the earth" (*The Creeds of Christendom*, ed. Philip Schaff, 3d ed. [London, 1877], 3:853). The Augsburg Confession has a parallel clause (app. VII).
68. Erasmus, *The Second Tome*, fol. xxxii; Diodati, *Pious and Learned Annotations*, sig. Yyy2v; Daniel Featley, *Annotations upon all the Books of the Old and New Testaments* (London, 1645), sig. uu4v; Marlorat, *A Catholike Exposition*, fol. 276v; and Napier, *A Plaine Discovery*, p. 294.
69. On Alsted see especially R. G. Clouse, "The Rebirth of Millenarianism," in *Puritans, the Millennium and the Future of Israel*, ed. Peter Toon (Cambridge, 1970), pp. 42–56.
70. The opposition was formed in the main by Anglicans like Bishop Joseph Hall

but included Presbyterians like Robert Baillie, professor of divinity at Glasgow and one of the Scottish representatives to the Westminster Assembly. See Baillie's *A Discursive from the Errours of the Time* (London, 1645), notably its last chapter ("The thousand yeares of Christ his visible Raigne upon earth, is against Scripture"), discussed within a broader context by A. R. Dallison, "Contemporary Criticism of Millenarianism," in *Puritans, the Millennium,* ed. Toon, chap. 6. On the more general developments, consult B. S. Capp, "The Millennium and Eschatology in England," *Past and Present* 57 (1972): 156–82, and his chapter in *The Apocalypse,* ed. Patrides and Wittreich, pp. 92–124.

71. Quoted in the anonymous tract *The Faithful Narrative of the Late Testimony* (London, 1655), p. 35; cited by B. S. Capp, "Extreme Millennarianism," in *Puritans, the Millennium,* ed. Toon, p. 71. My own emphasis, it may be noted, departs in fundamental respects from Christopher Hill's *Milton and the English Revolution* (London, 1977). Hill is exclusively concerned to proclaim Milton as a consistent and undeviating "radical Protestant heretic." The attempt is a salutary reminder of Milton's immediately contemporary context: but it is mounted with a commitment that often borders on monomania.

72. See Arthur E. Barker, *Milton and the Puritan Dilemma 1641–1660* (Toronto, 1942), chap. 12. Dobbins. *Milton and the Book of Revelation,* and Fixler, *Milton and the Kingdoms of God,* are in essential agreement.

73. *Prose Works,* 6:615.

74. *Prose Works,* 6:623ff.

75. As I argue in the essay on *Paradise Lost,* below, p. 217.

76. Revelation 6.16 conflated with Hosea 10.8; and *Paradise Lost* IX.1088–90, and X.723–24. The same Biblical verses inform the cry of Marlowe's Faustus, "Mountains and hills, come, come, and fall on me, / And hide from the heavy wrath of God" (*Doctor Faustus* XIV.143–44).

77. Revelation 19.17 and 1.4, respectively, of which the latter is an extension of Zechariah 4.10; and *Paradise Lost* III.648–51. It was even possible, it appears, to regard the seven spirits as a representation of the Holy Ghost. Thus the formidable William Perkins: "the holy Ghost may be called by the name of the seven spirits" (*A Godly and Learned Exposition or Commentarie upon the three first Chapters of the Revelation* [London, 1606], p. 16).

78. Brightman, *A Revelation of the Revelation,* sig. A3v.

79. *The Key to the Revelation,* sig. A8, and 1:30 et seq. On the more "theatrical" elements in *Paradise Lost,* see especially F. T. Prince, "Milton and the Theatrical Sublime," in *Approaches to "Paradise Lost,"* ed. C. A. Patrides (Toronto, 1968), pp. 53–63, and John G. Demaray, *Milton's Theatrical Epic* (Cambridge, Mass., 1980).

80. *Commentary,* p. 20. Pareus is also quoted and discussed by Barbara K. Lewalski, "*Samson Agonistes* and the 'Tragedy' of the Apocalypse," who additionally cites Hezekiah Holland, *An Exposition . . . upon the Revelation* (London, 1650), p. 146.

81. Revelation 19.7 and 17.1ff. The phrase is Richard Bernard's (*A Key of Knowledge,* p. 247).

82. For a more detailed exposition and further references, see my account in *"The Grand Design of God": The Literary Form of the Christian View of History* (London, 1972).
83. Walter Schmithals, *The Apocalyptic Movement,* trans. John E. Steely (Nashville, 1975), p. 33.
84. *A Key of Knowledge,* p. 12.
85. *The Key of the Revelation,* 2:45 and 7, respectively. Mede's basic premise is that "the interpretation of propheticall Symboles, is not easily to be attained other-where, then from those properties which the Scripture somewhere doth warrant" (2:33).
86. *Sermons,* 4:50.
87. Consult especially Jason P. Rosenblatt, "Structural Unity and Temporal Concordance: The War in Heaven in *Paradise Lost,*" *PMLA* 87 (1972): 31–41. On the exilic pattern in *Pardise Lost,* see also two other essays by Rosenblatt, of equally capital importance—"Adam's Pisgah Vision: *Paradise Lost,* Books XI and XII," *ELH* 39 (1972): 66–86; and "The Mosaic Voice in *Paradise Lost,*" *Milton Studies* 7 (1975): 207–32—and additionally: Harold Fisch, "Hebraic Style and Motifs in *Paradise Lost,*" in *Language and Style in Milton,* ed. R. D. Emma and John T. Shawcross (New York, 1967), chap. 2; and John T. Shawcross, *"Paradise Lost* and the Theme of Exodus," *Milton Studies* 2 (1970): 3–26.
88. Cf. the Father's statement to the Son: "two dayes are therefore past, the third is thine; / For thee I have ordained it" (VI.699–700). Consult especially William B. Hunter, "The War in Heaven: The Exaltation of the Son," in *Bright Essence: Studies in Milton's Theology,* by W. B. Hunter, C. A. Patrides, and J. H. Adamson (Salt Lake City, 1971), pp. 115–30.
89. William G. Madsen, *From Shadowy Types to Truth: Studies in Milton's Symbolism* (New Haven, 1968), p. 111.
90. Bullinger, *A Hundred Sermons,* p. 356. Also Pareus, *A Revelation of the Revelation,* p. 266; Diodati, *Pious and Learned Annotations,* sig. Xxx4; Franciscus Junius [François Du Jon] the Elder, *The Apocalyps . . . with a briefe and methodicall Exposition,* trans. Anon. (Cambridge, 1592), p. 148; Thomas Wilson, *A Christian Dictionarie* (London, 1622), sig. Hhh3; and others. The ultimate justification offered for the identification of Michael with Christ was "the composition of the word of three Hebrew particles, *Mi-ca-el, who is like* or *equall to the Lord,* that is onely Christ" (Edward Leigh, *Annotations upon all the New Testament* [London, 1650], p. 597; thus also Thomas Taylor, *Christs Victorie over the Dragon* [London, 1633], pp. 341–42; and others.) So far as I know, only Napier proposed another possibility: "*Michael* meaneth the holie Spirit" (*A Plaine Discovery,* p. 205). See further the details collected by Stella Revard, *The War in Heaven: "Paradise Lost" and the Tradition of Satan's Rebellion* (Ithaca, N.Y., 1980).
91. *A Revelation of the Revelation,* sig. A4.

Paradise Lost: The Language of Theology

> The brightest heaven of invention
> —*Henry V*

At the dawn of this century *Paradise Lost* was described as "a monument to dead ideas,"[1] and some three decades later Milton's total dislodgement was hailed as an accomplished fact.[2] Today, however, we are less in haste to make such categorical statements. Milton's consignment to oblivion has not, after all, been accomplished. The dead ideas of *Paradise Lost,* stirring beneath the forgetful snow, have come to life again. Already innumerable commentaries have accumulated about the poem, and though the commentators often seem like clouds of locusts bent on transforming a fertile plain into a wasteland, we can still say that we have gained much more than we have lost. Since none is endowed with the capacity for perfect illumination and since we all see "through a glass darkly," our hope of appraising *Paradise Lost* satisfactorily must depend on the concerted efforts of scholars and critics. As Milton himself declared in *Areopagitica,* the seekers after truth have to imitate Isis' careful search for the mangled body of Osiris, collecting it limb by limb.

I venture here some suggestions on the deployment in *Paradise Lost* of the language of theology. The subject is of some moment since Milton's poem is not only inextricably wedded to theology but also amounts to a "cosmic disclosure."[3] In demonstration I propose not to confine myself to Milton and his age but to consider also discussions now in progress concerning the nature of theological language. These discussions, stemming from the recent "revolution" in philosophy precipitated largely by logical positivists, have for some time been posing a challenge to Christianity.[4]

The Renaissance view of the Bible may not have comprehended awareness of "parallelism," the main formal characteristic of Hebrew poetry to which Robert Lowth first drew attention in 1753. Yet Renaissance scholars acknowledged that many books of the Bible were poems rather than prose works.[5] Nearly every Renaissance thinker subscribed readily to Donne's thesis that Biblical language is often poetic and consistently metaphorical:

[T]he Holy Ghost in penning the Scriptures delights himself, not only with a propriety, but with a delicacy, and harmony, and melody of language; with height of Metaphors, and other figures, which may work greater impressions upon the Readers, and not with barbarous or triviall, or market, or homely language.[6]

Yet enthusiasms of the moment bred many foolish notions, among them one claiming the superiority of Hebrew poets to those of ancient Greece and Rome. Milton himself held the perverse opinion that Hebrew lyric poems are incomparable "in the very critical art of composition," and Donne assured his congregation that while Virgil is "the King of the Poets," David remains "a better *Poet* than *Virgil.*"[7] Notwithstanding their convictions, neither Donne in his sermons nor Milton in *De doctrina christiana* found himself capable of responding to Hebrew poetry as poetry. Repeatedly they flatten the "height of Metaphors" they claim to have discerned in the Bible to the level terrain of their prosaic theology. Donne and Milton were hardly alone in this. Their unresponsiveness was shared by the host of Christian theologians who contributed so many inglorious chapters to the history of the Church. Interpreters of the Johannine Apocalypse and the hysteria they so often generated by their speculations come to mind. Luther, too, comes to mind, joining hands with his Catholic opponents to denounce the "new philosophy" of Copernicus by invoking Joshua 10:12–13, which is patently a poem. And last, there is Origen who, dramatizing in his own life a metaphorical statement by Jesus (Matthew 19:22), castrated himself.

Are we ourselves any more enlightened? Consider, for instance, Professor Maurice Kelley's *This Great Argument* (1941), where the prose of *De doctrina christiana* is used to bring a "gloss" to the poetry of *Paradise Lost* and to establish "parallels" between the two. Curious assumptions must yield curious results. Here, chosen at random from a page of Professor Kelley's study, are three of the numerous passages from the treatise and the poem presented to our scrutiny as "parallels." A statement from *De doctrina,* "It is clear that the world was framed out of matter of some kind or other,"[8] Professor Kelley claims is a parallel to the Father's address to the Son in *Paradise Lost:*

> ride forth, and bid the Deep
> Within appointed bounds be Heav'n and Earth,
> Boundless the Deep, because I am who fill
> Infinitude, nor vacuous the space.
>
> (VII.166–69)

He invites us at the same time to consider also part of Uriel's description of the creation of the universe:

>   I saw when at his Word the formless Mass,
>   This Worlds material mould, came to a heap. . . .
>
>   (III.708–9)

The statement from *De doctrina* affirms dogmatically the theory of *creatio ex materia praeexistente*. The two excerpts from *Paradise Lost* reiterate the providential creation of order from disorder, good from evil, life from death. Yet brutal disregard of context is the least offense committed here. Far more serious in its implications is Professor Kelley's calm juxtaposition of two passages from a poem with a passage from a prosaic treatise. Their modes of expression, however, are of course utterly different. Does not the poem, "outward-looking" as it is, expand constantly its circumference? Does not the treatise, "inward-looking" as it is, contract always its circumference until circumference and center touch? I have purposely called *De doctrina* a "prosaic" treatise for I am of the opinion that Milton found its subject to be "above the years he had, when he wrote it, and nothing satisfi'd with what was begun, left it unfinished." I am not arguing that Milton abandoned *De doctrina* in the same way or for the same reasons that he abandoned *The Passion* from which I have just quoted. I am arguing, rather, that *De doctrina* is unfinished in the sense that, Milton's expectations notwithstanding, it is a singularly gross expedition into theology. Not only is it strikingly unoriginal, but it is also utterly lacking in the two qualities which are, as we shall see, the very essence of theological language: an appropriate "oddness" combined with a certain logical behavior. In arguing against the doctrine of the Trinity, for instance, Milton denied that the Father and the Son are equal in "essentia" yet concurrently affirmed that they participate with the Holy Spirit in one common "substantia"; which in effect yields not unity but plurality—tritheism within the Godhead! Stylistically, too, the treatise might have been illumined by any number of outstanding precedents in manner equal to their great argument, for example the imposing orations of St. Athanasius against the Arians. But Milton preferred an arid style utterly devoid of literary grace, "resting in the meere element of the Text"—to quote what he himself had denounced as a pernicious habit in *The Doctrine and Discipline of Divorce*. The result is quite inauspicious, for it involves among other infelicities the improbable point that God the Father is greater than God the Son in much the same way, and for precisely the same reasons, that fathers are older than their sons! Was Milton—a poet, we recall with mounting despair—so totally unaware that "Father" and "Son" are only suggestive metaphors for the relations within the transcendent Godhead? The astonishing literalism of *De doctrina* would seem to disqualify it as a "gloss" to the poetry of *Paradise Lost* (see p. 266).

Milton, performing in the cool sphere of theology, largely met with disaster in *De doctrina*. The same is not, however, true of *Paradise Lost*. Indeed with that epic Milton compensated enormously the failure of his prosaic treatise. In the poem he burst his limitations as a theologian and became the great poet he truly was, answering the call, natural to him, of poetry. Ponder for a second Milton's discussion in *De doctrina* concerning the inequality of the "essentiae" within the Godhead. Consider not so much his deployment of the Biblical evidence as his insensitivity in trampling the metaphors "Father" and "Son" to their death.[9] Milton would have increased by one the number of the literalistic theologians whose corpses litter the highway of Church history but for "the inspired gift of God rarely bestowed," his abilities as a poet.

"All attempts to explain the nature and relations of the Deity," we have been told, "must largely depend on metaphor, and no one metaphor can exhaust those relations. Each metaphor can only describe one aspect of the nature or being of the Deity."[10] In *Paradise Lost* Milton was obviously illumined by such an awareness. Putting away in that poem the childish things of *De doctrina*, he embarked upon an exploration of the nature and relations of the Deity that took him voyaging through the Christian tradition he had so scrupulously avoided earlier, never failing to expound the very metaphors he had so insensitively ignored in his prosaic treatise. And so the thoughts of *De doctrina*—thoughts of a dry brain in a dry season—yielded to the throbbing metaphors in book III of *Paradise Lost*:

> Hail holy Light, ofspring of Heav'n first-born,
> Or of th' Eternal Coeternal beam
> May I express thee unblam'd? since God is Light,
> And never but in unapproached Light
> Dwelt from Eternitie, dwelt then in thee,
> Bright effluence of bright essence increate. . . .
>
> . . . .
>   on his right hand
> The radiant image of his Glory sat,
> His onely Son . . .
> . . . .
>   Divine Similitude,
> In whose conspicuous count'nance, without cloud
> Made visible, th' Almighty Father shines. . . .
> . . . .
>   Thron'd in highest bliss
> Equal to God, and equally enjoying
> God-like fruition.
>
>   (III.1–6, 62–64, 384–86, 305–7)

Milton's *De doctrina christiana* is a theological labyrinth. *Paradise Lost* is a window to the sun.

My thesis may be approached, too, from another direction, through the many modern studies of *Paradise Lost* that have so advanced our ability to "see" the poem properly that the giving famishes the craving. We have come to appreciate as never before the multitude of theological ideas underlying the whole of *Paradise Lost* and the significance of its various parts, down to phrases and words themselves. Thus the last two books of the poem, so frequently misunderstood, have emerged of late as indispensable components not only of its poetic movement but also of its theological content.[11] Again, we no longer look through a glass darkly at the seemingly ludicrous War in Heaven or the apparently pointless Jacob's Ladder and Paradise of Fools.[12] Phrases and words have also been given their due, yielding studies demonstrating why the Fall occurred "at the hour of Noon" (IX.739), why the prophecy of the woman's "seed" is important (X.181), as well as implications of Michael's reference to "types and shadowes" (XII.232ff.).[13] But for my purposes here one reading of *Paradise Lost* is particularly relevant. I refer to Roland M. Frye's study of the theory of accommodation in the poem.[14]

The theory of accommodation reached Milton with impressive credentials. Nearly all major theologians, trailed by a host of minor expositors, had already affirmed that God in the Scriptures "accommodated" himself to our low capacities of comprehension, that he has "so far tempered the language of his utterance as to enable the weakness of our nature to grasp and understand it."[15] The theory was obviously framed to justify the cruder instances of Biblical anthropomorphism, though it was also intended as an invitation to consider as metaphors all statements concerning God—"metaphors," wrote St. Gregory of Nyssa, "which contain a deeper meaning than the obvious one."[16] Milton accepted the invitation both in *De doctrina* and in *Paradise Lost*.[17] In the poem he made it "the basic mode of development," as Frye argues. In his prosaic treatise he resolutely shielded his eyes from its implications and wholly avoided the invitation when arguing against the equality of the "Father" and the "Son." I cannot believe that such spectacular differences between *De doctrina* and *Paradise Lost* are attributable to Milton's hesitation publicly to assert his private beliefs. He was never a man who lacked the courage of his convictions. Nor can I believe that these differences spring from his desire to avoid alienating the readers of his poem, since this would involve us in a charge of hypocrisy that might prove rather difficult to substantiate. I am not even prepared to accept the reasonable-sounding theory that such differences are "eventually due to differences in the media and aims of expository prose and epic poetry."[18] A theological treatise not only might, but *ought,* to avail itself of the theory of accommodation and, especially if it aspires to discuss the nature and relations of the Deity, of metaphorical language. We recall the practice of the great theologians who in their attempts to delineate the nature of the Christian "cosmic disclosure" resorted to the kind of metaphorical language that, for example, informs the treatises of St. Athanasius against the Arians.[19]

In the absence in Milton's *De doctrina* of such language, of any application of the theory of accommodation nominally endorsed in it, and because we can hardly be impressed by its espousal of a form of tritheism, I can only conclude that the treatise represents such an abortive venture into theology that Milton was forced drastically to alter his approach in *Paradise Lost*. It may be that Milton never actually abandoned *De doctrina*. It may be that he reverted to it often until his death in 1674. No matter. None of us is prepared to acknowledge total defeat, Milton least of all. In any case the treatise never resolved the problems it raised and, probably for that very reason, was never published.

The problems were resolved only in *Paradise Lost*. The achievement was due to several factors. The most decisive was certainly Milton's adoption of a language whose center of gravity is the "model"[20] or—depending on the dictates of our particular critical vocabulary—the image, the metaphor, the symbol or the archetype, the emblem or the icon, perhaps even parabolic language and possibly "myth."[21] Whichever term we finally endorse, it ought to be one that describes adequately the odd behavior of a language that is always more in intention than it is in existence and constantly points to something beyond itself, thereby enabling poet or theologian to be "articulate about an insight."[22] When the "model" is centrally located, it radiates outward in the manner of the passages from book III of *Paradise Lost* I quoted earlier. When the "model" is abandoned, however, articulation about an insight lapses into mere affirmation in the manner of *De doctrina*. Many readers of Milton would, of course, argue that in *Paradise Lost* he abandons the "model" in certain respects. This seems to be true notably in the last two books, but also in the prolonged attempts of the Father in book III to justify himself. But the interpretation of passages isolated from their context is surely a fruitless pastime. In such fragments all poets are inclined to nod. Consider T. S. Eliot in *East Coker:*

> You say I am repeating
> Something I have said before. I shall say it again.
> Shall I say it again? . . .
>
> (III.34–36)

or Yeats at the outset of *Lapis Lazuli:*

> I have heard that hysterical women say
> They are sick of the palette and fiddle-bow,

Of poets that are always gay,
For everybody knows or else should know
That if nothing drastic is done . . . .

(ll. 1–5)

These fragments, set within their proper context in the *Four Quartets* and *Lapis Lazuli,* change utterly. Similarly, the center of gravity of *Paradise Lost* is, as I see it, neither in the Father's address in book III nor in any other single part of the poem. "Other echoes / Inhabit the garden": it is the cumulative effect of these echoes, the total pattern of *Paradise Lost* that fuses leaf, blossom, and bole into one chestnut tree, one great-rooted blossomer.

My point is hardly novel. Frank Kermode has also invited us to see *Paradise Lost* "as a whole."[23] How else, indeed, can we appreciate the poem's marvelous tonal range? Only in the light of Raphael's courteous attitude toward Adam before the Fall, for example, can we best grasp the sense of Michael's manner when coldly he corrects the fallen Adam who misinterprets most aspects of the Vision unfolding before him, including the union between the sons of Seth and the daughters of Cain (XI.556–636). Kermode rightly concludes that Michael's attitude heralds a change in the divine arrangements: "the evidence of the senses, the testimony of pleasure, is no longer a reliable guide." As Michael pointedly observes,

> Judg not what is best
> By pleasure, though to Nature seeming meet . . . .
>
> (XI.603–4)

Here, in poetic affirmation of the fundamental Christian claim that fallen man errs constantly and constantly needs grace to repair mere nature, we have yet another instance of the marriage between poetry and theology in *Paradise Lost.* Michael's reproof of the fallen Adam is quite simply a "model," a "myth," a metaphor that draws a spiritual truth within the compass of our lowly apprehension. The incident by itself, seen out of context, is doubtless "odd"; but seen in context it has its own "distinctive logical behaviour," particularly because it gathers together many of the echoes we have been hearing throughout the poem. The "oddness" and the "logical behaviour" might indeed be said to describe the language of poetry. They certainly *do* describe the language of theology.[24]

Can we regard the prolonged attempts of the Father in book III to justify himself as an aspect of this pattern? It is a possibility. The theory of accommodation certainly offers an adequate precedent for Milton's seemingly "odd" conception of the Deity. We might with even more profit, however, invoke the context to attest the simple fact that Milton's

God appears for the first time not in books I or II but in book III. This strategy has several important implications. The very first line of book III ("Hail holy Light ofspring of Heav'n first-born") instantly marks the difference between Heaven and Hell, not simply in terms of light and darkness, but—let it be noted—in terms of life and death, fruition and decay, the natural and the perverse.[25] Thereafter the language of book III appears to be less "poetic" than the language of books I and II, though it has, in fact, become more subtle, more complex, more "outward-looking." The difference is by no means obvious. How could it be? We ascend most reluctantly from Hell to Heaven, already seduced by the sounds that have charmed our ears, the splendor that has dazzled our eyes, the rhetoric that has gorgonized our total being. We are barely in a position to recognize that Adam's predicament after the Fall has been our predicament and that Michael's reproof of Adam might as readily have been a reproof of ourselves, lately so tempted by the sights, the sounds, the rhetoric of Hell:

> Judg not what is best
> By pleasure, though to Nature seeming meet....
>
> (XI.603-4)

To observe Milton's strategy is better to appreciate the particular way that he is "articulate about an insight," the particular way that his language is always more in intention than it is in existence. Accordingly, the transition from book II to book III is a transition from the spectacular world of Hell, where might and grandeur are merely insubstantial reflections in the mirror of poetry, to the relatively still world of Heaven, where majesty and glory are the substantial reflections not of any mirror but the still center of the turning world. The basic "model" is now manipulated with deliberate care. Its effect is calculated. No longer is it permitted to lend support to its immediate object as in books I and II but is carefully designed to throw light on the whole universe of *Paradise Lost*. Thus it penetrates into Hell and undermines the insubstantial nature of its several claims, glances across history and invests it with meaning, reverts to Heaven and arrays the angels in enormous circles that connect the still point at the center to the turning world of the periphery. Even the generally decried forensic terms—justice and justification, imputed merit and propitiation, ransom and satisfaction[26]—explode far beyond book III to affect the entire structure of *Paradise Lost*. "Merit," for example, links four events: the exaltation of the Son (V.815; VI.43; cf. III.309); the rebellion of Satan (cf. I.98); the nocturnal temptation of Eve (V.80); and the sacrifice of the God-man (III.290ff.; cf. XII.408ff.). "Ransom" emerges implicitly during the debate in Heaven and explicitly during Michael's revelation of the future (III.287ff.; XII.424; cf. X.61), yet in between underlies Eve's offer to die in Adam's place (X.930ff.).[27] "Justice," which on the evidence of book III is usually related only to the Father, reappears in direct relation to the Son both during the War in Heaven (VI.824ff.) and in all visions of the Last Judgment (III.323ff.; XII.458ff., 545ff.). Such an exchange of roles confirms afresh a thesis I have argued elsewhere, that Milton's conception of the "Father" and the "Son" in *Paradise Lost* is neither poetry nor dogma; it is both.[28] We persist in distinguishing the dancer from the dance. Milton does not.

The theory of accommodation as it is used in *Paradise Lost* might, from another standpoint, be seen as a valid means of "knowing" God through the finite symbols common enough in religious poetry. Thus Louis A. Reid has authoritatively observed that:

> [T]he characteristic of religious poetry as such is that it is forever attempting to express the trans-phenomenal or the transcendent, and forever failing to do so. Perhaps it is fairer to say that it is always partially succeeding and partially failing. It must fail to do so in the sense that the trans-phenomenal, the transcendent, the infinite, can never be more than hinted at by phenomenal, finite symbols. Yet on the other hand it can in its own symbolism suggest or express this very inexpressibility. One gets something of this in the negative language of some mystics, and in the tumbled and contradictory imagery of much prophetic and eschatological writing.[29]

The language of *Paradise Lost* is not negative or even abstract. It is concrete and earth-bound, as is normally the language of the Bible.[30] We must, on the other hand, be alive to the affinities that exist between the language of *Paradise Lost* and the "tumbled and contradictory" imagery of Biblical apocalyptic literature, partly because we may then restrain our almost indecent readiness to see the entire poem as "baroque" and partly because we may resolve some of our difficulties over its alleged discrepancies.

The best report on these discrepancies has been ventured by William Empson in *Milton's God* (1961). One of the most significant examples he has cited concerns Milton's repetition of a metaphor with seemingly disastrous implications.[31] The metaphor first appears when God intervenes in the threatened conflict between Gabriel and Satan by hanging forth in Heaven the constellation of his golden scales (IV.996ff.). It reappears when God later "protests his innocence" over the Fall of Man:

> No Decree of mine
> Concurring to necessitate his Fall,

>   Or touch with lightest moment of impulse
>   His free Will, to her own inclining left
>   In even scale.
>
>   (X.43–47)

Empson feels that the metaphor is "unfortunate." But might it not be "fortunate" after all? Might not Milton have used it with studied deliberation? Surely we ought to inquire whether this metaphor, this "model," forms part of any larger model such as the "fortunate" Fall? This may seem at best the merest possibility. Yet possibility is transformed into certainty the moment we remind ourselves that *Paradise Lost* is "articulate about an insight" not simply in poetic terms but rather in poetic terms that are bound up inextricably with the whole vocabulary that goes to make up the language of theology. We have already seen this language called "odd." It is indeed *very* "odd"; it is "logically anomalous";[32] it is, in the last analysis, paradoxical—and "paradoxical and near-paradoxical language," we have been told, "is the *staple* of accounts of God's nature."[33]

The paradox of the "fortunate" Fall in *Paradise Lost* was first noted by Arthur O. Lovejoy in 1937 and has since been the subject of numerous studies.[34] But there are other paradoxes in the poem, among them Adam's sweeping confession that God is

>   Merciful over all his works, with good
>   Still overcoming evil, and by small
>   Accomplishing great things, by things deemd weak
>   Subverting worldly strong, and worldly wise
>   By simply meek,
>
>   (XII.565–69)

which in retrospect lends coherence to the entire epic as the divers activities of God, Man, and Satan fuse into one "logically anomalous" scheme.[35] Part of this scheme is the seemingly vexing problem of God's foreknowledge and man's free will, indeed the whole paradoxical situation that Rosalie L. Colie sees exemplified in the poem's action and demonstrated in its structure.[36] The technique is decidedly Milton's own, but the general method recalls the attempts of many poet-prophets—among them Isaiah, the creator of Job, and Dante—to absorb the merely natural into a far more comprehensive vision until all paradoxes merge into "one simple flame," until "the fire and the rose are one."[37]

Milton in *Paradise Lost* may often have failed to see beyond the dark mirror, to see "face to face." But this was inevitable. As Yeats said of another poet-prophet:

The technique of Blake was imperfect, incomplete, as is the technique of wellnigh all artists who have striven to bring fires from remote summits; but where his imagination is perfect and complete, his technique has a like perfection, a like completeness.[38]

NOTES

An earlier version of this chapter appeared in *Language and Style in Milton: A Symposium in Honor of the Tercentenary of "Paradise Lost,"* ed. Ronald David Emma and John T. Shawcross (New York: Frederick Ungar, 1967), pp. 102–119. Copyright 1967 by Frederick Ungar Publishing Co. Reprinted with permission. Milton's poetry is here quoted from *The Poetical Works of John Milton,* ed. Helen Darbishire (Oxford, 1952–55), 2 vols.; and his prose, from *The Works of John Milton,* gen. ed. Frank A. Patterson (New York, 1931–40), 20 vols.

1. Sir Walter A. Raleigh, *Milton* (London, 1900), p. 88.
2. I allude to the celebrated first sentence of F. R. Leavis's essay "Milton's Verse," *Scrutiny* 2 (1933): 123–36; reprinted in *Revaluation* (London, 1936), pp. 42–61.
3. I borrow the phrase—and much else besides—from I. T. Ramsey's *Models and Mystery* (London, 1964), and especially his *Christian Discourse* (London, 1965), *passim.*
4. See I. T. Ramsey, "The Challenge of Contemporary Philosophy to Christianity," *The Modern Churchman* 42 (1952): 252–69; and "The Challenge of the Philosophy of Language," *The London Quarterly & Holborn Review* (October, 1961): 243–49. Cf. H. D. Lewis, "Contemporary Empiricism and the Philosophy of Religion," *Philosophy* 32 (1957): 193–205, as well as his survey of "The Philosophy of Religion 1945–1952," *Philosophical Quarterly* 4 (1954): 166–81, 262–74. The challenge has all too often assumed the proportions of a frontal attack on theology, most notably in A. J. Ayer's *Language, Truth and Logic* (London, 1936), esp. chap. 6, "Critique of Ethics and Theology." See, further, the important collection of essays edited by A. J. Ayer, *Logical Positivism* (Glencoe, Ill., and London, 1959), and his paper "The Vienna Circle," in *The Revolution in Philosophy* (London, 1956), being essays by W. C. Kneale, G. A. Paul, D. F. Pears, *et al.*
5. See Israel Baroway, "The Bible as Poetry in the English Renaissance: An Introduction," *JEGP* 32 (1933): 447–80; "The Hebrew Hexameter: A Study in Renaissance Sources and Interpretation," *ELH* 2 (1935): 66–91; "'The Lyre of David': A Further Study in Renaissance Interpretation of Biblical Form," *ELH* 8 (1941): 119–42; and "The Accentual Theory of Hebrew Prosody: A Further Study in Renaissance Interpretation of Biblical Form," *ELH* 17 (1950): 115–35.
6. E. M. Simpson and G. R. Potter, eds., *The Sermons of John Donne* (Berkeley and Los Angeles, 1953–60), 6:55.
7. Milton, "The Reason of Church-Government," in *Works,* 3:238; and Donne,

Sermons, 4:167. Cf. *Paradise Regained* IV.356–60. For a similar statement by Luther and another one by Donne, see my *Milton and the Christian Tradition* (Oxford, 1966), p. 149.

8. Milton, *Works,* 15:19; quoted by Maurice Kelley, *This Great Argument* (Princeton, 1941), p. 124.

9. It should be noted that at this point I see *De doctrina* through the eyes of the Christian tradition generally. But as the treatise could, from another standpoint, be seen more precisely as the by-product of literalistic puritanism, one might convincingly argue that it is a far greater achievement than I intimate here. On *De doctrina,* see the following: George N. Conklin, *Biblical Criticism and Heresy in Milton* (New York, 1949); William B. Hunter, "The Theological Context of Milton's *Christian Doctrine,*" in *Achievements of the Left Hand,* ed. Michael Lieb and John T. Shawcross (Amherst, Mass., 1974), pp. 269–90; Dayton W. Haskin, "Milton's Strange Pantheon: The Apparent Tritheism of the *De Doctrina,*" *Heythrop Journal* 16 (1975): 129–48; C. A. Patrides, "Milton and the Arian Controversy," *Proceedings of the American Philosophical Society* 120 (1976): 245–72; William Shullenberger, "Linguistic and Poetic Theory in Milton's *De Doctrina Christiana,*" *ELN* 19 (1982): 262–78; and three essays by Gordon Campbell, "*De Doctrina Christiana:* Its Structural Principles and Its Unfinished State," *Milton Studies* 9 (1976): 243–60; "Alleged Imperfections in Milton's *De Doctrina,*" *Milton Quarterly* 12 (1987): 64–65; and "The Son of God in *De Doctrina* and *Paradise Lost,*" *MLR* 75 (1980): 507–14.

10. J. F. Bethune-Baker, *An Introduction to the Early History of Christian Doctrine,* 5th ed. rev. (London, 1933), quoted in I. T. Ramsey, *Religious Language* (London, 1957), p. 164.

11. See F. T. Prince, "On the Last Two Books of *Paradise Lost,*" *Essays and Studies,* n.s. 11 (1958): 38–52; L. A. Sasek, "The Drama of *Paradise Lost,* Books XI and XII," in *Studies in English Renaissance Literature,* ed. W. F. McNeir (Baton Rouge, 1962), pp. 181–96; Barbara K. Lewalski, "Structure and Symbolism of Vision in Michael's Prophecy: *Paradise Lost,* Books XI–XII," *PQ* 42 (1963): 25–35; H. R. MacCallum, "Milton and Sacred History: Books XI and XII of *Paradise Lost,*" in *Essays in English Literature,* ed. Millar MacLure and F. W. Watt (Toronto, 1964), pp. 148–68; Mary Ann Radzinowicz, " 'Man as Probationer of Immorality': *Paradise Lost* XI–XII," in *Approaches to "Paradise Lost,"* ed. C. A. Patrides (London, 1969), pp. 31–52; Balachandra Rajan, "*Paradise Lost:* The Hill of History," in his *The Lofty Rhyme* (London, 1970), chap. 6; Michael Cavanagh, "A Meeting of Epic and History: Books XI and XII of *Paradise Lost,*" *ELH* 38 (1971): 206–22; Mary B. Durken, "Iterative Figures and Images in *Paradise Lost,* XI and XII," *Milton Studies* 3 (1971): 139–58; Jason P. Rosenblatt, "Adam's Pisgah Vison: *Paradise Lost,* Books XI and XII," *ELH* 39 (1972): 66–86; Raymond B. Waddington, "The Death of Adam: Vision and Voice in Books XI and XII of *Paradise Lost,*" *MP* 70 (1972): 9–21; Lucretia B. Yaghjian, "Between the Alpha and the Omega," *Christian Scholar's Review* 6 (1976): 180–95; Robert L. Entzminger, "Michael's Options and Milton's Poetry: *Paradise Lost* XI and XII," *ELR* 8 (1978):

197–211; George E. Miller, "Archetype and History: Narrative Technique in *Paradise Lost,* Books XI and XII," *Modern Language Studies* 10.3 (1980): 12–21; and Thomas Amorose, "Milton the Apocalyptic Historian: Competing Genres in *Paradise Lost,* Books XI–XII," *Milton Studies* 17 (1983): 141–62.

12. See, for example, on Jacob's Ladder: C. A. Patrides, "Renaissance Interpretations of Jacob's Ladder," *Theologische Zeitschrift* 18 (1962): 411–18; on the Paradise of Fools: Joseph Horrell, "Milton, Limbo, and Suicide," *RES* 18 (1942): 413–27; Frank L. Huntley, "A Justification of Milton's 'Paradise of Fools,' " *ELH* 21 (1954): 107–13; and E. L. Marilla, "Milton's Paradise of Fools," *English Studies* 42 (1961): 1–6; reprinted in his *Milton & Modern Man* (University, Ala., 1968), pp. 106–13; on the War in Heaven: Arnold Stein, "Milton's War in Heaven: An Extended Metaphor," *ELH* 18 (1951): 201–20 reprinted in his *Answerable Style* (Minneapolis, 1953), pp. 17–37; Mason Tung, "The Abdiel Episode: A Contextual Reading," *SP* 62 (1965): 595–609; William B. Hunter, "The War in Heaven: The Exaltation of the Son," in *Bright Essence,* by Hunter et al. (Salt Lake City, 1971), pp. 139–56; Jason P. Rosenblatt, "Structural Unity and Temporal Concordance: The War in Heaven in *Paradise Lost,*" *PMLA* 87 (1972): 31–41; Anne T. Barbeau, "Satan's Envy of the Son and the Third Day of the War," *PLL* 13 (1977): 362–71; James G. Mengert, "Styling the Strife of Glory: The War in Heaven," *Milton Studies* 14 (1980): 95–115; and Stella P. Revard, *The War in Heaven:* Paradise Lost *and the Tradition of Satan's Rebellion* (Ithaca, N.Y., 1980).

13. The Fall at high noon is discussed by Albert R. Cirillo," Noon-Midnight and the Temporal Structure of *Paradise Lost,*" *ELN* 29 (1962), 372–95. There are four studies of the woman's "seed": by J. E. Parish in *Rice Institute Pamphlet* 40, no. 3 (1953): 1–24, and in *JEGP* 58 (1959): 241–47; by John M. Steadman in *SP* 56 (1959): 214–25; and by C. A. Patrides in *SEL* 3 (1963): 19–30. See also my discussion of the seed, pp. 300–301. The importance of typology was first discussed in relation to *Samson Agonistes* by F. Michael Krouse, *Milton's Samson and the Christian Tradition* (Princeton, 1949); it has since been related to the epic by William G. Madsen, "Earth the Shadow of Heaven: Typological Symbolism in *Paradise Lost,*" *PMLA* 75 (1960): 519–27, and "From Shadowy Types to Truth," in *The Lyric and Dramatic Milton,* ed. Joseph H. Summers (New York, 1965), pp. 95–114.

14. Roland M. Frye, *God, Man and Satan: Patterns of Christian Thought and Life in* Paradise Lost, Pilgrim's Progress *and the Great Theologians* (Princeton, 1960).

15. St. Hilary of Poitiers, *De Trinitate* VIII.43, in *Nicene and Post-Nicene Fathers,* 2d ser. (Oxford, 1899), 9:150. To the similar affirmations of the theory by Thomas Aquinas, Calvin, *et al.,* quoted by Frye (*ibid.*, pp. 7–13), I have added the statements by Augustine and numerous Renaissance writers in "*Paradise Lost* and the Theory of Accommodation," *Texas Studies in Literature and Language* 5 (1963): 58–63; and in *Milton and the Christian Tradition,* pp. 9ff. See also the quotations given by Stephen J. Brown, S.J., *The World of Imagery* (London, 1926), pt. II, chap. 5, "Metaphor and Theology." On the "distinctive poetic style" allotted to Milton's God, see George E. Miller, "Stylistic

Rhetoric and the Language of God in *Paradise Lost,* Book III," *Language and Style* 8 (1975): 111–26. See also Michael Murrin, "The Language of Milton's Heaven," in his *The Allegorical Epic* (Chicago, 1980), chap. 6. On the poet's evolving view of a deity who is at once process and fully realized, see Joan Webber, "Milton's God," *ELH* 40 (1973): 514–31.
16. *Contra Eunomium* I.23, in *Nicene and Post-Nicene Fathers,* 2d ser. (Oxford, 1893), 5:63.
17. In *De doctrina* he discusses the theory at some length (*Works,* 14:30ff.), and in *Paradise Lost* he uses it as the basis of the "extended metaphor" of the War in Heaven. See esp. *Paradise Lost* V.571–74, and VI.893–96; cf. Stein, "Milton's War in Heaven."
18. B. Rajan, Paradise Lost *and the Seventeenth-Century Reader* (New York, 1948), p. 35.
19. Lest it be thought that here I mean to imply a relationship between Arianism and Milton's treatise, please see the evidence I cite to disprove such a relationship in "Milton and Arianism," *Journal of the History of Ideas* 25 (1964): 423–29.
20. Max Black, *Models and Metaphors* (Ithaca, N.Y., 1962); I. T. Ramsey, *Religious Language,* and *Models and Mystery.*
21. On parabolic language, see note 30. On "myth," two readings of *Paradise Lost* may in particular be recommended: Isabel G. MacCaffrey, Paradise Lost *as "Myth"* (Cambridge, Mass., 1959), and Wayne Shumaker, "*Paradise Lost:* The Mythological Dimension," *Bucknell Review* 10 (1961): 75–86. As the term "myth" is highly elusive, however, particular care must be taken not to lose sight of the historical claims of the Christian faith.
22. While quoting from I. T. Ramsey, *Models and Mystery,* p. 53, I have also adapted two phrases from Philip Wheelwright, *The Burning Fountain: A Study in the Language of Symbolism* (Bloomington, Ind., 1954), p. 19, and Paul Tillich, "Theology and Symbolism," in *Religious Symbolism,* ed. F. Ernest Johnson (New York, 1955), p. 108.
23. Frank Kermode, "Adam Unparadised," in *The Living Milton,* ed. Frank Kermode (London, 1960), pp. 119ff.
24. Cf. I. T. Ramsey, *Religious Language,* chaps. 1–2. On the languages of poetry and theology, see esp. Austin Farrer, *The Glass of Vision* (London, 1948); Ronald W. Hepburn, "Poetry and Religious Belief," in *Metaphysical Beliefs,* ed. Alasdair MacIntyre (London, 1957), pt. II; and H. D. Lewis, *Our Experience of God* (London, 1959), chap. 13, "Art and Religion."
25. See esp. the exposition by Joseph H. Summers, *The Muse's Method* (London, 1962), chap. 4. On the light/dark opposition, see the discussion and further references by Merritt Y. Hughes, *Ten Perspectives on Milton* (New Haven, 1965), chap. 4.
26. I have outlined the traditional nature of these terms in "Milton and the Protestant Theory of the Atonement," *PMLA* 74 (1959): 7–13, and *Milton and the Christian Tradition,* pp. 130–42. Cf. Hughes, chap. 5. The same terms are discussed as "models" by I. T. Ramsey, *Christian Discourse,* chap. 2, "Atonement Theology."
27. The word *ransom* is particularly prominent in *Samson Agonistes* where it is an indispensable element of dramatic irony.

28. C. A. Patrides, "The Godhead in *Paradise Lost:* Dogma or Drama?" *JEGP* 64 (1965): 29-34.
29. Louis A. Reid, *Ways of Knowledge and Experience* (London, 1961), pp. 117-18.
30. For a convenient list of the most common clusters of Biblical images—all equally "concrete"—see Stephen J. Brown, S.J., *Image and Truth: Studies in the Imagery of the Bible* (Rome, 1955). The various studies of the parables of Jesus available in English—as by G. C. Morgan (1907), R. M. Lithgow (1914), H. B. Swete (1920), G. A. Buttrick (1928), A. T. Cadoux (1931), C. H. Dodd (1935), W. O. E. Oesterley (1936), Hugh Martin (1937), B. T. D. Smith (1937), G. C. Morgan (1943), J. A. Findlay (1950), F. L. Filas (1959), A. M. Hunter (1960), G. V. Jones (1964), *et al.*—might assist readers of Milton wishing to consider the substantial influence of the parabolic language of the New Testament on *Pardise Lost*.
31. William Empson, *Milton's God* (London, 1961), pp. 112, 116ff.
32. Cf. I. M. Crombie, "The Possibility of Theological Statements," in *Faith and Logic,* ed. Basil Mitchell (London, 1957), chap. 2.
33. Ronald W. Hepburn, *Christianity and Paradox* (London, 1958), p. 16. In addition to this entire study, see the symposium on "Paradox in Religion" by I. T. Ramsey and Ninian Smart, *Aristotelian Society Supplementary Volume,* 33 (1959): 195-232. Cf. Wheelwright, pp. 70ff. The reader may care to recall at this point Cleanth Brooks's argument that "the language of poetry is the language of paradox," in *The Language of Poetry,* ed. Allen Tate (Princeton, 1942), pp. 37-61; reprinted in *The Well Wrought Urn* (New York, 1947), chap. 1.
34. Arthur O. Lovejoy, "Milton and the Paradox of the Fortunate Fall," *ELH* 4 (1937): 161-79; reprinted in his *Essays in the History of Ideas* (Baltimore, 1948), chap. 14, and in *Criticism: The Foundations of Modern Literary Judgment,* ed. Mark Schorer *et al.* (New York, 1948), pp. 137-47. I have noted a number of other uses of the paradox in "Adam's 'Happy Fault' and XVIIth-Century Apologetics," *Franciscan Studies* 23 (1963): 238-43. The studies occasioned by Lovejoy's thesis range from William G. Madsen's brief though suggestive essay in *MLN* 74 (1959): 103-5, to Dick Taylor's extremely personal view in *Tulane Studies in English* 9 (1959): 35-51.
35. I have noted this paradox in *Milton and the Christian Tradition,* pp. 159-61. But see also its exposition by Thomas Greene, *The Descent from Heaven* (New Haven, 1963), pp. 388-94, and the relevant discussion by MacCaffrey, pp. 64ff.
36. Rosalie L. Colie, "Time and Eternity: Paradox and Structure in *Paradise Lost,*" *Journal of the Warburg and Courtauld Institutes* 23 (1960): 127-38. See also her more comprehensive study, *Paradoxia Epidemica: Studies in Renaissance Paradoxy* (Princeton, 1966). For another approach, cf. Roy Daniells, "*Paradise Lost:* Paradox and Ambiguity," in *Milton, Mannerism and Baroque* (Toronto, 1963), chap. 8. On the medieval predilection for paradox, see Walter J. Ong, S.J., "Wit and Mystery: A Revaluation of Mediaeval Latin Hymnody," *Speculum* 22 (1947): 310-41.
37. Cf. Dante's "un semplice lume" (*Paradiso* XXXIII.20), and the last verse of T. S. Eliot's *Little Gidding*. On Milton as poet-prophet, see, e.g., Austin Farrer, *The Glass of Vision* (London 1948), chap. 8; H. D. Lewis, *Our Experience*

of God (London, 1959), chap. 13; William Kerrigan, *The Prophetic Milton* (Charlottesville, Va., 1974); and Joseph Wittreich, *Visionary Poetics: Milton's Tradition and His Legacy* (San Marino, Calif., 1979).
38. William Butler Yeats, "William Blake and His Illustrations to the *Divine Comedy,*" in *Essays and Introductions* (London, 1961), p. 127.

Samson Agonistes: The Comic Dimension

> The lamentable change is from the best;
> The worst returns to laughter.
> —*King Lear*

I. "Horn-pypes and funeralls"

There is nothing new under the sun. Or so we tend to hold, inclined as we are to elevate familiar concepts into ultimate truths, and known modes of thought into vast generalizations. There is comfort in such gestures, and much assurance, until the creators in our midst forcefully remind us that literature as a matter of course resists the dogmatic. The habit of mind that sustains the confident generalizations whether of Aristotle's *Poetics* or Sidney's *Apology for Poetry* is not necessarily pernicious, however. It must on the contrary elicit our sympathetic response and command our ample respect. Yet it is injurious all the same, since the impulse in each work is fundamentally toward the categorical, the definitive, the absolute.

The *Poetics* and the *Apology for Poetry* alike claim, with characteristic assurance, that what is tragic appertains to tragedy and what is comic to comedy. We are of course considerably amused by Sidney's dichotomy since his consequent censure of what he called "mungrell Tragy-comedie" was penned on the eve—and indeed on the very day—of the most imaginative transposition of his terms conceivable (see pp. 47ff.). Armed with hindsight, we have not failed to note that the practicing playwrights of his age, drawing on the rich experience of their medieval predecessors, habitually merged the tragic and the comic; and our recognition has yielded several investigations of the convergence of the twain in Marlowe as in Shakespeare.[1]

But Sidney's capital concern was not with his immediate contemporaries. The polemical nature of his *Apology* demanded that he should celebrate the distant past which, he decided, had consistently eschewed the confluence of the tragic and the comic. He also decided that the evidence was clearly present in the plays of "the ancients" who "never, or very daintily, match horn-pypes and funeralls": a view not uncommon even today, our hindsight notwithstanding. But such a confident generalization was for him, as it is for us, a misjudgment of the first magnitude. True, Sidney merely echoed the opinions of the Italian critics who had themselves extended—and, it must be admitted, relentlessly codified—tendencies implicit or explicit in Aristotle's *Poetics*. But in the very act of echoing his predecessors Sidney revealed a distressing infatuation with critical dicta at the expense of the actual practice in ancient Greek literature. The consequences are clearly to be observed. By endorsing a wrong dictum at the wrong time in the wrong country, he failed utterly to affect Elizabethan drama, but did contribute heavily to a serious misconception of Greek drama and consequently to the widening of the wide enough gulf between literature and criticism. The line of descent from the archetypical Aristotle to the codifying Italian critics and their imitator Sidney reaches to our time; and also encompasses, during the seventeenth century, Milton.

Or rather one particular Milton: not indeed the superb dramatist who composed *Samson Agonistes,* but the prosaic author who compiled its narrow-minded preface. The prosaic author was of the unqualified opinion that to intermix "comic stuff with tragic sadness and gravity" is reprehensible in the extreme; but the dramatist promptly violated that dictum, cognizant as a creator that mere opinions—however sanctified by tradition—may be superseded in a play that aspires to reflect human experience. The discrepancy between the preface and the play looms very large indeed; nor am I distressed by it since Milton the poet has always impressed me as an altogether superior artist to Milton the left-handed prose writer. In the pages immediately following, therefore, while my primary aim will be to demonstrate the correspondence between Greek drama and *Samson Agonistes* in terms of their jointly upheld "mungrell Tragycomedie," a secondary but no less vital aim will be to maintain that the play's preface is monomaniacally polemical and may not be trusted as a categorical, definitive, or final judgment on the play itself. The parallel here, if I may appeal to the theologically inclined reader, is to the argument I ventured earlier, that Milton's prosaic theological treatise bears *as literature* no conceivable relationship to Milton's major poem: for while the prose of *De doctrina christiana* descends to theological grossness, the poetry of *Paradise Lost* is a window to the sun (see pp. 219ff.).

But to my argument.

II. "The comedy of the gods"

The intrusion of the comic upon the primary motifs of *Paradise Lost* is no longer, I expect, a matter of dispute: the recognition of its presence in the poem appears to be widespread even if it is variously conceived and diversely articulated.[2] Not surprisingly; for the epic was regarded during the Renaissance as all-inclusive by definition, "the best and most accomplished kind of poetry" as Sidney unhesitatingly proclaimed. Mindful though Milton must have been of such critical pronouncements, he would have invoked the far more significant precedent which was Spenser's actual deployment of the comic in *The Faerie Queene*.³ Yet he would have been aware of the comic in the Bible too,⁴ and, beyond the Bible, in Homer.

Our own knowledge of Homer is limited in that it is commonly filtered through Pope's version, and possibly even through Chapman's. But Milton, who had access to the original Greek, would have been alert to the comic in *The Odyssey* as in *The Iliad*. Penelope in the former epic, for instance, will upon consideration emerge neither as the ethereal prototype of the patient woman nor as the pitiful victim of the suitors' advances, but as the living embodiment of craft: the ingeniously inventive center of conspiracies which she herself initiates and habitually wins. Her mode of existence is by no means singular, however. It is on the contrary reflected on one plane in Odysseus himself, and on another in the goddess Athena—both brilliant performers, both consummate actors, both superbly adroit.

The delightful good will that in *The Odyssey* envelops several characters and reduces a goddess to the level of mere humanity, is in *The Iliad* amplified so generously that not to discern the implicit comic dimension is seriously to misconstrue Homer's intentions. Certainly no account of Achilles may bypass his extreme solemnity which Homer so obviously sets at the other extreme from the amusement generated by Nestor, while a variety of intermediate positions are assigned to Agamemnon and Odysseus among the other warriors. But mere translations, it should be emphasized, can rarely if ever convey the wondrously intricate balance between amicable laughter and perpetual admiration, witness the moment when the poet describes how Odysseus "looks short when he stands up and tall when he is sitting down."⁵ On the other hand, even the worst possible translation cannot fail to suggest the twofold aspect of the greatest of the gods. Zeus, it is obvious, is neither solely grave nor simply amusing; he is both: "the supreme and awful sovereign of all the universe," yet a comic "nursery-rhyme Zeus."⁶ This dual attitude was later to inform Greek art as well, most explicitly perhaps in the delightful terra-cotta statue of Zeus at Olympia, portrayed at the moment when clutching Ganymede in one arm he is fleeing the disapproval of Hera, his face the very picture of mischievousness. But *The Iliad* reserves much the same treatment for the lesser Olympians, jointly and justly described by one critic as "*agents provocateurs*, smart propagandists, heated partisans."⁷ The fuller account by the same critic deserves to be quoted at length:

> The quarrels and reconciliation of Zeus and Hera, the seduction scene in which, armed with Aphrodite's magic ribbon, she manages to make a fool of her husband, the scene where Zeus discovers his wife's trick as he wakes up and threatens to push her off the heights of Olympus and let her hang suspended in the ether, all these really

belong to musical comedy. But here, again, truth to human experience somehow moves this marital farce to a plane of more substantial reality. There is Hera with her big stupid eyes, her obstinacy more brutish than evil, and the real genius she shows while subjecting Zeus to a successful "war of nerves," from which she always comes off with the honors. There is Aphrodite, all smiles and whims, enchanting and futile in her weakness, yet not so defenseless as she seems. There is Pallas Athena, a warrior with a man's muscles, expert and treacherous, who can send Ares rolling to the ground with the force of a single blow, who knows how to harbor a grudge and let rancor steep within her until her revenge is brewed. These are the three goddesses involved in the judgment of Paris, and each in her own way reveals the other side of the eternal feminine whose tragic purity is embodied in Andromache, Helen, and Thetis.[8]

Students of Milton should in addition be reminded that "the comedy of the gods" which in the first book of *The Iliad* terminates in uncontrollable laughter, is comic especially because the light-hearted exchanges of the merry Olympians are couched in language that remains throughout grave, solemn, "epic." Intentions apart, the premeditated discrepancy between matter and manner at the heart of the Homeric account parallels the equally premeditated one in Milton's account of the relations within the infernal trinity of Satan, Sin, and Death.

It is not without warrant, then, that Milton would have invoked Homer as a major precedent for the introduction of the comic dimension in *Paradise Lost*. But did he also adapt the Homeric antecedents to the demands of *Samson Agonistes*? More important still, did he discern analogous patterns in Greek tragedy, the claims of Aristotle and Sidney to the contrary?

III. "O King, beware of Greeks!"

Post-Homeric thought and experience are so totally dominated by Homer that he is present even where he appears to be most evidently absent. Yet in the area under examination it would seem that his impact was minimal. Consider Aeschylus, solemnly proclaiming the primacy of Zeus, gravely espousing the cosmic relevance of divine law and justice, darkly espousing the reality of inherited guilt and its extension from generation to generation by individuals voluntarily implicated in its web. Could such an awesome poet-prophet be connected with the convergence of the tragic and the comic we have noted in Homer?

It should in the first instance be remembered, however, that Aeschylus was celebrated not only for his trilogies but for his satyr-plays. He had written fifteen such plays,⁹ all presented during the City Dionysia when each morning's performance of a cluster of three tragedies—closely related as a trilogy in the case of Aeschylus but less often interconnected in the case of Sophocles—would be promptly followed by the performance of a robustly comic and pretentiously "epic" satyr-play by the same dramatist: in sum, not a trilogy but a tetralogy. Not many examples of the unique genre of satyr-plays survive: we possess the complete text of only one, *The Cyclops* of Euripides; the nearly complete text of another, *The Searchers* of Sophocles; and mere fragments from the rest.¹⁰ But even these remnants suffice to indicate how stunning their impact must have been. "It is almost," we are told, "as if Shakespeare had written a *Punch and Judy* show to be presented as an after-piece to *Romeo and Juliet*"¹¹— or equally, I think, as if he had written a gross parody of *King Lear*, penned in the same style and presented immediately after that tragedy concludes. No less suggestive is the odd way that satyr-plays anticipate the efforts of the Attic poets of the New Comedy who later parodied the ancient myths, and of the craftsmen who represented on vases not the winged Pegasus but a winged donkey! The involvement of Aeschylus in these productions astonishes, to say the least; but alerts us also, I believe, to a proper understanding of his formal tragedies.

For curious things occur even within those "tragedies." Evidently composed while Aeschylus was μεδύων, "in a state of intoxication,"¹² they embrace the Dionysiac element which we will have the opportunity to observe on other occasions as well. Should "tragedy" be conceived in Aristotelian terms, the practice of Aeschylus certainly defies categorization since *Philoctetes* and *The Eumenides* alike end happily, and so apparently did *The Prometheia*.¹³ The latter trilogy survives, of course, solely in its first play, *Prometheus Bound*; and Aristotle, who must have sensed that it did not conform to his vision of tragedy, pointedly enrolled it among "tragedies depending upon spectacle" (*Poetics,* chap. XVIII). Horace Walpole was at least more honest when he protested that the play's leading lady is a cow!¹⁴ However absurd a remark, it does prevent us from accepting Aeschylus' characters at their face value. Oceanus—the god of the ocean—will then be more readily admitted to be what he is, "plainly half-comic in intention."¹⁵ In Robert Lowell's version of the play ("derived from Aeschylus"), Oceanus is not unjustly described as "a tall, fat god with a beautiful white curling beard—good-natured, but now and then, vexation and venom animate his great languor."¹⁶ According to the same version he enters riding a swan, but it appears that he should rather be conceived as riding one of his more amusing marine monsters, probably the hippocamp.¹⁷ His offer to intercede with Zeus should be seen (literally) in the light of our ocular view of him on the stage, hippocamp and all; for that offer is well meant but rather silly, not unlike the misguided efforts of Milton's Manoa. Prometheus responds warmly to Oceanus, as respond warmly he must; yet he sees through him after a minimum of reflection:

> *Oceanus:* Tell me, what danger do you see for me in loyalty to you, and courage therein?
> *Prometheus:* I see only useless effort and a silly good nature.[18]

We are tempted confidently to generalize that the comic element in primitive Greek drama was gradually "extruded from the tragedies," to be confined thereafter solely to the satyr-plays and eventually to the "new and independent outlet" of the comedies.[19] But such an "extrusion" is as inadmissible about Greek drama as it would be about medieval or Shakespearean drama, given the presence of Oceanus in *Prometheus Bound* on the one hand, and of Noah's wife in the mystery plays or the grave-diggers in *Hamlet* on the other. Great artists, prodigally creative, do not abide by theories elevated into dogmas. Intent upon realistic viewpoints beyond the simply comic or the expressly tragic, they are wont as in the case of Aeschylus to deploy satyr-plays as entities directly affecting the "tragedies" to which they are annexed. A robustly comic *Proteus,* converting the trilogy of *The Oresteia* into a tetralogy, would have transmuted our response radically; and so would *Prometheus the Fire-kindler,* reported to have been postfixed to the three plays constituting *The Prometheia.*

As with Aeschylus, so with Sophocles: the reputed intensification of the tragic atmosphere in the plays of the latter as in those of the former has deflected us into neglecting the numerous exceptions to the confident generalizations so freely dispensed on both. Sophocles, like Aeschylus, wrote several satyr-plays; and their very existence should as before raise certain expectations concerning the intrusion of the comic upon the tragic. Aristotle's comment on the chorus provides one avenue of approach. "The chorus," he declared, "should be regarded as one of the actors, as a constituent part of the whole, and should share in the action as Sophocles, and not as Euripides, has it do."[20] To share in the action as one of the actors means, of course, that the chorus must necessarily be a character endowed with a particular sensibility and therefore subject to the same oscillations as any of the other dramatis personae. This fact, so manifestly appreciated by Milton in *Samson Agonistes* as we will see, also led Sophocles to introduce a highly individualized chorus in each of his plays, varying their characterization to suit the circumstances surrounding the given protagonist. The result is often comic, not indeed because the behavior of the chorus is ever amusing but because, as in *Samson Agonistes,* there is a discrepancy between the progressive movement of the play in one direction and the regressive movement of the chorus in another.

Additionally, however, Sophocles introduced several minor characters who oddly resemble their counterparts not so much in Milton as in Shakespeare. The first of two such characters is encountered in the opening lines of *Electra*. He is the old servant who had once attended to the boy Orestes and now accompanies him and Pylades to Mycenae. As the play unfolds, he is brought before Clytemnestra whom he pretends not to recognize. Much to her delight, he reports the "pleasant news" of Orestes' death; and questioned more closely, he embarks on a very long and eminently realistic account of Orestes' lamentable end (ll. 679–763)—save that the account is not true. This brilliant inversion of the usual messenger's speech is at the same time an equally brilliant deployment of dramatic irony as Electra cries out in agony, Clytemnestra exults, and we knowingly await the next reversal which is to compel them to switch roles. But the comic dimension borne by the old servant in *Electra* is even more explicitly carried by the guard who in *Antigone* confronts Creon (ll. 223–331). The guard has the unenviable task of reporting to the autocratic king that Polyneices has been buried in violation of the royal decree. Within a few lines he reveals himself to be not a stereotype but an individual with traits decidedly his own:

> Lord, I can't claim that I am out of breath
> from rushing here with light and hasty step,
> for I had many haltings in my thought
> making me double back upon the road.
> My mind kept saying many things to me:
> "Why go where you will surely pay the price?"
> "Fool, are you halting? And if Creon learns
> from someone else, how shall you not be hurt?"
> Turning this over, on I dilly-dallied.[21]

The guard's "light and hasty step" is clearly neither light nor hasty; and the impatient Creon whose lack of *sophrosyne* has already been impressed on us, now confirms his limitations all too prodigally. The guard eventually delivers his report, embellishing his meandering narrative with numerous irrelevant details and ending with the complaint that his mates elected him to appear before Creon: "So here I am unwilling, / quite sure you people hardly wish to see me." Creon responds in kind, and there follows this comic variation on the traditional stichomythia:

> *Guard:* May I say something? Or just turn and go?
> *Creon:* Aren't you aware your speech is most unwelcome?
> *Guard:* Does it annoy your hearing or your mind?
> *Creon:* Why are you out to allocate my pain?

Guard: The doer hurts your mind. I hurt your ears.
Creon: You are a quibbling rascal through and through.

(ll. 315–20)

The guard represents a sophisticated application by Sophocles of the point discerned, however distantly, by Horace. To quote Jonson's version of *The Art of Poetrie*:

> The Comick matter will not be exprest
> In tragick Verse; no lesse *Thyestes* feast
> Abhorres low numbers, and the private straine
> Fit for the sock: Each subject should retaine
> The place allotted it, with decent thewes.
> ....
> Yet, sometime, doth the Comedie excite
> Her voyce, and angry *Chremes* chafes out-right
> With swelling throat: and, oft the tragick wight
> Complaines in humble phrase.[22]

When all is said, however, it is in Sophocles' last play that the comic intervenes on a massive scale; so much so, indeed, that *Oedipus at Colonus* can by no stretch of the usual critical criteria be regarded as a "tragedy." It is not simply that Oedipus is by the end of the play transmuted into a "hero" presiding over Colonus. Far more trenchant is the way that the cumulative details are handled by Sophocles. The highly individualized chorus—"one of the actors"—is initially less than pleased to see Oedipus trespassing the inviolate sanctuary, and in fact makes it clear that his very presence in Athens is altogether unwelcome. But Ismene intervenes to report the oracle's prophecy that Oedipus' eventual burial place will sanctify the land on which it stands. The chorus, profoundly impressed, hurriedly reconsiders the situation and later reminds King Theseus how very useful Oedipus is to prove once he dies. Theseus, having to his credit already extended hospitality to Oedipus, now proclaims him a citizen; and the chorus, much gratified, breaks into one of the most beautiful—and ironic because it is so exquisitely beautiful—choral poems in ancient Greek literature (ll. 668ff.). But the underlying comedy that so relentlessly exposes human selfishness proceeds apace. Creon, who had also learned of the oracle's prophecy, arrives to invite Oedipus back to Thebes with telling assurances that the erstwhile exile would now be most welcome (ll. 728ff.); but Oedipus unerringly perceives the motivation and violently denounces the transparent change of heart. Polyneices also comes, this time with a plea that Oedipus join the Argives against the Thebans (ll. 1284ff.); but Oedipus responds with a harsh and often misunderstood tirade which, within the play's context, is a pointed disclosure of man's greed. The death of Oedipus at Colonus emerges in the end as a parable likely to be misunderstood only by those who seeing see not, and hearing hear not.

Euripides' propensities should have yielded more satyr-plays than Aeschylus and Sophocles composed jointly, but in the event he wrote fewer than did either of the other two. *The Cyclops* is consequently not the rule but the exception. Instead, Euripides elected to project the terms normally reserved for satyr-plays to his drama at large. The result was confusion expertly confounded. *Alcestis,* for instance, can be defined rather negatively than positively. It is clearly not a tragedy; but neither is it a comedy, or even a tragicomedy, and may in the end only loosely be classed as a satyr-play. At the City Dionysia, at any rate, it was given the benefit of the doubt and performed as a satyr-play. The crucial factor must be presumed to be the presentation of Heracles, conceived that he is as a burlesque character with a sufficiently obvious progeny. He is on his way to cope with the mares of Diomedes—"a horse-stealing expedition," explains the most irrelevant critic of Greek drama[23]—but on visiting the household of Admetus he is confronted by Alcestis' imminent departure for Hades in lieu of her husband. A servant who is assigned to look after the travel-weary Heracles is not at all impressed:

> I have known all sorts of foreigners who have come in
> from all over the world here to Admetus' house,
> and I have served them dinner, but I never yet
> have had a guest as bad as this to entertain.

The trouble is that the omnicompetent and legendary Heracles indulges rather too freely in wine:

> [he] drank the wine of our dark mother, straight, until the flame of the wine went all through him, and heated him, and then he wreathed branches of myrtle on his head and howled, off key.[24]

Yet the comic dimension is not restricted to Heracles, not even after he enters the stage half-drunk. It is extended to include the return of the veiled Alcestis, the refusal of Admetus to consider "another" woman, and their joyous reunion. Should the play appear less than promising as a potential influence on other dramatists, we could do worse than ponder T. S. Eliot's acknowledgment that *Alcestis* was the "source" of one of his own plays, *The Cocktail Party*[25]—itself subtitled, in a calculated gesture of defiance, "A Comedy."

The other plays of Euripides also challenge our infatuation with classifications. In *The Heraclidae,* for instance, the superannuated Iolaus touches high comedy when an attendant helps him (more or less) to prepare for his improbable battle against the Argives:

> *Iolaus:* All right, come on; but keep my things all ready.
>   Now put the spear-shaft into my left hand
>   And take my right arm so, to guide my steps.
> *Attendant:* Ye gods! Am I to nursemaid you to war?
> *Iolaus:* No, but we'll watch our step. To fall's bad luck.
> *Attendant:* If only you could do what you can dream.
> *Iolaus:* Hurry! I can't afford to miss the fight.
> *Attendant:* You are the dawdler, though you think it's I.
> *Iolaus:* But don't you see how very fast I'm walking?
> *Attendant:* I see the speed is largely in your mind.
> *Iolaus:* You'll change your tune as soon as I get there.
> *Attendant:* What will you do? I want to see you win.
> *Iolaus:* You'll see me smash clean through somebody's shield.
> *Attendant:* If ever we arrive there, which I doubt.[26]

Two other plays, *Helen* and *Iphigenia in Tauris,* use a device which may be described as comic by osmosis. In the one, Helen tricks King Theoclymenus so that she can escape with her companions from Egypt; while in the other, Iphigenia does as much with King Thoas of Tauris— but not before she has advised him most earnestly, "O King, beware of Greeks!" (l. 1204). The mind at work on these occasions is veritably Homeric, and more specifically Odyssean, in that it mirrors the conduct of the versatile Odysseus, of his equally callid wife, and of their protector, the vulpine Athena. It is therefore not impossible to claim that *Helen* is "comedy from beginning to end,"[27] provided we are fully aware of the "comedy" we have in mind, and provided too we are not tempted to negate the gravity of Euripides' ultimate concerns. The dramatist has much fun in positing a real Helen in Egypt at the very time that the Greeks were sacking Troy to avenge the abduction of Helen's ghost! The deflation of the Trojan war is total: "O Troy, how you were brought down in vain!" (l. 1220). In other words, if in Aeschylus and Sophocles the comic intrudes upon the tragic, in Euripides the tragic emerges from the heart of comedy—nowhere more movingly than in Helen's passionate lament over the ravages effected by the folly of aggression and war:

> Ah, Troy, the unhappy,
> for things done that were never done
> you died, hurt pitifully . . .
> Mothers who saw their children die,
> maidens who cut their long hair

for kinsmen who were killed beside the waters
of Phrygian Scamander.
Hellas too has cried, has cried
aloud in lamentation,
beaten her hands against her head
and with the nails' track of blood
torn her cheeks' softness.[28]

Yet it would appear that Euripides at the end of his life abandoned his evident predilections in favor of a tragedy properly so called. But in regarding *The Bacchae* care must be had to understand—so far as it is possible to understand—the mystery of the presence which is the god Dionysus. Risible and harmless at first, but utterly potent and alarming by the end, Dionysus possesses a chilling smile that haunts the self-confident Pentheus to destruction, μεδύων. The ambivalence of Dionysus in *The Bacchae* parallels that which in *The Iliad* resulted in a "nursery-rhyme Zeus" who is yet "the supreme and awful sovereign of all the universe." Is it possible in such circumstances to seek, and much less to establish with assurance, any strict lines of demarcation between tragedy and comedy? The question answers itself when we recall that the marks borne by Dionysus in *The Bacchae* are also borne by Dionysus in *The Frogs* of Aristophanes.[29]

IV. "Consider who it is that speaks"

Samson Agonistes is a tolerant play. It has tolerated in particular a variety of critical claims, especially the large claims about the influence reputedly exerted on it by several Greek plays ranging from Sophocles' *Oedipus at Colonus* to Euripides' *Heracles*.[30] But since a dramatist responds to an aggregate of influences only in order to transmute them into novelties, we must remain skeptical of all singular claims that endeavor to reduce the larger framework or impoverish the richer texture.[31] The caveat applies equally to the preceding paragraphs where my tentative suggestions may have inadvertently appeared in the guise of categorical dicta. The given detail was in each instance intended but to suggest the general, exactly as the presence in *Samson Agonistes* of a character like Harapha is meaningful only in relation to the predicament of the protagonist.

Harapha's entry is heralded by a trumpet blast from the Chorus:

> I know him by his stride
> The giant Harapha of Gath, his look
> Haughty, as is his pile high-built and proud.
>
> (ll. 1067–69)

Harapha may or may not be "the high point of the drama" in that his presence effects "the necessary reversal in Samson's attitude."[32] If he is of such major importance, however, is it not very odd that Milton should have provided him with a literary progeny which includes the braggarts in the comic literature of the Continental Renaissance?[33] The consequences, after all, are unmistakable. So far as the play's preface is concerned, Harapha's progeny flatly contradicts—and, at the very least, neatly subverts—the militant censure of "the error of intermixing comic stuff with tragic sadness and gravity." So far as the play itself is concerned, on the other hand, the question must necessarily be posed whether Harapha's comic antecedents are meant to alert us to the concurrent presence of other comic elements.

Manoa's endeavors to ransom Samson, we noted earlier, are "not unlike" the well-meant if silly efforts of Oceanus to intercede with Zeus. The parallel—in itself hardly novel[34]—should not be pressed too far, however, since Manoa will always remain a rather distant cousin of his "plainly half-comic" predecessor. But an awareness of Aeschylus' intentions in Oceanus obliges us to inquire more closely into Milton's aims in Manoa. The first speech of Manoa (ll. 340-72) emotionally contrasts his erstwhile great expectations concerning Samson and his present shattering disappointment over the actual turn of events. Presently Manoa even threatens to induce despair by questioning divine justice; and as Samson is spontaneously driven to defend the ways of God, the roles are abruptly switched. The one who should have been comforted is now himself the comforter:

> Appoint not heavenly disposition, father,
> Nothing of all these evils hath befallen me
> But justly.
>
> (ll. 373-75)

Samson who is eyeless will eventually gain spiritual vision, but Manoa who possesses eyesight will remain blind to the end. He is tellingly made to carry the burden of the playwright's dramatic irony, anticipating the final outcome even as he himself is incapable of perceiving it. For instance:

> God,
> Nothing more certain, will not long defer
> To vindicate the glory of his name
> Against all competition, nor will long
> Endure it doubtful whether God be Lord,
> Or Dagon. But for thee what shall be done?
>
> (ll. 473-78)

Just as the initial affirmation here forecasts the play's actual resolution, so the final question—emphatically induced by the dichotomizing "But"—proclaims the impossibility that sealed eyes such as Manoa's can ever be made to see. A prisoner of his senses, Manoa credits only what he can see or touch or feel, whether in commending the "friends" in the Chorus who are in fact Samson's most dangerous enemies, or in prosecuting his plan to free his son through "ransom"—the very word which, in its theological context, pertains solely to the redemption of man by God. Samson's death is an occasion for Manoa contentedly to observe that his son is "on his enemies / Fully revenged" (ll. 1171–72); and as his blindness persists, he voices Milton's crowning instance of dramatic irony in the play by asking that the "heroic" Samson be carried to "his father's house" (l. 1733). But "heroism" involves much more than the slaughter of one's enemies, just as "Father" has more than the single point of reference upheld by Manoa.[35]

The comic aspects of Manoa, it might be said, center on the discrepancy between his own immobility and the onward movement of the world about him. What might in that case be proposed about the Chorus whose movement is less an arrested than a regressive one?[36] In the previous paragraph I proposed that the "friends" who constitute the Chorus are Samson's most dangerous enemies; nor would I now wish that premise to be dismissed lightly. The Chorus—"one of the actors"—is as highly individualized by Milton as it was by Sophocles. But the personality that emerges is meant to generate considerable disquiet, generously confirmed as it is by echoes of the Book of Job where the three "friends" militantly espouse a patently mistaken view of divine providence. The pattern in *Samson Agonistes* is most obvious in that extraordinary choral song which misleads precisely because it appears to duplicate the aspiration of *Paradise Lost* to justify the ways of God to man: "Just are the ways of God, / And justifiable to men" (ll. 293–94). But it is assuredly an error to equate an epic's invocation with a play's manifestly dramatic speech. As Milton himself observed on another occasion,

> We must not regard the poet's words as his own, but consider who it is that speaks in the play, and what that person says; for different persons are introduced, sometimes good, sometimes bad, sometimes wise men, sometimes fools, and they speak not always the poet's opinion, but what is most fitting to each character.[37]

That which is "most fitting" to the Chorus in *Samson Agonistes* becomes apparent in the startling affirmation that the universe is under the control of an authoritarian and capricious deity,

> Who made our laws to bind us, not himself,
> And hath full right to exempt

Whom so it pleases him by choice
From national obstriction, without taint
Of sin, or legal debt;
For with his own laws he can best dispense.

(ll. 309–14)

The speech can hardly be claimed to carry the approval of Milton, whose own efforts were, throughout his life, a relentless attack on the sinister theory propounded here. The Chorus is permitted to sustain it because each of the play's *dramatis personae* is individualized largely in terms of his (or her) attitude to divinity, whether positive as it is in most cases, or strictly negative as it is in the case of Dalila. But should the implications of the speech not register on us, Milton has other means to mark the vulgarity of the "friends." These means are partly thematic, as in the Chorus's omnipresent and vicious antifeminism,[38] and partly poetic—thus:

God of our fathers, what is man!
That thou towards him with hand so various,
Or might I say contrarious,
Temper'st thy providence through his short course.

(ll. 667–70)

It requires total insensitivity to poetry not to see that the line here italicized constitutes an arrant deviation from the most basic canons of poetic articulation; yet it is an insensitivity that the Chorus clearly possesses. I darkly suspect, indeed, that the Chorus would have responded with equal enthusiasm to Mrs. Browning's improbable lines: "Will you oftly / Murmur softly?" But in time the Chorus's regressive movement is inverted, bent toward that superb benediction that marks a new dimension in its experience:

Go, and the Holy One
Of Israel be thy guide
To what may serve his glory best.

(ll. 1427–29)

Where *The Iliad* predicates a "nursery-rhyme Zeus" who is yet "the supreme and awful sovereign of all the universe," and *The Bacchae* maintains as much in connection with Dionysus, *Samson Agonistes* reflects explicitly through its Chorus what is implicit in its protagonist: a gradual transition from risible vulgarities to the noble conception of a mysterious universe under the control of "th' unsearchable dispose of Highest Wisdom" (ll. 1746–47). The comic dimension is not thereby negated, however. It continues to illumine the human condition in that our follies—the greed exposed in *Oedipus at Colonus,* the martial endeavors condemned in *Helen,* the self-confidence of inconsequential man denounced in *The Bacchae,* the vulgarity of presumption censured in *Samson Agonistes*—such follies are best perceived through laughter. But laughter, as Henry More the Cambridge Platonist pointed out, is itself the gift of God,

> whose Gayete and Festivity is also so conspicuous in endowing us with that passion or property of Laughter, to entertain those lighter miscarriages with, whether in manners or fortune: As if Providence look'd upon her bringing Man into the World as a Spectatour of a Tragick-Comedy.[39]

Samson Agonistes sidesteps explicitness in that it is not a treatise but a dramatic poem. Yet it embraces the self-same mystery which a later poet also perceived when he wrote that "constellations indeed / Sing of some hilarity beyond / All liking and happening."[40]

NOTES

An earlier version of this chapter appeared as "The Comic Dimension in Greek Tragedy and *Samson Agonistes*" in *Milton Studies* 10 (1977): 3–21, ed. James D. Simmonds. Published in 1977 by the University of Pittsburgh Press. Used by permission. *Samson Agonistes* is here quoted from *The Poetical Works of John Milton,* ed. Helen Darbishire (Oxford, 1955), vol. 2.

1. On Marlowe, consult Robert Ornstein, "The Comic Synthesis in *Doctor Faustus,*" *ELH* 22 (1955): 165–72; John H. Crabtree, Jr., "The Comedy of Marlowe's *Dr. Faustus,*" *Furman Studies* 9.1 (1961): 1–9; Douglas Cole, *Suffering and Evil in the Plays of Marlowe* (Princeton, 1962), pp. 11ff., 141ff., 215ff., etc.; Gerald Morgan, "Harlequin Faustus: Marlowe's Comedy of Hell," *Humanities Association Bulletin* 18.1 (1967): 22–34; Donna Bobin, "Marlowe's Humor," *Massachusetts Studies in English* 2 (1969): 29–40; etc. On Shakespeare, see the various studies cited in the essay on pp. 47ff.
2. See Arnold Stein, *Answerable Style* (Minneapolis, 1953), pp. 19ff., 45ff., and *passim*; Roy Daniells, "Humour in *Paradise Lost,*" *Dalhousie Review* 33 (1953): 159–66; Carolyn Herbert, "Comic Elements in the Scenes of Hell in *Paradise Lost,*" *Renaissance Papers,* 1956, pp. 92–101; Joseph H. Summers, *The Muse's Method* (London, 1962), pp. 46ff.; Gregory Ziegelmaier, "The Comedy of *Paradise Lost,*" *College English* 26 (1965): 516–22; Roger B. Rollin, "*Paradise Lost:* Tragical-Comical-Historical-Pastoral," *Milton Studies* 5 (1973): 3–37; K. W. Gransden, "Milton, Dryden, and the Comedy of the Fall," *Essays in Criticism* 26 (1976): 116–33; Robert Crosman, *Reading "Paradise Lost"*

(Bloomington, Ind., 1980), chap. 6; Robert H. Bell, " 'Blushing like the morn': Milton's Human Comedy," *Milton Quarterly* 15 (1981): 47–55; and three studies by John Wooten: "Satan, Satire, and Burlesque in *Paradise Lost,*" *Milton Quarterly* 12 (1978): 51–58; "The Metaphysics of Milton's Epic Burlesque Humor," *Milton Studies* 13 (1979): 255–73; and "The Comic Milton and Italian Burlesque Poets," *Cithara* 22 (1982): 3–12.
3. See the studies listed on p. 46 (note 38).
4. See my essay on "The Biblical Comic and the Demands of Reality," *UTQ* 53 (1983): 72–84.
5. *The Iliad* III.209–11; here quoted in the paraphrase by W. F. Jackson Knight, *Many-Sided Homer* (London, 1968), p. 156. Pope's version obliterates the point altogether: "Erect, the Spartan most engaged our view; Ulysses seated, greater reverence drew." But even Richmond Lattimore's responsible version (1951) falters here: "when these . . . stood up, Menelaos was bigger by his broad shoulders / but Odysseus was the more lordly when both were seated."
6. Knight, *Many-Sided Homer,* pp. 114–15.
7. Rachel Bespaloff, "The Comedy of the Gods," in her *On the Iliad,* trans. Mary McCarthy (New York, 1947; reprint 1962), pp. 71–79. The broader background is detailed by Lawrence Giangrande, *The Use of Spoudaiogelion in Greek and Roman Literature* (The Hague, 1972).
8. Bespaloff, "The Comedy of the Gods," pp. 75–76.
9. Gilbert Murray, *Aeschylus: The Creator of Tragedy* (Oxford, 1940), pp. 146–47. Fragments survive from six of these plays: *The Heralds* and *The Lion* (subjects unknown); *Proteus, Prometheus the Fire-kindler,* and *The Sphinx* (the satyr-plays annexed to the trilogies of *The Oresteia, The Prometheia,* and *The Oedipodeia,* respectively); and *Lycurgus* (the satyr-play of the lost trilogy centered on Lycurgus). See *Aeschylus,* ed. Herbert W. Smyth, Loeb Classical Library (Cambridge, Mass., 1926), 2:419, 420, 453–54, 455, 460–61.
10. Trans. Roger L. Green in *Two Satyr Plays* (Harmondsworth, England, 1957). The Sophoclean satyr-play was first published in 1912; but the Euripidean one was extant during the Renaissance (see, among others, the Latin version by Melanchthon) and had been studied by Milton (see his marginal notes on it in *Works of John Milton,* gen. ed. Frank A. Patterson et al. [New York, 1931–38], 18:314–15).
11. From Green's introduction to *Two Satyr Plays,* p. 11. For a useful glance at satyr-plays, see Peter D. Arnott, *An Introduction to the Greek Theatre* (New York, 1963), chap. 7.
12. "Obviously," warns Gilbert Murray nervously, "the phrase is figurative"! (*Aeschylus: The Creator of Tragedy,* p. 147).
13. H. D. F. Kitto, *Greek Tragedy* (New York, 1955), p. 118.
14. A "mad cow" at that! (Letter to the Rev. William Mason, January 24, 1778, in *The Letters of Horace Walpole,* ed. Peter Cunningham [Edinburgh, 1906], 7:24). I am grateful to Professor Allen T. Hazen for assistance in locating this reference.
15. E. T. Owen, *The Harmony of Aeschylus* (Toronto, 1952), p. 58.
16. Lowell, *Prometheus Bound* (London, 1970), p. 12.
17. Jonson, in a marginal note to his *Masque of Blacknesse,* reminds us of still another possibility: "The ancients induc'd *Oceanus* always with a Bulls head"

(*Ben Jonson*, ed. C. H. Herford and Percy and Evelyn Simpson [Oxford, 1925–52], 7:170).
18. *Prometheus Bound*, ll. 381–83, trans. David Greene in *The Complete Greek Tragedies*, ed. David Greene and Richmond Lattimore (Chicago, 1956), *Aeschylus II*, p. 153.
19. George Thomson, *Aeschylus and Athens: A Study in the Social Origins of Drama*, 3d ed. (London, 1966), pp. 222–23. I owe this reference to Michael Moschos.
20. *Poetics*, chap. 18; trans. Preston H. Epps (Chapel Hill, 1942), p. 37. For a general view of the chorus, see T. B. L. Webster, *The Greek Chorus* (London, 1970).
21. *Antigone*, ll. 223–31, trans. Elizabeth Wyckoff in *The Complete Greek Tragedies*, ed. Greene and Lattimore, *Sophocles I*, p. 166.
22. *Ben Jonson*, ed. Herford and Simpson, 8:311, ll. 121–25, 132–35.
23. Jan Kott, *The Eating of the Gods: An Interpretation of Greek Tragedy*, trans. B. Taborski and E. J. Czerwinski (New York, 1974), p. 91. Kott's study is often amusing, in spite (or rather because) of his great expectations. It is otherwise "tiresome, silly and pretentious" (Hugh Lloyd-Jones, *TLS*, November 20, 1974, p. 1330).
24. *Alcestis*, ll. 747–50, trans. Richmond Lattimore in *The Complete Greek Tragedies*, ed. Greene and Lattimore, *Euripides I*, p. 37.
25. In *Poetry and Drama* (London, 1951), p. 31. See also his further remarks on "my Greek originals"—especially *Alcestis*—in *Writers at Work: The "Paris Review" Interviews*, 2d ser., intro. Van Wyck Brooks (New York, 1965), p. 103.
26. *The Heraclidae*, ll. 727–40, trans. Ralph Gradstone in *The Complete Greek Tragedies*, ed. Greene and Lattimore, *Euripides I*, p. 144.
27. H. D. F. Kitto, *Greek Tragedy* (New York, 1955), p. 328. For a thorough roll-call of Euripides' comic figures, consult Lydia Biffi, "Elementi comici nella tragedia greca," *Dioniso* 35 [i.e., 24] (1961): 89–102.
28. *Helen*, ll. 362–73, trans. Richmond Lattimore in *The Complete Greek Tragedies*, ed. Greene and Lattimore, *Euripides II*, p. 205.
29. The connection between Aristophanes and Euripides could be extended to include Aeschylus, whose *Pentheus* (now lost) had anticipated the Dionysus-centered story of *The Bacchae*. Cf. the reference in *The Eumenides* to Dionysus who "in divine form . . . led his Bacchanals in arms / to hunt down Pentheus like a hare in a deathtrap" (ll. 25–26, trans. Richmond Lattimore in *The Complete Greek Tragedies*, ed. Greene and Lattimore, *Aeschylus I*, pp. 135–36). A particularly sensitive assessment of Euripides' play is by Bernd Seidensticker, "Comic Elements in Euripides' *Bacchae*," *American Journal of Philology* 99 (1978): 303–20.
30. On Sophocles, see Martin Mueller, "Time and Redemption in *Samson Agonistes* and *Iphigenie auf Tauris*," *UTQ* 41 (1972): 227–45. Earlier, William R. Parker, in *Milton's Debt to Greek Tragedy in "Samson Agonistes"* (Baltimore, 1937), chap. 17, was concerned to establish that Milton's play "most resembles" *Oedipus at Colonus* in technical details and mere parallels. Neither critic appears cognizant of the comic dimension in the Sophoclean play noted earlier. On Milton's links with Euripides, see Carole S. Kessner, in "Milton's Hebraic Herculean Hero," *Milton Studies* 6 (1974): 243–58, who detects the "substance and spirit" of *Samson Agonistes* in *Heracles*, but gingerly bypasses

several fundamental and diametrically opposed aspects of the two plays, i.e., that Samson is not annihilated by his experience as Heracles is, that the brutality of Euripides is not even distantly matched by Milton, that the resolution in *Heracles* centers largely on a merely human agent (Theseus), and so on.

31. It is perhaps necessary to remind ourselves that Milton's respect for Euripides is well attested: see Philip W. Timberlake, "Milton and Euripides," in *The Parrott Presentation Volume,* ed. Hardin Craig (New York, 1935), pp. 315–40. But the evidence should be interpreted cautiously since Milton's favorable comments on Euripides on several occasions and in diverse contexts do not preclude his equal respect for Aeschylus and Sophocles when he came to write a play himself.
32. Nancy D. Libbey, "Milton's Harapha," *SAQ* 71 (1972): 521–29.
33. As D. C. Boughner conclusively demonstrated in "Milton's Harapha and Renaissance Comedy," *ELH* 11 (1944): 297–306.
34. Parker, *Milton's Debt to Greek Tragedy,* chap. 9, remarks that Oceanus may not be ignored as "a possible parallel" since his part in *Prometheus Bound* is "too strikingly like that of Manoa." Oceanus' comic aspects, at any rate, are downplayed ("to some readers he appears comic, or at least undignified").
35. Obviously I endorse the reading by Nancy Y. Hoffman in "Samson's Other Father: The Character of Manoa in *Samson Agonistes,*" *Milton Studies* 2 (1970): 195–210.
36. The ensuing argument, it should be made clear, reflects my respect for John Huntley's thesis in "A Revaluation of the Chorus' Role in *Samson Agonistes,*" *MP* 64 (1966): 132–45. Huntley understood implicitly the practice of the Greek dramatists which is here made explicit.
37. *Pro populo anglicano defensio* (1651), in *Selected Prose,* ed. C. A. Patrides, rev. ed. (Columbia, Mo., 1985), p. 403.
38. The most uncompromising claim of the Chorus reads:
    God's universal law
    Gave to the man despotic power
    Over his female in due awe,
    Nor from that right to part an hour,
    Smile she or lour.
    (ll. 1053–57)

    I admit to a lack of patience with those who detect here Milton's own voice. They have clearly never read his humane treatise *The Doctrine and Discipline of Divorce,* nor understood the presentation of Eve in *Paradise Lost.* Their reading is probably confined to the irrelevant novel by Robert Graves, *Wife to Mr. Milton* (London, 1943).
39. *Divine Dialogues* (London, 1668), 1:180. Cf. his *Antidote against Atheism* (1653): "if we could pierce to the utmost *Catastrophe* of things, all might prove but a *Tragick-Comedy*" (in *The Cambridge Platonists,* ed. C. A. Patrides [London, 1969], p. 269).
40. W. H. Auden, *Horae canonicae:* "Compline."

Milton's Prose: The Adjustment of Idealism

> Presume not that I am the thing I was
> —2 *Henry 4*

I. "The very visible shape and image of vertue"

Has there been a vast conspiracy uncritically to foster on us Milton's prose? Do we not feel at times much as Dr. Johnson felt about Congreve's novel, that we would rather praise it than read it?

To be more precise: would we have read Milton's prose works had he not been the author of *Paradise Lost?* True, we are fully aware of the intrinsic merits of *Areopagitica*; but what comparable claim can be advanced for the embarrassing histrionics of the ecclesiastical tracts, the apparent narrowness of outlook in *The Doctrine and Discipline of Divorce,* the laborious defensiveness of *The Tenure of Kings and Magistrates,* or the depressing dullness of the Latin treatise on Christian doctrine? Keats may have thought that Milton—"an active friend to Man all his Life"—had written "much delectable prose."[1] But might not Dr. Johnson have been more perceptive in his austere judgment on Milton's political convictions? In his words,

> Milton's republicanism was, I am afraid, founded on an envious hatred of greatness, and a sullen desire of independence; in petulance impatient of control, and pride disdainful of superiority. He hated monarchs in the State, and prelates in the Church; for he hated all whom he was required to obey. It is to be suspected that his predominant desire was to destroy rather than establish, and that he felt not so much the love of liberty as repugnance to authority.[2]

Dr. Johnson did not necessarily regard Milton as "an active friend to Man all his Life."

Shelley, on the other hand, praised exactly what Dr. Johnson had elected to denounce: "the sacred Milton was, let it be remembered, a republican, and a bold inquirer into morals and religion."[3] Wordsworth generalized even more. In 1802, adversely affected by the "vanity and parade" of England in contrast to the revolutionary zeal of France, he composed the celebrated sonnet beginning

> Milton! thou shouldst be living at this hour:
> England hath need of thee.

He continued:

> Thy soul was like a Star, and dwelt apart;
> Thou hadst a voice whose sound was like the sea:
> Pure as the naked heavens, majestic, free.
> So didst thou travel on life's common way,
> In cheerful godliness; and yet thy heart
> The lowliest duties on herself did lay.

But to be aware of Milton's activities is to realize the extent to which Wordsworth like everyone else created Milton in his own image. Whether Milton's voice during the revolutionary period of the seventeenth century was consistently majestic is debatable; and whether always pure, doubtful. Cheerful godliness was in evidence only spasmodically, whenever he managed to rise above the smoke and stir of passionate controversies. Perennially embattled, he would have found Wordsworth's notion of his apartness "like a Star" a travesty of his total commitment to the causes he had espoused throughout his life.

Shelley's view of Milton as "a bold inquirer into morals and religion" likewise defines tendencies latent not so much in Milton as in Shelley; while Dr. Johnson's judgment on Milton's republicanism is descriptive less of Milton's actual sentiments than of Dr. Johnson's obsessive partiality to the established order in Augustan England. To have hated monarchs in the State and prelates in the Church may have appeared dangerous to Dr. Johnson; but uncritically to have accepted either was, for Milton, unworthy of the dignity of man. As in *Paradise Lost* the Son of God reigns not so much by right of birth as by merit (III.309), so in *The Tenure of Kings and Magistrates* sovereignty is reserved for the individual who is worthy of the consent of the governed. Variations on this theme abound, yet the ethical orientation of the central concept was never surrendered by Milton: "queen truth ought to be preferred to king Charles" (p. 74). Equally, however persuasive the rhetoric that claims Milton felt "not so much the love of liberty as repugnance to authority," it is imperative to recognize how insistently Milton held that nothing is "of more grave and urgent importance throughout the whole life of man, than is discipline." I quote from the paean to discipline at the outset of *The Reason of Church-Government* (1642). It continues:

> What need I instance? He that hath read with judgement, of Nations and Common-wealths, of Cities and Camps, of peace and warre, sea and land, will readily agree that the flourishing and decaying of all

civill societies, all the moments and turnings of humane occasions are mov'd to and fro as upon the axle of discipline. So that whatsoever power or sway in mortall things weaker men have attributed to fortune, I durst with more confidence (the honour of divine providence ever sav'd) ascribe either to the vigor, or the slacknesse of discipline. Nor is there any sociable perfection in this life civill or sacred that can be above discipline, but she is that which with her musicall cords preserves and holds all the parts thereof together. Hence in those perfect armies of *Cyrus* in *Xenophon,* and *Scipio* in the Roman stories, the excellence of military skill was esteem'd, not by the not needing, but by the readiest submitting to the edicts of their commander. And certainly discipline is not only the removall of disorder, but if any visible shape can be given to divine things, the very visible shape and image of vertue, whereby she is not only seene in the regular gestures and motions of her heavenly paces as she walkes, but also makes the harmony of her voice audible to mortall eares. Yea the Angels themselves, in whom no disorder is fear'd, as the Apostle that saw them in his rapture describes [Revelation 7:1], are distinguisht and quaterniond into their celestiall Princedomes, and Satrapies, according as God himselfe hath writ his imperiall decrees through the great provinces of heav'n. The state also of the blessed in Paradise, though never so perfect, is not therefore left without discipline, whose golden surveying reed marks out and measures every quarter and circuit of new Jerusalem. Yet is it not to be conceiv'd that those eternall effluences of sanctity and love in the glorified Saints should by this meanes be confin'd and cloy'd with repetition of that which is prescrib'd, but that our happinesse may orbe it selfe into a thousand vagancies of glory and delight, and with a kinde of eccentricall equation be as it were an invariable Planet of joy and felicity, how much lesse can we believe that God would leave his fraile and feeble, though not lesse beloved Church here below to the perpetuall stumble of conjecture and disturbance in this our darke voyage without the card and compasse of Discipline.

(Columbia ed., 3:184–86; Yale ed., 1:751–53)

Yet Milton's celebration of discipline at the cosmic level does not terminate here. It reverberates across his prose and poetry, vesting man with that majesty of responsibility which is commensurate to his dignity as the favorite of God.

II. "Receiv'd with written Encomiums"

The best account of Milton's life and work is in the three interpretations composed by himself: the idealistic account of his aspirations to contribute "to Gods glory by the honour and instruction of my own country" in *The Reason of Church-Government* (1642); the extension of the same view in terms of the poet as himself "a true Poem" in *An Apology for Smectymnuus* (1642); and the detailed exposition of his visit to the Continent and of his eventual commitment to the republican cause in the *Defensio Secunda* (1654).[4] The rest is commentary.

But commentary should suggest in particular the cumulative impressions registered by the more recent activities of our scholars. Yet as it is no less perilous to be categorical than impossible fully to represent the diversities of opinion, one development may be cited as providing testimony to the conclusions now laboriously arrived at. It concerns Milton's visit to the Continent from the spring of 1638 to the late summer of 1639, and the presence especially of five names among the numerous individuals he befriended: Hugo Grotius, Lucas Holstein, Pietro Frescobaldi, Antonio Malatesti, and Francesco Cardinal Barberini.

Grotius at the time of Milton's visit to Paris was Queen Christina's ambassador to the French Court. Among his achievements he could already count *Adamus Exul* (1601), a play in Latin on the Fall of Man, but also a vast reputation as the founder of international law in *De jure belli ac pacis* (1625). Later, in Rome, Milton also befriended the learned Lucas Holstein, secretary and librarian to Cardinal Barberini, and later librarian of the Vatican.[5] Might Milton have discussed with Grotius the problems inherent in the literary treatment of the Fall of Man, and with Holstein the visual representations of the same subject by Raphael in the Stanze della Segnatura and especially by Michelangelo in the Sistine Chapel? Of these possibilities Milton himself is silent; yet his contacts with Grotius and Holstein are certainly significant, immediately because of their ready acceptance of Milton's company, and mediately because of the evolutionary nature of his plans for a major poem.

To credit the conventional view of Milton as a grim Puritan is to expect him fanatically to have eschewed the company of the representatives of the Antichrist in Rome. On the contrary, however, his Florentine friends included the devout Frescobaldi, soon to become a prince of the Catholic Church; while in Rome he not only dined at the English Jesuit College but even entered the circle of the one man certainly to have been regarded as anathema by any committed Puritan, Cardinal Barberini, prime minister and chief counselor to his uncle, Pope Urban VIII. Milton was impressed as much by Barberini's "submissive loftiness of mind" as by the musical entertainments which, performed at the theater recently completed (1632) in the Cardinal's palace, evinced those exuberant elements that constitute the *grandiosità monumentale* of the baroque. It was the period of Rome's transformation by Borromini and Bernini.[6]

No less instructive is Milton's friendship with the Florentine Antonio

Malatesti, author of *La Tina,* a cycle of fifty amusingly obscene sonnets in the baroque idiom. *La Tina* was dedicated to Milton. Yet the expected strictures of that grim Puritan never materialized; instead, on his return to England, he sent Malatesti his warm regards.[7].

What do Milton's encounters on the Continent reveal? Above all, I think, a developing catholic taste, since the five men referred to represent achievements not so much incompatible as mutually exclusive: Milton in France and Italy had been studying the nature of multiform reality. But even more significant is the authority with which Milton on his return home articulated his future expectations:

> In the privat Academies of *Italy,* whither I was favor'd to resort, perceiving that some trifles... were receiv'd with written Encomiums, which the Italian is not forward to bestow on men of this side the *Alps,* I began thus farre to assent both to them and divers of my friends here at home, and not lesse to an inward prompting which now grew daily upon me, that by labour and intent study (which I take to be my portion in this life) joyn'd with the strong propensity of nature, I might perhaps leave something so written to aftertimes, as they should not willingly let it die. (P. 54)

Thus inspired, Milton extended the range of his activities spectacularly. For the first time he set down detailed outlines of several subjects for a major poem, even if, mindful less of Renaissance critical theory than of the practice of Grotius in *Adamus Exul,* the preferred form in each case is not an epic but a play—and in one particular instance a play on the Fall of Man under the title *Adam Unparadis'd.*[8] Shortly, too, Milton commenced writing in prose a number of works which by the end of his life were to include treatises on a vast range of subjects. He himself described them as labors of his left hand, yet they remain the most complete program actually carried out by any of the equally ambitious "universal men" of the English Renaissance. Reduced to its essentials, the program involved "three species of liberty": ecclesiastical, domestic, and civil (p. 71).

III. "The best way to bring men to their senses"

By the middle of the 1640s royalists tended increasingly to lament the plight of "poore, miserable, distracted, almost destroyed *England.*"[9] But to others—were they the majority?—the Civil War offered the opportunity to confirm the self-evident truth that England was favored of God. In a sermon delivered less than a year before the execution of Charles I, Paul Knell upheld the widespread persuasion that we may compare with *Israel* for a fruitfull scituation, being neither under the torrid nor the frozen Zone, neither burned away with parching heat, nor benummed away with pinching cold, but seated in a temperate climate & a fertile soile; our folds are full of sheep, our rallies stand so thick with corne that we may laugh and sing. God hath also fenced us about, like the *Israelites* in the red sea with a wall of water, the waters are as a wall unto us on our right hand, and on our left. But especially God hath fenced us by his protection, salvation hath the Lord appointed for wals and bulwarks. He hath likewise gathered the stones out from us, he hath cast out the *Romish* rabble, and hath planted our Land with the choicest Religion, that of Protestants.[10]

Yet the Reformation was far from complete. The process initiated a century earlier by Luther was now threatened by the episcopalian or prelatical form of ecclesiastical government whose hierarchical structure and elaborate church services were in appearance, and plausibly in fact, extensions of Roman Catholicism. In the early 1640s one of the most vociferous attacks on episcopalianism was mounted by a group of five Presbyterians improbably signing themselves "Smectymnuus" (from the initials of their names: Stephen Marshall, Edmund Calamy, Thomas Young, Matthew Newcomen, William Spurstow). Arranged on the other side were in the main Archbishop James Ussher of Armagh and Bishop Joseph Hall of Norwich. Milton was perhaps drawn into the controversy by one of the Smectymnuans, Thomas Young, who was once his tutor. Five pamphlets later, in any case, Milton's initially enthusiastic commitment was displaced by wary disenchantment, even acerbic disquiet.

Milton's experience parallels that of several of his contemporaries, for example, Henry More the Cambridge Platonist. More was in the 1650s to engage in a bitter controversy with Thomas Vaughan, the poet's brother; but his ambitious effort to curtail his antagonist's "preposterous and fortuitous imaginations" resulted first in Vaughan's abusive counterattack in *The Man-Mouse taken in a Trap,* then in More's bitingly satiric *Second Lash,* and finally in Vaughan's virulent attempt at a *Second Wash, or the Moore scour'd once more!* A badly shaken More sounding retreat concluded ruefully: "if ever *Christianity* be exterminated, it will be by *Enthusiasme.*"[11]

Idealism adjusted in the face of brutal reality was also the lesson that embittered controversy impressed on Milton. His first tract, *Of Reformation touching Church-Discipline* (1641), combines a serene assurance that an appeal to reason would prove decisive, with an apocalyptic persuasion that the Primal Reason could hardly fail to intervene on behalf of so just a cause as Milton's. The tract ends with a prolonged prayer that looks back to the denunciation of the corrupt clergy in *Lycidas* (1637) and ahead to the celebration of the eventual triumph of goodness in *Paradise Lost* (1667):

> Thou therefore that sits't in light & glory unapproachable, *Parent of Angels* and *Men*! next thee I implore Omnipotent King, Redeemer of that lost remnant whose nature thou didst assume, ineffable and everlasting *Love*! And thou the third subsistence of Divine infinitude, *illumining Spirit,* the joy and solace of created *Things*! one *Tripersonall* GODHEAD! looke upon this thy poore and almost spent and expiring *Church,* leave her not thus a prey to these importunate *Wolves,* that wait and thinke long till they devour thy tender *Flock,* these wilde *Boares* that have broke into thy *Vineyard,* and left the print of thir polluting hoofs on the Soules of thy Servants. . . . (P. 108)

The fervent prayer concludes first with the consecration of Milton's personal aspirations to the service of the Divine Purpose, and finally with the celebration of the beatific vision beyond the confines of time.[12]

But Milton's opponents were not impressed; and as their replies filled the air with barbarous dissonance, he tried again with a scholarly study *Of Prelatical Episcopacy* as well as with some satirical *Animadversions* (1641), and next with the rational and patient discourse entitled *The Reason of Church-Government urg'd against Prelaty* (1642). Frequently able to ascend from the immediate controversy to general principles, Milton relates once more his personal aspirations to the larger pattern by outlining his expectations and defining the role of the poet within a narrowly partisan society. Yet already Milton's reasonable tone is decreasingly in evidence. Enthusiasm—the "enthusiasm" of the fanatic which Henry More would soon learn to fear—has intervened to sacrifice principles on the questionable altar of ephemeral abuse. Milton's opponents have now grown into a "whippe of Scorpions," else "a continuall *Hydra* of mischiefe, and molestation," or "unctuous, and epicurean paunches."[13] However, Milton's abusive vocabulary and devastating scorn was common to any number of his contemporaries who likewise opposed the Anglicans' lukewarm *via media* by "the language of zeal." The justification was apparently Biblical: "because thou art lukewarm, and neither cold nor hot, I will spew [lit., vomit] thee out of my mouth" (Revelation 3:16).[14] Equally, however, the justification was broadly traditional, witness in particular Pascal's lengthy exposition of the way in which "mockery is sometimes the best way to bring men to their senses, and in that case is a righteous action."[15] Milton's view is not unlike Pascal's:

> Although in the serious uncasing of a grand imposture (for to deale plainly with you Readers, Prelatry is no better) there be mixt here

and there such a grim laughter, as may appeare at the same time in an austere visage, it cannot be taxt of levity or insolence: for even this vaine of laughing (as I could produce out of grave Authors) hath oft-times a strong and sinewy force in teaching and confuting; nor can there be a more proper object of indignation and scorne together then a false Prophet taken in the greatest dearest and most dangerous cheat, the cheat of soules.[16]

Later, in *Paradise Lost,* Milton would confine "blind Zeal" to the Limbo of Vanity (III.452); yet he retained scorn, boldly asserting that it is deployed by God in his derisive attitude towards the vain pursuits of Satan (II.188–91; V.735–37; VIII.75–79). Biblical precedent was again not far to seek: "The kings of the earth set themselves, and the rulers take counsel together, against the Lord. . . . He that sitteth in the heavens shall laugh: the Lord shall have them in derision" (Psalm 2:2–4). Embarrassed by the implications, Biblical commentators often tried to evade the issue ("God laughs figuratively," Alexander Ross suggested nervously in 1652).[17] But the "ever-memorable" John Hales of Eton perceptively concluded that

> It is a sport, and as it were a kind of recreation to God to discover false play, to wash off the colour and paint from disguised actions, and openly expose them to the laughter and scorn of Men and Angels.[18]

Another Biblical precedent often invoked ("answer a fool according to his folly") was annotated by a commentator in 1638 thus:

> *Answer therefore such a foole* lest hee thinke himself victorious, because there appeareth no one in the field against him. But if thou doe answer him, let it be *according to his folly,* and in such a manner as that it may declare his error and folly unto him, and that as it doth reproove him, for it may teach him the truth.[19]

Here as elsewhere, the consideration of Milton's activities in the light of seventeenth-century assumptions and practice should restrain our indecent haste to misconstrue as personal bias attitudes in fact widely upheld. More important aspects would then be readily apparent: that Milton's wary disenchantment after his last contribution to the controversy meaningfully testifies to vital experience gained; that such experience contributed greatly to his subsequent activities; and that it was a richly endowed poet who finally turned to *Paradise Lost.* To learn to temper "enthusiasm" and exorcise zeal are no mean achievements.

IV. "A command above all commands"

Milton in the five antiepiscopal tracts is increasingly emotional, even hysterical; yet he should have lapsed into insensate incoherence after his next experience, when, far more personally involved, he lifted his pen in defense of divorce. Married to Mary Powell in 1642, he was abandoned by her before the year was out; and faced with the unlikelihood of a divorce unless adultery was proved, he launched four treatises including in particular *The Doctrine and Discipline of Divorce* (1643, rev. ed. 1644). The four treatises should have been hastily prepared, ill considered, and highly partisan. Yet they are fully scanned, carefully wrought, and exceptionally liberal.

The background to *The Doctrine and Discipline of Divorce* is partly the vast Puritan literature on domestic conduct, partly the infinity of courtesy books, but especially the liberal tradition of Christian humanism emanating from Erasmus.[20] Had Milton been chained to the emotions that Mary Powell's departure must have aroused, he should have argued for divorce on the grounds of desertion. But he consciously chose the far more difficult and controversial task of pleading for divorce on the basis of mental incompatibility. Its "first protagonist in Christendom,"[21] he anticipated the more compassionate laws of our own day by three centuries. But the price he paid for this distinction was certainly high. Instantly denounced by a number of his shocked contemporaries, he remained tarnished in reputation until the end of his life.[22]

The violent reaction of Milton's contemporaries is understandable. For centuries the single valid ground for divorce had been adultery; and as this was taken to be the attitude of Christ himself (Matthew 19:9), its "flat contradiction" by Milton naturally horrified his contemporaries and obliged them to protest against his defense of divorce "for many other causes besides that which our Saviour only approveth, namely, in case of Adultery."[23]

Milton rested his case in part upon an appeal to the often used (and as often abused) "fundamentall law book of nature" (p. 147). Here as elsewhere the basic premise was the well-known idea that "the first and most innocent lesson of nature [is] to turn away peaceably from what afflicts and hazards our destruction" (*Tetrachordon*, Columbia ed. 4:117). But existing laws of divorce, Milton protested, violate "the reverend secret of nature" by frequently forcing "a mixture of minds that cannot unite." Surely the spiritual aspect of marriage ought to take precedence over the physical? "In marriage," St. Thomas Aquinas had written, "the union of souls ranks higher than union of bodies." Humanists agreed. According to the widely respected Juan Luis Vives, "There canne be [no] maryage or concorde" where man and wife "agree not in wyll and minde, the whyche twoo are the beginning & seate of all amitie & friendship."[24]

Therefore, as in *Paradise Lost,* Raphael insists that where there is no love there can be no happiness but only gratification of the senses, mere bestiality (VIII.579ff., 621), so *The Doctrine and Discipline of Divorce* maintains that "where love cannot be, there can be left of wedlock nothing, but the empty husk of an outside matrimony; as undelightfull and unpleasing to God, as any other kind of hypocrisie" (p. 140). God did not institute marriage "to remedy a sublunary and bestial burning," to have man and wife "grind in the mill of an undelighted and servil copulation" (pp. 144, 141).

> God in the first ordaning of marriage, taught us to what end he did it, in words expresly implying the apt and cheerfull conversation [i.e., association] of man with woman, to comfort and refresh him against the evill of solitary life, not mentioning the purposes of generation till afterwards, as being but a secondary end in dignity, though not in necessity. (P. 124)

The generous compass of Milton's thesis was widened as he went on to comprehend his belief in the potentialities of "the divine and softening breath of charity." "Our Saviours doctrine," he affirmed in *Tetrachordon,* "is, that the end, and the fulfilling of every command is charity; no faith without it, no truth without it, no worship, no workes pleasing to God but as they partake of charity" (Columbia ed., 4:96 and 135). Charity is "a command above all commands," "the supreme dictate," "whose grand commission is to doe and to dispose over all the ordinances of God to man; that love & truth may advance each other to everlasting" (pp. 180, 135, 168). As the concluding sentence of *The Doctrine and Discipline of Divorce* has it, "God the Son hath put all other things under his own feet; but his Commandments hee hath left all under the feet of Charity."

Milton's treatises on divorce have twice reappeared in English literature, first in the unexpected context of Farquhar's *The Beaux' Stratagem* (1707), and later as "the tragic machinery of the tale" in Hardy's *Jude the Obscure* (1895).[25] But we read *The Doctrine and Discipline of Divorce* not because of its influence on Farquhar or Hardy, much less as an excursion in autobiography. It is above all a remarkable testimony to a man's ability so to transcend his towering passions as to formulate principles of universal validity. At once a plea for liberty and a protest against institutionalism, it warrants also Milton's right proudly to claim: "Let not England forget her precedence of teaching nations how to live" (p. 120).

V. "According to conscience above all liberties"

A year later, in 1644, the precedence was further confirmed in *Of Education* and *Areopagitica*. The obvious differences between the two works forcefully remind us how impossible it is to generalize on Milton's style. Each work possesses a style appropriate to the given occasion. *Of Education,* in assuming the reader's familiarity with humanist educational theories, does not argue; it posits. But *Areopagitica,* in professing a thesis contrary to received opinion, displaces assertion by argument, and mere allegation by cogent analysis. The stylistic consequences cannot possibly be missed. *Of Education* is authoritative in appearance, categorical in manner, and almost entirely devoid of rhetoric since its thesis is, as it were, self-evident. But *Areopagitica* advances cumulatively in a series of waves, until the gathered force of argument and rhetorical patterns overwhelms our reservations and commands our assent.

Of Education was, like the treatises on divorce, the direct result of Milton's experience. The experience was two-fold: on the practical level, the education and instruction of his sister's two sons; and on the theoretical, the extensive discussions then under way concerning the methods of Comenius, the great Czech educational reformer who had visited England in 1641 possibly at the invitation of Parliament and who numbered among his English friends Samuel Hartlib, the recipient of Milton's address. Milton's participation in these discussions significantly assumed the form of a reiteration of the great ideals of Renaissance humanism. The vast compass of the educational scheme he endorses is by no means peculiar to himself but displays the humanist aspiration to create the "universal man." The countless precedents include the idealistic vision which in Rabelais informs Gargantua's famed letter to Pantagruel (bk. II. chap. 8); the all-encompassing nature of Vives' treatise *De disciplinis* in 1531; and, in England, Sir Philip Sidney's outline of a course of studies which extends from the Scriptures ("the foundation of foundations, the Wisdome of Wisdomes") to works on moral philosophy as on the art of war, and on geography as on history—the latter including all the major historians of ancient Greece, Rome, Byzantium, and Renaissance Europe! Milton like every humanist would have agreed with Sidney's disarming remark: "To me, the variety rather delights me, then confounds me."[26]

The program of studies outlined in *Of Education* is placed in *Areopagitica* within an even broader framework, the necessity of unlimited access to reading in order to exercise man's talents and issue in discrimination. The talents themselves, and man's ability to exercise them properly, are not called into question. Firm in his faith in man, Milton reserves the full weight of his ire against those who hubristically tamper with the individual's right to decide for himself. The emphasis is humanistic in general even while it is Protestant in particular: "Give me liberty to know, to utter, and to argue freely according to conscience above all liberties" (p. 241). It is noteworthy that fifteen years later, in *A Treatise of Civil Power in Ecclesiastical Causes* (1659), the plea was voiced yet again, on that occasion more particularly on behalf of religious liberty.

Originality of argument need not be sought in *Areopagitica* for it will not be found. Commonplaces, indeed, abound; but they are commonplaces raised to the level of great literature. Bishop Joseph Hall, Milton's antagonist in the antiepiscopal tracts, rephrased a familiar notion thus: "Ther can be but one truth: and that one Truth oft-times must be fetcht by peece-meal out of divers branches of contrary opinions."[27] But Milton's restatement is a touchstone of English prose:

> Truth indeed came once into the world with her divine Master, and was a perfect shape most glorious to look on: but when he ascended, and his Apostles after him were laid asleep, then strait arose a wicked race of deceivers, who as that story goes of the *Ægyptian Typhon* with his conspirators, how they dealt with the good *Osiris,* took the virgin truth, hewd her lovely form into a thousand peeces, and scatter'd them to the four winds. From that time ever since, the sad friends of Truth, such as durst appear, imitating the carefull search that *Isis* made for the mangled body of *Osiris,* went up and down gathering up limb by limb still as they could find them. We have not yet found them all, Lords and Commons, nor ever shall doe, till her Masters second coming; he shall bring together every joynt and member, and shall mould them into an immortal feature of loveliness and perfection. (P. 234)

The style *is* the work. It looks beyond Milton's other works—and other styles—to the only other classical oration in English literature, Sidney's *Apology for Poetry*. *Areopagitica* like the *Apology* weds style and argument in such a manner that while style and structure reflect the practice of classical rhetoricians, the thesis appeals to the most liberal instincts in man. Milton has appreciated by now what he would later transmute into poetry, that rhetoric by itself may be put to perverse uses, witness its deployment by Satan in *Paradise Lost*. But rhetoric exerted on behalf of truth—the truth of moral precepts immemorially upheld—could so imprint a cause upon the consciousness of men as they should not willingly let it die.

VI. "Pure Zeale to the Liberty of Mankind"

The liberty of the individual, threatened in Milton's time as in ours by societies militantly bent on conformity, was further defended by Milton in his several expressly political works. Whatever their nominal subjects, their one constant theme coincides with Blake's visionary denunciation of each and every effort to curtail the prerogatives of the individual ("One Law for the Lion and Ox is Oppression"). The fundamental principle of

Milton's thought is lucidly stated: "No man who knows ought, can be so stupid as to deny that all men naturally were born free" (p. 255).

The Tenure of Kings and Magistrates (1649), published within two weeks of the execution of Charles I, could be read as a straightforward justification of regicide. As with the treatises on divorce, however, Milton ascends beyond the immediate episode to formulate general principles, in this instance that free men having once entered into a voluntary contract with their governors may terminate it whenever tyranny is palpably in evidence. But *The Tenure* is also concerned with a development that was becoming increasingly apparent ever since the abolition of episcopacy in 1646: the tendency of the victorious Presbyterians "to sit the closest & the heaviest of all Tyrants, upon the conscience, and fall notoriously into the same sinns, wherof so lately and so loud they accus'd the Prelates" (p. 284). In the memorable words of a poem Milton wrote at this time, "*New Presbyter* is but *Old Priest* writ Large" ("On the New Forcers of Conscience under the Long Parliament," l. 20).

As *The Tenure* was followed by the two *Defenses* of the republican regime (1651–54), and they by *The Readie and Easie Way to Establish a Free Commonwealth* (1660), Milton's thinking appears to have become less flexible until his endorsement in the latter work of government by a self-perpetuating grand council of the "worthiest." But wildest undulations in Milton's stated attitudes cannot obscure either his insistence that sovereignty may never be "transferrd, but delegated only," or his consistent and even exclusive opposition to rule by any single person, whether Charles I or Cromwell.[28] On the very eve of the monarchy's restoration he warned: "that people must needs be madd or strangely infatuated, that build the chief hope of thir common happiness or safetie on a single person," "corruptible by the excess of his singular power and exaltation" (pp. 336, 348). The sage conclusion of John Aubrey in his brief life of Milton is apposite:

> Whatever he wrote against Monarchie was out of no animosity to the King's person, or owt of any faction or interest, but out of a pure Zeale to the Liberty of Mankind, which he thought would be greater under a free state than under a Monarchiall government.[29]

Not that the consistency of Milton's opposition to rule by any single person should mislead us into thinking that his political views remained static. Development there was, partly in the inevitable disillusionment when his great expectations for a radical reformation were shattered, but especially in the increasing realization that his apocalyptic entreaties for an external reformation—the rule of the saints exorcizing malefic prelates and authoritarian monarchs—should be preceded by an internal reformation, "a paradise within."[30]

Milton's political thought may also be approached by way of its opposition to that of Hobbes. After the appearance of Salmasius' royalist apologia in *Defensio regia* (1649) and Milton's reply in the first *Defense*— the *Pro populo anglicano defensio* (1651)—Hobbes wrote:

> I have seen them both. They are very good Latin both, and hardly to be judged which is better; and both very ill reasoning, hardly to be judged which is worse.[31]

Milton's judgment of Hobbes was equally generous. It is reported by Aubrey:

> His widowe assures me that Mr. T. Hobbs was not one of his acquaintance, that her husband did not like him at all, but he would acknowledge him to be a man of great parts, and a learned man. Their Interests and Tenets did run counter to each other.[32]

Hobbes was a materialist, Milton an idealist. Hobbes upheld determinism in a universe obedient to inflexible laws, Milton maintained that the liberty of man is an inalienable right granted by God in perpetuity. Hobbes endorsed absolute authoritarianism, Milton vehemently rejected any doctrine that deprived man of his independence. The power of kings, argued Milton, is "derivative, transferr'd and committed to them in trust from the People, to the Common good of all" (p. 257). Hobbes would have agreed but for the crucial qualification "in trust." It measures the abyss dividing two mutually exclusive responses to the predicament of man.

Milton also divides from Hobbes—and indeed from every other political philosopher of the seventeenth century—in terms of style. The magniloquent voice of the epic poet is heard throughout the two *Defenses* beginning with the preface to the first:

> I shall relate no common things, or mean; but how a most puissant king, when he had trampled upon the laws, and stricken down religion, and was ruling at his own lust and wantonness, was at last subdued in the field by his own people, who had served a long term of slavery; how he was thereupon put under guard, and when he gave no ground whatever, by either word or action, to hope better things of him, was finally by the highest council of the realm condemned to die, and beheaded before his very palace gate. I shall likewise relate (which will much conduce to the easing men's minds of a great superstition) under what system of laws, especially what laws of Eng-

land, this judgement was rendered and executed; and shall easily defend my valiant and worthy countrymen, who have extremely well deserved of all subjects and nations in the world, from the most wicked calumnies of both domestic and foreign railers, and chiefly from the reproaches of this utterly empty sophister [i.e., Salmasius], who sets up to be captain and ringleader of all the rest. For what king's majesty high enthroned ever shone so bright as did the people's majesty of England, when, shaking off that age-old superstition which had long prevailed, they overwhelmed with judgement their very king (or rather him who from their king had become their enemy), ensnared in his own laws him who alone among men claimed by divine right to go unpunished, and feared not to inflict upon this very culprit the same capital punishment which he would have inflicted upon any other.

As always in Milton, however, an apparently secular event is promptly placed within a metaphysical context. The preface to the first *Defense* continues:

Yet why do I proclaim as done by the people these actions, which themselves almost utter a voice, and witness everywhere the presence of God? Who, as often as it hath seemed good to his infinite wisdom, useth to cast down proud unbridled kings, puffed up above the measure of mankind, and often uprooteth them with their whole house. As for us, it was by His clear command we were on a sudden resolved upon the safety and liberty that we had almost lost; it was He we followed as our Leader, and revered His divine footsteps imprinted everywhere; and thus we entered upon a path not dark but bright, and by His guidance shown and opened to us. I should be much in error if I hoped that by my diligence alone, such as it is, I might set forth all these matters as worthily as they deserve, and might make such records of them as, haply, all nations and all ages would read. For what eloquence can be august and magnificent enough, what man has parts sufficient, to undertake so great a task? Yea, since in so many ages as are gone over the world there has been but here and there a man found able to recount worthily the actions of great heroes and potent states, can any man have so good an opinion of himself as to think that by any style or language of his own he can compass these glorious and wonderful works—not of men, but, evidently, of almighty God?

(*Pro populo anglicano defensio,* trans.
Samuel L. Wolff, Columbia ed., 7:3ff.)

The two *Defenses* like the five antiepiscopal tracts are intimately related to the point of view which, as we shall see, also pervades *The History of Britain*.

But the two *Defenses* and especially the third *Defense of Himself* (1655) are considerably marred by the frequently intemperate language which readers have often remarked, and as often deplored. Milton's earlier treatment of the bishops, indeed, pales before his personal attacks both against Salmasius, the author of the *Defensio regia,* and Alexander More, the presumed author of the *Regii sanguinis clamor* (1652). But here Milton appears to have relied not only on the weapons furnished by the traditional forms of mockery we noted in Pascal; he also depended on classical precedents, particularly the vituperation which in Cicero among others is intimately related to the ethical orientation of one's opponents.[33] The resort to abuse, at any rate, never propelled Milton towards distortion. Whether immersed in the broad argument of *The Tenure* or the narrow attacks on Salmasius and Alexander More, he remained throughout remarkably faithful to his sources.[34]

VII. "According to his Divine retaliation"

We do not know when Milton composed *The History of Britain* or the controversial theological treatise *De doctrina christiana*. The former was published for the first time in 1670; the latter, following its discovery a century and a half after Milton's death, in 1825.

The History of Britain may well have been written in the early 1640s. Edward Phillips, Milton's nephew, appears to have thought so, and at least one modern scholar places it even earlier.[35] But the work bears the mark of substantial revisions prior to its publication in 1670, most obviously in connection with the parallels Milton frequently and pointedly drew between the past and the present. Such "parallelism" was far from unknown during the Renaissance in England. Historians were adequately conditioned by Plutarch's *Parallel Lives* to agree with Thomas Heywood that "If wee present a forreigne History"—or indeed the history of Britain—"the subject is so intended, that in the lives of *Romans, Grecians,* or others, either the vertues of our Country-men are extolled, or their vices reproved."[36]

Milton's endorsement of the same approach resides partly in his account of the usurpation of Britain by William the "outlandish Conquerer"—an obvious parallel to the restoration of the monarchy in 1660— but also in his more emphatic representations of sovereigns with a moral authority entirely lacking in Charles II, for instance that "mirror of Princes" Alfred the Great, whose life advanced "not idely nor voluptuously, but in all vertuous emploiements both of mind and body" (Columbia ed., 10:315,

223, 220; Yale ed., 5:402, 292, 289). But the "lessons" of history also comprehended the traditional belief that historical events are a record of divine mercies and judgments. This expressly Christian view of history reappears in Milton's work mostly in connection with the periodic invasions of Britain, now firmly interpreted as so many judgments on a wayward nation:

> When God hath decreed servitude on a sinful Nation, fitted by thir own vices for no condition but servile, all Estates of Government are alike unable to avoid it. God hath purpos'd to punish . . . according to his Divine retaliation; invasion for invasion, spoil for spoil, destruction for destruction.
>
> (Columbia ed., 10:198; Yale ed., 5:259)

Even while embracing traditional beliefs, however, Milton pursued "truth" in accordance with the highest ideals of humanist historiography. Fables like Britain's mythical origins were not eschewed, "be it for nothing else but in favour of our English Poets, and Rhetoricians, who by thir Art will know, how to use them judiciously"; yet even then Milton drew the line, firmly, at Arthur ("who *Arthur* was, and whether ever any such reign'd in *Britain,* hath bin doubted heertofore, and may again with good reason" [Columbia ed., 10:3, 127–28; Yale ed., 5:3, 164]). On the other hand, Britain's documented past since the Roman invasion was so diligently and constructively researched that Milton is now generally regarded as "a judicious and conservative scholar."[37] Style was made subservient to truth. "I affect," he wrote in opposition to no less an authority than Thucydides,

> I affect not set speeches in a Historie, unless known for certain to have bin so spok'n in effect as they are writt'n, nor then, unless worth rehearsal; and to invent such, though eloquently, as some Historians have done, is an abuse of posteritie, raising, in them that read, other conceptions of those times and persons then were true.
>
> (Columbia ed., 10:68; Yale ed., 5:80)

The pursuit of truth also led Milton boldly to question widely held beliefs, and even sacrosanct dogmas, in *De doctrina christiana.* As observed earlier (p. 217), Milton tampered with the doctrine of the Trinity, denying the equality of the Father and the Son; he argued that the soul dies with the body; and he claimed that polygamy is not contrary to divine law.

De doctrina christiana began to be compiled sometime after Milton's return from the Continent in 1639, as Edward Phillips testifies; but there is evidence to suggest that it was being amended well into the 1650s, and possibly into the 1660s. Yet Milton never published it. Did he hesitate because aware of the furor its controversial arguments would have generated? Where totally committed, however, Milton utterly disregarded the possibility of the public's disapprobation, witness his bold publication of the treatises on divorce and the perilous reaffirmation of his republican convictions mere weeks before the restoration of the monarchy. It may be that he simply regarded *De doctrina* as incomplete, still seeking on his death a way out of the labyrinthine mazes he had entered in pursuit of "truth."

Stillborn though the treatise may be, it merits our scrutiny because Milton's achievement in prose cannot be divorced from his sporadic failures in the same medium. Moreover, the opportunity to compare the ideas expressed in *De doctrina* and *Paradise Lost* may not be bypassed. Obvious differences in mode of expression, and more subtle ones in intent, will not lead us to regard the treatise as a "gloss" upon the poem but ought to clarify those vital issues which, boldly explored in *De doctrina*, were finally resolved only through the poetry of *Paradise Lost*.

VIII. "The serious and hearty love of truth"

Milton's literary criticism is severely circumscribed, for he remarked on prose and poetry only occasionally, and sometimes almost accidentally. His brief remarks, extracted from their context, make an impressive if misleading collection;[38] but lengthy statements are extremely rare, except where called for by the immediate occasion. Instances include his views on the aims of scorn (quoted on pp. 255–56), the well-known passage in *The Reason of Church-Government* on his personal aspirations and the nature of poetry generally, and of course the preface to *Samson Agonistes*.

The passage in *The Reason of Church-Government* and the preface to *Samson* are alike meaningful in the light of Renaissance thought. Implicit in the first is the widespread fear that the abuse of poetry by inconsequential "poet-apes" (to borrow Sidney's term in the peroration of the *Apology for Poetry*) threatens not simply the art of poetry but, given Milton's idealistic view of the poet's mission, the very fiber of national life. Should the personal terms of Milton's utterance irritate us, it is well to remember that other Renaissance humanists display much the same vaulting pride in their achievements. But the personal "I" may also be regarded as an assumed persona expediting the transition from the particular to the general, from the merely personal to the expressly universal. In such a reading, the concluding statement on the office of the poet (p. 57) appears as a pronouncement of a poet-prophet, not unlike the dramatic peroration in Sidney's *Apology for Poetry*.

The preface to *Samson Agonistes* is similarly comprehensible within the context of critical opinion in its time. In appearance but a personal defense of Milton's practice, it is in fact a "highly compressed treatment of complex critical problems" involving the major issues of English neoclassical criticism.[39] Incidentally, however, the preface also highlights the difference between Milton's poetry and Milton's prose; for while the preface censures the mixture of the tragic and the comic, the play itself reaches its crisis in the introduction of the giant Harapha whom we earlier discerned to be a distant relative of the braggarts in Continental comic literature (see the discussion on p. 242).

The discrepancy—if indeed it is a discrepancy—has far-reaching implications. If Milton's engagement with prose differs in kind from his engagement with poetry, we would be well advised to hesitate before accepting the preface to *Samson* as entirely relevant to the play itself—or, further afield, before equating the prose of *De doctrina christiana* with the poetry of *Paradise Lost*. Milton's prose is after all unremittingly multiform, as noted in connection with *Of Education* and *Areopagitica*. Vastly different in style because vastly different in intent, *Of Education* and *Areopagitica* disarm any effort to generalize on Milton's prose. The "total effect" of this prose has been said to depend "more on an accumulation of convictions gained from individual sentences than on the logical progress of the argument through the complete work."[40] But however accurate an observation on Milton's polemical pamphlets, the statement misrepresents the method and effect of the eminently logical *Doctrine and Discipline of Divorce*, the fully sustained *Tenure of Kings and Magistrates*, the relatively unemotional *Treatise of Civil Power*, the serenely progressive *History of Britain*, or the relentlessly unrhetorical *De doctrina christiana*. Only one generalization pertains to Milton's multiform prose, that it is distinguished by its impressively variable tonal range.

The multiformity of Milton's prose can best be defined negatively. Eschewing Senecan laconisms, it is not given to "Sentences by the Statute, as if all above three inches long were confiscat."[41] At the other extreme, it avoids also the stylistic extravagances that Milton enumerates in *Of Reformation* as

> knotty Africanisms, the pamper'd metafors; the intricat, and involv'd sentences of the Fathers; besides the fantastick, and declamatory flashes; the crosse-jingling periods which cannot but disturb, and come thwart a setl'd devotion worse then the din of bells, and rattles.
>
> (Columbia ed., 3:34; Yale ed., 1:568)

Milton's own prose advances along the path marked by Cicero and his imitators. "I cannot say," he once wrote in a rare understatement, "that

I am utterly untrain'd in those rules which best Rhetoricians have giv'n, or unacquainted with those examples which the prime authors of eloquence have written in any learned tongue (*An Apology for Smectymnuus*, Columbia ed., 3:362; Yale ed., 1:948–49). Yet the best precedent for the multiformity of his own prose Milton discovered not in "the prime authors of eloquence" but in the Bible. His claim deserves to be quoted at length:

> Our Saviour who had all gifts in him was Lord to express his indoctrinating power in what sort him best seem'd; sometimes by a milde and familiar converse, sometimes with plaine and impartiall home-speaking regardlesse of those whom the auditors might think he should have had in more respect; otherwhiles with bitter and irefull rebukes if not teaching yet leaving excuselesse those his wilfull impugners. What was all in him, was divided among many others the teachers of his Church; some to be severe and ever of a sad gravity that they may win such, & check sometimes those who be of nature over-confident and jocond; others were sent more cheerefull, free, and still as it were at large, in the midst of an untrespassing honesty; that they who are so temper'd may have by whom they might be drawne to salvation, and they who are too scrupulous, and dejected of spirit might be often strengthn'd with wise consolations and revivings: no man being forc't wholly to dissolve that groundwork of nature which God created in him, the sanguine to empty out all his sociable livelinesse, the cholerick to expell quite the unsinning predominance of his anger; but that each radicall humour and passion wrought upon and correct as it ought, might be made the proper mould and foundation of every mans peculiar guifts, and vertues. Some also were indu'd with a staid moderation, and soundnesse of argument to teach and convince the rationall and sober-minded; yet not therefore that to be thought the only expedient course of teaching, for in times of opposition when either against new heresies arising, or old corruptions to be reform'd this coole unpassionate mildnesse of positive wisdome is not anough to damp and astonish the proud resistance of carnall, and false Doctors, then (that I may have leave to soare a while as the Poets use) then Zeale whose substance is ethereal, arming in compleat diamond ascends his fiery Chariot drawn with two blazing Meteors figur'd like beasts, but of a higher breed then any the Zodiack yeilds, resembling two of those four which *Ezechiel* and S. *John* saw, the one visag'd like a Lion to express power, high authority and indignation, the other of count'nance like a man to cast derision and scorne upon perverse and fraudulent seducers; with these the invincible warriour Zeale shaking loosely the slack reins drives over the heads of Scarlet Pre-

lats, and such as are insolent to maintaine traditions, brusing their stiffe necks under his flaming wheels. Thus did the true Prophets of old combat with the false; thus Christ himselfe the fountaine of meeknesse found acrimony anough to be still galling and vexing the Prelaticall Pharisees.

(*An Apology for Smectymnuus,* Columbia ed., 3:312–14; Yale ed., 1:899–900)

The close relationship here said to exist between rhetoric and truth is emphasized throughout Milton's prose and poetry. In the *Apology for Smectymnuus,* for instance, Milton maintained that

> true eloquence I find to be none, but the serious and hearty love of truth: And that whose mind so ever is fully possest with a fervent desire to know good things, and with the dearest charity to infuse knowledge of them into others, when such a man would speak, his words (by what I can expresse) like so many nimble and airy servitors trip about him at command, and in well order'd files, as he would wish, fall aptly into their own places.[42]

The principle, applied in *Paradise Lost,* issues in Milton's invitation that we discriminate sharply between Satan's seductive eloquence and his ambition to ruin man, a discrepancy amply confirmed in the harrowing episode involving the infernal trinity (II.648ff.). Satan's eventual reappearance in book IX as the representative of corrupt eloquence (ll. 665–76) links with the Christ's pointed contrast in *Paradise Regained* between the orators of Greece and the prophets of Israel:

> Thir Orators thou then extoll'st, as those
> The top of Eloquence, Statists indeed,
> And lovers of thir Country, as may seem;
> But herein to our Prophets farr beneath,
> As men divinely taught, and better teaching
> The solid rules of Civil Government
> In thir majestic unaffected stile
> Then all the Oratory of *Greece* and *Rome.*
> In them is plainest taught, and easiest learnt,
> What makes a Nation happy, and keeps it so,
> What ruins Kingdoms, and lays Cities flat;
> These onely with our Law best form a King.
>
> (IV.353–64)

The possession of a kingdom within that Milton's last poems persistently celebrate had been the aim of the poet himself many years since. As he wrote in 1642, "he who would not be frustrate of his hope to write well hereafter in laudable things, ought him selfe to bee a true Poem" (p. 62).

To what extent the poem has been realized will continue to be debated. But the aspiration itself commands respect.

NOTES

Earlier versions of this chapter served as the introductions to *John Milton: Selected Prose* (Harmondsworth, Middlesex, England: Penguin, 1974), pp. 15–45; rev. ed. (Columbia: University of Missouri Press, 1985), pp. 15–46. Copyright 1974, C. A. Patrtides; copyright 1985, the Curators of the University of Missouri. Reprinted with permission. Milton's prose is here quoted largely from the revised edition of *Selected Prose.* It is additionally quoted from *Works,* gen. ed. Frank A. Patterson (New York, 1931–40), 20 vols., and *Complete Prose Works,* gen. ed. Don M. Wolfe (New Haven, 1953–82), 8 vols., hereafter abbreviated as "Columbia ed." and "Yale ed.," respectively.

1. Letter to James Rice, March 24, 1818.
2. *Lives of the English Poets,* Everyman ed. (London, 1925), 1:92–93. Edgar Allan Poe in 1845 firmly separated Milton's subject from Milton's style: "independently of the subject-matter, his treatises are among the most remarkable ever written" (in *Selected Prose and Poetry,* ed. T. O. Mabbot [New York, 1951], 362).
3. Preface to *Prometheus Unbound* (1818–19).
4. *The Early Lives of Milton,* ed. Helen Darbishire (London, 1932, reprint 1965), is also an indispensable collection.
5. See Milton's letter to Holstein in the Columbia ed., 12:38–45, and the holograph discussed by J. McG. Bottkol in *PMLA* 68 (1953): 617–27.
6. On Frescobaldi, see the account by Roland M. Frye in *Milton Quarterly* 7 (1973): 74–76; on Milton's visit to the Jesuit College, Leo Miller, *Milton Quarterly* 13 (1979), 142–46; and on Barberini, John Arthos, *Milton and the Italian Cities* (London, 1968), pp. 55f., 69ff.
7. Columbia ed., 12:53; Yale ed., 2:765. *La Tina* has been translated by Donald Sears in *Milton Studies* 13 (1979): 275–317.
8. The outlines are in the manuscript now in the library of Trinity College, Cambridge (reproduced in the Columbia ed., 18:231–32).
9. John Harris, *Englands Out-cry* (London, 1644), p. 1.
10. *Israel and England Paralelled* (London, 1648), p. 15. The sermon was delivered at Gray's Inn on April 6, 1648.
11. See the account of this controversy in the introduction to my edition of *The Cambridge Platonists* (London, 1969; reprint Cambridge, 1980).
12. The imagery of warfare in *Of Reformation,* often present in Milton's more militant prose works, has been noted frequently. See Theodore H. Banks,

Milton's Imagery (New York, 1950), pp. 76–92; James H. Hanford, *John Milton: Poet and Humanist* (Cleveland, 1966), chap. 5; and Joan Webber, *The Eloquent "I"* (Madison, Wis., 1968), pp. 204ff. Consult also the broader contexts provided by Robert T. Fallon, *Captain or Colonel: The Soldier in Milton's Life and Art* (Columbia, Mo., 1984), and James A. Freeman, *Milton and the Martial Muse: "Paradise Lost" and European Traditions of War* (Princeton, 1980).

13. These are only three of the phrases rather lovingly collected in the Yale edition (1:113) as testimony to Milton's "bitter hatred." But they should be judged in the light of the period's vocabulary in controversy. Well into the Restoration, for example, Andrew Marvell, having written *The Rehearsal Transpros'd* (1672), was denounced in Samuel Parker's *Reproof* as "Thou Rat-Divine! thou hast not the Wit and Learning of a Mouse...."
14. See the excellent study by Thomas Kranidas, "Milton and the Rhetoric of Zeal," *Texas Studies in Literature and Language* 6 (1965): 423–32.
15. *The Provincial Letters,* trans. A. O. Krailsheimer (Harmondsworth, England, 1967), p. 165 [letter 11, dated August 18, 1656].
16. From the Preface to *Animadversions* (Columbia ed., 2:107; Yale ed., 1:663–64). Milton's "grave Authors" are fully set forth by Pascal (in *Provincial Letters,* 164ff.). Elsewhere Milton sought support in the origin and nature of satire: "a Satyr as it was borne out of a Tragedy, so ought to resemble his parentage, to strike high, and adventure dangerously at the most eminent vices among the greatest persons" (*An Apology for Smectymnuus,* in Columbia ed., 3:329; Yale ed., 1:916).
17. *Arcana Microcosmi* (London, 1652), p. 177.
18. *Sermons preach'd at Eton,* 2d ed. (London, 1673), p. 36. The first edition appeared posthumously in 1660.
19. Proverbs 26.5; as annotated by Michael Jermin, *Paraphrasticall Meditations, by Way of Commentarie, upon the Whole Booke of the Proverbs of Solomon* (London, 1638), p. 598.
20. The Puritan literature is emphasized by Chilton L. Powell, *English Domestic Relations 1487–1653* (New York, 1917), pp. 147–48, and William and Malleville Haller, "The Puritan Art of Love," *HLQ* 5 (1941–42): 235–72; the courtesy books, by John Halkett, *Milton and the Idea of Matrimony* (New Haven, 1970); and the Christian humanist tradition, by V. Norskov Olsen, *The New Testament Logia on Divorce: A Study of their Interpretation from Erasmus to Milton* (Tübingen, West Germany, 1971).
21. Edward A. Westermarck, *Christianity and Morals* (London, 1939), p. 385. One of the best studies of the treatises on divorce is Halkett's *Milton and the Idea of Matrimony* to which I am indebted; but I have also drawn liberally on my own remarks in *Milton and the Christian Tradition* (Oxford, 1966), pp. 178–86.
22. See William Haller, *Tracts on Liberty in the Puritan Revolution* (New York, 1934), vol. I, appendix B, and the passages collected by William R. Parker, *Milton's Contemporary Reputation* (Columbus, Ohio, 1940), pp. 73ff., 170ff. Cf. Milton's two sonnets, XII ("I did but prompt the age to quit their cloggs") and XI ("A Book was writ of late call'd *Tetrachordon*").
23. Ephraim Pagitt, *Heresiography,* 3d ed. (London, 1647), p. 150, and Daniel Featley, *The Dippers Dipt,* 5th ed. (London, 1647), sig. A4.

24. St. Thomas, *Summa theologica* III.1v.1, trans. by the English Dominican Fathers (London, 1911–25), and Vives, *The Office and Duetie of an Husband*, trans. Thomas Paynell (London, 1550?), sigs. K8–K8v.
25. See M. A. Larson, "The Influence of Milton's Divorce Tracts on Farquhar's *Beaux' Stratagem*," *PMLA* 39 (1924): 174–78. Milton's influence on Hardy has not yet been studied.
26. John Buxton, "An Elizabethan Reading List: An Unpublished Letter from Sir Philip Sidney," *TLS*, March 24, 1972, pp. 343–44. Vives' treatise is available in English, trans. Foster Watson (London, 1913, reprint Totowa, N.J., 1971). The humanist burden of Milton's *Of Education* is most ably expounded by William R. Parker, "Education: Milton's Ideas and Ours," *College English* 24 (1962): 1–14.
27. *Holy Observations* (London, 1607), p. 52.
28. The thesis is persuasively argued by Merritt Y. Hughes, *Ten Perspectives on Milton* (New Haven, 1965), pp. 267–68. See also his essay "Milton's *Eikon Basilike*," in *Calm of Mind*, ed. Joseph Wittreich (Cleveland, 1971), pp. 1–24.
29. *Brief Lives*, ed. Oliver L. Dick, 3d ed. (London, 1960), p. 203.
30. *Paradise Lost* XII.587. For an interpretation of Milton's development along the lines suggested, see Michael Fixler, *Milton and the Kingdoms of God* (London, 1964). See also my discussion of the nature of Milton's apocalyptic emphases on pp. 181–214.
31. *English Works*, ed. Sir William Molesworth (London, 1839), 6:368; quoted by Don M. Wolfe, "Milton and Hobbes: A Contrast in Social Temper," *SP* 41 (1944): 410–26.
32. *Brief Lives*, pp. 203.
33. See Diane P. Speer, "Milton's *Defensio Prima*: Ethos and Vituperation in a Polemic Engagement," *Quarterly Journal of Speech* 56 (1970): 277–83.
34. See Hughes, *Ten Perspectives*, chap. 9. Milton's charges against More have been largely substantiated: consult the studies by Kester Svendsen in *Texas Studies in Literature and Language* 1 (1959): 11–29; *JEGP* 60 (1961): 796–807; and *Th' Upright Heart and Pure*, ed. A. P. Fiore (Pittsburgh, 1967), pp. 117–30.
35. As early as 1632–38, according to Lloyd E. Berry in *RES*, n.s. 11 (1960): 150–56.
36. *An Apology for Actors* (London, 1612), sig. F3v.
37. Harry Glicksman, "The Sources of Milton's *History of Britain*," *University of Wisconsin Studies in Language and Literature* 11 (1920): 105–44.
38. Ida Langdon, *Milton's Theory of Poetry and Fine Arts* (New Haven, 1924).
39. See Annette C. Flower, "The Critical Context of the Preface to *Samson Agonistes*," *SEL* 10 (1970): 409–23.
40. K. G. Hamilton, "The Structure of Milton's Prose," in *Language and Style in Milton*, ed. R. D. Emma and John T. Shawcross (New York, 1967), chap. 10.
41. That is, like the style of Milton's opponent Joseph Hall, the so-called "English Seneca" (*An Apology for Smectymnuus*, in the Columbia ed., 3:268, and the Yale ed., 1:873).
42. The passage is crucial to the antiprelatical tracts because of Milton's insistent censure of the bishops' abuse of language. See Thomas Kranidas's exposition of Milton's "*decorum*" in *The Fierce Equation* (The Hague, 1965), chap. 2.

Andrew Marvell: Engagements with Reality

> Sunshine and rain at once
> —*King Lear*

I. "A rich and nervous poet"

That agreeable gossip, John Aubrey, had a theory about Marvell's inspiration. Marvell, he reported, "kept bottles of wine at his lodgeing, and many times he would drinke liberally by himselfe to refresh his spirits, and exalt his Muse."[1]

Aubrey is of course describing not so much Marvell as Aubrey. The transposition is perfectly understandable, however, since Marvell's poetry habitually elicits rather personal confessions than aesthetic responses: we ascribe to him, that is to say, assumptions characteristic of ourselves. The persuasion of Gerard Manley Hopkins that Marvell is "a rich and nervous poet"[2] was after all professed by a poet equally as rich, and no less nervous.

Judgments on Marvell should be attempted within the framework suggested. True, we have grown much in perception of late, for we look with some hesitation on the opinion of Victoria Sackville-West that Marvell wrote, as she elegantly maintained, "preposterous rubbish."[3] To our further credit, we also regard Samuel Parker with some suspicion because, having been pursued by Marvell "thorow thick and thin, hill or dale, over hedge and ditch,"[4] he extracted ample revenge in the portrait of Marvell he sketched later ("A vagabond, ragged, hungry Poetaster, being beaten at every tavern, he daily receiv'd the rewards of his sawciness in kicks and blows").[5] But other opinions, elevated into doctrines just as readily, are admitted without even a minimum of reflection. We endorse for example T. S. Eliot's vast generalizations on Marvell (1921), apprehensive though we should have been that in his second essay (1923) Marvell was proclaimed a lesser talent than the distinctly minor poet Henry King.[6] Eliot's pronouncements are nevertheless permitted to pandiculate, even to the extent that his considered vision of Marvell's "alliance of levity and seriousness" has become yet another dogma, what one critic unhappily calls Marvell's "joco-serious approach."[7] There is finally the view, also inspired by Eliot and rather too casually articulated by others, that "Marvell may have written a few great poems, but he was not a great poet."[8] Applied prodigally, the measure of greatness here proffered would presently affect other major poets as well, among them Mallarmé.

Embarrassing questions are also raised by the several claims on the diverse influences said to have been exerted on Marvell. Such claims, necessary if we are to appreciate Marvell's remarkable powers of assimilation, are nevertheless so often ventured in absolute terms that they yield not clarity but confusion. Where cautiously phrased claims illumine—that "Clorinda and Damon" is a "predominantly Spenserian poem," "The Coronet" intimates the presence of Herbert, and that several other poems suggest "certain resemblances" with Herrick[9]—categorically stated opinions merely obscure. T. S. Eliot, for example, imposed on Marvell "the vast and penetrating influence of Ben Jonson"; yet another critic has asserted that Marvell's "master" was in fact Donne, even as a third denied the same premise altogether ("Marvell has no connection with Donne").[10] Judgments on individual poems vex equally. "On a Drop of Dew," for instance, is said to have affinities with Herbert on the one hand, and Crashaw on the other;[11] while "Eyes and Tears" is alleged to have been "derived" from Crashaw's "The Weeper" when it patently manifests the entwined influences of Marino, Góngora, and Cleveland, as much as that of Donne.[12]

Details do matter; but we are also in need of the larger picture. We may remind ourselves that a great poet exposes himself to a diversity of particular influences in order promptly to transcend them, annihilating all that's made to his given sensibility, else adjusting tradition to his individual talent. Once properly considered, the larger context in Marvell's case should provide us with his characteristic achievement, the intricate balance between his personal predilections and the aggregate of literary precedents: the embroidered luxuriance of Spenser, the temperate umbrage of Jonson, the intellectual foliations of Donne, the daedalian animation of Herrick, the expansive lushness of Crashaw, the indesinent fecundity of Herbert.

Marvell did not draw solely on these poets, however. His affinities demonstrably lie elsewhere as well, with Shakespeare and Milton within English literature, and the Greek and Roman poets without. To appreciate this range of reference as I propose to do in part here, is to confirm that Marvell's poems are all-inclusive yet utterly unique, and in consequence passionately committed to a reality duly variegated.

II. "What luckless Apple did we tast. . . ?"

It will I know seem odd to impute a sense of reality to a poet who on the face of it is full of sounds and sweet airs that give delight and hurt not. Is there not in Marvell "a strong tinge of escape"?[13] Was he not happiest when conferring with birds and trees in the grounds of Nun Appleton, and happier still when he dwelt in the solitariness of his garden? He even confronted a coy but panic-stricken mistress with his "vegetable love"—a sort of lecherous cabbage, solemnly said by a critic to be "an ironic version of dendro-eroticism."[14]

Marvell's pastoral poems will engage us presently.[15] But I should initially prefer to consider his expressly political poems, not only because in them commitment to reality is necessarily substantial but because they exhibit most lucidly Marvell's adjustment of literary precedents to his sensibility. The best example in this respect is also the most predictable one, "An Horatian Ode upon Cromwell's Return from Ireland."

The Ode is in the first instance Horatian because of its external demeanor: it uses the four-line structure also employed by Marvell's friend Milton on three occasions.[16] But the Ode is especially Horatian in that it accommodates within its circumference elements internal to Horace's poems. It may indeed be said of Marvell what has been asserted of Horace, that

> he is extremely clever at disposing his novelties so that they are not obtrusive and the style appears uniform. Stylistic tact and appropriateness are Horace's outstanding qualities, but for this to be appreciated the reader's ear needs to be constantly attuned to the tone of the poet's voice, for it is in such small-scale works as the *Odes* that significant tonal effects, often dependent on but a single word, are possible. This splendid movement and complexity of tone is an exact counterpart to the complexity of ideas, and together they make an adequate reading of the *Odes* a rich (and varied) poetic experience.[17]

Marvell likewise has that within which passes show. The apparent uniformity of his verses constantly belies their actual agitation as the tone veers suddenly if imperceptibly to oblige reconsideration of "but a single word." The innocuous monosyllables are particularly suspect, as in the lines on Cromwell's likely progress after the execution of Charles:

> Nor yet grown stiffer with Command,
> But still in the *Republick's* hand:
>
> (ll. 81–82)

where the second word in each line, if stressed in accordance with the regular iambic rhythm, will suggest the least attractive of the possible alternatives:

> Nor *yet* grown stiffer with Command,
> But *still* in the Republick's hand.

Marvell's espousal of more than a single point of view echoes the similar tendency in Horace, who could celebrate martial endeavors (III.2) even as he reproached Iccius for pursuing them (I.29), or joy at the prospect of the death of Cleopatra, the "wild Queen" who opposed the designs of Rome, even as he admired the nobility of her final gesture:

> Yet she preferred a finer style of dying:
> She did not, like a woman, shirk the dagger
>   Or seek by speed at sea
> To change her Egypt for obscurer shores,
>
> But, gazing on her desolated palace
> With a calm smile, unflinchingly bid hands on
>   The angry asps until
> Her veins had drunk the deadly poison deep ....[18]

Marvell did not merely echo the Horatian patterns, however. He also amended them slyly, thereby promoting an irony that informs every line of his Ode. Horace lauded Octavius without qualification ("While Caesar stands guard, peace is assured, the peace / No power can break" [IV.15]), but Marvell praised Charles as well as Cromwell, even as he modulated his judgments on both. In similar fashion, Horace acclaimed the imperial arts of war, but Marvell transferred that praise from the sovereign to the usurper and chillingly warned of the potential consequences. A passage from Lucan, whose *Pharsalia* includes a hostile portrait of Caesar (I.143–55) and an encomiastic one of Pompey (IX.192–200), best illumines Marvell's intricate balance. Lucan's Caesar is poised to wield

> His forward Sword; confident of successe,
> And bold the favour of the gods to presse;
> Overthrowing all that his ambition stay,
> And loves that ruine should enforce his way:
> As lightning by the wind forc'd from a cloud
> Breakes through the wounded aire with thunder loud,
> Disturbes the Day, the people terrifies,
> And by a light oblique dazels our eyes ....[19]

Marvell's Ode similarly begins with the analogy to the "forward" youth, and advances on Cromwell who

>   through adventrous War
>   Urged his active Star.
> And, like the three-fork'd Lightning, first

> Breaking the Clouds where it was nurst,
>   Did thorough his own Side
>   His fiery way divide . . .
> Then burning through the Air he went,
> And Pallaces and Temples rent . . . .
>
> (ll. 11–12)

Granted the evident affinities between Lucan's Caesar and Marvell's Cromwell, it is I believe no less imperative to discern their fundamental differences. The lightning in Lucan provides a naturalistic context; but the three-forked lightning in Marvell endows that context with a further dimension, palpably supernatural and fraught with apocalyptic implications. Were Cromwell's cyclonic activities divinely sanctioned? If so, the warning that follows seems entirely apposite:

> 'Tis Madness to resist or blame
> The force of angry Heavens flame.
>
> (ll. 25–26)

But what if we are to regard the lightning as a merely earthbound phenomenon? Cromwell's self-urged "active Star" would then be transformed into a blasphemous presumption and a blight on the natural order. The warning itself, moreover, would be abruptly qualified with shattering irony:

> 'Tis Madness to resist or blame
> The force of angry Heavens flame:
>   And, if we would speak true,
>   Much to the Man is due . . . .

Lucan afforded Marvell a framework much as Horace did; but the final structure is entirely Marvell's own.

The Horatian features of the "Horatian Ode" must then be understood in a particular sense, much qualified as they were by pressures exerted on Marvell from other directions. The Ode's *color romanus*, in fact, need not be sought only in Rome when it was readily accessible in London as well, in an obvious yet so far neglected place: Shakespeare's *Julius Caesar*. The emphases in the Ode as in the play run at times along lines sufficiently parallel to raise expectations that they will eventually meet. Yet barring the obvious concern in both works with political assassination and its consequences, how far may one venture in pursuit of closer affinities? I am not myself prepared to argue that Marvell's three-forked lightning is related to the equally symbolic testimony of Cassius that "the cross blue lightning seem'd to open / The breast of heaven" (I.iii.50). Nor am I inclined to posit the connection between the advent of Marvell's fiery

278 / Figures in a Renaissance Context

Cromwell and Calphurnia's supernatural forebodings ("Fierce fiery warriors fight upon the clouds . . ." [II.ii.19]), much less to pontificate on the link between Marvell's "Royal Actor" (l. 59) and Brutus' exhortation to his fellow-conspirators to act "as our Roman actors do" (II.i.226)—even if the latter should confirm the ironic reversal of roles basic to the "Horatian Ode" and frequent enough in Marvell's other poems. Equally, I would resist the claim that the spectators' response to the king's performance in the Ode ("the armed Bands / Did clap their bloody hands") is connected in any way to the emphasis in *Julius Caesar* on hands, from the moment that the conspirators seal their pact by joining hands (II.i.112) to the moment that Mark Antony with a similar gesture pretends—"as our Roman actors do"—to endorse the murder (III.i.184–90 and 218). It is nevertheless worthy of note that after the assassination Brutus' blasphemous invitation to the other assassins is followed by ominous prophecies that the "scene," acted once in Rome, would be reenacted thereafter:

Brutus: Stoop, Romans, stoop,
   And let us bathe our hands in Caesar's blood
   Up to the elbows, and besmear our swords:
   Then walk we forth, even to the market-place,
   And waving our red weapons o'er our heads,
   Let's all cry, "Peace, freedom, and liberty!"
Cassius: Stoop, then, and wash. How many ages hence
   Shall this our lofty scene be acted over,
   In states unborn, and accents yet unknown!
Brutus: How many times shall Caesar bleed in sport,
   That now on Pompey's basis lies along,
   No worthier than the dust!
                              (III.i.105–16)

One observes that the "memorable Scene" enacted in Marvell's Ode concludes in the vision of Cromwell holding aloft a sword only recently besmeared with Irish blood. It is done for "effect" (l. 116).

The ambiguities surrounding Cromwell encase King Charles too. Just before his execution, we are told, the Royal Actor "with his keener Eye / The Axes edge did try" (ll. 59–60). The calculated defiance is an obvious attempt to elicit the reader's admiration. But the detail provided may also be a recollection of the execution of Sir Walter Ralegh, himself a victim of Stuart injustice. Like Charles on the scaffold in 1649, so Ralegh on his in 1618 had "felt along the edge" of his axe; and it is at least conceivable that we are meant to see the one execution in the light of the other.

Marvell's vision of history is veritably Aeschylean in the way crime is seen to link with crime, and bloodshed to merge with bloodshed. It is also Shakespearean, at least to the extent that it vibrates in response to John of Gaunt's celebrated paean to England as the happy and dear isle, a "fortress," a latter-day garden of Eden bound in with the triumphant sea, yet self-conquered and expiring in shame (*Richard II*, II.i.40ff.). The narrator in *Upon Appleton House* gathers up the echoes and molds them within the Fall of Man:

> Oh Thou, that dear and happy Isle
> The Garden of the World ere while,
> Thou *Paradise* of four Seas,
> Which *Heaven* planted us to please,
> But, to exclude the World, did guard
> With watry if not flaming Sword;
> What luckless Apple did we tast,
> To make us Mortal, and The[e] Wast[e]?
>
> (st. 41)

Judged against this background, the execution of Charles is not endorsed. Neither is it deplored. It is accepted. Realistic in the extreme, Marvell was not in the least concerned with what might or should have been; and temperamentally disinclined to indulge in utopian speculations, he would have agreed with Milton's sentiment we heeded earlier in *Areopagitica:* "To sequester out of the world into *Atlantick* or *Eutopian* polities, which never can be drawn into use, will not mend our condition; but to ordain wisely as in this world of evil, in the midd'st whereof God hath plac't us unavoidably."[20] If Marvell is concerned with the past, it is only because he wishes to understand how that past has shaped the present, and how both could—but *need* not—affect the future. Cromwell and Charles are therefore observed in the Ode as they ride their different assumptions on the way to their historic confrontation. The terrain is marked by the poem's well-attested ironies which suggest that we may honor the qualities inherent in exalted ideals yet dread their enactment, and that we may admire the nobility of soaring visions yet fear the fanaticism that so often attends them. Like the visionaries in Yeats's poem, Cromwell and Charles embody "a terrible beauty."

The confrontation of Marvell's protagonists change both radically. Charles, who is but a shadow until his great performance on the scaffold, unexpectedly seizes the opportunity to create subsequent history to his image; and becomes, in death, a much more commanding presence than he ever was in life. Cromwell, who believed that he could direct history at will, discovers that he has inadvertently helped his opponent to greatness; and the more he seeks to resume his role as director, the more he finds himself obliged to "act" (in both senses of the word). At this moment in time, as Marvell pauses to suggest the options still open, the poem once more bristles with ambiguities. As already noted, monosyllabic words are crucial:

> Nor *yet* grown stiffer with Command,
> But *still* in the Republick's hand.
>
> (ll. 81–82)

The warning sounded here ranges across the analogy introduced within a few lines to elucidate the relations between Cromwell and the State:

> So when the Falcon high
> Falls heavy from the Sky,
> She, having kill'd, no more does search,
> But on the next green Bow to pearch;
>   Where, when he first does lure,
>   The Falckner has her sure.
>
> (ll. 91 96)

We are often enough assured that the falcon is Cromwell, and the falconer the State.[21] Might not the reverse be equally true, however? Cromwell "kill'd" in Ireland; but so did the State in condemning Charles to the scaffold. The word "lure," it may be added, appertains as much to the State as to Cromwell's increasingly brilliant performance.

The implications of the Ode are frequently proclaimed with some abandon. We have been told, for instance, that Marvell endorsed a necessitarian view of history ("freedom is the knowledge of necessity"), and that therefore he urged "the subordination of self to political purposes."[22] With respect, however, I cannot credit that Marvell was, even by anticipatory osmosis, a Marxist. History is not determined by impersonal forces latent within it. History is determined solely by individuals; and though individuals may be destroyers or redeemers or (most likely) both, they are nevertheless free to pursue the course of their choice. The subordination of self is indeed advocated by Marvell, but it is a subordination to moral not to political purposes. Hence the Ode's Roman parallels and mounting ambiguities. The Roman parallels are not supplied in order ironically to concatenate two political experiences; they are especially meant to remind us of a moral order whose violation in time past remains a constant threat to times future. The ambiguities, similarly, are not only intended to celebrate Marvell's retrospective political insights: they are especially designed to admonish that individuals who accept that past events could be acted over in states unborn and accents yet unknown, have already predetermined the occurrence of those events and are self-ordained to relive them. The past belongs to the past, unalterably so; but its cumulative experiences forcefully warn us that the luckless apple will be tasted yet again unless opportunities in the present are used to "mend our condition" in the future. Freedom is the knowledge, but also the exercise, of moral options.

III. "A Traitor-Worm, within it bred"

Marvell wrote two other poems on Cromwell, one on the first anniversary of Cromwell's accession to absolute power (1655), the other on his death (1658). They are not universally admired as poems, nor widely respected as profound analyses of the strained years under the protectorate. Each is indeed singular, in that the sublunar Cromwell of the "Horatian Ode" has now yielded to "Angelique *Cromwell*," "*Heavens Favorite*," a cosmic figure "nearer to the Skyes," "like a Star," and ever-impelled by "A secret Cause," "an higher Force."[23] The changed emphasis in the argument coincides with the displacement of the Horatian four-line structure by the heroic couplet. Our response is qualified accordingly; for here, certainly, the heroic couplet is for Marvell largely what blank verse was for Milton. It celebrates. It is acclamatory, ceremonial, ritualistic, even sacramental. It is consequently dedicated to idealistic issues consciously articulated in sublime terms. The still center is not time but eternity, not the historical Cromwell but a transcendent authority of impeccably moral credentials. The demanding vision disturbs; and we protest, suspicious as we are of those who gaze as if admonished from another world. We therefore dismiss the vision as artificial, until we summon up remembrance of Sir Thomas Browne: "all things are artificiall, for nature is the Art of God" (*Religio Medici* I.17).

The cosmic morality that bolsters the two poems on the Lord Protector illumines the varieties of human imperfection delineated elsewhere: implicitly in the tactful measures of the Ode as we have seen, explicitly in the telling ludicrous rhythms of "Clarendon's House-Warming," in the crushing satire of the three "painter poems"—especially the stunning *Last Instructions to a Painter*—and in the merciless prosecution of the demented Mr. Bayes, alias Samuel Parker, in *The Rehearsal Transpros'd* (e.g., "the Church of *England* is much obliged to Mr. *Bayes* for having proved that Nonconformity is the Sin against the Holy Ghost" [p. 91]). But the same cosmic morality informs too the rest of Marvell's poems, equally concerned as they all are with the reality of imperfection within the created order.

The reality so designated is, in theological terms, the fact of the Fall.

As a datable historical event, the Fall is nowhere expressly formulated in Marvell's poetry; but as an ever-present human experience, it is never absent from his consciousness. Its figurations are manifold. "Bermudas," for instance, implies that perfection "in this world of evil" (to quote Milton again) is beyond the realm of possibility. True, such is the enchantment of the isles that they hardly appear to warrant their traditional appellation as "still-vexed"; and we are prone rightly to regard them as partaking of the isle of Prospero, and indeed the prelapsarian world. However, just as Shakespeare and Milton introduced discordant elements in their respective visions, so Marvell suggests the distant threat of the huge sea-monsters and of the roaring waves—and may even have meant us to recall not so much Spenser's Garden of Adonis as his ominous Bower of Bliss.[24] The threat presses even harder upon the precarious domain of "The Picture of Little T. C. in a Prospect of Flowers," where an idealized young girl is invited to reform "the errours of the Spring" introduced by the Fall, yet is warned that she is no less mortal than the flowers and buds she gathers. Death brought into the world by the luckless apple tasted, casts its maleficent shadow over any number of other poems as well: "Young Love" and "The Match," "The Unfortunate Lover" and "The Nymph complaining for the death of her Faun"—and of course "To his Coy Mistress," where an initially light-hearted variation on a common enough theme (*carpe diem,* in short, seduction) progresses expeditiously along unforeseen tracts to an alarming apprehension of the ravenous nature of time and death. Such emphases are brilliantly hypostasized in "The Coronet" which, read as it must be in the light of Herbert's aspiration to dedicate poetry to religious uses, pleads for the Christ's intercession because mere man—fallen man—is prevented by other interests from consecrating the flowers of poetry to the Creator:

> Alas I find the Serpent old
> That, twining in his speckled breast,
> About the flowers disguis'd does fold,
> With wreaths of Fame and Interest.
>
> (ll. 13–16)

It is a measure of Marvell's ambidextrous art, however, that a poem which confesses its inability to praise the Christ is nevertheless a poem in praise of the Christ.

Mortality intimated in the midst of life is also the common theme of the four mower poems. These displant the benevolent shepherd of traditional pastoral poetry by the destructive mower who in his indiscriminate decimation of the natural order is said to resemble death ("Death thou art a Mower too" ["Damon the Mower," l. 88]). The four poems are essentially dramatic, beginning with "The Mower against Gardens" where the narrator fiercely denounces "luxurious man" for having imposed art on nature and the formal garden on the wilderness:

> He first enclos'd within the Gardens square
>   A dead and standing pool of Air:
> And a more luscious Earth for them did knead,
>   Which stupefi'd them while it fed.
>
> (ll. 5–8)

The burden of the actual argument is carried in the first instance by the word "luxurious," which is to say lecherous or lascivious (one recalls the appearance of "luxurie" from *The Pardoner's Tale* [l. 897] to *King Lear* [IV.vi.116] with the crucial extensions in *The Revenger's Tragedy* inclusive of the aptly named Lussurioso). But as the word also meant outrageous or excessive, we are invited to observe that it applies most ineluctably to the strident tone of the narrator himself. His language, indeed, is compulsively possessed of sexual references—"seduce," "luscious," "eunuchs," and the like—so that the effect is not dissimilar to that of the central panel of Bosch's *Garden of Delights* where the frantic sexuality of the ravelled figures disarranges the natural order. In this respect "The Mower against Gardens" is best annotated by the three poems appended to it: "Damon the Mower," in which Damon suffers "hot desires" under Juliana's "scorching beams"; "The Mower to the Glow-Worms," in which the narrator's mind is "displac'd" by his sexual passion; and "The Mower's Song," in which the mind so affected considers wreaking "revenge" on the innocent flowers and grass—"Depopulating all the Ground," as Damon had earlier remarked with savage clarity ("Damon the Mower," l. 74). Thus introduced, the mower appears yet again in the very different context of *Upon Appleton House*.

    The difference resides in that poem's apparent affinities with the tradition-bound celebrations of country houses. Nun Appleton in Yorkshire, the seat of the Lord General Fairfax and his home after his resignation as commander of the Parliamentary army (1650), was intimately known to Marvell who lived there for two years as tutor to young Mary Fairfax. Sustained by an adequate history, the house could also claim that its present master was a poet responsible for several verses—to be exact, "one hundred and twenty five couplets and thirty five quatrains"—collectively entitled *Honny dropps*. Here is one drop:

> A good man questionless was never hee
> That strives nott always better for to be.

Or to quote from the ambitious "Songe of Prayse" to the providence of God:

> The East the West tast of his Care
> Hott Affrick nor the freezinge Beare
> From his al seeinge eye is hidd.[25]

Upon Appleton House discreetly avoids any reference to Fairfax's extraordinary muse, but extols his considerable talents in architectonic horticulture. Marvell's Fairfax is rather like Sir Thomas Browne's Cyrus, "Not only a Lord of Gardens, but a manuall planter thereof: disposing his trees like his armies in regular ordination."[26] The retired general is said to have laid out his garden "in sport / In the just figure of a Fort"; and the respectful flowers

>   as at *Parade*,
> Under their *Colours* stand displaied:
> Each *Regiment* in order grows,
> That of the Tulip Pinke and Rose.
>
>   (ll. 285–6, 309–12)

The house itself, moreover, responds to its master in no uncertain terms:

>   the laden House does sweat,
> And scarce indures the *Master* great:
> But where he comes the swelling Hall
> Stirs, and the *Square* grows *Spherical.*
>
>   (ll. 49–52)

    T. S. Eliot was not amused. The image, he declared, "is more absurd than it was intended to be."[27] But the poem should perhaps be judged in the light of Browne's whimsical *Garden of Cyrus;* for we might then recognize that absurdity in the one, like whimsicality in the other, is pressed to the service of a larger design. This design suggests that *Upon Appleton House* praises Fairfax to the same extent that the "Horatian Ode" praises Cromwell, and that consequently both poems are involved in the reality of the Fall "in this world of evill."

    Upon Appleton House may not be regarded as "an extended jest."[28] True, it has moments of lightheartedness, deployed with great tact and even greater good will; but it remains a most earnest examination of profound issues profoundly affirmed. We may consider the crucial stanza (71) at the end of the narrator's somber reflections on the "Traitor-Worm" which ravages "the tallest Oak" from within:

> Thus I, *easie Philosopher,*
> Among the *Birds* and *Trees* confer:
> And little now to make me, wants
> Or of the *Fowles,* or of the *Plants.*
> Give me but Wings as they, and I
> Streight floting on the Air shall fly:
> Or turn me but, and you shall see
> I was but an inverted Tree.

"Easie," we are informed, means "at ease, detached from care, free from pain, annoyance, or burden, free from pressure or hurry";[29] and we are mildly amused, I suppose, by the narrator's evident attempt at self-reproach. But "easie" could also mean on the one hand credulous, which considerably strengthens the self-reproach, and on the other gentle, which considerably weakens it. By the same token, the apparently amusing vision of the narrator turned upside down to resemble an inverted tree—itself no less comic—should be placed within the context of the time-honored idea that "man may be compared to an inverted tree: for he has his roots, or his hair, in the air, while other trees have their hairs, or their roots, in the earth."[30] Should these examples not suffice to deflect us from precipitous responses, we ought certainly not disregard the narrator's admonition:

> Thrice happy he who, not mistook,
> Hath read in *Natures mystick Book.*
>
> (ll. 583–84)

"Not mistook" affirms, if any single phrase can be said to affirm, the precise nature of Marvell's commitment to reality.

The Fall is diversely delineated in *Upon Appleton House.* It confronts us first in the unlikely episode of "the Suttle Nunns," residents of Nun Appleton when it was still a monastic retreat. Extreme in length, the episode is also extreme in tone; but forewarned by its forceful exposition of the nature of retreat and its consequences, we are better able to evaluate two later manifestations of retreat in the same grounds: Fairfax's retirement into his artificial fort (st. 44), and shortly thereafter the experiences of the narrator himself (st. 47 et seq.). The word "artificial" should not be misconstrued: it intimates here as before the natural order, "the Art of God," now extended by Fairfax with agreeably good humor ("in sport"). On the other hand, Fairfax's actual retreat sets off reverberations emanating largely from the statement that he "might" have made "our Gardens spring / Fresh as his own" (ll. 347–48). His retirement from the affairs of England—"The Garden of the World ere while"—is perilously analogous to his retirement from the meadow within reach of the

House proper, "the Abbyss" whose "unfathomable Grass" is abandoned to the mercy of a particular breed of men, the mowers:

> With whistling Sithe, and Elbow strong,
> These Massacre the Grass along:
> While one, unknowing, carves the *Rail,*
> Whose yet unfeather'd Quils her fail.
>
> (ll. 393–96)

The natural order, wearing man's smudge, is reduced to its original chaos; and with the mowers in command of the field, the narrator eventually takes "sanctuary" in the wood. But the nightmare continues as the natural order in turn duplicates the destructiveness of man, and incarnadines all making the green one red. The menace now is an internal one. It is enclosed within "the tallest Oak":

> the Tree ...
> A *Traitor-Worm,* within it bred.
> (As first our *Flesh* corrupt within
> Tempts impotent and bashful *Sin.*)
> And yet that *Worm* triumphs not long,
> But serves to feed the *Hewels young.*
> While the Oake seems to fall content,
> Viewing the Treason's Punishment.
>
> (st. 70)

The apparently innocuous monosyllable "seems" speaks for itself.

The narrator is understandably alarmed. He therefore leaves the wood, only to descend into the ultimate retreat of self-deception. After assuming the cloak of the "easie Philosopher," he meets young Maria and explodes in hyperbolic praise to the point of incredulity (ll. 651ff.).

Maria has been welcomed with immense enthusiasm, and evident relief, by a battalion of critics. She has been hailed as "a true representative of purity and innocence," as the embodiment of "the ideal union of active and contemplative virtues," as "the epitome of beauty, law, and harmony," and even as the conjunction of the wisdom of Pallas Athena ("the virgin of virgins") and Sophia ("the graver and more potent daughter of Jehovah").[31] With respect, however, I am not certain I understand how a poem that proceeds from a cry of despair over the luckless apple tasted to a harrowing vision of fallen man's rampant destruction of nature, can abruptly introduce an idealized figure and expect us to assent without protest. The evidence on the contrary points to a figure which the poet—but not the narrator, I should insist—qualifies substantially. Elaborate praise, after all, was not a habit Marvell indulged in aimlessly; nor was he prepared to abscind from his general view of fallen humanity an individual however young and innocent. In associating Maria with a comet (l. 683), the poet intended that we regard not only the "flame which purifies because it is heavenly"[32] but the menacing overtones which the passing of comets through Renaissance literature invariably suggests. Our suspicions once aroused, we perceive that Marvell's Maria is removed from Donne's Elizabeth Drury thrice as far as is the center from the utmost pole:

> Hence *She* with Graces more divine
> Supplies beyond her *Sex* the *Line;*
> And, like a *sprig* of *Misleto,*
> On the *Fairfacian Oak* does grow;
> Whence, for some universal good,
> The *Priest* shall cut the sacred Bud;
> While her *glad Parents* most rejoice,
> And make their *Destiny* their *Choice.*
>
> (st. 93)

Such are the echoes that inhabit a major poem that we cannot dispart "the Fairfacian Oak" from the account earlier given of "the tallest Oak" enclosing a traitor-worm. Moreover, be the associations attendant upon the mistletoe what they may, we cannot ignore that it is also parasitic— "baleful Misseltoe," in Shakespeare's common phrase (*Titus Andronicus* II.iii.95). In other words, even as Maria amasses praise rightly lavished, Marvell's realistic vision interposes a reminder that as a member of the postlapsarian world she is, potentially at least, a threat. To deem otherwise is to credit that Marvell sequestered "out of the world into *Atlantick* or *Eutopian* polities, which never can be drawn into use."

Maria is therefore not the "resolution" of *Upon Appleton House.* Just as Milton's *Comus* transcends the Lady and her brothers as much as Comus and his crew to acclaim the joyous dance of life, so Marvell's poem courses beyond Maria and her family as much as the mowers to celebrate the delightfully lighthearted prospect of the last stanza:

> But now the *Salmon-Fishers* moist
> Their *Leathern Boats* begin to hoist;
> And, like *Antipodes* in Shoes,
> Have shod their *Heads* in their *Canoos.*
> How *Tortoise like,* but not so slow,
> Those rational *Amphibii* go?
> Let's in: for the dark *Hemisphere*
> Does now like one of them appear.

Except for the two poems on the cosmic figure of the Lord Protector, Marvell circumscribed mere idealism by the circle of reality. But his ambidextrous art also suggests, as it does here, that sublunar reality must on the one hand induce disquiet because the dark hemisphere remains dark, yet on the other instill confidence because the same hemisphere could "appear" like the protective shell of the amiable tortoise within the natural order.

IV. "Such sweet and wholsome Hours"

Marvell's art, comprised in part of elements selectively drawn from a variety of poets as noted earlier, depends in the final analysis on the practice of his Greek and Roman predecessors. The poet whom Milton described as "a scholar and well read in the Latin and Greek authors"[33]—spectacular praise considering the source!—applied his direct knowledge of classical poetry partly to his Latin poems and consistently to his English. The qualities harvested are readily apprehensible: respect for form, restraint in the use of language, economy in phraseology, and discretion in the display of emotions.

So much for appearances. For Marvell also evinces a Donne-like theatricality, especially when he wishes pointedly to call attention to a deviation from the titular norms. The nominal serenity of the verse is not thereby negated; it is confirmed, not in spite but because of the currents that seethe beneath the surface. The effect is oddly reminiscent of the stylized Racine who could as in *Bajazet* abruptly lash out with incredible savagery. It puzzles readers, inviting questions raised with mounting irritation. What is the issue debated in "A Dialogue between the Soul and Body"? Is the poem a dialogue at all? Are its two protagonists "a comic duo" perhaps?[34] By the same token, is "The Definition of Love" a proper definition, or indeed about love? Was its title "attached to the poem by mistake"?[35] Equally, is "The Nymph complaining for the death of her Faun" fraught with religious overtones, or is it strictly pagan, what a German critic ever so impressively calls "eine bacchantisch-erotische Szene zwischen Nymphen und Faunen"?[36]

But no poem has forced critical hairs to stand on end more than "The Garden." Its background has been said to be Platonic in general or Plotinian in particular, and Hermetic as well as Epicurean or even Cartesian, while the narrator in the foreground has been conflated with any number of mythological figures inclusive of the androgynous Adam.[37] Marvell's vexatious garden scarcely confirms Bacon's view that a garden is "the purest of human pleasures, . . . the greatest refreshment to the spirits of man."[38]

"The Garden" may be described best after the fashion of the *theologia negativa,* that is, not what it is but what it is not. Marvell's theology is after all like Shakespeare's, not dogmatic but suggestive, entirely subordinate to the demands of an art which is nevertheless founded upon a given order of theological premises. Thus the poem's fifth stanza—the evocation of the garden's sensuous fruits like the "curious" peach—concludes with the narrator's "fall on Grass" and thereby may be said to insinuate the Fall. It is on the other hand rather odd that such an intensely personal experience should occur after the exorcism of "Passions heat" mentioned in the previous stanza, and indeed after the indication ventured even earlier that the garden encloses not uncessant labor but repose, not toil but quiet, not action but contemplation. The chronology of the poem, I am suggesting, does not accord with the sequence of events in the "historical" Fall; and because it does not, we are cautioned against any identification of the narrator with Adam, androgynous or not. As if to admonish us further, Marvell deploys throughout the poem a cluster of irksome adjectives, and in this stanza one in particular: "curious," presented in improbable modification of the peach. Could "curious" mean only delicate or dainty? But there are any number of other meanings, all relevant, and alike dementing: anxious, attentive, careful, cautious, concerned, eager, ingenious, recondite, skilful, solicitous, studious—and the like.

The Fall may of course be present in the fifth stanza not "historically" but mythically, as the ubiquitous experience that it is. If so, what is its connection with the concurrent movement described in the next stanza?

> Mean while the Mind, from pleasure less,
> Withdraws into its happiness:
> The Mind, that Ocean where each kind
> Does straight its own resemblance find;
>
> Yet it creates, transcending these,
> Far other Worlds, and other Seas;
> Annihilating all that's made
> To a green Thought in a green Shade.

The monosyllabic "less" of the first line, initially obscured by the outward serenity of the verse, distracts by its excess of clarity. Does the phrase "from pleasure less" mean that the mind withdraws "from a pleasure that is inferior," or "from the lessening of pleasure" (in the sense that it is "made less by pleasure")[39]—or indeed "from the lessening of pleasure induced by its incapacity to feel pleasure"? Moreover, does "annihilating" mean reducing, possibly even obliterating, or—in diametric contrast—transcending? Our answers will in each case determine the reading immediately of the import of "a green Thought in a green Shade," and mediately of the entire poem. The greenness should in any case not be stressed to the exclusion of other elements,[40] lest we elevate a transient detail to Armado's generalizations in *Love's Labour's Lost* ("Green indeed is the colour of lovers" [I.ii.87]), or reduce it to Gonzalo's perception in *The Tempest:*

> *Gonzalo:* How lush and lusty the grass looks! how green!
> *Antonio:* The ground indeed is tawny.
> *Gonzalo:* With an eye of green in 't.
> *Antonio:* He misses not much.
>
> (II.i.52–55)

The tenor of "The Garden" to the end of the sixth stanza conditions our response to what ensues. In the seventh stanza we run into the soul. It has glided into the boughs where, "like" a bird, it is self-consciously engaged in an uncessant labor:

> it sits, and sings,
> Then whets, and combs its silver Wings;
> And, till prepar'd for longer flight,
> Waves in its Plumes the various Light.

The hyperbole is best assessed if the soul's pastime here is referred to the echoes it collects from wisdom's activities in *Comus:*

> Wisdoms self
> Oft seeks to sweet retired Solitude,
> Where with her best nurse Contemplation
> She plumes her feathers, and lets grow her wings
> That in the various bussle of resort
> Were all to ruffl'd, and sometimes impair'd.
>
> (ll. 375–80)

The soul in Marvell's poem is also "ruffl'd," and perhaps even "impair'd"; but its predicament is largely the result of its own "bussle." Strictly intent upon itself, the soul is only vaguely considering the possibility ("till") that it might eventually be "prepar'd" for longer flight. Earthbound for the foreseeable future, it is oddly similar to the garden's other sublunar representatives of "mortal Beauty"—Daphne and Syrinx among them—who also ended in the boughs, in their case literally (ll. 27–32).

The transmuted Daphne and Syrinx are not the only members of the fair sex who inhabit Marvell's garden. There are two more: Quiet and her "sister dear" Innocence (ll. 9–10). The narrator therefore deludes himself when in the penultimate stanza he compares his circumstances to "that happy Garden-state, / While Man there walk'd without a Mate." Having retreated into self-deception—much as his counterpart in *Upon Appleton House* does—he can now only revert to the natural order which alone (as Milton said) "can be drawn into use." Hence the last stanza:

> How well the skilful Gardner drew
> Of flow'rs and herbes this Dial new;
> Where from above the milder Sun
> Does through a fragrant Zodiack run;
> And, as it works, th' industrious Bee
> Computes its time as well as we.
> How could such sweet and wholsome Hours
> Be reckon'd but with herbs and flow'rs!

The "Dial new" is not in fact new at all. The natural order of the poem's outset—the order of palms and oaks and bays (l. 2)—is of the self-same universe which the Creator endowed upon its inception with extraordinary beauty and perfection. The change is solely in the narrator's recognition that the natural order is indeed perfect, indeed beautiful. For a while the sun appeared to be less mild, and the zodiac less fragrant, because several experiences intervened to suggest so: the narrator's own extreme responses, or the mutilation of the garden of the world by the mower-like "cruel" lovers (ll. 19–20). The man-induced horrors of "this world of evil," it is clear, are not bypassed. Acknowledged as a fact of our existence, they are concurrently placed within the larger context of the time-bound universe of "sweet and wholsome Hours" under the supervision of "the skilful Gardner."

Marvell's theology, here as elsewhere, trembles on the brink of nonexistence. Yet it is vital to his poetry all the same, in measure equal to his agreement with Sir Thomas Browne that "the greatest mystery of Religion is expressed by adumbration."[41] The adumbration in Marvell's case involves a sustained vision not of the supernatural order, however, as of the pendant world. He seems always prepared for longer flight, it is true; but he'd much rather sit and sing, then whet and comb his silver wings.

NOTES

An earlier version of this chapter appeared as " 'Till Prepared for Longer Flight': The Sublunar Poetry of Andrew Marvell," in *Approaches to Marvell: The York*

Tercentenary Lectures, ed. C. A. Patrides (London: Routledge and Kegan Paul, 1978), pp. 31–55. Copyright 1978, Routledge and Kegan Paul Ltd. Reprinted by permission of the publishers. Marvell's poetry is here quoted from *The Poems and Letters of Andrew Marvell,* ed. H. M. Margoliouth, 2d ed. (Oxford, 1952), vol. 1.

1. *Brief Lives,* ed, Oliver L. Dick, 3d ed. (London, 1960), p. 196.
2. February 27, 1879; in *Correspondence of Gerard Manley Hopkins and Richard Watson Dixon,* ed. C. C. Abbott (London, 1935), 2:23.
3. In her biography of the poet (1929); in John Carey, ed., *Andrew Marvell,* Penguin Critical Anthologies (Harmondsworth, England, 1969), p. 33.
4. *The Rehearsal Transpros'd,* ed. D. I. B. Smith (Oxford, 1971), p. 187.
5. Samuel Parker, *History of His Own Time,* trans. Thomas Newlin (London, 1727), p. 332.
6. The first essay was published in *TLS* on March 31, 1921; the second, in *The Nation and the Athenaeum* on September 29, 1923. Both are available in *Andrew Marvell,* ed. Carey, pp. 46–60, and in *Marvell,* ed. Michael Wilding, "Modern Judgements" (London, 1969), pp. 45–59.
7. Eliot, in *Andrew Marvell,* ed. Carey, p. 50, and in *Marvell,* ed. Wilding, p. 49. The critic quoted is Maren-Sofie Røstvig, "Andrew Marvell and the Caroline Poets," in *English Poetry and Prose, 1540–1674,* ed. Christopher Ricks (London, 1970), p. 223.
8. A. Alvarez, *The School of Donne* (London, 1961), p. 104; also in *Marvell,* ed. Wilding, p. 182.
9. J. B. Leishman, *The Art of Marvell's Poetry* (London, 1966), p. 119; Joseph H. Summers, "Marvell's 'Nature,'" *ELH* 10 (1953): 135; and Kitty Scoular, *Natural Magic* (Oxford, 1965), p. 176; respectively.
10. Eliot, in *Andrew Marvell,* ed. Carey, p. 55; Pierre Legouis, *Andrew Marvell,* 2d ed. (Oxford, 1968), pp. 42, 62, etc.; and J. B. Broadbent, *Poetic Love* (London, 1964), p. 252; respectively.
11. Joseph H. Summers, in *Andrew Marvell,* ed. Carey, p. 140; and J. B. Leishman, *The Art of Marvell's Poetry,* p. 202; respectively.
12. The case for "The Weeper" was proposed by Legouis, *Andrew Marvell,* p. 35. The sane judgment involving Marino et al. is by Donald M. Friedman, *Marvell's Pastoral Art* (London, 1970), p. 46.
13. Patrick Cruttwell, *The Shakespearean Moment* (New York, 1960), p. 199.
14. Harold E. Toliver, *Marvell's Ironic Vision* (New Haven, 1965), p. 159.
15. My inversion of the accepted chronology of the poems' composition is intentional. Save for poems on public occasions, I see no reason for admitting that Marvell's "real poetry" (as Cruttwell calls it, in *The Shakespearean Moment*) was written before, and his satires after, the Restoration. "The Garden," for instance, need not belong to the years at Nun Appleton.
16. Twice in Latin (the elegies on the Bishop of Ely and the Vice-Chancellor at Cambridge), and once in English (the translation of Horace's *Ode* I.5):
    What slender Youth, bedew'd with liquid odours
    Courts thee on Roses in some pleasant Cave,

> *Pyrrha* for whom bind'st thou
> In wreaths thy golden Hair . . .?

17. Gordon Williams, *The Nature of Roman Poetry* (London, 1970), p. 174. For an introduction to the extraordinary range of sound patterns in Horace's odes, see L. P. Wilkinson, *Horace and His Lyric Poetry,* 2d ed. (Cambridge, 1951), chap. 5, "The Horatian Ode."
18. *The Odes of Horace,* I.37; trans. James Michie (Harmondsworth, England, 1967).
19. From Thomas May's translation of Lucan (1627); quoted and discussed by R. H. Syfret, "Marvell's 'Horatian Ode,' " *RES,* n.s. 12 (1961): 160–72. Syfret also remarks perceptively on Marvell's affinities with Horace.
20. *Selected Prose,* ed. C. A. Patrides, rev. ed. (Columbia, Mo., 1985), p. 219. Also quoted on p. 192.
21. E.g., Muriel C. Bradbrook and M. G. Lloyd Thomas, *Andrew Marvell* (Cambridge, 1940, reprint 1961), p. 75; et al.
22. Christopher Hill, *Puritanism and Revolution* (London 1958), pp. 362, 364. The Ode has also been reduced to a document in support of Cromwell, else a treatise in censure of his Machiavellianism. The first theory is by John M. Wallace, *Destiny His Choice: The Loyalism of Andrew Marvell* (Cambridge, 1968), chap. 2; the second, by Joseph A. Mazzeo, *Renaissance and Seventeenth-Century Studies* (New York, 1964), chap. 8 (initially published in *Journal of the History of Ideas* 21 [1960]: 1–17, where it was severely criticized by Hans Baron in a subsequent issue the same year, pp. 450–51).
23. *The First Anniversary of the Government under O. C.,* ll. 46, 101, 126, 239; and *A Poem upon the Death of O. C.,* ll. 101, 157.
24. As R. M. Cummings argues in "The Difficulty of Marvell's 'Bermudas,' " *MP* 67 (1969–70): 338. The poem's remarkable political background is explicated by Philip Brockbank, "The Politics of Paradise: 'Bermudas,' " in *Approaches to Marvell,* ed. C. A. Patrides (London, 1978), chap. 8.
25. *The Poems of Thomas Third Lord of Fairfax,* ed. Edward B. Reed, in *Transactions of the Connecticut Academy of Arts and Sciences* 14 (1909): 261–62.
26. *The Garden of Cyrus,* in *The Major Works,* ed. C. A. Patrides (Harmondsworth, England, 1977), p. 327.
27. In *Andrew Marvell,* ed. Carey, p. 51, and *Marvell,* ed. Wilding, p. 50.
28. Robin Grove, in *Andrew Marvell,* ed. Carey, p. 296.
29. Louis L. Martz, *The Wit of Love* (South Bend, Ind., 1969), p. 186.
30. From *The Hermetic Museum* (1677), quoted together with other references by A. B. Chambers, " 'I was but an inverted tree': Notes Toward the History of an Idea," *Studies in the Renaissance* 8 (1961): 291–99. The idea harks back to Plutarch's view of man "inverted to point to heaven" (*De exilio* V [600F]).
31. Maren-Sofie Røstvig, in *English Studies* 42 (1961): 350; Frederic H. Roth, Jr., in *Texas Studies in Literature and Language* 14 (1972): 281; Barbara K. Lewalski, in her *Donne's "Anniversaries" and the Poetry of Praise* (Princeton, 1973), p. 359; and Don C. Allen, in his *Image and Meaning* (Baltimore, 1960), pp. 149ff.; respectively. Only one critic has shrewdly observed that Maria's portrait is sketched with "affectionate gaiety," "a distinct jocularity" (Frank J. Warnke, *Versions of Baroque* [New Haven, 1972], pp. 121–22).

32. Kitty Scoular, *Natural Magic,* p. 178.
33. From Milton's recommendation of Marvell for employment by the republican government, February, 1653.
34. Peter Berek, "The Voices of Marvell's Lyrics," *MLQ* 32 (1971): 144.
35. Frank Kermode, "Definitions of Love," *RES,* n.s. 7 (1956): 184.
36. Werner Vordtriede in his translation of the poem in *Die Neue Rundschau* 72 (1961): 869.
37. On the latter, See Lawrence W. Hyman in *ELH* 15 (1958): 13–22. Plotinus is invoked by Milton Klonsky in *Sewanee Review* 58 (1950): 16–35; the Hermetic tradition by Maren-Sofie Røstvig in *English Studies* 40 (1959): 65–76; Epicureanism by John M. Potter in *SEL* 11 (1971): 137–51; and Cartesianism by Daniel Stempel in *Journal of the History of Ideas* 28 (1967): 99–114. The Platonic dimension is averred with various emphases, depending on the thesis argued.
38. "Of Gardens," XLVI in *Essays* (1625); in *Works,* ed. James Spedding et al., (London, 1861), 6:485–92.
39. The first alternative was espoused by Legouis (in *Andrew Marvell,* ed. Carey, p. 267), who is followed by Leishman and Summers; and the second by William Empson (in *Andrew Marvell,* ed. Carey, p. 239). See also Kermode (in *Andrew Marvell,* ed. Carey, p. 260) and Warnke, *Versions of Baroque,* pp. 117f.
40. Cf. Stanley Stewart: "greenness in itself does not present the final statement of value in the poem" (*The Enclosed Garden* [Madison, Wis., 1966], p. 162).
41. *The Garden of Cyrus,* in *The Major Works,* ed. Patrides, p. 376.

The Experience of Otherness: Theology as a Means of Life

> more things in heaven and earth
> —*Hamlet*

I. "We have chosen the Lord God Almighty"

The landscape of the Renaissance has many prominent features, each impressive in itself. But theology dominates them all, its mighty shadow falling on the political dimension as on the social, and on the literary as on the scientific. Omnipresent in the intellectual and emotional life of the period, theology exerted a salutary influence in several directions—and no less adverse in others.

"Theology," it should be made clear, does not encompass only the aggregate of strictly defined dogmas, nor even the diverse interpretations attendant upon them. Theology also encompasses emotional engagements with modes of experience illumined, in one form or another, by an order of ideas whose ultimate appeal is to Otherness. The reference here is not to the faculty peculiar to the mystic. It is to the ongoing awareness of the realist who recognizes the need to respond to demands of authorities beyond himself and of quarters beyond the visible. Such an attitude could lead, and did lead, to fanaticism; and so far it can only be deplored. But where the experience was properly channeled, it yielded a commitment to life in all its manifestations. The terminal points are well attested even where they were not attained: socially, the ambition to reform the existing patterns within the State at large and the family in particular; and personally, the dedication to an impressive purity in moral behavior. Inevitably reflected in the period's literature, these thrusts are demonstrably present not only in explicitly political poems such as Marvell's "Horatian Ode" but, equally, in any number of major literary works similarly informed by a socially oriented fervor, be they Shakespeare's *The Tempest* (1611) or Ben Jonson's *Epigrammes* (1616) or Herbert's *The Temple* (1633)—and of course the sum total of Milton's endeavors in poetry as in prose.

But if cognizance of Otherness led the period's major minds superbly to articulate issues of perennial import, the same cognizance induced in minor minds the deplorable fanaticism already noted. Risible in itself, such fanaticism should be marked because its demonic proportions loom quite large in the background against which Shakespeare and Jonson and Milton wrote. Self-appointed moralists abounded, hysterically denouncing "this hard iron age" with its "monstrous pride of apparell, of [at]tyres, of bracelets, of Jewels, overflowing our nation like a generall deluge," the maidens "standyng tootyng twoo howers by the Clocke, lookyng now on this side, now on that, least any thyng should be lackyng needefull to further Pride," while the "proud plumed gallants . . . do seeme as if they scornde both heaven and hell"—and all indulging, it was said, in "practices of wantonesse, as stage-playes, which serve for nothing but to nourish filthinesse."[1] Indignation of this order was not addressed solely to a few social issues, nor was it voiced by a handful of self-righteous individuals. It covered, on the contrary, the entire circumference of thought and behavior, and was often sanctioned by formally instituted agents. One example is the ruthless theocracy forged by Calvin in Geneva from 1541; another, the intolerance displayed by conservative Catholicism through the Counter-Reformation which the Council of Trent launched from 1545. True, both Calvinism and the Counter-Reformation contributed much of enormous and lasting benefit; yet it is advisable to remember in what ensues that the two movements were at times alike vicious, witness the burning at the stake for "heresy" of Michael Servetus in Geneva (1553) and of Giordano Bruno in Rome (1600), the one condemned for his antitrinitarian views, the other for his wild flights of fancy. Earlier, at Münster in Westphalia, an extreme group of extreme Anabaptists had indulged in frenetic activities which, distinguished as they were by their lunacy and brutality, were justly condemned both by Protestants and by Catholics. But Protestants and Catholics were themselves no less barbarous, not only in their mutually fervent dedication to censorship but in their manifest zeal in the significantly increased persecution of "witches."

To what extent were such activities theologically oriented? The persecution of "witches," for instance, has been attributed rather to social than to expressly theological reasons in that the hapless victims were dissidents whose extermination was dictated by the need to find "a scapegoat for social frustration."[2] Even more sweepingly, the controversies of the Renaissance have been declared to be primarily social and political in their orientation, the theological language commonly deployed being incidental and ultimately of slight relevance.[3] Such efforts to demythologize the Renaissance must be approached with caution, however. In our secular age, theology is suspect; and we seek, with an excess of sophistication, to neutralize the force of theological impulses. The potency of the political, social, and economic motives behind the metaphysical claims of the Renaissance can scarcely be denied; yet to question the earnestness and the significance of those claims *as claims* is to risk an imbalance likely to terminate in gross misrepresentation. The vast literature directed against witchcraft, however incredible the arguments and terrifying their application, may not be reduced to so many instances of "social frustration" so long as it enlisted the support of the misguided but otherwise brilliant Jean Bodin (*De la démonomanie des sorciers,* Paris, 1580) and of the brilliant but otherwise misguided King James (*Daemonologie,* Edinburgh, 1597). We should consider that even the very few skeptics who dared oppose the prevalent views—Johann Wier in 1563 or Reginald Scott in 1584—adamantly refused to deny the reality of witches. Even the irenic Sir Thomas Browne was in the 1630s to agree: "I have ever beleeved, and doe now know, that there are Witches; they that doubt of these, doe not onely deny them, but Spirits; and are obliquely and upon consequence a sort, not of Infidels, but Atheists." Browne was certainly not inclined to harden hearts against the victims of fanatics. As his statement makes clear, he was primarily concerned lest a negation of the demonic should involve a negation of the spiritual—and thence a negation of God.

By the same token, our tendency to displace the theological by the purely political and economic in the controversies of the Renaissance disturbs the balance sought even by a substantial number of the Levellers, the period's most obviously "secular" political party. But the habitual appeal to Otherness was not a mere rhetorical flourish. It was the foundation which sustained much of the idealism in the political contexts of the Renaissance, whether we focus on the Levellers' view of the Christian brotherhood of all men or on the Diggers' independence under the sovereignty of the ultimate taskmaster ("We have chosen the Lord God Almighty to be our king and protector"). So, too, the Anabaptists—not the religious fanatics at Münster but the pacifists of the communes, whether in Moravia (Hutterites) or the Netherlands and north Germany (Mennonites)—in severing themselves from conventional social life aspired to change society politically, yet they remain, as their most recent historian concludes, "primarily a religious movement rather than a political one."[4] We may add that they were also, like the countless other minor groups of the period, specifically Protestant. Their common appeal was, after all, to the Bible, which the Reformation elevated into the foremost if not the exclusive authority in all matters of doctrine as of conduct.

II. "The verie Soule of Protestancie"

The Reformation is supposed to have begun on October 31, 1517, when Luther fastened to the door of the castle church at Wittenberg his ninety-five theses against papal abuses. Like all vulgar suppositions, however, this one is also untenable. At the time, none of the doctrines characteristic of Protestantism had been formulated; the German princes had not yet perceived Luther's usefulness in furthering their political autonomy from Rome; and Rome's eventually militant conservatism was a development reserved for the future. In 1517, certainly, Luther was not even remotely inclined to question his loyalty to the Catholic Church. He was only indulging in the widespread clamor to reform the Church from within, much like the scholarly Lorenzo Valla (d. 1457), who questioned the authenticity of documents such as the "Donation of Constantine" upon which the papal claims to temporal power rested, or the saintly John Colet (d. 1519), who attacked abuses on several fronts by living the very pattern of the upright Christian humanist, or the fervently moral Juan Luis Vives (d. 1540), who in each of his brilliant works palpitated with an unqualified devotion to "puritanism." Twenty years before the episode at Wittenberg, indeed, another "reformer" had tellingly denounced the "pseudo-theologians of our time, whose brains are rotten, their language barbarous, their intellects dull, their learning a bed of thorns, their manners rough, their life hypocritical, their talk full of venom, and their hearts as black as ink." The zeal is similar to Luther's; but the voice is that of the mighty Erasmus.[5]

There were, in other words, numerous efforts at reformation before the Reformation. Even so, however, the Reformation is a re-formation in the sense that it proved a radical revolution which recast the religious map of Europe and affected the commitment to Otherness as much outside the Catholic Church as within it. But we must guard against perilous generalizations. In terms of the individual's devotional life, for instance, there was a difference not in kind but in degree: while Protestantism commended the worship capitally of the Christ, Catholicism had already intensified that worship—and after the Council of Trent intensified it even further—to include the Virgin in the first instance and the pantheon of saints in the second. Expectations to the contrary, moreover, Protestants did not substantially increase the quality of Biblical and theological studies: Biblical scholarship reached its apogee with two major contributions by Catholics—the edition of the Greek New Testament by Erasmus (1516) and the Polyglot Bible supervised by Cardinal Ximénez (1522)—while Catholic theology responded to the challenge of the Reformation with impressive spokesmen of the order of Robert Bellarmine and Edmund Campion, both of whom we shall encounter again later. Finally, Protestantism may not be regarded as a liberal force in a world of monkish papists bent on confining the free spirit of man. As before noted, the Catholic Church was by no means the solitary guardian of illiberal conduct.

Positively, we expect, the quintessence of Protestantism should be sought in the writings of Luther. But they are far too many and far too long, and the modern reader must be equipped with patience to withstand his histrionics, tact to overlook his lack of coherence, and sympathy to understand the issues he articulates with enormous passion. However, three of his treatises may be commended as still readable: the address *To the Christian Nobility of the German Nation*, which urges the secular authorities to support the Reformation; *The Babylonish Captivity of the Church*, which attacks the seven sacraments; and *The Liberty of a Christian Man*, which expounds his central conviction about "justification by faith." But as none of these treatises testifies to Luther's reckless courage, a fourth may also be commended as the foremost of the many blunders he committed during his turbulent life: his espousal of the absolute supremacy of Divine Grace in response to Erasmus' reasoned defence of man's free will. Stylistically and philosophically, Luther was annihilated by the infinitely superior grace and intelligence of his opponent. But as *felt* theology—theology as a means of life—Luther's thesis convinces because his commitment to Otherness was so total. His celebrated view of man's free will may offend or, at best, amuse;[6] but as Luther himself ruefully observed on one occasion, if the province of Erasmus was style without the truth, that of Luther was the truth without style.[7]

It was a question not of the single truth, however, but of two diametrically opposed attitudes to Otherness. Where Luther proclaimed man's total dependence on God, Erasmus gloried in man's initiative under God. Where Luther condemned the earthbound works of independent man, Erasmus saw in those same works evidence of past achievements and future promise. Where Luther vehemently insisted on the sovereign relevance of the Bible, Erasmus serenely commended the authority even of non-Christians (e.g., "from Cicero's enchiridion alone flows forth a divine source of virtue which suffices for all our spiritual need").[8] Even more tellingly, where Luther like all Protestants favored among the early Fathers especially St. Augustine, Erasmus reserved his respect particularly for St. Jerome.[9] St. Augustine appealed to Luther and became the guiding spirit of the Reformation partly because of his providential vision of history in *The City of God*, partly because of his affirmation of the elemental authority of Divine Grace in opposition to Pelagius—an early if crude prototype of Erasmus—but especially because of his sense of personal sinfulness as detailed in his remarkable *Confessions*. St. Jerome appealed to Erasmus, on the other hand, for equally personal reasons; for alike humanists, alike great scholars, they were also alike in that their commitment to the Christian faith was an intellectual exercise, an experience not of the heart but of the mind. Zeal was not absent from the horizons of St. Jerome, much less of Erasmus; but it was a zeal conditioned habitually by their concern with the learned few, and finally determined more by their response to the outward text than to the inner life of the Scriptures: the word, that is to say, in decisive preference to the Word.

Protestantism as molded by Luther was, then, directly personal, explicitly Augustinian, and ultimately Biblical. But its Biblical orientation was not nearly as comprehensive as we might expect. The Epistle of James, for instance, was thoroughly disliked by Luther because of its emphasis on works ("by works a man is justified, and not by faith alone").[10] At the other extreme, St. Paul's epistles were allotted such a central place in Protestant thought and experience that we may describe the Reformation as fundamentally Pauline. Here the crucial factor was Paul's insistence on the primacy of faith, which eventually led to the specifically Protestant dogma of "justification by faith." Rightly proclaimed by Catholics like Campion to be "the verie Soule of Protestancie,"[11] the dogma asserted the individual's salvation not through any good works he might undertake or any external acts of worship he might perform but solely through faith in the redeeming powers of Christ (*sola fide*). In the ensuing controversy, Catholics charged that Protestants dismissed works as irrelevant. Not quite. The "justified" individual was impelled to an active life, not paralyzed into a passive one. "The life of a Christian is his faith," it was said in 1623, but "the life of his faith, is his good workes." Even more perceptively, John Donne annexed the theological terms to the two commandments: "love God, and love thy Neighbour, that is, faith and works."[12]

The Protestant declaration of the primacy of faith had as an inevitable consequence the formulation of another fundamental dogma, the priesthood of all believers. Intended as a redefinition of "the church" in radical opposition to Catholic claims, it redefined also the nature of universality:

> The Churche is called the whole societie of people that acknowledge the Gospell of Christe and beleve in him. And this Church not to be of one time only but of all tymes & ages, as Adam and Eve hys wife, his son Abel & his familie was the church, Noah with his familie was the churche, Melchizedek with his familie was the Churche, Abraham also with his familie. Likewyse Isaac, Jacob, David, the Prophetes and Apostles with their Auditours that beleeved in the Gospell of Christ were the churche, and where soever at this daye the Gospel of Christ is receyved and beleved there is also the church of Christ.[13]

The sweeping enlistment of the Hebrew patriarchs under the Christian banner may surprise; but it was, for all that, a natural corollary to the dogma of justification *sola fide*. The widespread acceptance of Adam as a Christian, for instance, centered on the premise that he believed in the Christ and was thereby justified "by faith only." The evidence? The prophecy in Genesis (3.15) that Satan would be crushed by "the seed of the woman," which Protestants consistently interpreted as a reference to the

Christ-to-come. In the words of the popular Swiss theologian Rudolf Gwalter,

> It is evident that [Adam] put his whole hope and trust in Jesus Chryst alone, which was that promised seede of the woman. Therefore *Adam was a christian man*, and beleeved that he and his posteritie should be delivered and saved from the tyrannie of the Divell, through the merite of Chryst onely.[14]

Consenting, Milton elevated the prophecy of the "seed" into the single most important motif of the last two books of *Paradise Lost*, the vision of the future unfolded by Michael, terminating in Adam's moving acceptance of the "seed" as his "Redeemer ever blest" (XII.573). For Milton, as for Protestants generally, Adam was indeed "a christian man"—and more specifically, a Protestant.[15]

The primacy of faith presupposed, for all Protestants, a deeply felt conviction of personal sinfulness reminiscent at its most intense of the experiences of Luther. Whatever the psychological motivation behind such a conviction, the purely theological dimension appealed in the first instance to "original sin" and, in the second, to its reenactment in daily life. Original sin is scarcely comprehensible to the modern mind, since it involves the hereditary transmission of Adam's guilt to the sum total of his descendants. Passionately experienced during the Renaissance, however, it was with equal passion described as "an hereditary vitiousnesse" or "*epidemicall* contagion" issuing from Adam and reducing all men into so many "ungracious bastards" or, even less flatteringly, "nothing else but a filthy dunghill of all abominable vices."[16] Should the total terms, so totally uncompromising, distress us by their extravagance, we may consider that in positing man's "fallenness" they assent to a fact of experience we can hardly question ourselves, namely, that man's conduct tends on the whole toward the imperfect. This universal proclivity, translated into theological language, confronts us also in Donne: "man was sour'd in the whole lump, poysoned in the fountain, perished at the chore, withered in the root, in the fall of *Adam*."[17]

The consequences were generally agreed upon: man inclines toward a reenactment of the primal disobedience, much as the narrator in Herbert's "The Collar" duplicates both the experience of Adam ("there is fruit, / And thou hast hands") and its immediate afterlife ("I rav'd and grew more fierce and wilde"). Variations upon the same theme abound. Milton in *Paradise Lost* delineated the prototype of the Fall, somberly warning of its effects on the universe at large. Donne in the *Holy Sonnets* lashed about wildly, confirming a general principle repeatedly echoed across the Renaissance ("the *Essence* of *sinne* [is] merely ἀταξία: *Disor-*

der").[18] Others—Donne once again among them—marked with mounting despair the way the macrocosm mirrors the restlessness of man:

> All the creatures are upon a wheele, and in motion; there is not a creature since *Adam* sinned, sleepeth sound. Wearinesse and motion is laid on *Moon* and *Sunne,* and all *creatures* on this side of the *Moon. Seas* ebbe and flow, and that's trouble; *winds* blow, *rivers* move, *heavens* and *stars* these five thousand yeares, except one time,[19] have not had six minutes rest; living creatures walk apace toward death; Kingdomes, Cities, are on the wheele of changes, up, and down.... The great *All* of heaven and earth, since *God* laid the first stone of this wide Hall, hath been groning, and weeping....[20]

Still others issued a call to arms; and borrowing St. Paul's recurrent martial imagery—especially in the Epistle to the Ephesians—they provided massive treatises like John Downame's *The Christian warfare Against the Devill World and Flesh Wherein is described their nature, the maner of their fight and meanes to obtaine victorye,* which by its fourth edition (1633–34) exceeded eleven hundred folio pages. Enterprises of this order may appear unlikely, and at best useless, until we recall that their tediously spun imagery was essential to the purposes of more refined spirits. Erasmus in his exceedingly popular *Enchiridion* (1503), similarly addressed to Christ's soldiers, had already enlisted St. Paul's armory to the services of Christian "philosophy" (see above, p. 14). But the same images were in due course to be depicted to advantage in *The Faerie Queene,* in *Paradise Lost,* in *The Pilgrim's Progress,* and even in Marvell's redaction of the same tradition in "A Dialogue between the Resolved Soul, and Created Pleasure."

The war against the devil, the world and the flesh was an experience which Luther lived in delicious agony and Calvin mapped with relentless logic. Personally most unattractive as he was intellectually most impressive, Calvin had by the late 1530s hammered the flexible views of Luther into the rigid framework of his awe-inspiring *Institutes* (1536, revised in 1539, and translated into French by Calvin himself in 1541). Original sin was now magnified into a total experience with total consequences, reducing man to a creature capable of thoughts and deeds strictly evil in both intent and execution. The absolute primacy of faith was moreover made subordinate to the absolute primacy of Grace, transforming "justification" from a promise into an improbability except where the offended and alienated Deity inscrutably elected ("predestined") some to salvation and the rest to eternal damnation. Not surprisingly, man's free will was abrogated altogether, the Divine Wisdom retaining unqualified priority not only in that the Fall was foreseen but that it was indeed decreed. Could such a scheme have attracted anyone? And where accepted, was it not bound to paralyze its partisans into inaction? Our expectations to the contrary, however, the scheme generated a phenomenal energy as Calvinists under the assumption of their own "election" propelled themselves into action with missionary zeal. Self-confidence, not the lack of it, accounts for Calvinism's widespread appeal, which by the middle of the sixteenth century had seized the initiative from Lutheranism and for wellnigh a hundred years affected the manner of life and the mode of thinking throughout northern Europe inclusive of England and especially Scotland.

There were changes, certainly. The more uncompromising aspects of Calvin's thought were in reiteration much qualified, less perhaps by Theodore Beza, who succeeded him as head of Geneva's theocracy (from 1564), than by the numerous theologians who constructed Protestant equivalents of the massive "cathedrals of the mind" characteristic of medieval Catholicism. These theologians drew liberally on Calvin's *Institutes*, yet they were equally influenced by the less rigid framework of a work Luther regarded as second in importance to the Bible: the *Common Places* (1521) of his genial friend, the humanist Philipp Melanchthon. The most noteworthy consequence was the manual of theology compiled by the successor to Zurich's great reformer Zwingli, the moderate Heinrich Bullinger (d. 1575), and translated into English as *Common Places* (1572). Other labors included Wolfgang Musculus' *Common Places*, which in its English version (1563) exceeded one thousand folio pages, Peter Martyr Vermigli's *Common Places* (1583), Zacharias Ursinus' *Summe of Christian Religion* (1587), Gulielmus Bucanus' *Institutions* (1606), Lucas Trelcatius' *Common Places* (1610), Hieronymus Zanchius' *Body of Christian Religion* (1659)—and a host of still other works variously designated "system," "exposition," "body," "anatomy," "apology," "model," "sum," and the like. Protestants in England as on the Continent were well-enough equipped for any eventuality.

But so were Catholics. The Council of Trent (in three sessions in 1545–48, 1551–52, and 1562–63) may have been a victory for the conservative elements within the Catholic Church, and its decrees may have been inflexibly authoritarian. But it signaled the recovery of Catholic self-confidence, which in the ensuing Counter-Reformation strengthened spirituality by emphasizing the very aspects so thoroughly detested by Protestants: the intense veneration of saints, the increased celebration of the sacraments, the elaborate liturgy, the exuberant music, the explosive baroque in the ornate churches and in the sensuous arts both visual and plastic. Mariolatry proliferated, its sheer physicality ("Her sacred breasts were as two Pearly-bottels, tipped with rich rubies")[21] best mirrored in the experiences which St. Teresa of Avila (d. 1582, canonized 1622) testifies in her celebrated confrontation with the angel "in corporall forme":

> He was not great but litle, very beautifull, his face so glorious, that he seemed to be one of the higher angells. . . . I did see in his hand

a long darte of gold, and the end of the yron head of it seemed to have a litle fyre, this he seemed to pass through my heart sometimes, and that it pierced to my entrayles, which me thoght he drew from mee, when he pulled it out agayne, & he left me whole enflamed in great love of God, the payne was so great that it made me complayne greevously, & the sweetnesse was so excessive, which this exceeding great payne causeth, that I could not desyre to have it taken away. . . .[22]

Catholic self-confidence is also evident in the refusal of Elizabethan England's foremost Catholic poet, Robert Southwell (d. 1595), to compromise his extreme language. Crashaw in the next generation was to prove even more confident, his rousing lyricism centered not on expostulation as on meditation, nor on analysis as on celebration (see pp. 141ff.).

Two other developments strengthened Catholic resolve even further. One was the introduction of Catholicism into the Far East by the Portuguese and into the Americas by the Spaniards, in the latter case under exceptionally vicious circumstances which very few—notably the Dominican Bartolomeo de Las Casas—were prepared to question. The other development was the advent of the Jesuits under Ignatius Loyola (d. 1556, canonized 1622), whose efforts in every direction were so impressively successful that their very mention among Protestants induced a torrent of virulent denunciations. The ardent response is understandable, especially among Calvinists, who unerringly perceived that the Jesuits had by the outset of the seventeenth century regained the initiative for the Catholic church precisely as Calvinism had already seized the initiative within Protestantism. Typically, as a result, the English Jesuit Robert Parsons was described on his death (1610) as "a most Diabolicall, unnaturall, and barbarous butcherlie fellow"[23]—an estimate which in his case was not altogether misplaced, even if he did compose the most popular work of devotion produced by the Counter-Reformation in England (*A Christian Directorie* [Rouen, 1585]). Partisan hysterics apart, however, Jesuits like Campion (d. 1581, canonized 1970) and Bellarmine (d. 1621, canonized 1930) command the highest possible respect. Campion in addition to his personal courage was responsible for one of the most succinct defences of Catholicism (*The Ten Reasons*), while Bellarmine was the period's most brilliant controversialist, all the more effective because he was so irritatingly courteous to his opponents. His worthiest antagonist in England, William Whitaker, Regius Professor of Divinity at Cambridge, freely acknowledged that Bellarmine was "unquestionably learned, possessed of a happy genius, a penetrating judgment, and multifarious reading." In turn, Bellarmine kept a picture of Whitaker in his study because, he said, the English divine was "the most learned Heretick that ever he read."[24] The compliments, it should be emphasized, are an exception to the usual manner of engaging in controversies, since Protestants normally attacked Catholic spokesmen as so many "Bastards borne of one Whore," and Catholics with equal zeal claimed that "never any man writ more filthily, more uncivilly, more lewdly, and that beyond all boundes of Christian modesty and temperance &c. then did *Luther.*"[25]

Of the major Catholic theologians, the one least often accommodated by either side was St. Thomas Aquinas. True, his magisterial exposition of the God-descended hierarchy of laws exerted a lasting influence on every Christian writer, including Richard Hooker in Elizabethan England and the Cambridge Platonists in the mid-seventeenth century.[26] Generally speaking, however, Catholics preferred the aggregate of their theological tradition to any single spokesman, quite unlike Protestants, who so highly favored St. Augustine as before noted. The reputation of Thomism is adequately represented by John Colet's response to the suggestion of Erasmus that St. Thomas was the best of the medieval theologians:

> Why do you praise to me a man who, had he not had so much arrogance, would never have defined everything in such a rash and supercilious way, and who, had he not had a worldly spirit, would never have contaminated the teaching of Christ with his profane philosophy?[27]

III. "A metaphoricall God"

Protestants appealed to but a single authority, the Bible. But in practice, as we have seen, they invoked with readiness St. Augustine, as indeed they also resorted to St. Bernard of Clairvaux (d. 1153), in whom they respected his passionately expressed pleas for moral purity, and to St. John Chrysostom (d. 407), in whom they admired his strikingly articulated expositions of Christianity's paradoxes. Notwithstanding, the Bible remained for Protestants the court of constant appeal, dictated as it was believed to have been by the Holy Spirit, and indeed "licensed by the Omnipotent," as Thomas Dekker proclaimed in his preface to *The Seven Deadly Sinnes of London* (1606). The accessibility of the Bible became, in consequence, a normative Protestant commitment. Here the way was again led by Luther, who translated the entire Bible into German by 1534. The corresponding achievement in England, the King James ("Authorized") Version of 1611, was prepared with royal approval by a committee of the best available experts, who labored for nearly seven years. Generous use was made of all previous translations, notably the pivotal versions by John Wycliffe and William Tyndale, witness the evolution of four verses from St. Paul's "hymn to charity" (1 Corinthians 13.4–7):

Charite is pacient, it is benyngne, charite enuyeth not, it doth not wickidli it is not blowun it is not coueitous, it sekith not the thingis that ben his owne, it is not stired to wraththe, it thenkith not yuel, it ioieth not on wickidnesse, but it ioieth to gidre to truthe, it suffrith alle thingis: it bileueth alle thingis, it hopith alle thingis it susteyneth alle thingis.

(John Wycliffe, 1380s)

Love suffreth longe, and is corteous. Love envieth not. Love doth not frowardly, swelleth not dealeth not dishonestly asketh not her awne, is not provoked to anger, thynketh not evyll, reioyseth not in iniquite: but reioyseth in the trueth, suffreth all thynge, beleveth all thynges, hopeth all thynges, endureth in all thynges.

(William Tyndale, 1525ff.)

Loue suffreth longe, and is curteous. Loue enuyeth not. Loue doth not frowardly, swelleth not, dealeth not dishonestly seketh not her awne, is not prouoked to anger, thinketh no euyll, reioyseth not in iniquitie: but reioyseth in the trueth, suffreth all thynges, beleueth all thynges, hopeth all thynges, endureth all thynges.

(Thomas Cranmer ["The Great Bible"], 1539

Loue suffreth long, is courteous: loue enuieth not: loue doth not boast it selfe, swelleth not, Disdaineth nothing as vnbeseming, seketh not her owne things, is not prouoked to anger, thinketh not euil, Reioyseth not in iniquitie, but reioyseth in the trueth. Suffreth all thinges, beleueth all thinges, hopeth all thinges, endureth all thinges.

(The Geneva Bible, 1st complete ed. 1560)

Charitie is patient, is benigne: Charitie enuieth not, dealeth not peruersly: is not puffed vp, is not ambitious, seeketh not her owne, is not prouoked to anger, thinketh not euil: reioyseth not upon iniquitie, but reioyseth with the truth: suffereth al things, beleeueth al things, hopeth al things, beareth al things.

(The Rheims New Testament [Catholic version], 1582)

Charitie suffereth long, and is kinde: charitie enuieth not: charitie vaunteth not it selfe, is not puffed vp, Doeth not beuave it selfe vnseemly, seeketh not her owne, is not easily prouoked, thinketh no euill, Reioyseth not in iniquitie, but reioyseth in the trueth: Beareth all things, beleeueth all things, hopeth all things, endureth all things.

(The King James Version, 1611)

It should be noted that one of the Protestant versions, the extremely popular Geneva Bible of 1560, carried marginal notes for the edification of the elect. Even more nervously, the Catholic version of the New Testament published at Rheims—eventually merged with the version of the Old Testament published at Douai (1609–10)—provided marginal notes as well as extensive "annotations," often longer than the verses and chapters annotated. Comparison is invariably illuminating, even where only the text itself is involved. For example, the "prophecy" in Genesis of "the seed of the woman" reads in the Geneva Bible thus: "I wil also put enmitie betwene thee and the woman, and betwene thy sede and her sede. He shal breake thine head, and thou shalt bruise his heele." In the Douai Bible, however, the second sentence reads: "she shall bruise thy head in peeces, & thou shalt lye in waite of her heele." An accompanying annotation, lengthy as usual, remarks on *She shall bruise:* "Protestants wil not admitte this reading . . . lest our Blessed Ladie should be said anie way to bruise the serpents head. . . ." The different readings, it is clear, support radically different doctrines: in the Protestant version, "justification by faith"; and in the Catholic, the status of Mary as coredemptrix with the Christ. Such issues loomed very large in the horizons of the Renaissance, arousing passions whose intensity we cannot even begin to comprehend. We may remind ourselves that the Bible was not a minor appendix to life. Easily the foremost "best seller" of the period, its English versions alone are estimated to have appeared in over six hundred thousand copies by 1640, and as many again by the end of the century.[28]

So far as the interpretation of the Bible is concerned, Protestants commonly endorsed "the literal sense." As Donne categorically maintained, "the word of God is not the word of God in any other sense than literally."[29] The emphasis was especially voiced in connection with the Book of Genesis, since a denial of its historicity might have mythologized the Christian claims about the presence of God—even of the God-man Jesus—within history. Hence the reiterated warnings that

> histories in scripture, as that of creation, of paradise, of mans fall, of *Adams* progenie, *Abraham* his leaving his country, and many such are uttered in plaine wordes and proper without allegories, or other figures. Because that would make the scripture to bee laughed at, and breede infinite absurdities, if one should attempt to make all tropicall [i.e., figurative], and turne every thing into Allegoricall senses, as some wanton unsanctified wittes too much do endeavor it.[30]

Foremost among the "wanton unsanctified wittes" was the brilliant Origen (d. ca. 254), whose allegorical interpretations continued through the Renaissance to vex theologians into nightmares. Later, radicals such as Samuel Fisher would in works like *The Rustics Alarm* (1660) additionally demonstrate how the mythologization of the Bible could be used as a powerful weapon against authority in general.[31] Aware of the dangers, "orthodox" Protestants maintained with William Tyndale that the literal sense includes all other senses ("the scripture hath but one sence which is yᵉ literall sence. And yᵉ literall sence is yᵉ rote and grounde of all"), much as in the sacraments the outward ceremony and the inner spiritual truth are two indivisible aspects of the same unity.³² "The literall sense," we have earlier seen Donne to assert, "is always to be preserved. . . . But the literall sense of every place, is the principall intention of the Holy Ghost, in that place: And his principall intention in many places, is to express things by allegories, by figures; so that in many places in Scripture, a figurative sense is the literall sense."³³

The sense which is at once literal and figurative is most apparent in the domain of typology. A time-honored approach to the Bible, typology—to be exact, historical typology—was used as early as the New Testament to assert the linearity of the onward-moving, nonrecurring historical processs in terms of the Messiah's prefiguration in the activities of numerous predecessors ("types"). As elaborated over the centuries, typology designated the extensive anticipatory "premonstration" of the Christ argued among others by Bishop Griffith Williams in 1624:

> [Christ] is the *First*, hee is the *Last*. . . . Veyled and shadowed in the Old, reveiled and exhibited in the New Testament; *promised* in that, *preached* in this; there *shewed* into the Fathers in *Types*, here *manifested* unto us in *Truths:* for the *Tree* of *Life*, the *Arke* of *Noah*, the *Ladder* of *Jacob*, the *Mercy Seat*, the *Brazen Serpent*, and all such mysticall *Types*, and typicall *Figures* that we reade of in the Old *Testament*; what were they else but *Christ;* obscurely *shadowed* before he was fully *reveiled;* and so all the men of Note, *Noah, Isaac, Joseph, Moses, Aaron, Josua, Sampson, David, Salomon,* Kings, Priests, Prophets, Titles of Dignities, *Names of Honour,* . . . belong unto this *King of Kings*.³⁴

Poetic adaptations are legion. Explicitly formulated, typology underlies in *Paradise Lost* the progressive revelation of the Christ's advent in terms of "types and shadowes" (XII.239f.), and in Crashaw the lyrical celebration of the single moment in history when "Types yield to TRUTHES":

> Lo, the full, finall SACRIFICE
> On which all figures fix't their eyes.
> The ransom'd ISACK, and his ramme;
> The MANNA, and the PASCHAL Lamb . . . .
>   ("Lauda Sion Salvatorem," st. XII)

But typology will also be discerned to have affected the total fabric of poems, as in *Paradise Lost* the "types and shadowes" encompass not only "historical figures" but the very sound patterns and clusters of images until, thus juxtaposed, they complete Milton's aesthetic vision. In *The*

Temple, too, Herbert deploys a strategy whose eucharistic burden is, like Grace, omnipresent and "prevenient" or anticipatory, witness the way that the lengthy poem "The Sacrifice" anticipates through its liturgical stanzas each given narrator's emergent anguish by placing it—in advance of its enunciation—within the context of Christ's Passion (see pp. 130ff.).

The figurative nature of much of the Bible could hardly have escaped the scrutiny even of the most committed partisan of the literal sense. That portions of the Bible are poems—for example the Psalms and the Proverbs in their entirety, the Book of Job exclusive of its prologue and epilogue, and shorter units such as the Song of Moses (Exodus 15) and the Song of Deborah (Judges 5)—was fully recognized during the Renaissance.[35] Donne, in fact, did not hesitate to describe God as "a *figurative, a metaphoricall God*":

> A *God* in whose words there is such a height of *figures,* such *voyages,* such *peregrinations* to fetch remote and precious *metaphors,* such *extensions,* such *spreadings,* such *Curtaines* of *Allegories,* such *third heavens* of *Hyperboles,* so *harmonious eloquutions,* so *retired* and so *reserved expressions,* so *commanding perswasions,* so *perswading commandments,* such *sinewes* even in thy *milke,* and such *things* in thy *words,* as all *prophane Authors,* seeme of the seed of the *Serpent,* that *creepes,* thou art the *Dove,* that *flies.*[36]

There was moreover the recognition that the language of the parables in the New Testament, in itself concrete enough to satisfy "the literal sense," is ultimately symbolic, iconic, emblematic, hieroglyphical. The link was averred, for instance, by Valeriano at the outset of his *Hieroglyphica* (1575). But it also informs the definition of an emblem by Francis Quarles:

> An *Embleme* is but a silent Parable. Let not the tender Eye check, to see the allusion to our blessed Saviour figured in these Types. In holy Scripture, he is sometimes called a Sower; sometimes, a Fisher; sometimes a Physician: and why not presented so as well to the eye as to the ear? Before the knowledge of letters God was known by *Hieroglyphicks* and *Emblemes* of His Glory.[37]

The impact of such an attitude on literature was decisive. The creative form which Spenser and Milton and Donne imposed on words appealed in the end to the prototypical activities of the creative Word. For the poets of the English Renaissance, and for prose-writers like Sir Thomas Browne, the universe was "historical" yet figurative, "literal" yet emblematic—and essentially sacramental.

The interpretation of the Bible might have presented very few problems had it not been for the enigmatic material comprising the Book of Revelation. It could hardly be "history" since it appertained to the future. If "prophecy," however, in what sense was it to be interpreted? Donne valiantly resorted to a distinction:

> In the first book of the Scriptures, that of Genesis, there is danger in departing from the letter; In this last book, this of the Revelation, there is much danger in adhering too close to the letter. . . . As then to depart from the literall sense, that sense which the very letter presents, in the book of Genesis, is dangerous, because if we do so there, we have no history of the Creation of the world in any other place to stick to; so to binde our selves to such a literall sense in this book, will take from us the consolation of many spirituall happinesses, and bury us in the carnall things of this world.[38]

Undeterred, numerous commentators ventured to "open up the mysteries of this Revelation, . . . both Paraphrastically expounded and Historically applyed." I quote from John Napier (cf. p. 182), who, as the discoverer of logarithms, reminds us that the Book of Revelation was by no means the province of theologians only, witness *inter alia* the subsequent labors of Sir Isaac Newton. Napier's own effort, first published in 1593 as *A Plaine Discovery of the Whole Revelation of Saint John,* enjoyed by 1645 four editions as well as an *Epitome* (1641). Other expositions were no less popular,[39] their ambition endorsed by none other than King James as already noted ("of all the scriptures, the buik of Revelatioun is maist meit for this our last age, as ane prophecie of the letter [i.e., latter] tyme").[40] The book is a prophecy, it was widely claimed among Protestants, in that it details the victory of the elect over the sinister forces of impiety, inclusive of the activities of the Antichrist (Revelation 13.11ff., cf. 1 John 2.18) who was commonly identified with the Pope.[41] It is also a prophecy, according to an increasing number of clamorous militants, in that its promise of the Christ's temporal reign of a thousand years (Revelation 20.6) was about to be realized. In short, the literal meaning once enforced, the Book of Revelation yielded as many interpretations of history as there were spokesmen prepared to entertain them.

Donne pretended not to be concerned. Since several of the early Fathers had also accepted the prophecy of Christ's millenarian reign "in all temporall abundances," any parallel belief during the Renaissance was not a heresy so much as "an opinion, which is no word of heavy detestation." With equal assurance Bishop Joseph Hall maintained that the "opinion" of the latter-day millenarians was not "so deadly and pernicious in it selfe, as to make ship-wrack of their own or others faith."[42] In fact, however, millenarianism—chiliasm, according to its alternative designation—was potentially a very serious threat indeed. Millenarian expectations, for one, sustained the questionable theoretical premises of the events at Münster. Within the seventeenth century, moreover, a partiality to the number 666—fraught with supernatural import on the basis of the Book of Revelation (13.18)—resulted in a veritable "Itch of prophecying" ("*O Sixty-six!* Thou center of human Prophecies! Thou Ocean, into which all the Rivers of Conjectural Predictions did run!") which at the approach of 1666 unleashed a phenomenal hysteria as London was struck first by the devastating plague of the year before and then, in the apocalyptic year itself, by the Great Fire.[43] As the Book of Revelation was additionally read in connection with the Book of Daniel—both contain, it was widely believed, "historicall prophecies"[44]—the thousand years' temporal reign of Christ in the one was identified with the "fifth monarchy" at the end of history in the other (Daniel 2.44). The political consequences were formidable. At the risible level, violent disputes often centered on whether the beast in Revelation was Charles I or Parliament, and whether the "fifth monarchy" was to be established by Christ or—an improbable candidate at best—Charles II.[45] The actuality, of course, was far different, involving as it did political ambitions fired by emotional commitments on the part of radicals generally and the fifth Monarchy men in particular, who similarly embraced millenarianism with revolutionary zeal.[46] In the moment's "enthusiasm"—to use the word in the strictly pejorative sense it had assumed by the later Renaissance—the Book of Revelation was further conflated with extrabiblical "prophecies." The most notable of these, first propounded by Joachim of Fiore (d. 1202) and codified by his wilder disciples into the *Evangelium aeternum,* divided history into three temporal Ages of which the third and last, expected to endure for a thousand years, was said to have begun under the supervision of the Holy Ghost. Attacked as a "most detestable and blasphemous book" by John Foxe during the Elizabethan era and by Donne during the Jacobean, the "everlasting gospel" was resuscitated by the radicals of the mid-seventeenth century—and beyond, stripped of its theological attire, by Hitler's Third Reich, which was also expected to last a thousand years.[47]

Is it at all credible that such promiscuous interpretations of the Book of Revelation had any influence on literature? Yet the evidence is conclusive: not only Spenser but Shakespeare and Milton alike labored under the shadow of apocalyptic thought,[48] as if intent on demonstrating the Protestant claim of the Bible's all-encompassing authority. The literature of the English Renaissance is in its commitment to Otherness essentially Biblical.

IV. "The visible sign of an invisible grace"

The experiential life of Protestantism centered on the proclamation of the Word through preaching and its symbolic confirmation through the sacrament of the Lord's Supper, the Eucharist. Preaching was the capital medium of evangelization, and though frequently used for transparently political purposes, it consisted by and large of expositions of doctrine and counsel for behavior. Several manuals provided generous advice on technical details such as the sermon's length and form, and on substantive matters such as procedure.[49] Least heeded, alas, was the advice appertaining to length ("Every Sermon ought to be briefe").[50] Otherwise, however, the most responsible preachers elevated their sermons to high-aspiring art fully commensurate to their noble aims. The principal aim was best set forth by Donne in 1627:

> The Preacher doth so infuse the feare of God into his Auditory, that first, they shall feare nothing but God, and then they shall feare God, but so, as he is God; and God is Mercy; God is Love; and his Minister shall so spread his wings over his people, as to defend them from all inordinate feare, from all suspition and jealousie, from all diffidence and distrust in the mercie of God.[51]

So far as the mode of articulation was concerned, the Marburg theologian Andreas Gerardus (Hyperius) invoked St. Augustine's endorsement of the sermon as a studied oration: "the whole craft of varienge the Oration by *Schemes and Tropes*, pertaineth indifferently to the Preacher and Orator."[52] In England, the highly respected William Perkins in *The Arte of Prophecying. Or a Treatise concerning the Sacred and Onely True Manner and Method of Preaching*—translated from its original Latin in 1606 by Thomas Tuke— advanced a vital consideration no less relevant to poetry such as Herbert's:

> *Humane wisdome* must be concealed, whether it be in the matter of the sermon, or in the setting forth of the words: because the preaching of the word is the *Testimonie of God, and the Profession of the knowledge of Christ,* and not of humane skill. . . . If any man thinke that by this meanes barbarisme should be brought into pulpits; he must understand that the Minister may, yea & must privately use at his libertie the artes, philosophy, and varietie of reading, whilest he is in framing his sermon: but he ought in publike to conceale all these from the people, and not to make the least ostentation. *Artis etiam est celare artem; it is also a point of Art to conceale Art.*[53]

A widely credited misconception accepts that "Anglicans" and "Puritans"— designations which themselves call for annotation—delivered sermons "eloquent" in the former instance, "plain" in the latter. Yet Perkins, who commended the use of implicit eloquence, was a Puritan. In actual practice, moreover, eloquence was by no means the exclusive province of celebrated Anglican preachers like Lancelot Andrewes, Donne, Humphrey Sydenham, Jeremy Taylor, or Thomas Fuller, in that the same quality manifests itself throughout the evocative sermons of the Puritan Thomas Adams as well as in one of the period's greatest performances by the equally Puritan Ralph Cudworth.[54] By the same token, "plainness" is very much in evidence among Anglican preachers, not only Archbishop James Ussher of Armagh but—the ultimate evidence!—-that archenemy of all Puritans, Archbishop William Laud of Canterbury. The most categorical affirmation of the virtues of "plainness" in opposition to the elaborately structured sermon, finally, was also ventured by an Anglican: George Herbert (see p. 119).

Response to preaching by the believing Protestant led to the symbolic confirmation of his faith through the Eucharist. One of the two sacraments recognized by Protestants as warranted by the Bible,[55] the Eucharist occasioned acrimonious controversies which turned Protestant against Protestant and permanently affected the divisions among the Reformers. But the central issue—the nature of the "Real Presence" of Christ in the sacrament—need concern us less than the emphasis which Protestants upheld in opposition to Catholics. For where Catholics regarded the sacrament as dispensing grace irrespective of the attitude of the minister or the recipient, Protestants insisted on the prior condition of the recipient's faith. Equally important, where Catholics maintained that the sacrament as "an efficacious sign of sanctifying grace" imparts salvation of itself, Protestants claimed that as "the visible sign of an invisible grace" it is but symbolic of the actual blessings.[56] Translated into literature, the Protestant interpretation figures diversely in *The Faerie Queene* during the spiritual arming of the Redcross Knight for his ensuing victory over Orgoglio (I.xi.36 and 46), and in *Samson Agonistes* during the gradual transformation of its protagonist into the believer who, inwardly illumined, correctly perceives "the visible sign of an invisible grace." But when all is said the poet who responded most fully to the sacramental life was Herbert. Words whether intimately or remotely related to the Eucharist are jointly drawn into the experiences recounted in *The Temple,* yielding a cumulative unity which is fundamentally eucharistic (see pp. 129ff.).

Whatever our preconceptions, then, the importance of the Eucharist in Protestantism should not be underestimated. True, the devotional life of Protestants appears minimal when compared to that of Catholics; and so indeed it is, but rather in its extent than in its intensity. Mariolatry, as before noted, was intensified in Catholicism especially after the Council of Trent. Mariology, on the other hand, was by no means ostracized from Protestantism, the Reformers themselves commending it in no uncertain terms, and Anglicans even more explicitly.[57] We also expect Anglicans to have been far more devotional than Puritans; and we point to the very dimensions so violently denounced at the time by Puritans: the fulsome celebration of the Virgin in Anthony Stafford's *The Femall Glory* (1635), the "monastic" community at Little Gidding dedicated under Nicholas Ferrar to sustained prayers and ritualistic night-long vigils, the introduction of distinctly "popish" elements into the liturgy by Archbishop Laud— and beyond, the powerful influence which the devotional writings of St. Ignatius Loyola and St. Francis of Sales are said to have exerted on Anglican poets[58] or the composition of a fervent poem like Joseph Beaumont's *Psyche* (1648) under the shadow of St. Teresa.[59] Yet extreme forms of devotion were not unknown among Puritans. Thus a leading Cromwellian, Francis Rous, indulged in prayers for "heavenly excesse," "divine extasie," and the like,[60] even as Samuel Petto described his "witnessings of the spirit" in *The Voice of the Spirit,* adding for good measure several "sweet experiences" under the title *Roses from Sharon* (1654). Significantly, too, a virulent anti-Catholic like William Crashaw—the Catholic poet's most Protestant father—managed to attack the papal Antichrist even in his will,[61] yet he was not at all disinclined, creditably to translate several devotional Catholic hymns and meditations in his *Manuall Catholicorum* (1611). Just as telling, finally, is the report of a parliamentary committee which visited Cambridge probably early in 1641 to investigate the suspect new chapel at Peterhouse (consecrated in 1634), which, they discovered, "hath bene so dressed up and ordered soe Ceremoniously, that it hath become ye gaze of ye University & greate invitation to strangers." Worse still, students from that preeminent Puritan stronghold, Emmanuel College, responded to the sinister practices at Peterhouse with distressing eagerness:

> Some of ye Schollers have received harme by theire frequent goeing to Peterhowse chapp[ell] . . . as appeareth by theire Novel gestures in the Chappell [of Emmanuel], as bowing at their rising up at *gloria patri* or ye Gospell as also by crucifixe[s] wch have bene occasionally discovered in two or three of theire Chambers. . . .[62]

Details of this order are imperative if we ever hope to appreciate the frequent confluence of apparently opposed attitudes. Yet these same details should not prevent us from recognizing several tendencies which differentiate Anglican poets like Donne and Herbert from Puritan ones like Milton. The Passion, for instance, elicited the response of Donne and Herbert in measure equal to its absence from the emotional world of Milton. Not a defect in Milton but a mark of his particular sensibility, his response was reserved for the effects of divine omnipotence within history, whether he celebrates in the Nativity Ode the impact of Christ on the universe at large, in *Comus* the joyous dance of the created order, in *Lycidas* the actual harmony within the apparent dissonance, or in *Paradise Lost* the constant displacement of demonic disorder by effectual Grace—the Eucharist projected, as it were, on a cosmic canvas.

V. "Made miserable, but not desperate"

Theology as a commitment to Otherness is clearly not an abstraction. It partakes fully of multifoliate life, however diverse the experiences recounted and the literary forms deployed. We should therefore regard with skepticism any generalization which channels responses in a single direction at the expense of reality's infinite complexity. The terms "Anglican" and "Puritan," for instance, are often used—and have been used even here—as if they were absolute entities that do not admit qualification. Yet we may consider that "Anglican" is anachronistic in that it is a term of later vintage, while "Puritan" is misleading in that it was by the early seventeenth century already a term of abuse, "for the most part held a *name of infamie*," "used (most commonly) for any Zealous Person."[63] More to the point, the two terms are not in fact opposed, since they do not designate modes of thought and experience alike theological. "Anglican" is indeed descriptive of the theology and ecclesiology of the Church of England, but "Puritan" alludes rather to antiritualism in church services and dedication to moral uprightness than to any specific theological tenet. In theology as such, "Anglican" is properly opposed by "Calvinist"—save that most Anglicans during Elizabeth's reign (but not later) were very sympathetic to Calvinist theology, just as many Calvinists like William Perkins were sufficiently open-minded to have been admired by Anglicans. In matters of Church government, "Anglican"—here, more accurately, "episcopalian"—initially stood in opposition to "Presbyterian," itself a term whose theological horizons terminated in Calvin; but when the presbyters on displacing the bishops proved no less obsessed with ecclesiastical hierarchy (*"New Presbyter* is but *Old Priest* writ Large," Milton protested),[64] the lines of demarcation shifted yet again so that by the 1640s decentralized Church government was in the main espoused by the Independents or Congregationalists. Throughout these developments the term "Puritan" remained at its best suggestive of personal experiences centered on "immediacy in relation to God."[65] As such, it is an essentially Protestant phenomenon; and William Bradshaw rightly observed in 1605 that Puritanism includes the rejection of "all Ecclesiasticall actions invented & devised by man," the acknowledgment solely of the Bible's "absolute perfection," and the participation through faith in the priesthood of all believers ("every Companie, Congregation or Assemblie of man, ordinarilie joyneing together in the true worship of God, is a true *visible church* of Christ").⁶⁶ The perceptive student of Puritanism will seek its Protestant roots in basic principles equally as much as in the categorical language, the confident poise, the tone of finality.

Developments in the early seventeenth century involve yet another expressly theological term, "Arminian." Deriving from the doctrinal positions of the Dutch Protestant theologian Jacobus Arminius (d. 1609), the term was accurately used at the time to represent anti-Calvinism at its most sustained. Alarmed, the Calvinists who monopolized the Synod of Dort (Dordrecht) in 1618–19 condemned Arminianism with predictable indignation. Their anxiety is best attested by their rhetoric. "I desire," Francis Rous warned in 1629,

> I desire we may consider the increase of Arminianism, an error that makes the grace of God lackey after the will of man. I desire we may look into the belly and bowels of this Trojan horse, to see if there be not men in it ready to open the gates to Romish tyranny, for an Arminian is the spawn of a Papist, and if the warmth of favour come upon him, you shall see him turn into one of these frogs that rise out of the bottomless pit.⁶⁷

Not in the least intimidated, however, the "ever-memorable" John Hales of Eton decided during the Synod of Dort to bid Calvin good night.⁶⁸ It was by no means a solitary decision. Anglicans were already moderating their erstwhile flirtation with Calvinist theology; so much so that when Bishop George Morley of Winchester was asked what the Arminians held, he could blandly reply that they held the best bishoprics and deaneries in the country. Yet the liberal theology represented by Arminianism influenced even "Puritans" like John Goodwin. It is also mirrored in *Paradise Lost*, whose reiterated proclamations of man's free will (III.98ff.; V.234ff., 524ff.; IX.343ff.; X.43ff.) would have been condemned early in the Renaissance as Arminian at best, "the spawn of a Papist" at worst. By 1667, when the poem was published, however, Calvinism had by and large ceased to be the most pronounced influence on English theology.

Here as elsewhere the change may be measured in terms of the rhetoric used. Earlier in the seventeenth century the articulation of the prevalent views differed but in degree from Gabriel Powel's language in *The Resolved Christian* (1616):

> Man is made of the earth, conceived in sinne, and borne to paine, *Man is evill, wretched, corrupt and abhominable, doing nothing that is good, mortall, vaine* and *wicked, unprofitable, vanity, altogether lighter than vanitie, sinfull, miserable, dust and ashes, sown in corruption, dishonour and weaknes, deceitfull, naked, subject to death, dead in sin, a liar,*

> *an hypocrite, an enemy unto God,* a creature that *drinketh iniquity like water, a pilgrime, grasse, ignorant, a stranger & sojorner, of no continuance, compassed with the snares of death, water spilt on the ground.* By birth *uncleane, a child of wrath, a worker of iniquity, an open sepulchre, a worm, the meat of wormes, dung and wormes, deprived of Gods glory.* . . . True it is, that some few sparks of the Image of God doe yet remaine in Man, but they are few indeede, very small, and of no strength. . . .[69]

By the middle of the century, however, attitudes were already inclining towards Milton's eventual efforts to justify the ways of God. Typically, Jeremy Taylor in his *Deus justificatus* (1656) could in measured tones firmly deny that "when we all fell in *Adam,* we fell into the dirt," "broken all in pieces." He added:

> We by [Adam's] fall received evill enough to undoe us, and ruine us all; but yet the evill did so descend upon us, that we were left in powers & capacities to serve and glorifie God; Gods service was made much harder, but not impossible; mankind was made miserable, but not desperate, we contracted an actuall mortality, but we were redeemable from the power of Death; sinne was easie and ready at the door, but it was resistable; Our *Will* was abused, but yet not destroyed; our Understanding was cosened, but yet still capable of the best instructions; and though the Devill had wounded us, yet God sent his Son, who like the good Samaritan poured Oyle and Wine into our wounds. . . .[70]

Milton's concurrent partiality to the demands of Divine Justice after the fall of man—"Die he or Justice must" (III.210)—is also typical of the period's evolving thought. Alexander Gil the elder, High Master of St. Paul's School when Milton was there in the early 1620s, anticipated the militancy of Milton's God by providing the following "gloss":

> Either the whole race of mankinde must be lost and perish being tainted with the sinne of *Adam,* or the infinite justice against which the sinne was done, must for ever stand violated and broken, or else a Mediator must bee found who was able to satisfie the infinite justice that was offended. The first is against the wisdome, goodnesse, and love of God to his creatures; either to make mankinde in vaine, that is to destroy it againe, or to make it unto eternall punishment. The second is impossible, that an infinite justice infinitely able to avenge it selfe should endure it selfe for ever to remaine violate and offended: for so should it prize a thing finite, and wicked, before it selfe infinite in justice: therefore there behoves to be a

Mediatour who should fully satisfie the justice offended, and utterly blot out the guilt of sinne. Now an infinite justice offended must be satisfied by a punishment answerable, that is infinite: but no finite creature could any way be, or be accounted infinite. Therefore *when none was found worthy either in heaven, or in earth, or under the earth; the Lambe slaine from the beginning of the world tooke upon him our flesh,* to satisfie for the sinne of his creature, and so by his infinite obedience . . . was the infinite justice satisfied.[71]

The statement is an adequate summary of the Protestant theory of the Atonement. Yet it is significant that its burden was so qualified by Milton that the more brutal aspects of Calvinist logic were eschewed in favor of the moderate theology increasingly characteristic of English thought.

The decline and fall of Calvinism owed much to purely political factors. Yet theological considerations once again dominate the scene. The advent of Arminianism is crucial, certainly. But most thinkers, Milton among them, could as readily have adapted the liberal strain in Christian theology which reaches through Erasmus back to early Fathers like the enticing St. Clement of Alexandria (d. *ca.* 215). The line of descent is most evident in the Cambridge Platonists; for whatever their links with Renaissance thought, they shared in particular an undeviating commitment to the more generous aspects of Christianity's vision. The approval that the Cambridge Platonists extended to Eastern theologians like Origen at the expense of Western ones like St. Augustine and especially Calvin was based on the conviction that the latter upheld a dichotomy between the natural and the supernatural, the rational and the spiritual, the will of man and the grace of God. In opposition it was now argued that "God hath left us as *Free* as we may be"; so much so, added Henry More, that it is impossible for any Christian properly so called to "swallow down that hard Doctrine concerning *Fate . . . or Calvinistick Predestination.*"[72] The cumulative result was a dramatic change in the attitudes to Otherness. Peter Sterry, for instance, penned A *Discourse of the Freedom of the Will* (1675), which is not so much a discourse as an extravagantly lyrical hymn to "all the Beauties, all the Sweetnesses of the Divine Holiness, the Divine Love and Goodness." "The Wrath and the Contrariety now ceaseth," he sang, "being reconciled and charmed by these Divine Harmonies into the Unity of eternal Love."[73]

It may nevertheless be doubted whether the Cambridge Platonists would have approved of Sterry's lyricism, suspicious as they were of any form of "enthusiasm." Their efforts were, after all, directed toward the eradication of fanaticism, which in effect meant an assault both on extreme principles as such and on their presentation in extreme language. The extreme principles were frontally attacked by Henry More in *Enthusias-*

mus triumphatus (1656), the blueprint as it were of the Restoration's consistently adverse attitude toward "enthusiasts." The extreme language, on the other hand, was most effectively censured through the controlled tone used in particular by Benjamin Whichcote and John Smith to demonstrate the advantages of reasonableness. Style, indeed, became an indispensable weapon against "enthusiasm" as related writers resorted to a variety of strategies, none more devastating in its immediate consequences than the satire which Marvell in *The Rehearsal Transpros'd* (1672–73) directed against the Anglican "enthusiast" Samuel Parker.[74]

The fall of Calvinism may or may not have been a felicitous development. But the concurrent annihilation of "enthusiasm"—the suspension not only of the irrational but of the prophetic in religious experience and of the radical in political thought—was eventually to be regarded with passionate regret. One's thoughts race beyond "the peace of the Augustans" to Blake. But that, as they say, is another story.

Terminat hora diem; terminat Author opus.

NOTES

An earlier version of this chapter appeared in *The Age of Milton: Backgrounds to Seventeenth-Century Literature,* ed. C. A. Patrides and Raymond B. Waddington (Manchester: Manchester University Press; Totowa, N.J.: Barnes and Noble Books, 1980), pp. 170–196. Copyright C. A. Patrides and R. B. Waddington. Reprinted by permission.

1. John Swift, *The Divine Eccho* (London, 1612), sig. M2; Matthew Brookes, *The House of God* (London, 1627), p. 29; Thomas Salter, *A Mirrhor mete for all Mothers* (London, 1579), sigs. A6–A6v; Robert Pricket, *Times Anotomie* (London, 1606), The Epistle to the Reader; and John Dod with Robert Cleaver, *Exposition of the Ten Commandements,* 19th ed. (London, 1635), p. 269; respectively.
2. See H. R. Trevor-Roper, "The European Witch-Craze of the Sixteenth and Seventeenth Centuries," in his *Religion, the Reformation and Social Change, and Other Essays* (London, 1967).
3. Christopher Hill, *The World Turned Upside Down: Radical Ideas during the English Revolution* (London, 1972). It is not irrelevant that Hill is a Marxist.
4. Claus-Peter Clasen, *Anabaptism: A Social History, 1525–1618* (Ithaca, N.Y., 1972), p. 425.
5. *The Epistles of Erasmus,* trans. Francis M. Nichols (London, 1901), 1:44 (ep. 59).
6. "Man's will is like a beast standing between two riders. If God rides, it wills and goes where God wills.... If Satan rides, it wills and goes where Satan wills. Nor may it choose to which rider it will run, or which it will seek; but the riders themselves fight to decide who shall have and hold it" (*De servo*

arbitrio [1525], trans. J. I. Packer and O. R. Johnston [New York, 1957], pp. 103–4).
7. "Verba sine re Erasmus; res sine verbis Lutherus" (quoted in Wilhelm Pauck, *Luther and Melanchthon,* ed. Vilmos Vajta [Philadelphia, 1961], p. 26).
8. Quoted in Albert Hyma, "The Continental Origins of English Humanism," *HLQ* 4 (1940): 17.
9. "I consider Jerome," wrote Luther, "as much inferior to Augustine as Erasmus thinks he is superior" (*Luther's Correspondence,* trans. Preserved Smith [Philadelphia, 1913], 1:43 [ep. 21], quoted in Elmore H. Harbison, *The Christian Scholar in the Age of the Renaissance* (New York, 1956), p. 106. The fundamental opposition I posit between Erasmus and Luther is also endorsed—as I discovered subsequently—in the sophisticated core of Richard McKeon's "Renaissance and Method in Philosophy," in *Studies in the History of Ideas* (New York, 1935), 3: esp. pp. 71–107.
10. James 2.24. Consult Luther's *Reformation Writings,* trans. B. L. Woolf (New York, 1956), 2:306–308, and the observations by Willem J. Kooiman, *Luther and the Bible,* trans. John Schmidt (Philadelphia, 1961), pp. 110–15.
11. *Campian Englished. Or . . . the Ten Reasons,* anon. trans. (Douai? 1632), p. 134. A useful way to approach the dogma is through *A Reformation Debate,* ed. John C. Olin (New York, 1966) which contains the exchanges between Jacopo Cardinal Sadoleto and Calvin (1539) as well as the formal statements by the Council of Trent (1547) and Calvin in his *Institutes* 3:xi (1559).
12. Jerome Phillips, *The Fisherman* (London, 1623), p. 7, and Donne, *Sermons,* ed. E. M. Simpson and G. R. Potter (Berkeley, 1953–62), 2:256.
13. John Dawes, in the dedicatory epistle of his translation of Heinrich Bullinger's *Hundred Sermons upon the Apocalips* (London, 1561).
14. *Homelyes . . . uppon Actes,* trans. John Bridges (London, 1572), pp. 852–53.
15. See my essay "The First Promise Made to Man: The Edenic Origins of Protestantism," in *Premises and Motifs in Renaissance Thought and Literature* (Princeton, 1982), chap. 6.
16. Lucas Trelcatius, *Common Places of Sacred Divinitie,* trans. John Gaven (London, 1610), p. 509; Anthony White, *Truth and Error* (Oxford, 1628), p. 41; Thomas Morton, *The Three-fold State of Man* (London, 1629), p. 209 (211); and William Whately, *The New Birth* (London, 1618), p. 7; respectively.
17. *Sermons,* 8:176.
18. Anthony Fawkner, Εἰρηνογονία (London, 1630), p. 17.
19. I.e., the time of Christ's birth, when it was said that nature was uniquely peaceful (cf. Milton's account in the Nativity Ode 11.61ff.). The "five thousand yeares" designates the agreed span of time insofar as the world was normally said to have been created some time within the millennium ending this side of 4000 B.C. See my essay " 'The Exact Compute of Time': Estimates of the Year of Creation," in *Premises and Motifs,* chap. 3.
20. Samuel Rutherford, *Christ Dying and Drawing Sinners to Himselfe* (London, 1647), p. 12. Donne's *Anatomy of the World* ("The First Anniversary") clearly partakes of this manner of thought.
21. John Falconer, *The Mirrour of Created Perfection* (St. Omer, 1632), p. 136. Most Catholic books in English were during this period printed by the sem-

inary for English Catholic scholars at Douai in Flanders and the Jesuit College of St. Omer in Artois.
22. *The Lyf of the Mother Teresa of Jesus,* trans. W. M. (Antwerp, 1611), p. 239 (chap. 29).
23. Quoted in John E. Parish, "Robert Parsons and the English Counter-Reformation," *Rice University Studies* 52 (1966): 1.
24. Whitaker, *Disputatio de Sacra Scriptura* (1588, trans. William Fitzgerald [Cambridge, 1849]), p. 6, and Anthony à Wood, *Athenae Oxonienses* (London, 1691): 1:303; respectively. On Whitaker's treatise see below, note 32. Bellarmine's major work was his *Disputations against the Heretics of our Time* (Ingolstadt, Germany, 1586–93), 3 vols.; but he also wrote numerous devotional and expository works, including the cogent *Dottrina christiana,* translated by Richard Gibbons as *A Short Catechisme* and illustrated with exquisite plates (Augsburg, Germany, 1614).
25. John Weemes, *The Christian Synagogue* (London, 1623), p. 271, and Lawrence Anderton (?), *Epigrammes* (Rouen, ca. 1630), p. 61. Weemes is specifically referring to "the three pillars of popery," all of the twelfth century: Gratian, the father of canon law; Peter Lombard, author of the *Sentences,* the standard textbook of theology during the Middle Ages; and Peter Comestor, author of *Historia scholastica,* the standard work on Biblical history.
26. See my remarks in *Milton and the Christian Tradition* (Oxford, 1966), pp. 81ff., and in the introduction to my edition of *The Cambridge Platonists* (London, 1969; reprint Cambridge, 1980).
27. *Opus epistolarum Des. Erasmi,* ed. P. S. and H. M. Allen (Oxford, 1922), 4:520 (ep. 1211); trans. in Harbison, *Christian Scholar,* p. 75. Even of the panegyrics in honor of St. Thomas, one—Lorenzo Valla's *Encomium* of 1457—was in fact a critical antipanegyric, an antieulogy (see John W. O'Malley, "Some Renaissance Panegyrics of Aquinas," *Renaissance Quarterly,* 27 [1947], 174–92, and Hanna H. Gray's remarks on Valla's performance in *Essays in History and Literature,* ed. Heinz Bluhm [Chicago, 1965], pp. 37–51). In consequence, John K. Ryan's enthusiastic study of "The Reputation of St. Thomas Aquinas among English Protestant Thinkers of the Seventeenth Century," *New Scholasticism* 22 (1948): 1–33, 126–208, is quite unreliable, given in particular the author's absurd claim that St. Thomas is "the peer of Plato and Aristotle and Augustine"!
28. C. John Somerville, "On the distribution of Religious and Occult Literature in Seventeenth-Century England," *The Library,* 5th ser. 29 (1974): 220–25.
29. *Essays in Divinity,* ed. E. M. Simpson (Oxford, 1952), p. 39. By way of contrast, cf. Erasmus' commendation of the "hidden" sense at the expense of the literal (*Enchiridion,* trans. Raymond Himelick [Bloomington, Ind., 1963], p. 105).
30. Thomas Wilson, *Theologicall Rules* (London, 1615), p. 26.
31. Consult Christopher Hill, *The World Turned Upside Down,* pp. 142ff., 261ff.
32. Tyndale, "The iiii. sences of ye scripture," in *Obedience of a Christen Man* (Antwerp, 1528), fols. 129–37. The analogy with the sacraments, argued by Whitaker, *Disputatio,* discussed by Charles K. Cannon in *HLQ* 25 (1962): 129–38.

33. Donne, *Sermons,* 6:62. Also quoted on p. 183.
34. *Seven Goulden Candlestickes* (London, 1624), p. 258. For one of the most detailed expositions of the typological approach, see William Guild, *Moses Unveiled* (London, 1620). Modern studies include G. W. H. Lampe and K. J. Woolcombe, *Essays in Typology* (London, 1957), and Jean Daniélou, *From Shadows to Reality,* trans. Wulstan Hibberd (London, 1960).
35. See, for instance, the sufficiently accurate list in Ferdinando Parkhurst, *Masorah* (London, 1660), p. 128. Consult also the standard essays by Israel Baroway in *JEGP* 32 (1933): 447–80, and in *ELH* 2 (1935): 66–91, 8 (1941): 119–42, and 17 (1950): 115–35.
36. *Devotions* (1624), ed. John Sparrow (Cambridge, 1923), p. 113.
37. *Emblemes* (London, 1658), "To the Reader." Valeriano's view of the esoteric language of hieroglyphics as of parables is noted by D. P. Walker, "Esoteric Symbolism," in *Poetry and Poetics,* ed. G. M. Kirkwood (Ithaca, N.Y., 1975), p. 227.
38. *Sermons*, 6:62.
39. For example, Thomas Brightman, *A Revelation of the Revelation,* 2d ed. (London, 1615); Arthur Dent, *The Ruine of Rome: or a Exposition of the Whole Revelation* (London, 1603); Joseph Mede, *The Key of the Revelation,* trans. Richard More (London, 1643); David Pareus. *A Commentary upon . . . Revelation,* trans. E. Arnold (Amsterdam, 1644); etc.
40. *Ane fruitfull meditatioun . . . of the 20 chap. of the Revelatioun* (Edinburgh, 1588), fol. A3; also quoted on p. 181. The allusion to the "last age" partakes of the widespread expectation that the end of the world was imminent.
41. See pp. 184ff.
42. Donne, *Sermons,* 4:77–78; cf. 6:62–63, 7:122, 8:81, etc.; and Hall, *The Revelation Unrevealed: Concerning the Thousand-Yeares Reigne of the Saints with Christ upon Earth* (London, 1650), p. 6.
43. The sentiments quoted are by Samuel Rolls, *The Burning of London in the Year 1666* (London, 1667), 2:90 and 96. See further Edward N. Hooker, "The Purpose of Dryden's Annus Mirabilis," *HLQ* 10 (1946–47): 49–67.
44. Wilson, *Theologicall Rules,* p. 62.
45. William Aspinwall, *A Brief Description of the Fifth Monarchy* (London, 1653), and Arise Evans, *The Bloudy Vision . . . also a refutation of . . . Aspinwall* (London, 1653).
46. See Christopher Hill, *The World Turned Upside Down,* and Bernard Capp, *The Fifth Monarchy Men* (London, 1972); respectively.
47. On the Joachimist tradition, see my remarks in *"The Grand Design of God": The Literary Form of the Christian View of History* (London, 1972), pp. 30–32. Foxe and Donne were quoted at my instigation by Marjorie Reeves, *The Influence of Prophecy in the Late Middle Ages: A Study of Joachimism* (Oxford, 1969), pp. 108–9. On the radicals, consult Christopher Hill, *The World Turned Upside Down,* pp. 147–48, 390, and Arthur L. Morton, *The World of the Ranters* (London, 1970), pp. 126ff. On the period's eschatological expectations generally, see in particular Bryan W. Ball, *A Great Expectation: Eschatological Thought in English Protestantism to 1660* (Leiden, 1975).
48. See the essays by Florence Sandler on Spenser, Joseph Wittreich on Shakespeare, and myself on Milton, in *The Apocalypse in English Renaissance Thought*

and Literature, ed. C. A. Patrides and Joseph Wittreich (Manchester, England, 1984), chaps. 6–8. My essay on Milton is also on pp. 181ff.
49. See William Chappell, *The Preacher, or the Art and Method of Preaching* (London, 1656); Joseph Hall, *Arte of Divine Meditation* (London, 1606); Andreas Gerardus Hyperius, *The Practis of Preaching,* trans. John Ludham (London, 1577); William Perkins, *The Art of Prophecying or, a Treatise concerning . . . Preaching* (London, 1606); etc.
50. Hyperius, *Practis of Preaching,* fol. 15v.
51. *Sermons,* 8:44.
52. *Practis of Preaching,* fol. 9.
53. *Art of Prophecying,* 2:759.
54. *A Sermon preached before the Honourable House of Commons* (Cambridge, 1647), reprinted in *The Cambridge Platonists,* ed. C. A. Patrides (London, 1969; reprint Cambridge, 1980), pp. 90ff.
55. The other is baptism. Catholics accept an additional five: confirmation, penance, orders, matrimony, and extreme unction.
56. The former statement is by Peter Lombard; the latter by St. Augustine (quoted in my *Milton and the Christian Tradition,* p. 218).
57. See A. M. Allchin, "Our Lady in Seventeenth-Century Anglican Devotion and Theology," in *The Blessed Virgin Mary,* ed. E. L. Mascall and H. S. Box (London, 1963), chap. 4; and so far as the Reformers are concerned: the texts collected, and the further studies cited, in *Das Marienlob der Reformatoren,* ed. Walter Tappolet (Tübingen, West Germany, 1962).
58. See Louis L. Martz, *The Poetry of Meditation* (New Haven, 1954); and in radical opposition, Barbara K. Lewalski, *Protestant Poetics and the Seventeenth-Century Religious Lyric* (Princeton, 1979).
59. See Paul G. Stanwood, "St. Teresa and Joseph Beaumont's *Psyche,*" *JEGP* 62 (1963): 533–50.
60. In Marc F. Bertonasco, *Crashaw and the Baroque* (University, Ala., 1971), pp. 47–51. Rous's work was significantly entitled *The Mysticall Marriage. Experimentall Discoveries of the Heavenly Marriage, betweene a Soule and her Saviour* (London, 1635). The parallel with developments on the Continent is instructive: the foremost Calvinist lyric poet of the Netherlands, Jacobus Revius, used in several poems the sort of language one might have expected rather of Crashaw than of any Protestant; see especially his poems "The Lord's Supper" and "Bloody Sweat" in *Jacobus Revius: Dutch Metaphysical Poet,* trans. Henrietta Ten Harmsel (Detroit, 1968), pp. 102–3 and 108–9.
61. "I accounte Poperie (as howe it is) the Heape and Chaos of all Heresies and the Channell whereinto the fowlest impieties and Heresies that have bene in the Christian world have runne and closelye emptied themselves. I beleeve the Popes seale and power to be the power of the greate Antichriste . . ." (P. J. Wallis, "The Library of William Crashawe," *Transactions of the Cambridge Bibliographical Society* 2 [1954–58]: 216). See also the senior Crashaw's view of the Catholic Church ("a spirituall leprosie") in *The Sermon preached at the Crosse, Feb. xiij, 1607* (London, 1608).
62. Allan Pritchard, "Puritan Charges against Crashaw and Beaumont," *TLS,* July 2, 1964, p. 578. See also p. 147.
63. Owen Felltham, *Resolves,* 5th ed. (London, 1634), p. 10, and Moses Capell,

Gods Valuation of Mans Soule (London, 1632), p. 36; respectively.
64. In "On the New Forcers of Conscience under the Long Parliament."
65. See Geoffrey F. Nuttall, *The Holy Spirit in Puritan Faith and Experience* (Oxford, 1946).
66. See his *English Puritanisme* (Amsterdam [?], 1605).
67. Quoted in A. W. Harrison, *Arminianism* (London, 1937), p. 140.
68. Consult James H. Elson, *John Hales of Eton* (New York, 1948), chap. 4, "The Synod of Dort."
69. *The Resolved Christian* (London, 1616), pp. 5 and 7.
70. *Deus justificatus* (London, 1656), pp. 15–16.
71. *The Sacred Philosophie of the Holy Scripture* (London, 1635), art. II, pp. 136–37. For a similar statement, see p. 125. See further the exposition in my *Milton and the Christian Tradition,* chap. 5.
72. Whichcote, *Several Discourses* (London, 1701–7), 3:328, and Richard Ward, *The Life of . . . Henry More* (London, 1610), p. 6; respectively.
73. *A Discourse* etc. (London, 1675), p. 220.
74. Raymond A. Anselment, "Satiric Strategy in Marvell's *Rehearsal Transpros'd,*" *MP* 68 (1970): 137–50. On the larger context, see George Williamson, "The Restoration Revolt against Enthusiasm," *SP* 30 (1933): 571–603.

Bibliography of C.A. Patrides

Books

The Phoenix and the Ladder: The Rise and Decline of the Christian View of History. Berkeley and Los Angeles: University of California Press, 1964.
Milton and the Christian Tradition. Oxford: Clarendon Press, 1966. Reprint. Hamden, Conn.: Archon Books, 1979.
With William B. Hunter and John H. Adamson. *Bright Essence: Studies in Milton's Theology.* Salt Lake City: University of Utah Press, 1971.
"The Grand Design of God": The Literary Form of the Christian View of History. London: Routledge and Kegan Paul; Toronto: University of Toronto Press, 1972.
Premises and Motifs in Renaissance Thought and Literature. Princeton: Princeton University Press, 1982.
An Annotated Critical Bibliography of John Milton. Brighton, England: Harvester Press, 1987.

Editions of Primary Sources

The Cambridge Platonists. The Stratford-upon-Avon Library. London: Edward Arnold Ltd.; Cambridge, Mass.: Harvard University Press, 1969. Reprint Cambridge: Cambridge University Press, 1980.
Sir Walter Ralegh. *The History of the World.* London: Macmillan; Philadelphia: Temple University Press, 1971.
General Editor. *The Poetry of John Milton.* 5 vols. London: Macmillan, 1972-74.
John Milton. *Selected Prose.* Harmondsworth, England: Penguin, 1974. Rev. ed. Columbia: University of Missouri Press, 1985.
The English Poems of George Herbert. Everyman's Library. London: Dent; Totowa, N.J.: Rowman and Littlefield, 1974.
Sir Thomas Browne: The Major Works. Harmondsworth, England: Penguin, 1977.
John Smith the Cambridge Platonist. *Select Discourses.* Delmar, N.Y.: Scholars' Facsimiles and Reprints, 1979.
George Herbert: The Critical Heritage. London and Boston: Routledge and Kegan Paul, 1983.
The Complete English Poems of John Donne. Everyman's Library. London: Dent, 1985.

Editions of Critical Studies

Milton's "Lycidas": The Tradition and the Poem. New York: Holt, Rinehart and Winston, 1961. Rev. ed. Columbia: University of Missouri Press, 1983.
Milton's Epic Poetry: Essays on "Paradise Lost" and "Paradise Regained." Harmondsworth, England: Penguin, 1967.

Approaches to "Paradise Lost": The York Tercentenary Lectures. London: Edward Arnold; Toronto: University of Toronto Press, 1969.
Aspects of Time. Manchester, England: Manchester University Press; Toronto: University of Toronto Press, 1976.
Approaches to Marvell: The York Tercentenary Lectures. London and Boston: Routledge and Kegan Paul, 1978.
With Raymond B. Waddington. *The Age of Milton: Backgrounds to Seventeenth-Century Literature.* Manchester, England: Manchester University Press; New York: Barnes and Noble, 1980.
Approaches to Sir Thomas Browne: The Ann Arbor Tercentenary Lectures and Essays. Columbia: University of Missouri Press, 1982.
With Joseph A. Wittreich. *The Apocalypse in English Renaissance Thought and Literature.* Manchester, England: Manchester University Press; Ithaca, N.Y.: Cornell University Press, 1984.

Articles

"A Note on Renaissance Plagiarism." *Notes and Queries,* n.s. 2 (1956): 438–39.
"*Paradise Lost* and the Mortalist Heresy." *Notes and Queries,* n.s. 4 (1957): 250–51.
"Renaissance Ideas on Man's Upright Form." *Journal of the History of Ideas* 19 (1958): 256–58.
"Milton and His Contemporaries on the Chains of Satan." *Modern Language Notes* 73 (1958): 257–60.
"Renaissance and Modern Thought on the Last Things: A Study in Changing Conceptions." *Harvard Theological Review* 51 (1958): 169–85.
"Bacon and Feltham: Victims of Literary Piracy." *Notes and Queries,* n.s. 5 (1958): 63–65.
"The Numerological Approach to Cosmic Order during the English Renaissance." *Isis: An International Review of the History of Science* 49 (1958): 391–97.
"Milton and the Protestant Theory of the Atonement." *Publications of the Modern Language Association* 74 (1959): 7–13.
"Renaissance Thought on the Celestial Hierarchy: The Decline of a Tradition." *Journal of the History of Ideas* 20 (1959): 155–66.
"Thomas Heywood and Literary Piracy." *Philological Quarterly* 39 (1960): 118–22.
"The Microcosm of Man." *Notes and Queries,* n.s. 7 (1960): 54–56, and 10 (1963): 282–86.
"Creation and the Self in *Paradise Lost,*" edited from an incomplete study by Charles Monroe Coffin. *ELH* 39 (1962): 1–18. Reprint, with a Note by John Crowe Ransom, in *Kenyon Alumni Bulletin* 20, no. 4 (1962): 11–17.
"Renaissance Interpretations of Jacob's Ladder." *Theologische Zeitschrift* 18 (1962): 411–18.
"The Tree of Knowledge in the Christian Tradition." *Studia Neophilologica* 34 (1962): 239–42.
"Renaissance Views on the 'Vnconfused Orders Angellick.' " *Journal of the History of Ideas* 23 (1962): 265–67.

"As Relacoes do Milton com Portugal." *Revista da Faculdade de Letras da Universidade do Lisboa* 6 (1962): 413–19.
"The 'Protevangelium' in Renaissance Theology and *Paradise Lost.*" *Studies in English Literature* 3 (1962): 19–30.
"Psychopannychism in Renaissance Europe." *Studies in Philology* 60 (1963): 227–29.
" 'The Bloody and Cruell Turke': The Background of a Renaissance Commonplace." *Studies in the Renaissance* 10 (1963): 126–35.
"*Paradise Lost* and the Theory of Accommodation." *Texas Studies in Literature and Language* 5 (1963): 58–63.
"Renaissance Estimates of the Year of Creation." *Huntington Library Quarterly* 26 (1963): 315–22.
"Adam's 'Happy Fault' and XVIIth-Century Apologetics." *Franciscan Studies* 23 (1963): 238–43.
"The 'Universal and Publik Manuscript' of Commonplaces." *Neophilologus* 47 (1963): 217–20.
"The Renaissance View of Time: A Bibliographical Note." *Notes and Queries,* n.s. 10 (1963): 408–10.
"The Scale of Nature and Renaissance Treatises on Nobility." *Studia Neophilologica* 36 (1964): 63–68.
"Renaissance Commentaries on the Passion." *Theologische Zeitschrift* 20 (1964): 125–35.
"Milton and Arianism." *Journal of the History of Ideas* 25 (1964): 423–29.
"Renaissance and Modern Views on Hell." *Harvard Theological Review* 57 (1964): 217–36.
"The Godhead in *Paradise Lost:* Dogma or Drama?" *Journal of English and Germanic Philology* 64 (1965): 29–34.
"The Cessation of the Oracles: The History of a Legend." *Modern Language Review* 60 (1965): 500–507.
" 'The Beast with Many Heads': Renaissance Views of the Multitude." *Shakespeare Quarterly* 16 (1965): 241–46.
"I nove ordini degli angeli: storia di una idea." *Sophia: Rassegna critica di filosofia e storia della filosofia* 33 (1965): 341–48.
"John Milton: The Poet Who Gave Us Paradise." *The Observer Magazine* (London), 13 August 1967, pp. 3–9.
"The Salvation of Satan." *Journal of the History of Ideas* 28 (1967): 467–78.
"*Paradise Lost* and the Language of Theology." In *Language and Style in Milton: A Symposium in Honor of the Tercentenary of "Paradise Lost,"* edited by Ronald D. Emma and John T. Shawcross, pp. 102–119. New York: Frederick Ungar, 1967.
"Milton." *Year's Work in English Studies* 50 (1969): 231–40.
"Milton." *Year's Work in English Studies* 51 (1970): 231–40.
"Milton." *Year's Work in English Studies* 52 (1971): 235–44.
"On the Ode, the Masque, and the Pastoral Elegy." In *John Milton: The Minor Poems in English.* General editor C. A. Patrides, pp. 343–57. London: Macmillan, 1972.
"Milton." *Year's Work in English Studies* 53 (1972): 239–49.
"Hierarchy and Order." In *Dictionary of the History of Ideas.* 5 vols. Edited by Philip P. Wiener, 2:434–49. New York: Scribner's, 1973.

"The Renascence of the Renaissance: T. S. Eliot and the Pattern of Time." *Michigan Quarterly Review* 12 (1973): 172–96. Revised in *Aspects of Time*. Ed. C. A. Patrides, pp. 159–71. Manchester, England: Manchester University Press; Toronto: University of Toronto Press, 1976.
"Milton." *Year's Work in English Studies* 54 (1973): 242–51.
"John Milton." In *New Cambridge Bibliography of English Literature*. 4 vols. Edited by George Watson, 1:1237–96. Cambridge: Cambridge University Press, 1974.
"Milton." *Year's Work in English Studies* 55 (1974): 282–96.
"Milton." *Year's Work in English Studies* 56 (1975): 210–20.
"Milton and the Arian Controversy: Or, Some Reflections on Contextual Settings and the Experience of Deuteroscopy." *Proceedings of the American Philosophical Society* 120 (1976): 245–52.
"Milton." *Year's Work in English Studies* 57 (1976): 178–84.
"The Comic Dimension in Greek Tragedy and *Samson Agonistes*." *Milton Studies* 10 (1977): 3–21.
"Milton." *Year's Work in English Studies* 58 (1977): 200–209.
"'Till Prepared for Longer Flight': The Sublunar Poetry of Andrew Marvell." In *Approaches to Marvell*, edited by C. A. Patrides, pp. 31–55. London and Boston: Routledge and Kegan Paul, 1978.
"Milton." *Year's Work in English Studies* 59 (1978): 203–16.
"The Atonement." "The Fall and Redemption of Man." "Nature." "The Scale of Nature." In *A Milton Encyclopedia*. 8 vols. General editor William B. Hunter, 1:110–11; 3:89–97; 5:189–94; 7:175–77. Lewisburg, Pa.: Bucknell University Press, 1978–79.
"Sir Walter Ralegh." In *Great Writers of the English Language: Poets*, edited by James Vinson, pp. 796–99. London: Macmillan, 1979.
"Sir Thomas Browne." In *Great Writers of the English Language: Novelists and Prose Writers*, edited by James Vinson, pp. 175–77. London: Macmillan, 1979.
"Milton." *Year's Work in English Studies* 60 (1979): 209–18.
"The Achievement of Edmund Spenser." *Yale Review* 69 (1980): 427–43.
"The Experience of Otherness: Theology as a Means of Life." In *The Age of Milton*, edited by C. A. Patrides and Raymond B. Waddington, pp. 170–96. Manchester, England: Manchester University Press; New York: Barnes and Noble, 1980.
"Platoniker von Cambridge." In *Theologische Realenzyklopadie*. 25 vols. Edited by Gerhard Krause and Gerhard Muller, 8:598–601. Berlin and New York: Verlag Walter de Gruyter, 1980.
"Milton." *Year's Work in English Studies* 61 (1980): 208–19.
"The Epistolary Art of the Renaissance: The Biblical Dimension." *Philological Quarterly* 60 (1981): 357–67.
"Milton." *Year's Work in English Studies* 62 (1981): 234–39.
"Spenser: The Contours of Allegorical Theology." *Centennial Review* 26 (1982): 17–32.
"'The Best Part of Nothing': Sir Thomas Browne and the Strategy of Indirection." In *Approaches to Sir Thomas Browne*, edited by C. A. Patrides, pp. 31–48. Columbia: University of Missouri Press, 1982.
"'Something Like Propheticke Strain': Apocalyptic Configurations in Milton." *English Language Notes* 19 (1982): 193–207.

"A Poet Nearly Anonymous." In *Classic and Cavalier: Essays on Jonson and the Sons of Ben*, edited by Claude J. Summers and Ted-Larry Pebworth, pp. 3–16. Pittsburgh: University of Pittsburgh Press, 1982.
"Milton." *Year's Work in English Studies* 63 (1982): 214–23.
"The Biblical Comic and the Demands of Reality." *University of Toronto Quarterly* 53 (1983): 72–84.
" 'The Greatest of the Kingly Race': The Death of Henry Stuart." *Historian* 47 (1985): 402–8.
"John Donne Methodized: Or, How to Improve Donne's Impossible Text with the Assistance of his Several Editors." *Modern Philology* 82 (1985): 365–73.
"Erasmus and More: Dialogues with Reality." *Kenyon Review*, n.s. 8, no. 1 (1986): 34–48.
"The Legacy of Patristic Humanism: Some Probabilities." *Christianity and Literature* 25, no. 4 (Summer, 1986): 19–30.
"Gaiety Transfiguring All That Dread: The Case of Yeats." *Yeats: An Annual of Critical and Textual Studies* 5 (1987): 117–32.
"T. S. Eliot: Alliances of Levity and Seriousness." *Sewanee Review* 96 (1988): 77–94.
"Shakespeare: The Comedy Beyond Comedy." *Kenyon Review*, n.s. 10, no. 2 (1988): 38–57.
"Homer: The Invention of Reality." *Michigan Quarterly Review* 28 (1989): 305–22.
"Angels" and "The Fall and Restoration of Man." In *A Spenser Encyclopedia*. General editor A. C. Hamilton. Toronto: University of Toronto Press, in press.

Reviews

Sir Thomas Browne, by Joan Bennett. *Renaissance News* 16 (1963): 242–45.
Sir Thomas Browne, by Frank L. Huntley. *Modern Philology* 61 (1964): 243–44.
The Descent from Heaven: A Study in Epic Continuity, by Thomas M. Greene. *Italian Quarterly* 8, no. 31 (1965): 79–82.
If This Be Heresy: A Study of Milton and Origen, by Harry F. Robins. *Journal of English and Germanic Philology* 64 (1965): 586–89.
Five Essays on Milton's Epics, by Northrop Frye. *Review of English Studies*, n.s. 21 (1970): 212–15.
The Race of Time: Three Lectures on Renaissance Historiography, by Herschel Baker. *English Language Notes* 6 (1969): 209–12.
Milton: A Biography, by William R. Parker. *Review of English Studies*, n.s. 21 (1970): 212–15.
Pagan Myth and Christian Tradition in English Poetry, by Douglas Bush. *Modern Language Review* 65 (1970): 868–69.
Milton Studies I, ed. James D. Simmonds. *Studia Neophilologica* 42 (1970): 233–34.
John Milton: An Annotated Bibliography 1929–1968, by Calvin Huckabay. *Studia Neophilologica* 42 (1970): 471–73.
Paradise Lost: A Tercentenary Tribute, ed. B. Rajan. *Yearbook of English Studies* 1 (1971): 254–55.

Divine Providence in the England of Shakespeare's Histories, by Henry A. Kelly. *English Language Notes* 9 (1971): 139–41.

Milton's Creation: A Guide Through "Paradise Lost," by Harry Blamires. *General Education,* no. 18 (Spring, 1972): 70.

Jeremy Taylor and the Great Rebellion, by Frank L. Huntley. *Renaissance Quarterly* 26 (1973): 88–89.

The Christian Poet in "Paradise Lost," by William G. Riggs. *Christian Scholar's Review* 3 (1973): 88–89.

"An Open Letter on the Yale Edition of *De Doctrina Christiana.*" *Milton Quarterly* 7 (1973): 72–74.

Christian Mortalism from Tyndale to Milton, by Norman T. Burns. *Renaissance Quarterly* 27 (1974): 375–76.

Sir Walter Ralegh by Robert Lacey, and *Sir Walter Ralegh: The Renaissance Man and His Roles,* by Stephen J. Greenblatt. *Renaissance Quarterly* 28 (1975): 269–71.

Touches of Sweet Harmony: Pythagorean Cosmology and Renaissance Poetics, by S. K. Heninger. *Seventeenth-Century News* 33 (1975): 97.

Typology and Seventeenth-Century Literature, by Joseph A. Galdon. *Modern Language Review* 72 (1977): 397–98.

Epic and Tragic Structure in "Paradise Lost," by John M. Steadman. *Times Literary Supplement,* 8 July 1977, p. 838.

Literary Uses of Typology from the Late Middle Ages to the Present, ed. Earl Miner. *Christian Scholar's Review* 8 (1978): 158.

A Milton Encyclopedia, gen. ed. William B. Hunter. *Review of English Studies* 30 (1979): 215–17.

John Donne: An Annotated Bibliography and *George Herbert: An Annotated Bibliography,* by John R. Roberts. *Seventeenth-Century News* 37 (1979): 73.

Andrew Marvell: The Critical Heritage, ed. Elizabeth S. Donno. *Renaissance Quarterly* 32 (1979): 442–45.

"Paradise Lost" and the Classical Epic, by Francis C. Blessington. *Milton and His Epic Tradition,* by Joan M. Webber. *Clio* 10 (1980): 101–2.

The Renaissance: Essays in Interpretation, ed. Andre Chastel et al. *Spenser Newsletter* 14 (1983): 30–31.

Milton and Scriptural Tradition, ed. James H. Sims and Leland Ryken. *Renaissance Quarterly* 38 (1985): 382–84.

Index

Adams, Robert M., 23, 25, 26
Adams, Thomas, 187, 209, 313
Addison, Joseph, 34
Aeschylus, 234–36, 242, 246, 247, 248, 278–79
Agrippa, Heinrich Cornelius, 171, 179
Alfred, King, 264
Allchin, A. M., 323
Allen, Don C., 286, 293
Allen, Peter A., 26
Allison, A. F., 158, 159
Alpers, Paul J., 45
Alsted, Johann Heinrich, 202, 212
Alvarez, A., 273, 292
Amorose, Thomas, 227
Anacreon, 155
Anderson, Judith M., 46
Anderton, Lawrence, 305, 321
Andreasen, N. J. C., 115
Andrewes, John, 197, 211
Andrewes, Lancelot, 119, 120, 136, 313
Anselment, Raymond A., 137, 324
Antiochus IV Epiphanes, 186, 209
Archilochus, 79–80, 81
Ardolino, Frank, 180
Ariosto, 12
Aristophanes, 18, 20, 75, 79, 85, 241, 247
Aristotle, 231, 232, 234, 235, 236, 247, 321
Arminius, Jacobus, 316
Arnott, Peter D., 246
Arthos, John, 270
Arthur, King, 265
Ashe, T., 45
Aspinwall, William, 322
Athanasius, St., 217
Aubrey, John, 118, 135, 261, 262, 272, 273, 292
Auden, W. H., 54, 55, 69, 72, 245, 248
Augustine, St., 94, 138, 227, 299, 300, 305, 312, 313, 318, 320, 321, 323
Ayer, A. J., 225

Bacon, Nicholas, 167
Bacon, Sir Francis, 119, 136, 157, 192, 288, 294

Baillie, Robert, 213
Baker, Sir Richard, 113
Bald, R. C., 113
Bale, John, 208
Ball, Bryan W., 322
Banks, Theodore H., 211, 270–71
Barbeau, Anne T., 227
Barberini, Francesco, 252, 270
Barker, Arthur E., 213
Barksdale, Clement, 158
Baron, Hans, 293
Baroway, Israel, 225, 322
Bate, Walter Jackson, 44
Battenhouse, Roy W., 69–70, 71
Bauckman, Richard, 209
Bayley, John, 70
Bayley, Peter, 44
Beals, Ralph L., 72
Beaumont, Joseph, 157, 314, 323
Becon, Thomas, 209
Bell, Ilona, 87
Bell, Robert H., 246
Bellarmine, Robert, 298, 304, 321
Bembo, Pietro, 94
Berek, Peter, 294
Berger, Harry, 45
Bernard, John D., 46
Bernard, Richard, 210, 204, 213
Bernard of Clairvaux, St., 305
Bernini, Gian Lorenzo, 252
Berry, Lloyd E., 272
Bertonasco, Marc F., 158, 323
Bespaloff, Rachel, 233–34, 246
Bethel, S. L., 70
Bethune-Baker, J. F., 218, 226
Beza, Theodore, 303
Bible
    Acts, 128
    1 Corinthians, 71, 122, 128, 167, 178, 305–6
    2 Corinthians, 128, 132
    Daniel, 174, 209, 311
    Ecclesiasticus, 122
    Ephesians, 302
    Exodus, 309
    Ezekiel, 188

Bible (*continued*)
  Genesis, 300–301
  Gospels, 120, 121, 136–37, 190, 211
  Hebrews, 137, 211
  Hosea, 213
  Isaiah, 128, 176, 195, 224
  James, 320
  Jeremiah, 197–98, 212
  Job, 224, 243, 309
  John, 128, 137
  1 John, 184, 310
  2 John, 184
  Joshua, 216
  Judges, 309
  Lamentations, 110, 111
  Luke, 204
  1 Maccabees, 209
  Mark, 122, 128, 197, 202
  Matthew, 128, 137, 197, 202, 216, 257
  2 Peter, 174
  Proverbs, 120, 256, 271, 309
  Psalms, 110, 120, 121, 122, 128, 137, 142–43, 256, 309
  Revelation, 181–214, 216, 251, 255, 310–11
  Romans, 125
  Song of Solomon, 110, 116
  2 Thessalonians, 184, 186
  1 Timothy, 184
  Wisdom of Solomon, 127
  Zechariah, 213
Biffi, Lydia, 247
Billingsley, Nicholas, 210
Black, Max, 220, 228
Blake, Ann, 67
Blake, William, 33, 36, 44, 84, 225, 230, 260, 319
Bloch, Chana, 136
Blunden, Edmund, 136
Bobin, Donna, 245
Bodin, Jean, 297
Bonicatti, Maurizio, 24
Bornkamm, Heinrich, 209
Borromini, Francesco, 252
Bosch, Hieronymus, 24, 283
Boswell, James, 43
Bottkol, J. McG., 270
Bottrall, Margaret, 137
Boughner, D. C., 248
Bowman, Phyllis S., 158
Bradbrook, Muriel C., 293

Braden, Gordon, 85
Bradley, A. C., 68
Bradshaw, William, 315–16, 324
Bramante, Donato di Angelo, 210
Brant, Sebastian, 12, 24
Brater, Enoch, 44
Bridgett, T. E., 25
Brightman, Thomas, 181, 207, 208, 213, 214, 322
Brinkley, Robert A., 46
Broadbent, J. B., 292
Brock, D. Heyward, 86–87
Brockbank, Philip, 293
Brookes, Matthew, 296, 319
Brooks, Cleanth, 44, 229
Bross, Addison C., 115
Brown, Charles Armitage, 44
Brown, Stephen J., 137, 227, 229
Browne, Sir Thomas, 2, 3, 4, 5, 30, 95, 121–22, 124, 128, 132, 136, 154, 161–80, 184, 197, 208, 212, 281, 284, 291, 293, 294, 297, 309
  The Garden of Cyrus, 30, 95, 161, 167–72, 173–74, 176, 284, 291, 293, 294
  Hydriotaphia, 30, 163–67, 168, 172, 173, 174, 212
  Musaeum Clausum, 161–63
  Religio Medici, 121–22, 124, 128, 132, 136, 161, 162–63, 168, 172–78, 184, 197, 208, 211, 281, 297
Browning, Elizabeth Barrett, 244
Browning, Robert, 94–95
Brucher, Richard T., 67
Bruegel, Pieter (the Elder), 24
Bruno, Giordano, 94, 100–101, 296
Bucanus, Gulielmus, 303
Bullinger, Heinrich, 171, 180, 181, 206, 210, 212, 214, 303, 320
Bunyan, John 30, 35, 43, 188, 210, 302
Burton, Henry, 197, 212
Bush, Douglas, 44
Busiris, 12
Buttrick, G. A., 229
Buxton, John, 272

Cadoux, A. T., 229
Caesar, Julius, 276, 277
Calamy, Edmund, 197, 254
Calvin, John, 184, 187, 201, 208, 209, 212, 227, 296, 302–3, 304, 315, 316, 318, 319, 320, 323

Cambridge Platonists, 2, 4, 65, 72, 154, 192, 211, 212, 245, 248, 254, 270, 305, 318–19, 321
Campbell, Gordon, 5, 226
Campion, Edmund, 298, 300, 304, 320
Cannon, Charles K., 321
Capp, Bernard, 208, 213, 322
Car, Thomas, 159
Carew, Thomas, 83, 86, 89–90, 112, 152, 159
Carey, John, 114
Carnes, Valery, 137
Cassirer, Ernst, 26
Castelli, E., 24
Castiglione, Baldassarre, 94
Catullus, 76, 77, 81, 85, 153
Cavanagh, Michael, 226
Cervantes, Miguel de, 12
Chambers, A. B., 116, 293
Chambers, Leland, 159
Champion, Larry S., 67, 69
Chapman, George, 31, 233
Chappell, William, 323
Charles I, King, 135, 144, 186, 250, 253, 261, 275, 276, 278–80, 311
Charles II, King, 264, 311
Charlton, Kenneth, 208
de Chateaubriand, Francois René, 29
Chaucer, Geoffrey, 37, 283
Chew, Samuel C., 209
Christian, Lynda G., 24, 25
Christianson, Paul, 198, 208, 212
Christina, Queen, 252
Cicero, 29, 71, 136, 264, 267, 299
Cinthio, Giraldi, 51
Cirillo, Albert R., 159, 227
Clapham, Henoch, 209
Clasen, Claus-Peter, 297, 319
Cleaver, Robert, 296, 319
Clement of Alexandria, St., 318
Cleopatra, 276
Cleveland, John, 157, 274
Clouse, R. G., 212
Coffin, Charles M., 1
Coghill, Nevil, 68
Cole, Douglas, 245
Coleridge, S. T., 39, 48, 68, 78, 84, 101, 119, 157, 160, 163, 170, 171, 176, 177, 179, 180
Colet, John, 298, 305, 321
Colie, Rosalie, 116, 138, 224, 229

Comenius, Johannes Amos, 259
Comestor, Peter, 321
Congreve, William, 249
Conklin, George N., 226
Copernicus, Nikolaus, 216
Corbett, Margery, 180
Cotton, Charles, 118–19
Court, Benoît, 170
Court, Franklin E., 46
Cowden Clarke, Charles, 31, 44
Cowden Clarke, Mary, 44
Cowley, Abraham, 30, 31, 43, 157
Crabtree, John H., Jr., 245
Craig, Martha, 45
Cranmer, Thomas, 306
Crashaw, Richard, 3, 4, 77–78, 84, 113, 119, 132, 135, 138, 141–60, 274, 292, 304, 308, 323
  "An Apologie for the [Hymn to Saint Teresa]," 148–49, 152, 158
  Carmen Deo Nostro, 147, 148, 159
  "Charitas Nimia," 152
  "Death's Lecture," 149, 159
  "Dies Irae," 155, 156
  "An Elegy upon the death of Mr. Stanninow," 153
  Epigrammata sacra, 158
  Epigrammatum sacrorum liber, 144, 158
  "An Epitaph upon Mr. Ashton," 155
  "Epithalamion," 149
  "The Flaming Heart," 148, 158
  "His Epitaph," 143
  "The Hymn of Sainte Thomas," 142, 143, 157
  "A Hymn to Sainte Teresa," 148–49, 150, 151, 158, 159
  "In cicatrices Domini Jesu," 150
  "In the Glorious Epiphanie," 154, 159, 156
  "In the Holy Nativity," 151, 154, 156, 159
  "In vulnera Dei pendentis," 146
  "Lauda Sion Salvatorem," 308
  "Letter to the Countess of Denbigh," 159
  "Loves Horoscope," 149
  "Luc. 2. Quaerit Jesum suum beata Virgo," 145
  "Luc. 24. In cicatrices Domini ad hunc superstites," 150
  "Luke 11. Blessed be the paps," 141

Crashaw, Richard (*continued*)
"Matth. 8:13. Absenti Centurionis," 145, 158
"Matth. 11. Onus meum leve est," 145
"Musicks Duel," 153
"New Year's Day," 154, 156
"Ode on a prayer booke," 144, 150, 152, 157, 159
"Office of the Holy Cross," 151, 156
"O Gloriosa Domina," 154, 156
"On Mr G. Herberts booke," 132, 138
"On the Assumption," 154, 156
"On the bleeding wounds of our crucified Lord," 146–47
"Our Lord and his Circumcision," 154
"Out of Catullus," 77–78
"Out of the Greeke *Cupid's* Cryer," 149–50
"Psalme 23," 143, 144, 155, 158
"Pulchra non diuturna," 145
"Sancta Maria Dolorum," 154, 156
"A Song: Lord, when the sense," 150, 159
Steps to the Temple, 145, 147, 151, 158
"The Suspicion of Herod," 153
"To [Mrs. M.R.] Councel Concerning her Choise," 144, 149, 159
"To the Morning," 156
"To the Name of Jesus," 149, 151, 152–53, 154, 156, 157, 159
"Upon the Asse that bore our Saviour," 152
"Upon the bleeding crucifix," 146–47
"Upon the death of a freind," 145–46
"Upon the Kings Coronation," 144
"Upon the Sepulchre of our Lord," 145
"Vexilla Regis," 158
"The Weeper," 151, 154, 156, 159, 274, 292
"Wishes to his (supposed) Mistresse," 149
"With Some Poems sent to a Gentlewoman," 153
Crashaw, William, 314, 323
Crofts, J. E. V., 114, 115
Crombie, I. M., 229
Cromwell, Henry, 159
Cromwell, Oliver, 186, 202, 213, 261, 275–81, 284
Crosman, Robert, 245–46
Cruttwell, Patrick, 274, 292
Cubeta, Paul M., 70
Cudworth, Ralph, 72, 313, 323
Cummings, R. M., 293

Dallison, A. R., 213
Daniel, Samuel, 89
Daniells, Roy, 229, 245
Daniélou, Jean, 322
Dante, 33, 39, 68, 224, 229
Danvers, Sir John, 118
Davenant, William, 37
Dawes, John, 300, 320
Dean, Leonard, 25
Dee, John, 178
Dekker, Thomas, 305
Demaray, John G., 213
Democritus, 9, 17
Dent, Arthur, 181, 201, 208, 212, 322
Dick, Aliki L., 85
Dickey, Franklin L., 67
Dickinson, Emily, 119
Diodati, Charles, 188
Diodati, Giovanni, 188, 189, 202, 210, 211, 212, 214
Dobbins, Austin C., 190, 210, 211
Dod, John, 296, 319
Dodd, C. H., 136, 229
Doebler, Bettie Anne, 114
Donne, John, 2, 3, 5, 11, 65, 72, 77, 82, 83, 84, 86, 89–116, 118, 119, 121, 122, 126, 128, 132, 134, 135, 157, 160, 162, 168, 178–79, 181, 183, 205, 208, 210, 214, 215–16, 225, 226, 274, 287, 288, 300, 301, 302, 307, 308, 309, 310, 311, 312, 313, 314, 320, 321, 322, 323
"Aire and Angels," 100
"Amicissimo, et meritissimo Ben. Jonson," 82
"The Anniversarie," 92, 99
The Anniversaries, 104, 107–9
Biathanatos, 109
"The Canonization," 93, 99, 110, 114
Catalogus Librorum Aulicorum, 162, 168
"Communitie," 92, 97
"Confined Love," 93
"La Corona," 110, 135
"The Crosse," 110
Devotions, 322
"Elegie on Mistris Boulstred," 102–3
"Elegie to the Lady Bedford: You that are she," 100
Elegies, 104, 106–7, 112
"Elegy II. The Anagram," 98, 101
"Elegy III. Change," 98
"Elegy IV. The Perfume," 106–7

"Elegy VIII. The Comparison," 107
"Elegy IX. The Autumnall," 92, 106
"Elegy X. The Dreame," 107
"Elegy XI. The Bracelet," 107
"Elegy XII. His parting from her," 99, 100, 107
"Elegy XIII. Julia," 107
"Elegy XV. The Expostulation," 83, 86, 107
"Elegy XVI. On his Mistris," 107
"Elegy XVII. Variety," 107
"Elegy XVIII. Loves Progress," 107
"Elegy XX. Loves Warre," 106
Essays in Divinity, 307, 321
"The Extasie," 100–101
"The First Anniversary," 107–9, 320
"The Flea," 95, 96
"A Funerall Elegie," 107
"Good Friday, 1613," 110
"The good-morrow," 96–97
"Holy Sonnet II. As due by many titles," 111
"Holy Sonnet V. I am a little world," 111
"Holy Sonnet VII. At the round earths," 103, 112
"Holy Sonnet X. Death be not proud," 103
"Holy Sonnet XIII. What if this present," 112
"Holy Sonnet XIV. Batter my heart," 111
"Holy Sonnet XVII. Since she whom I lov'd," 111
"Holy Sonnet XVIII. Show me deare Christ," 111
Holy Sonnets, 103, 109–12, 301
"A Hymne to God the Father," 11, 110
"The Indifferent," 98
"The Lamentations of Jeremy," 110–11
"The Legacie," 93
Letters to Severall Personages (verse letters), 104, 112
Letters to Severall Persons of Honour, 99, 102, 104, 107, 109
"The Litanie," 109, 110
"Loves Alchymie," 98
"Loves growth," 100
"Loves infinitenesse," 99
"The Message," 94
Metempsychosis, 91
"Negative Love," 91
"On himself," 104

"Satyre II," 104
"Satyre III," 105
"Satyre IV," 106
Satyres, 104–6, 112, 179
"The Second Anniversary," 108–9
Sermons, 118, 121, 126, 128, 135, 181, 183, 205, 208, 210, 214, 215–16, 225, 226, 300, 301, 308, 310, 312, 320, 322, 323
"Song: Goe, and catche," 93
"Song: Sweetest love I do not goe," 90
Songs and Sonnets, 97, 104, 112
"The Sunne Rising," 99
"To Mr R.W.: If, as mine is," 91
"To Mr R.W.: Kindly I envy," 105
"To Mrs M.H.: Mad paper stay," 135
"To Mr Tilman after he had taken orders,", 110
"To Sir Henry Wotton: Sir, letters more then kisses," 104, 115
"To the Countesse of Huntingdon: Man to Gods image," 100
"To the Countesse of Salisbury," 104
"To the Lady Magdalen Herbert," 135
"The Triple Fool," 97
"The undertaking," 100
"Upon the Translation of the Psalmes," 110
"A Valediction forbidding mourning," 90–92, 94, 100
Donner, H. W., 27
Doran, Madeleine, 67, 68
Dorp, Martin, 16, 23
Dorsch, T. S., 23, 27
Downame, John, 302
Downham, George, 209
Drayton, Michael, 155
Draxe, Thomas, 196–97, 212
Drummond, William, 45, 75, 113
Drury, Elizabeth, 107, 108, 116, 287
Dryden, John, 30, 31, 36–37, 43, 49, 90, 92, 97, 112, 114
Dugmore, C. W., 138
Dundas, Judith, 46, 179
Duns Scotus, John, 30
Du Perron, Jacques, 95
Durken, Mary B., 226
Dürrenmatt, Friedrich, 51, 68
Dyke, Daniel, 210

Ebreo, Leone, 94
Edel, Leon, 115
Edwards, J. Kelley, 23

Eisenstein, Sergei, 39
Eliot, T. S., 1, 38, 84, 95, 112, 119, 126, 132, 134, 136, 149, 159, 161, 190, 220, 221, 229, 239, 247, 273, 274, 284, 292, 293
Elizabeth, Queen of Bohemia, 136
Elliott, Robert C., 25
Ellrodt, Robert, 136
Ellwood, Thomas, 16, 25
Elson, James H., 324
Emerson, Ralph Waldo, 163, 179
Emma, Ronald D., 5
Empson, William, 223, 224, 229, 294
Endicott, Annabel M., 137
Ennius, 34, 44
Entzminger, Robert L., 226–27
Epictetus, 10
Epstein, Harry, 68
Erasmus, Desiderius, 3, 5, 7–27, 71, 85, 166, 170, 177–78, 180, 202, 209, 212, 257, 298, 299, 302, 305, 318, 319, 320, 321
  Ciceronianus, 7, 8, 16
  Convivium religiosum, 7
  De duplici copia verborum ac rerum, 25
  Enchiridion militis christiani, 9, 10, 14, 15, 23, 25, 302, 321
  Julius exclusus, 7–8, 16, 23
  Letter to Martin Dorp, 16, 23, 24, 25
  Moriae encomium, 8, 11–17, 20, 21, 22, 23, 24–25, 71, 170, 177–78, 180
  Opuscula, 16
  Paraphrase upon the Newe Testament, 202, 209, 212
  Sileni Alcibiadis, 9–11, 24
Erskine-Hill, Howard, 115
Euripides, 85, 235, 236, 239–41, 244, 245, 246, 247, 248
Evans, Arise, 322
Evans, Gareth Lloyd, 71
Evans, Maurice, 45
Evans, Robert O., 46

Fairfax, Mary, 283, 286–87
Fairfax, Thomas, 283–84, 285–86, 293
Falconer, John, 303, 320
Fallon, Robert T., 271
Farnham, Willard, 25
Farquhar, George, 258, 272
Farrer, Austin, 209, 210, 228, 229
Favorinus, 12

Fawkner, Anthony, 301–2, 320
Featley, Daniel, 202, 212, 257, 271
Felltham, Owen, 315, 323–24
Ferrar, John, 136
Ferrar, Nicholas, 17, 117, 121, 136, 138, 314
Filas, F. L., 229
Finch, Jeremiah S., 179
Findlay, J. A., 229
Firth, Katharine R., 208, 212
Fisch, Harold, 214
Fisher, Samuel, 307
Fixler, Michael, 189, 190, 210, 211, 272
Fletcher, John, 51, 157
Flower, Annette C., 272
Forbes, William, 138
Foreman, Walter C., Jr., 68
Fowler, Alistair, 45, 180
Foxe, John, 208, 311, 322
François de Sales, St., 158, 314
Françon, Marcel, 114
Fraser, Russell A., 68
Freeman, James A., 271
Freeman, Rosemary, 114, 136
Freer, Coburn, 136
French, A. L., 68
French, Carolyn F., 71
Frescobaldi, Francesco, 252, 270
Friedman, Donald M., 292
Frye, Northrop, 45, 70
Frye, Roland Mushat, 2, 5, 72, 219, 227, 270
Fuller, Thomas, 313

Galileo, 94
Gardiner, Samuel, 212
Gardner, Helen, 114, 135
Garrod, H. W., 135
Gavin, J. Austin, 24
Giangrande, Lawrence, 179, 246
Gil, Alexander (the elder), 317–18, 324
Gilbert, Allan, 67
Giles, Peter, 18
Gill, Roma, 115
Giorgi, Francesco, 127–28
Glauco, 12
Glicksman, Harry, 272
Golder, Harold, 43
Goldsmith, Robert H., 71
de Góngora y Argote, Luis, 274
Goodman, Godfrey, 196, 212

Goodwin, John, 316
Goodyer, Sir Henry, 102
Gordon, Walter M., 25-26
Gransden, K. W., 245
Gratian, 321
Graves, Robert, 248
Gray, Hanna H., 321
Greek Anthology, The, 78, 85
Green, Roger L., 235, 246
Greene, Thomas, 229
Greenfield, Thelma N., 71
Gregory of Nazianzus, St., 163
Gregory of Nyssa, St., 219, 228
Grew, Nehemiah, 162, 178
Grotius, Hugo, 252
Grove, Robin, 284, 293
Guarini, Giambattista, 51, 68, 113
Guild, William, 322
Guillory, John, 44
Gum, Coburn, 85
Gunther, R. T., 178
Gwalter, Rudolf, 301, 320

Hakewill, George, 138
Hales, John, 256, 271, 316, 324
Halkett, John, 271
Hall, Joseph, 113, 212, 254, 260, 272, 310, 322, 323
Hallam, Henry, 89
Haller, Malleville, 271
Haller, William, 271
Hamilton, A. C., 45, 46
Hamilton, K. G., 272
Hanford, James H., 211, 271
Harbison, Elmore H., 320
Hardy, Thomas, 258, 272
Harpsfield, Nicholas, 25
Harris, John, 253, 270
Hartlib, Samuel, 197, 259
Hartwig, Joan, 68, 69
Haskin, Dayton W., 226
Hassel, R. Chris, Jr., 71
Hawthorne, Nathaniel, 30, 43
Hayward, Sir John, 123
Hazen, Allen T., 246
Hazlitt, William, 157, 160
Hegel, G. W., 68
Helgerson, Richard, 44
Heninger, S. K., Jr., 45
Henrietta Maria, Queen, 147
Hepburn, Ronald W., 224, 228, 229

Herbert, Carolyn, 67, 245
Herbert, George, 1, 2, 3, 5, 17, 78, 83-84, 87, 110, 113, 117-39, 141, 142, 144, 150, 151, 152, 153, 154, 159, 160, 274, 282, 295, 301, 308-9, 312, 313, 314
"Aaron," 123
"Affliction I," 126, 132, 137
"Affliction IV," 131
"The Altar," 130
"The Answer," 123
"Antiphon II," 125
"Artillery," 125
Briefe Notes on Valdesso's "Considerations," 138
"Charms and Knots," 120
"Christmas," 121
"The Church," 126, 129-30
"The Church Militant," 126-27, 133, 137
"The Church-porch," 120, 123, 126, 133, 137
"Clasping of Hands," 124
"The Collar," 123, 130, 131, 134, 301
"Deniall," 123
"Discipline," 131
"Dooms-day," 132
"Easter," 124, 137
"Easter-wings," 131
"Even-song," 122
"Faith," 126
"The Flower," 132
"The Forerunners," 123
"Grace," 131
"The H. Communion," 125, 129
"Heaven," 124, 133
"Jordan I," 137, 152
"Jordan II," 124
"Judgement," 132
"Longing," 132
"Love III," 121, 130, 133
"Love unknown," 121, 125
"Man," 126
Memoriae matris sacrum, 135
"Mortification," 137
Musae Responsoriae, 121, 133, 138
"Nature," 126
Outlandish Proverbs, 120
"Paradise," 124
Passio discerpta, 138
"Peace," 121

Herbert, George (*continued*)
  "The Pearl," 134
  "Prayer I," 124, 152
  A Priest to the Temple, 119–20, 121, 124, 129
  "Providence," 137
  "The Pulley," 121, 123, 134
  "The Quidditie," 135
  "Redemption," 121, 122, 125
  "Repentance," 126
  "The Sacrifice," 130, 131, 134, 309
  "Sighs and Grones," 131
  "Sinne I," 126
  "The Sinner," 131
  "Sion," 126, 129
  "The Star," 137
  "Sunday," 124, 125
  "The Sunne," 124
  "Superliminare," 130
  The Temple, 119, 121, 126–29, 130, 131, 132, 133–35, 137, 295, 308–9
  "The Thanksgiving," 131
  "Time," 121
  "To the Lady Elizabeth Queen of Bohemia," 135
  "To the Same [i.e., Elizabeth of Bohemia]. Another," 136
  "The 23d Psalme," 142
  "The World," 126
  "A Wreath," 110, 124, 130, 137
Herbert, Henry, 119
Herbert, Magdalen, 118, 135
Herbert of Cherbury, Edward, 118
Hermes Trismegistus, 176
Herrick, Marvin T., 67, 68
Herrick, Robert, 3, 35, 274
Herrys, William, 143
Hester, M. Thomas, 115
Hexter, J. H., 26
Heywood, Thomas, 264, 272
Hibbard, G. R., 25, 211
Hicks, William, 182, 208
Hilary of Poitiers, St., 219, 227
Hill, Christopher, 213, 280, 293, 319, 321, 322
Hill, John M., 46
Hinman, Robert B., 137
Hippocrates, 168
Hitler, Adolph, 311
Hobbes, Thomas, 120, 262, 272
Hoffman, Nancy Y., 248

Holbein, Hans, 24
Holland, Hezekiah, 213
Holleran, James V., 46
Holstein, Lucas, 252, 270
Homer, 12, 168, 170, 233–34, 240, 241, 244, 246
Hooker, Edward N., 322
Hooker, Richard, 65, 130, 138, 305
Hopkins, Gerard Manley, 94, 111, 119, 142, 273, 292
Horace, 74, 83, 105, 238, 275, 276, 277, 292, 293
Horrell, Joseph, 227
Howell, A. C., 179
Hughes, John, 33, 43
Hughes, Merritt Y., 228, 272
Hughes, Richard E., 115–16
Huizinga, Johan, 179
Hull, John, 209
Hunt, Leigh, 33, 40, 43, 44
Hunter, A. M., 229
Hunter, William B., 214, 226, 227
Huntley, Frank L., 179, 210, 227
Huntley, John, 248
von Hutten, Ulrich, 9, 17, 25, 26
Hyman, Lawrence W., 294
Hyperius, Andreas Gerardus, 312, 323

Iccius, 276
Ignatius Loyola, St., 108, 304, 314
Ignatius of Antioch, St., 110
Isocrates, 12

Jack, Ian, 115
James, Henry, 115
James I, King, 118, 133, 181, 208, 297, 305, 310, 322
Janelle, Pierre, 159
Jermin, Michael, 256, 271
Jerome, St., 299, 320
Joachim of Fiore, 311, 322
John Chrysostom, St., 305
Johnson, Lee A., 137
Johnson, Samuel, 30, 43, 48–49, 51, 54–55, 66, 68, 69, 95, 170, 179, 249, 250, 270
Jones, G. B., 229
Jonson, Ben, 3, 5, 33–34, 37, 44, 45, 73–87, 89, 107, 108, 153, 157, 238, 246–47, 274, 295, 296
  "And must I sing," 83

"A Celebration of Charis," 74
Conversations with Drummond, 75, 81–82, 89
Discoveries, 44, 73, 74–75, 81
"An Elegie" (*Under-wood* 38), 83
"An Elegie" (*Under-wood* 39), 83, 86, 107
"An Elegie" (*Under-wood* 40), 83
"An Elegie" (*Under-wood* 41), 83
"An Elegy on the Lady Jane Pawlet," 83
Epigrammes, 295
"Epode," 82
"An Execration upon Vulcan," 81
"An Expostulation with Inigo Jones," 83
The Forrest, 76, 77, 83
"Horace, of the Art of Poetry," 74, 83, 238
Hymenaei, 75
"A Hymne on the Nativitie of My Saviour," 83
"A Hymne to God the Father," 83–84
Masque of Blacknesse, 246
"A Nymphs Passion," 84
"An Ode: Helen, did Homer never see," 76
"Ode to Himselfe," 76
"An Ode to James Earle of Desmond," 76
"Song: To Celia," 76, 77
"A Speech according to Horace," 83
"To the Memory of . . . Shakespeare," 82
"To the same [i.e., Celia]" 77
The Under-wood, 83
Volpone, 76, 82
Joyce, James, 38, 64, 72, 89
Jungman, Robert E., 85
Junius, Franciscus (the Elder), 214
Juvenal, 105

Kaiser, Walter, 25, 71
Kautsky, Karl, 26
Kay, W. David, 24
Keats, John, 30, 31, 34, 44, 108, 113, 133, 134, 249
Kelley, Maurice, 216–17, 226
Kelly, T. J., 115
Kermode, Frank, 221, 228, 294
Kerrigan, William, 230
Kessner, Carole S., 247–48
Kincaid, Arthur N., 26

Kincaid, James R., 44
King, Henry, 273
Kinney, Daniel, 25
Kirchheim, Astrid, 68
Kitto, H. D. F., 240, 246, 247
Klein, Robert, 24
Klonsky, Milton, 294
Knell, Paul, 253–54, 270
Knight, G. Wilson, 70, 71, 72
Knight, W. F. Jackson, 246
Knights, L. C., 86
Knott, John, 1
Knox, R. A., 160
Koelb, Clayton, 68
Könneker, Barbara, 24
Kooiman, Willem J., 320
Kott, Jan, 247
Kranidas, Thomas, 271, 272
Krouse, F. Michael, 227

Labriola, Albert C., 114
Lampe, G. W. H., 322
Langdon, Ida, 272
Larsen, Kenneth J., 158
de Las Casas, Bartolomeo, 304
Latimer, Kathleen, 69
Lattimore, Richmond, 246
Laud, William, 158, 186, 313, 314
Lauritsen, John R., 115
Lawrence, D. H., 66, 72, 98
Leavis, F. R., 215, 225
Lebans, W. M., 115
Leda, Jay, 45
Lederer, Josef, 114
Leech, Clifford, 69, 70
Legouis, Pierre, 292, 294
Leibowitz, Herbert A., 43
Leigh, Edward, 214
Leishman, J. B., 44, 113, 292, 294
Lewalski, Barbara K., 71, 115, 211, 213, 226, 286, 293, 323
Lewis, C. S., 26, 45, 210
Lewis, H. D., 225, 228, 229–30
Libbey, Nancy D., 242, 248
Lightbrown, Ronald, 180
Linden, Stanton J., 113–14
Listrius, Girardus, 11, 12, 24
Lithgow, R. M., 229
Lloyd, David, 151, 159
Lloyd Thomas, M. G., 293
Lodge, Thomas, 210

Lombard, Peter, 313, 321, 323
Lovejoy, Arthur O., 224, 229
Lovelace, Richard, 77
Lowell, James Russell, 45
Lowell, Robert, 235, 246
Lowth, Robert, 215
Lucan, 276, 277, 293
Lucian, 8–9, 10–11, 12, 13, 23
Lucretius, 9
Lucy, St., 108
Luther, Martin, 8, 184, 201, 208, 209, 216, 226, 297, 298–300, 301, 302, 303, 305, 319–20
Lyle-Scoufos, Alice, 211

Macaulay, Thomas, 35
MacCaffrey, Isabel G., 228, 229
MacCallum, H. R., 226
McCombie, Frank, 71
McCutcheon, Elizabeth, 26
McDonald, Russ, 67
McFarland, Thomas, 68, 69
McGinn, Bernard, 208
Mack, Maynard, 69
McKeon, Richard, 320
MacLure, Millar, 210
McNamara, Peter L., 70
McPeek, James A. S., 85
McPherson, David, 85
Maddison, Carol, 159
Madsen, William G., 214, 227, 229
Mahony, Patrick, 116
Mahood, M. M., 137
Malatesti, Antonio, 252–53, 270
Mallarmé, Stéphane, 273
Mallett, Phillip, 70
Malone, Edmund, 49, 68
Manley, Frank, 115
Marijnissen, R. H., 24
Marilla, E. L., 227
Marino, Gianbattista, 153, 157, 159, 274, 292
Markels, Julian, 69
Marlorat, Augustin, 202, 210, 212
Marlowe, Christopher, 69, 213, 231, 245
Marshall, Stephen, 197, 254
Martin, Hugh, 229
Martin, L. C., 158
Martz, Louis L., 26, 114, 115, 116, 136, 137, 285, 293, 323
Marvell, Andrew, 2, 3, 5, 33, 38, 44, 53, 84, 113, 117, 123, 134, 271, 273–94, 295, 302, 319, 324
  "Bermudas," 134, 282, 293
  "Clarendon's House-Warming," 281
  "Clorinda and Damon," 33, 44, 274
  "The Coronet," 274, 282
  "Damon the Mower," 282–83
  "The Definition of Love," 288, 294
  "A Dialogue between the Resolved Soul, and Created Pleasure," 302
  "A Dialogue between the Soul and Body," 288, 294
  "Eyes and Tears," 274
  "The First Anniversary," 281, 288, 293
  "The Garden," 288, 291, 292, 294
  "An Horatian Ode," 53, 275–81, 284, 295
  "Last Instructions to a Painter," 281
  "The Match," 282
  "The Mower against Gardens," 282–83
  "The Mower's Song," 282–83
  "The Mower to the Glow-Worms," 282–83
  "The Nymph complaining," 282, 288, 294
  "On a Drop of Dew," 274
  "The Picture of Little T.C.," 282
  "A Poem upon the Death of O.C.," 281, 288, 293
  The Rehearsal Transpros'd, 271, 273, 281, 292, 319, 324
  "To his Coy Mistress," 134, 275, 282
  "The Unfortunate Lover," 282
  "Upon Appleton House," 279, 283–88, 291
  "Young Love," 282
Mason, Thomas, 195, 211
Mason, William, 246
Maus, Katharine, 85
May, Thomas, 293
Maycock, Alan L., 136
Mazzeo, Joseph A., 293
Mede, Joseph, 181, 182, 197, 205, 208, 212, 214, 322
Melanchthon, Philipp, 9, 246, 303
Melville, Andrew, 138
de Mendonça, Barbara Heliodora C., 67
Mengert, James G., 227
Mesnard, Pierre, 24
Metsys, Quentin, 24
Michelangelo Buonarroti, 252

Miles, Leland, 26
Miller, George E., 227–28
Miller, Henry K., 24
Miller, Leo, 270
Miller, Lewis H., Jr., 45
Miller, Ronald F., 70, 72
Milton, John, 1, 2, 3, 5, 12, 16, 20, 25, 30, 31, 33, 36, 38, 39, 43, 44, 55, 66, 73, 74, 75, 84, 85, 86, 105, 112, 113, 117, 120, 122, 123, 125, 133, 138, 144, 154, 157, 166, 169, 179, 181–272, 274, 275, 279, 281, 282, 284, 287, 288, 290, 291, 292–93, 294, 295, 296, 301, 302, 308, 309, 311, 313, 314–15, 316, 317, 318, 320, 323, 324
  Adam Unparadis'd, 253, 270
  Animadversions, 181, 195, 197, 198, 208, 211, 255–56, 266, 271
  An Apology for Smectymnuus, 252, 254, 267–69, 270, 272
  Areopagitica, 43, 192, 201, 207, 211, 212, 215, 249, 258–60, 267, 279
  "At a Solemn Musick," 193, 207
  "A Book was writ of late," 271
  Comus, 192, 193–94, 207, 211, 290, 315
  De doctrina christiana, 184, 202, 207, 209, 213, 216–21, 226, 232, 249, 264, 265–66, 267
  Defense of Himself, 264, 272
  The Doctrine and Discipline of Divorce, 217, 248, 249, 257–58, 267
  The History of Britain, 264–65, 267
  "How soon hath Time," 192
  "I did but prompt the age," 271
  Lycidas, 85, 86, 123, 192, 194–96, 197, 201, 207, 212, 254, 315
  Nativity Ode, 191–92, 207, 314–15, 320
  Of Civil Power, 209, 259, 267
  Of Education, 197, 258–59, 267
  Of Prelatical Episcopacy, 255
  Of Reformation, 184, 198–201, 202, 212, 254–55, 267, 270–71
  "On the Late Massacre in Piedmont," 185–86, 207
  "On the New Forcers of Conscience," 315, 324
  "On Time," 192–93
  Paradise Lost, 1, 3, 5, 20, 38, 55, 105, 125, 166, 169, 185, 186, 187–88, 189–91, 192, 193, 194, 201, 202, 203–7, 210, 211, 213, 214, 215–30, 232, 234, 243, 248, 249, 250, 255, 256, 258, 260, 262, 266, 267, 269, 272, 301, 302, 308, 315, 316, 317
  Paradise Regained, 25, 33, 44, 122, 179, 202, 207, 226, 269
  The Passion, 217
  Il Penseroso, 192, 197
  Pro populo anglicano defensio, 243, 248, 261, 262–63, 272
  Pro populo anglicano defensio secunda, 252, 253, 261, 262, 264, 272
  The Readie and Easie Way, 261
  The Reason of Church-Government, 73, 133, 185, 189, 197–98, 209, 210, 212, 216, 225, 250–51, 252, 253, 255, 266
  Samson Agonistes, 3, 5, 39, 157, 179, 189, 190, 207, 211, 227, 228, 231–48, 266–67, 272, 313
  The Tenure of Kings and Magistrates, 249, 250, 261, 262, 264, 267
  Tetrachordon, 257, 258, 271
Milton, Mary Powell, 257
Mirollo, James V., 159
Mnasalkes, 78–79
de Montaigne, Michel, 163
Montrose, Louis A., 71
More, Alexander, 264, 272
More, Henry, 182–208, 245, 248, 254, 255, 318–19, 324
More, Sir Thomas, 3, 5, 7–27, 192
  Dialogue concerning Heresies, 19, 25–26
  A Dialogue of Comfort, 18, 19
  History of King Richard III, 26
  Utopia, 9, 18, 19–23, 25–26, 192
Morgan, G. C., 229
Morgan, Gerald, 245
Morgan, Margery M., 67
Morley, George, 316
Morris, Brian, 67
Mortimer, Anthony, 85
Morton, Arthur L., 322
Morton, Thomas, 301, 320
Moschus, 149–50
Mozart, W. A., 39–40, 68
Mueller, Martin, 247

Mulder, John R., 137
Murray, Gilbert, 246
Murrin, Michael, 208, 210, 228
Musculus, Wolfgang, 303

Napier, John, 181, 182, 188–89, 201, 202, 208, 210, 212, 214, 310
Nardo, Anna K., 179
Narne, William, 210
Naunton, Sir Robert, 118
Neill, Kerby, 159
Nelson, William, 45, 46, 180
de Nerval, Gérard, 183
Nethercot, Arthur H., 116
Nethersole, Francis, 118
Neuse, Richard, 179
Nevo, Ruth, 69
Newcomen, Matthew, 254
Newton, Sir Isaac, 181, 310
Nicolson, Marjorie H., 116, 210, 212
Noble, Richmond, 71
Norris, Sylvester, 129, 138
Nosworthy, J. M., 68
Nuttall, Geoffrey F., 315, 324

Octavius Caesar, 276
Oesterley, W. O. E., 136–37, 229
Oley, Barnabas, 25, 118
Olsen, V. Norskov, 271
O'Malley, John W., 321
Ong, Walter J., 229
Orange, Linwood E., 46
Origen, 216, 307, 318
Ornstein, Robert, 245
Otto, Walter F., 46
Overall, John, 138
Ovid, 12, 76, 106, 114
Owen, E. T., 235, 246
Owen, W. J. B., 46

Pace, Richard, 17, 25
Pagitt, Ephraim, 257, 271
Palatine Anthology, 85
Palmer, D. J., 71
Palotto, Giovanni, 147
Panofsky, Erwin, 24
Pareus, David, 181, 208, 189–90, 203–4, 210, 212, 213, 214, 322
Parish, J. E., 227, 321
Parker, Samuel, 273, 281, 292, 319
Parker, William R., 25, 210, 242, 247, 271, 272

Parkhurst, Ferdinando, 322
Parr, Elnathan, 125, 137
Parrish, Paul A., 159
Parsons, Elsie C., 72
Parsons, Robert, 304, 321
Partee, Morris H., 68, 70
Pascal, Blaise, 255–56, 264, 271
Pasquier, Etienne, 114
Patrides, C. A., 45, 46, 72, 116, 136, 137, 180, 209, 211, 213, 226, 227, 228, 229, 270, 271, 320, 321, 322, 323, 324
Pebworth, Ted-Larry, 5, 86, 87, 115, 136, 138
Peck, Russell A., 70
Pelagius, 299
Pelikan, Jaroslav, 208
Pennell, Charles A., 137
Pepys, Samuel, 209
Perella, Nicolas J., 159
Perkins, William, 213, 312, 315, 323
Persius, 105
Person, David, 171, 180
Petrarch, 76, 100, 108
Petto, Samuel, 314
Phidias, 79
Philip Neri, St., 159
Phillips, Edward, 264, 265
Phillips, Jerome, 300, 320
Phillips, Margaret Mann, 23
Pico della Mirandola, Giovanni, 178
Pindar, 80–81, 83, 155–56
Pineas, Rainer, 26
Pineau, J. B., 23
Pirandello, Luigi, 49, 68
Plato, 7, 9, 21, 81, 100, 114, 121, 288, 294, 321
Pliny, 9
Plotinus, 288, 294
Plutarch, 264, 293
Poe, Edgar Allan, 270
Polycrates, 12
Pompey, 276
Pope, Alexander, 30, 31, 33, 41, 43, 44, 84, 94–95, 105–6, 112, 115, 155, 159, 233, 246
della Porter, Giambattista, 170
Portoghesi, Paolo, 210
Potter, Francis, 209
Potter, John M., 294
Poulet, Georges, 210
Pound, Ezra, 78

Powel, Gabriel, 316–17, 324
Powell, Chilton L., 271
Praxiteles, 79
Praz, Mario, 113, 114, 115, 156, 159, 160
Preston, Viscount, 44
Price, Daniel, 130, 138
Pricket, Robert, 296, 319
de la Primaudaye, Pierre, 171, 179–80
Prince, F. T., 213, 226
Pritchard, Allan, 158, 323
Propertius, 76
Proust, Marcel, 115
Puttenham, George, 21, 127
Pythagoras, 170–71, 174, 178

Quanbeck, Warren A., 208
Quarles, Francis, 309, 322
Quilligan, Maureen, 44
Quistorp, Heinrich, 208, 212

Rabelais, François, 12, 15, 162–63, 166, 179, 259
Racine, Jean Baptiste, 288
Radzinowicz, Mary Ann, 226
Rahner, Hugo, 179
Rajan, Balachandra, 179, 219, 226, 228
Ralegh, Sir Walter, 2, 4, 39, 45, 172, 180, 187, 209, 278
Ralegh, Sir Walter A., 215, 225
Ramsey, I. T., 225, 226, 228, 229
Rand, Edward K., 27
Randolph, Thomas, 157
Ransom, John Crowe, 1, 86, 92
Raphael (Raffaelo Santi), 252
Rauter, Herbert, 138
Reeves, Marjorie, 208, 322
Reid, Louis A., 223, 229
Reuchlin, Johann, 9
Revard, Stella, 214, 227
Revius, Jacobus, 323
Reynolds, Edward, 138
Reynolds, Henry, 34
Reynolds, John Hamilton, 44, 139
Rhenanus, Beatus, 18, 25
Rice, James, 270
Richmond, H. M., 70
Rickey, Mary E., 136, 144, 158
Riggs, William G., 138
Robbins, Robin, 178
Roche, Thomas P., Jr., 45
Rollin, Roger B., 245

Rolls, Samuel, 311, 322
de Ronsard, Pierre, 76
Roper, William, 18, 19, 25, 26
Rosenblatt, Jason P., 214, 226, 227
Ross, Alexander, 256, 271
Rossiter, A. P., 69, 70
Roston, Murray, 113, 114
Røstvig, Maren-Sofie, 286, 292, 293, 294
Roth, Frederic H., Jr., 286, 293
Rous, Francis (the Elder), 197, 212, 314, 316, 323, 324
Rozett, Martha T., 67
Rudwin, Maximilian, 209
Ruffo-Fiore, Sylvia, 116
Rutherford, Samuel, 302, 320
Ryan, John K., 321

Sackville-West, Victoria, 273, 292
Sadoleto, Jacopo, 320
Saintsbury, George, 113
Salingar, Leo, 67, 69
Salmasius, Claudius, 262, 264
Salter, Thomas, 296, 319
Sanders, Wilbur, 116
Sandler, Florence, 322
Sandys, George, 31, 182, 208
Sappho, 80, 81, 86
Sasek, L. A., 226
Saxl, F., 24
Schaar, Claes, 159
von Schlegel, A. W., 68
Schmithals, Walter, 214
Schoeck, R. J., 26
Schöne, Annemarie, 71
Schönfeld, Hermann, 24
Schwartz, Helen, 70
Scott, Reginald, 297
Scoular, Kitty, 287, 292, 294
Sears, Donald, 270
Seaton, Ethel, 1
Seidel, Max, 74
Seiden, Melvin, 72
Seneca, 267, 272
Servetus, Michael, 296
Sessions, William A., 136
Shafer, Robert, 159
Shakespeare, William, 3, 4, 5, 12, 30, 33, 47–72, 81, 82, 91, 111, 157, 166, 178, 181, 215, 231, 235, 236, 245, 249, 273, 274, 277–78, 279, 282, 283, 287, 289, 290, 295, 296, 311, 322–23

Shakespeare, William (*continued*)
  All's Well That Ends Well, 52, 59, 66, 71
  Antony and Cleopatra, 47, 48, 59, 67–68, 161
  As You Like It, 52, 59–61, 71
  The Comedy of Errors, 52, 53, 69
  Coriolanus, 50
  Cymbeline, 50–51, 52, 54
  Hamlet, 47, 48, 52, 53, 54, 69, 70, 71, 73, 117, 178, 236, 295
  I Henry IV, 52, 54–56
  II Henry IV, 52, 55–56, 63, 64, 249
  Henry V, 52, 56–57, 60, 69–70, 215
  I Henry VI, 52, 69
  II Henry VI, 52, 69
  III Henry VI, 52, 53, 69
  Julius Caesar, 277–78
  King Lear, 47, 50, 52, 56, 57–66, 68, 69, 70, 71–72, 166, 178, 231, 235, 273, 283
  Love's Labour's Lost, 69, 71, 290
  Macbeth, 47, 48, 50, 181
  Measure for Measure, 47, 48, 53–54, 55, 64, 67, 68
  Merchant of Venice, 47
  A Midsummer Night's Dream, 29, 71
  Othello, 47, 48, 54, 63, 67, 166
  Pericles, 48, 51
  Richard II, 47, 49–50, 52, 53, 55, 68, 279
  Richard III, 52, 53, 55, 69, 70, 89
  Romeo and Juliet, 47–48, 67, 235
  Sonnets, 91, 111
  The Tempest, 7, 47, 50, 51, 52, 53, 56, 69, 282, 290, 295
  Titus Andronicus, 47, 48, 67, 287
  Troilus and Cressida, 47, 52, 57, 67, 141
  Twelfth Night, 47, 51, 52, 53, 54, 59–61, 63, 68, 69, 70, 71
  The Winter's Tale, 51, 69
Shawcross, John T., 5
Shelley, Percy B., 249, 250, 270
Sheriff, William E., 69
Shroeder, John W., 43
Shullenberger, William, 226
Shumaker, Wayne, 228
Sibbes, Richard, 186, 209
Sicherman, Carol M., 116
Sidney, Sir Philip, 3, 37, 76, 120, 137, 157, 231–32, 234, 259, 260, 266, 272
Simmonds, James D., 5
Simmons, J. L., 67–68
Simpson, Evelyn, 86, 178–79
Sims, James H., 211
Smart, Ninian, 229
Smith, A. J., 116
Smith, B. T. D., 229
Smith, Hallett, 136
Smith, John, 72, 212, 319
Smith, Preserved, 23
Smith, Samuel, 211
Snyder, Susan, 67, 68, 70, 72
Socrates, 7, 9, 10, 19, 81
Somerville, C. John, 321
Sophocles, 235, 236–39, 241, 243, 245, 246, 247, 248
Southwell, Robert, 153–54, 159, 304
Speer, Diane P., 272
Spence, Joseph, 44
Spenser, Edmund, 3, 5, 20, 29–46, 84, 153, 170, 179, 186, 187, 190, 210, 232–33, 274, 282, 302, 309, 311, 313, 322
  Amoretti, 179
  Epithalamion, 179
  The Faerie Queene, 20, 29–30, 31, 32, 34–37, 38, 39–43, 44–46, 186, 190, 210, 233, 282, 302, 313
  Muiopotmos, 46, 170
  The Shepheardes Calender, 37
Spoure, Edmund, 191, 211
Spurstow, William, 254
Stafford, Anthony, 314
Stanenough, James, 153
Stanwood, P. G., 158, 323
Steadman, John M., 227
Stein, Arnold, 114, 227, 245
Stempel, Daniel, 294
Stenger, Genevieve, 24
Sterne, Laurence, 138
Sterry, Peter, 138, 318, 324
Stewart, Douglas, 67
Stewart, Randall, 43
Stewart, Stanley, 116, 294
Stock, A. G., 44
Stockholder, Katherine, 70, 72
Stone, Darwell, 138
Strada, Famianus, 153
Suckling, Sir John, 77
Suleiman the Magnificent, 186, 209
Summers, Claude J., 5, 70, 86, 87, 115, 138

Summers, Joseph H., 136, 137, 228, 245, 292, 294
Svendsen, Kester, 272
Swan, John, 210
Swanston, Hamish, 159
Swete, H. B., 229
Swift, John, 296, 319
Swift, Jonathan, 20
Sydenham, Humphrey, 313
Syfret, R. H., 293
Sylvester, Richard, 24, 26
Synesius, 12

Tansillo, Luigi, 159
Tasso, Torquato, 39
Taylor, Dick, 229
Taylor, Jeremy, 313, 317, 324
Taylor, Thomas, 214
Telle, Emile V., 23
Tennyson, Alfred Lord, 33, 44, 84
Teresa of Avila, St., 148–49, 303–4, 314, 321, 323
Thomas of Aquinas, St., 30, 141–42, 227, 257, 272, 305, 321
Thompson, Craig R., 23, 25
Thompson, Francis, 89
Thompson, Geraldine, 25
Thomson, George, 236, 247
Thucydides, 120
Tibullus, 76
Tillich, Paul, 228
Tillotson, Kathleen, 113
Timberlake, Philip W., 248
Toliver, Harold E., 292
Tolstoy, Leo, 70
Tomarkin, Edward, 69
Tonkin, Humphrey, 45
Tourneur, Cyril, 283
Tradescant, John, 162, 178
Traherne, Thomas, 135
Trelcatius, Lucas, 301, 303, 320
Trevor, Meriol, 159
Trevor-Roper, H. R., 296, 297, 319
Trimpi, Wesley, 85
Tromly, F. B., 71
Tuke, Thomas, 312
Tung, Mason, 227
Tuve, Rosemond, 136
Tuveson, Ernest L., 212
Twisse, William, 181, 208
Tymme, Thomas, 171, 179

Tyndale, William, 182–83, 208, 305, 306, 307–8, 321

Urban VIII, Pope, 252
Ursinus, Zacharias, 303
Ussher, James, 138, 254, 313

de Valdés, Juán, 138
Valeriano, Piero, 309, 322
Valla, Lorenzo, 298, 321
Vaughan, Dorothy, 209
Vaughan, Henry, 3, 113, 117–18, 119, 135
Vaughan, Thomas, 254
Vergil, Polydore, 127, 138
Vermigli, Peter Martyr, 303
Vickers, Brian, 116
Victoria, Queen, 143
Virdis, Caterina L., 24
Virgil, 12, 30, 34, 44, 121, 170, 216
Vives, Juan Luis, 257, 259, 272, 298
Vordtriede, Werner, 288, 294

Waddington, Raymond B., 226
Wade, Clyde G., 46
Waith, Eugene M., 68
Walker, D. P., 322
Walker, John W., 137
Wall, John M., Jr., 116
Wallace, John M., 293
Wallerstein, Ruth C., 141, 158, 159
Wallis, P. J., 323
Walpole, Horace, 235, 246
Walpole, Michael, 209
Walsh, Thomas M., 24
Walton, Izaak, 105, 117, 118, 119, 124, 134, 135, 136
Ward, Richard, 324
Warnke, Frank J., 179, 293, 294
Warren, Austin, 158, 159, 160
Warren, Roger, 68
Watkins, W. B. C., 46
Watson, Donald G., 24, 69
Watts, Robert A., 67
Webbe, William, 44–45
Webber, Joan, 228, 271
Webster, John, 98
Webster, T. B. L., 247
Weemes, John, 114, 305, 321
Weiner, Andrew D., 46
Weismiller, Edward, 160
Wells, Stanley, 67

Welsford, Enid, 72
Westermarck, Edward A., 271
Whately, William, 301, 320
Wheelwright, Philip, 228, 229
Whichcote, Benjamin, 72, 318, 319, 324
Whitaker, William, 304, 321
White, Anthony, 301, 320
White, Helen C., 134, 139, 143, 158
Whiting, George W., 211
Wier, Johann, 297
Willeford, William, 72
Willet, Andrew, 183, 186, 208, 209
William I, King, 264
Williams, Aubrey L., 115
Williams, Charles, 69
Williams, Gordon, 275, 293
Williams, Griffith, 308, 322
Williams, Gwyn, 69
Williams, Kathleen, 43, 44, 45
Williams, William P., 137
Williamson, George, 86, 116, 136, 324
Wilson, Elkin C., 71
Wilson, F. P., 113
Wilson, Thomas, 214, 307, 311, 321, 322
Wittreich, Joseph A., 189, 191, 201, 210, 211, 212, 230, 322

Wolfe, Don M., 272
Wood, Anthony â, 321
Wood, Glena D., 72
Wooden, Warren W., 23, 25, 26
Woolcombe, K. J., 322
Woolf, Virginia, 29, 30, 31, 39
Wooten, John, 246
Wordsworth, William, 37, 249–50
Wotton, Sir Henry, 99, 115
Wycherley, William, 115
Wycliffe, John, 305, 306

Xenophon, 251
Ximénez, Francisco, 298

Yaghjian, Lucretia B., 226
Yeats, William Butler, 1, 32–33, 35, 36, 37, 39, 40, 44, 66, 72, 84 178, 190, 220–21, 224–25, 230, 279
Young, Thomas, 254

Zanchius, Hieronymus, 303
Ziegelmaier, Gregory, 245
Zucker, Wolfgang M., 72
Zwingli, Huldrych, 303

OHIO UNIVERSITY LIBRARY

Please return this book as soon as you have finished with it. In order to avoid a fine it must be returned by the latest date